The World of Jak Smyrl

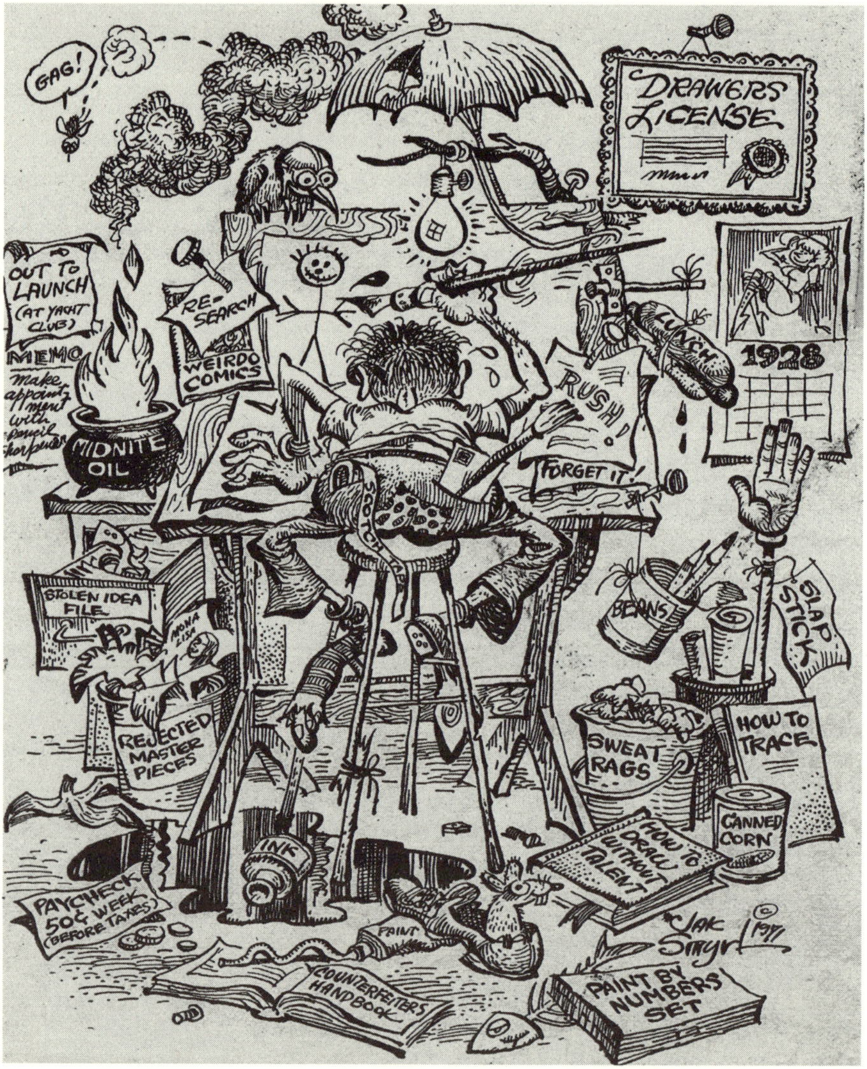

GAG!
DRAWERS LICENSE
OUT TO LAUNCH (AT YACHT CLUB)
MEMO
Make appointment with pencil sharpener
MIDNITE OIL
RE-SEARCH
WEIRDO COMICS
LUNCH
1928
RUSH!
FORGET IT!
SCOTCH TAPE
STOLEN IDEA FILE
MONA LISA
BEANS
SLAP STICK
REJECTED MASTER PIECES
SWEAT RAGS
HOW TO TRACE
CANNED CORN
INK
HOW TO DRAW WITHOUT TALENT
PAYCHECK 50¢ WEEK (BEFORE TAXES)
PAINT
COUNTERFEITERS HANDBOOK
PAINT BY NUMBERS SET
Jak Smyrl © 1977

The World of JAK SMYRL

South Carolina Artist, Journalist, Cartoonist

Joan A. Inabinet AND L. Glen Inabinet

THE UNIVERSITY OF
SOUTH CAROLINA PRESS

Published by the University of South Carolina Press
Columbia, South Carolina 29208

www.sc.edu/uscpress

Manufactured in the United States of America

29 28 27 26 25 24 23 22 21 20
10 9 8 7 6 5 4 3 2 1

Library of Congress Cataloging-in-Publication Data
can be found at http://catalog.loc.gov/.

This book was printed on recycled paper
with 30 percent postconsumer waste content.

Publication of this book is made possible in part by the
Caroline McKissick Dial Publication Fund of the South Caroliniana Library
and the University Libraries of the University of South Carolina.

ISBN: 978-1-64336-049-2 (cloth)
ISBN: 9768-1-64336-050-8 (ebook)

Frontispiece: Self-caricature of Jak burning the
midnight oil ©1971. Courtesy of the family.

For all who lighten hearts with faith, goodwill, and smiles

Contents

Acknowledgments

The subject of this biography was himself the grand source of information on his life and times. Close ties aside, the authors, having interviewed Jak a number of times for other projects, now recognize that unknowingly they were then also collecting information for his biography. Jak was a source for us in our writing of *A History of Kershaw County, South Carolina*, University of South Carolina Press, 2011, and a source for Joan (his niece) in compiling a family history.

To help tell his story, Jak left invaluable records, described in the biography. Most of them, along with many of his art pieces, are now in the Oscar Jackson "Jak" Smyrl, Jr., Papers in the South Caroliniana Library at the University of South Carolina. Those papers include Jak's handwritten outline of incidents, themes, and opinions for an intended but unwritten autobiography from his childhood into retirement and senior activities. The papers also include several decades of insightful contemporary correspondence between Jak and his friends and family.

In working with the Smyrl collection at Caroliniana, we have appreciated the assistance, advice, and encouragement of the following present or former associates of USC or the South Caroliniana Society: Edward Blessing, Henry Fulmer, Andrea L'Hommedieu, Tom McNally, Jason Shaiman, Allen Stokes, Harvey Teal, and others. To the University of South Carolina Press and those there who have guided our journey from concept to publication, we express hearty appreciation.

We also value our research reading newspaper content, especially the *State* (also formerly associated with the *Columbia Record* and the *State Magazine*) and the *Chronicle-Independent* (formerly the *Camden Chronicle*). We thank present newspaper staff members who aided and encouraged us in our manuscript and publication process. We also thank the Camden Archives and Museum staff for decades of clipping files so helpful in navigating microfilm dates.

We are deeply indebted to many other individuals for assisting us by providing or discussing documents, photographs, artwork, anecdotes, and memorabilia in the progress of our work. Professional associates of Jak's in this group included Robert Ariail, Johnny Baughman, Jim Holton, Bob Kaminer, Sam McCuen, Bill McDonald, Tom McLean, Tom Nebbia, Tom Priddy, Ray Twork, and many others, some now deceased. A reference herein made simply as "an interview" with any of these persons is one with the authors between 2011 and the present, and it included note taking, or sound recording, or both.

We thank the following personal friends and associates of Jak, some now deceased, who likewise were interviewed between 2011 and the present: Anna Shuler Bynum, Laura Sloan Crosby, Dick Goodwin, Alan Holden, Lynn Holden, F. N. "Mac" McCorkle, Ann McCrickard, Franda Pedlow, Mary Sloan Robey, Ed Royall, Bert Rush, Nick Varnam, and others who have graciously responded to questions.

The following members of the extensive Smyrl family, some now deceased, were especially generous with their information, some of them having been interviewed prior to 2011 for family or local history projects: Lewis F. Anderson, Sara Shaw Benson, Mary Ann Anderson Blaskowitz, Henry Brown, Nettie Ogburn Brown, Alvin Creed, Richard Creed, Bobbie Brown Daniels, Steve Kelly Sr., Linda Brown Layman, Gary Ogburn, Larry Ogburn, Onnie Ogburn, Dianne Edwards Smyrl, Marilyn Watts Tsirigotis, Cleo Smyrl Watts, Louise Smyrl Watts, and others. Collections of family materials compiled by kin deceased prior to 2000 were also invaluable: Lottie Smyrl Anderson, Robert A. "Bob" Love, Mamie Smyrl, and Jak's parents, Oscar and Mae Smyrl.

The two living persons to whom we are most indebted are those who knew Jak the best: his brother, Willie Alfred Smyrl, and Jak's wife for nearly half a century, Betty Spires Smyrl. Their recollections, identifications, and clarifications have been invaluable. The authors also thank collectively our children and grandchildren who have graciously shared us with this endeavor.

Our hearts are filled with gratitude to all.

Editorial Note

Readers no doubt will easily recognize that "Jack" as a child and young man is the same as "Jak" in later life. For most of his long professional career, artist Jak Smyrl publicly and privately used the three-letter spelling. Straight-faced, he denied changing his name: "Oh, I've been called *Jak* all my life!"

The biographers have spelled their subject's name in general consistency with his chronological usage. For ease of reading, the chronological narrative uses "Jack" in the story of his early years and shifts to "Jak" in chapter 19 ("A Career Beginning") since early in this period he adopted the three-letter spelling and used it thereafter. A favorite quip of his was: "I was just a poor artist. I couldn't afford a 'C.'"

While recognizing that artists have their own ways of doing things, the narrative sometimes for sake of clarity standardizes spelling and Jak's punctuation system, characterized by frequent dashes. Variances judged not confusing were left to stand within quotations as found.

Jak's own voice emerges in the narrative through quotations of his words as preserved in his own writing, in interviews and recordings of him, in interviews and memories of others who knew him, and in the biographers' research and personal association. These patterns were also used for others speaking of Jak. When quotations within the book stem from such informal sources, individual items for these do not appear in the bibliography.

Chapter 1

Lightening the Hearts

"So glad you're here"

Jak dressed carefully that morning in a natural linen sports coat, his favorite striped shirt, and a deep-blue tie. It was June 6, 2007, and temperatures in humid Columbia, South Carolina, soared as expected into the nineties. By the time he arrived at the State House, the combination of heat, extra exertion, and pleasant anticipation had restored color to his face. Most days now it was pallid.

In his right hand, the polished cane he had selected was as whimsical as useful. It was of his own carving, a sturdy burled twist with a long-beaked bird's head that fit into his palm. Seeing Jak Smyrl that day, even if recognizing him as a man of eighty-four, a casual observer might have thought the cane a mere fashion touch.

The visitors heading toward the spectators' gallery for the morning legislative session moved slowly, talking among themselves. Jak was at ease with the pace, especially with his wife, Betty, and brother, Alfred, on either side and with a half dozen nieces and nephews following. Jak smiled with pleasure when he recognized familiar faces and stopped more than once to speak. He rested only lightly on his cane. In conversation he inclined his white head carefully to favor small round hearing aids and peered through modest glasses with gold wire rims. For many years large dark frames had enhanced his distinctive, heavy-lidded eyes, which drooped downward at the outer corners. At the entrance to the gallery above the House of Representatives, he exchanged greetings and joked a few minutes with a hometown pal from Camden who had long worked as a greeter in these halls.

Taking a seat in the spectators' gallery, Jak spoke first to each family member seated about him, "Are you comfortable? Can you see? So glad you're here." He scanned with admiration the formal oil portraits, gleaming brass, and polished mahogany. "Look at all that . . . so grand . . . this place looks terrific." On the floor below, conversing legislators milled among rows of paper-strewn desks. A sharply pounded gavel summoned the hubbub to order and called for business.

Representative Laurie Funderburk stepped forward to the podium. For the record she announced a formal document already adopted in both the House and the Senate. Jak heard the words ring as she read the title on the printed page: "A Concurrent Resolution—to Recognize and Honor Jak Smyrl, of Kershaw County, for His Distinguished Career as an Artist and Writer." She then read aloud the words of the document. It first recounted the influences of his childhood:

> Whereas, Oscar Jackson Smyrl, Jr., born in 1923 in Camden, grew up in an active, loving family, where laughter and storytelling helped shape him into the artist Jak Smyrl; and
> Whereas, in his childhood during the Great Depression, when rural youngsters learned to make their own fun, young Smyrl sketched funny pictures to amuse his siblings as they sat together evenings by the light of an oil lamp centered on the kitchen table . . .

Jak heard the resolution detail achievements, and that "in his lifetime, he has turned to all arts, including conversation, music, and writing, that bring people closer together and enlarge their world with pleasure." The document traced the years of his early manhood:

> The Southern outdoor world of his youth nurtured an enduring love for natural beauty and a sympathy for nature's creatures, later seen in Jak's cartoon strips that for several years illustrated *South Carolina Wildlife* magazine's early Carolina Sports columns. Called by duty from his college classroom in World War II, he served in the United States Marines during the Pacific island invasions and afterwards in the occupation army in North China, his pencil, brush, and camera going with him everywhere. During post-war college and studio studies, Jak

landed a job with *The State* and *The Columbia Record* newspapers in Columbia and entered the working world of the commercial artist.

The resolution summarized his long career and touched on his private life:

> Staff artist at *The State* and *The Columbia Record* for thirty-seven years, as well as a free-lance illustrator for dozens of books and hundreds of other projects, Jak Smyrl has made an indelible mark on South Carolina and beyond. He was a sustaining contributor to the long-time survival of *The State Magazine,* one of the defining publications of the Palmetto State; the state and local maps he illustrated with comic sketches record valuable details of historic and contemporary locales; his was the first logo of the University of South Carolina to depict the gamecock in fighting stance. . . .
>
> With his devoted wife, interior designer Betty Spires, whom he married in 1958, Jak Smyrl has traveled the world and lived both simply and grandly, collecting friends everywhere, his trips frequently becoming the basis for detailed travel articles and sketches published on return. Jak and Betty's Camden and Holden Beach, North Carolina, homes are filled with memorabilia, objects of nature, his artworks, and often with family and friends.

Jak heard then the conclusion:

> Whereas, through his lifework, Jak, who referred to himself as "the pore man's Picasso," has given legions of South Carolinians insight into important issues, all delivered up with a smile and designed to engender chuckles in those enjoying his creations, the General Assembly takes great pleasure in recognizing this eminent artist and son of South Carolina for his contributions to this great State.
>
> Now, therefore,
> Be it resolved by the House of Representatives, the Senate concurring:
>
> That the members of the South Carolina General Assembly, by this resolution, recognize and honor Jak Smyrl, of Kershaw County, for his distinguished career as an artist and writer and thank him for lightening the hearts of uncounted South Carolinians with his cartoon humor.

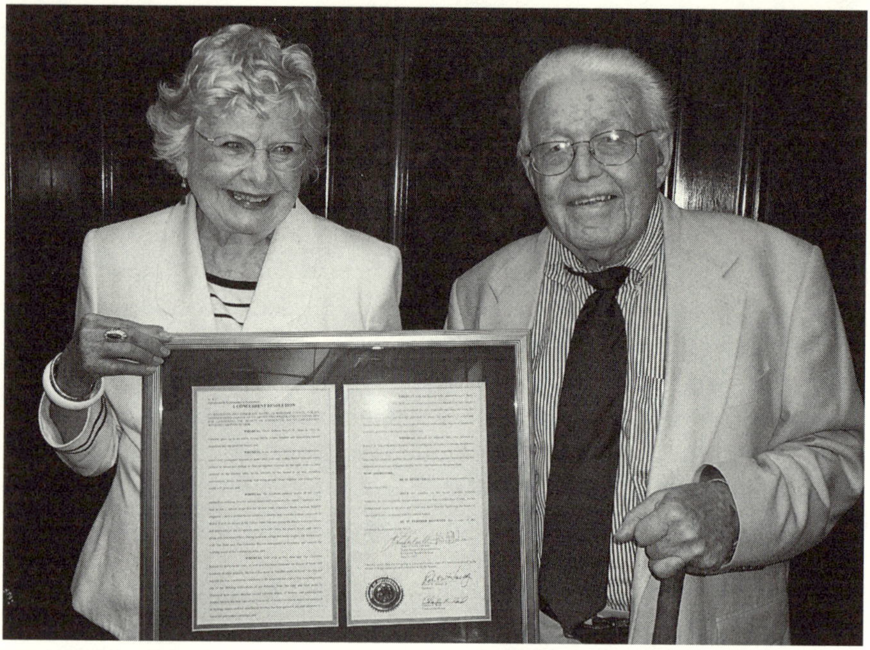

Betty and Jak with the resolution just presented him by the South Carolina General Assembly in 2007. Photograph by L. Glen Inabinet.

"For lightening the hearts of uncounted South Carolinians with his cartoon humor . . ." The words echoed. Jak heard thunderous applause—from his family seated around him, from the other spectators, and from the legislators who rose to their feet and turned to the gallery to look up at him. Standing slowly, his damp eyes shining, he waved, smiling in appreciation.

Amid a flurry of camera flashes he was led next to the Senate chamber, where the resolution was recognized by Senator Vincent Sheheen and followed by more resounding applause and more appreciative, upturned faces. From that gallery, too, Jak savored the response. He had always relished the pleasures of living in the moment, and this experience of so many smiling faces was one to enjoy. Again he raised his arm to wave to them. For the time being, the daily struggles of the cancer that isolated him on so many days of his life were put at a distance.

Chapter 2

Heritage

"To live up to a good man"

The life of artist Jak Smyrl began in Camden in the early-morning darkness of Saturday, May 5, 1923. Inside a pleasant cottage a short distance from the small town's main intersection, lights had burned since late Friday night. In the bedroom, where an oil lamp softened the direct circle of an electric bulb dangling overhead, Dr. S. C. Zemp delivered a well-formed but unresponsive baby boy. Expertly the doctor tilted the sluggish infant heels high, turned him over, thumped his back, slapped his bottom—once, twice, again—and massaged him confidently until Oscar Jackson Smyrl, Jr., drew his first breath with a healthily protesting squall. His mother watched with relief as the infant's bluish skin grew pink, marked briefly with the prints of the doctor's working fingers.

Monday morning at the Kershaw County courthouse, Dr. Zemp recorded the time of the birth as 11:25 P.M., May 4. He had been delivering babies for nearly three decades, but only in the last seven years had South Carolina law required the recording of their births. It would be twenty-one years before the boy whom the family would call "Jack" would need a copy of his birth certificate. Only then would the family learn that the sleepy doctor had made note of the time he had arrived to attend the mother—shortly before midnight—rather than the later time of the actual delivery.

All his life Oscar Jackson Smyrl, Jr., would report May 5 as his birth date. If a question arose about the difference on his birth certificate, he simply asserted, "My *mother* said I was born May 5." At times he jested as evidence, "My mother would know. She was there." Schools, the military,

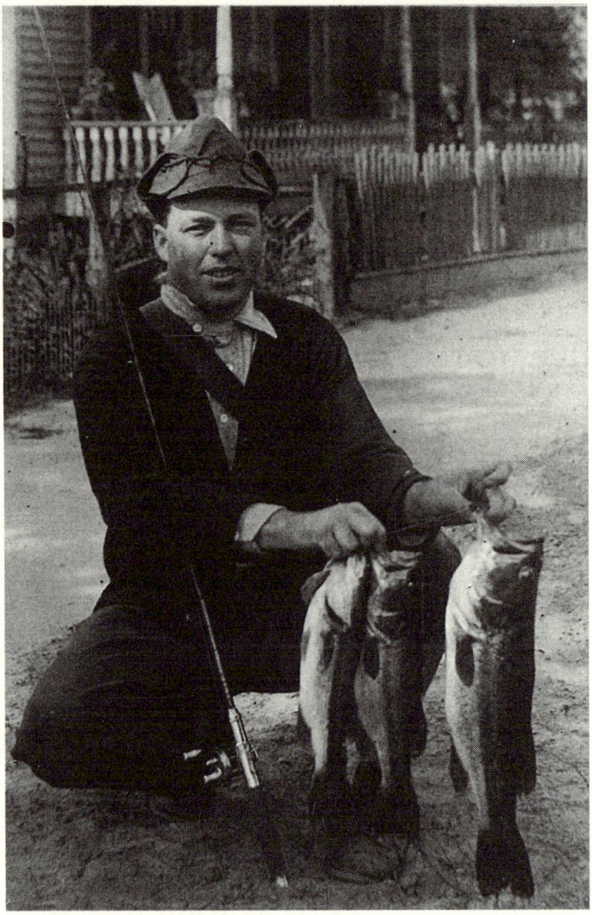

Oscar at home with good-luck catch celebrating the birth of his son "Jack." Courtesy of the family.

even Social Security would accept the explanation and record May 5 on their records. Only his passport would one day read May 4 to correspond with the birth certificate. Jack shrugged off occasional inconvenience from the discrepancy. "Mama told me the doctor was busy saving my life. He didn't have time to look at his watch."

In 1923 it was not the custom to photograph newborns nor to invite visitors in to greet recently delivered mothers, protectively hovered over by womenfolk. Young Jack's proud father celebrated the arrival of his first son and namesake by going fishing later on the morning he was born. Although no photograph was taken of the newborn, a snapshot was made of beaming papa Oscar Jackson Smyrl Sr. back at home with a fine string of largemouth bass. For a lifelong outdoorsman, the activity was a natural celebration of pride and good fortune. He was eager to introduce the world of nature to his son.

Neighbors around the Smyrl home soon learned of the new arrival. Some of them stopped by at the smell of fresh-cooked fish that Oscar fried outside in a pan of bubbling hot grease. Dishes prepared from neighbors' spring gardens began to appear at the Smyrl door. Good wishes were sent inside to the mother, who was expected to remain respectfully and quietly isolated for a couple of weeks more, watched over by a nursemaid approved of by the doctor and the womenfolk.

Three of Oscar's five sisters were living with their families only short blocks away from the Smyrl cottage, so infant Jack's two-year-old sister, Lottie, was kept happily playing nearby with older cousins surnamed Campbell, Creed, and Shaw. In an age when infection and contagion were more feared than preventable, cautions were prudent to protect an infant and a new mother from too much exposure or excitement. In a routine case, such care made home delivery with an attending doctor preferable to the comings and goings that a mother and infant might encounter in a hospital at the time.

Mae Smyrl took childbirth precautions seriously. She had been nine months old when her own mother died, and thus Mae knew the effects of such a loss on a child. Through the upbringing of her devout and energetic grandmother Davis, and through schooling encouraged by her father, a former educator, Mae held traditional values as well as beliefs in sanitation, order, and scientific learning. She valued the Bible, common sense, and sound information. To her, good manners included decent treatment of others and were as vital to admirable character as "putting on airs" was destructive to it. As a young mother, she felt her natural place was home, and she embraced care of it, husband, and children with a missionary devotion. As they grew the focus of her concern would expand. Were not her community and her country the enlarged spheres of the family circle that were her responsibility as a woman?

Oscar had been only ten years old when he openly announced that he intended to marry Mae. She was a stranger to him, and he did not even know her name. It was 1905 in rural Kershaw County when barefoot Oscar wandered into his family's sitting room. Here a bevy of visiting adults excitedly chattered among themselves about the upcoming home wedding of his sister Nannie, the first of his siblings to marry. Ignored, the boy listened for a while, feeling left out. Wanting attention he abruptly pointed to a photograph propped among others on the fireplace mantel.

His mother, fond of visiting and writing family and friends, was proud of her large collection of their photos she had neatly arranged on a lacey scarf.

"See that girl up there in the white dress?" piped up Oscar. "*I'm* going to marry *her.*"

There was a stunned silence before the adults broke into hearty laughter at the unexpected comment from someone his age. "Oscar," chuckled his mother, Lottie, picking up the photograph of a small girl, shyly posed standing on a large chair. She was the daughter of a deceased friend. "You don't even know this little girl. She doesn't live here."

"Well," protested Oscar stubbornly, glowering at the display of more familiar faces on the mantel. "I *do* know all them other girls, and I know for sure I won't marry none of *them!*"

For a while Oscar had to endure good-natured teasing as the story made its rounds. "Hey, buddy, where's your bride?" Eventually the incident faded into the background of congenial storytelling in the rural farming community where he grew up. Learning to joke and to take joking—it was part of his education in the familiar society of his childhood.

Nine miles northwest of Camden, that close-knit country neighborhood around Flint Hill Baptist Church undulated over red clay hills above the nearby Wateree River. Its postal and voting addresses varied over the years—Flat Rock, Cantey, Shaylor's Hill—and families such as the Smyrls near the church called their section "Flint Hill." Here Oscar grew into a sturdy, comely youth popular with the young ladies and ambitious enough to leave home for two years to earn a degree at a Columbia business college by 1915. By instinct he was a lover of nature and of the slow pace of agricultural seasons, but the modern world was changing. Not yet twenty he moved to Camden to work, boarding in the home of sister Nannie and her husband, Frank D. "Ted" Campbell. Oscar started as a bookkeeper for lien merchants Springs and Shannon and soon advanced to bookkeeper at the First National Bank.

In April 1917, a somber President Woodrow Wilson called for Americans to prepare for "a war to end all wars." The men of Oscar's family were not professional soldiers, but in every generation they had volunteered in defense of home. Oscar responded to natural duty. Activated in early October at Camp Jackson in Columbia, he was commissioned a corporal and qualified as a sharpshooter. In Officers Training School, he earned his second lieutenant's bar.

In November 1918, the Great War, the World War, ended while Oscar's unit was waiting to be shipped overseas. Held over six months for postwar duty, he was one of a small number of officers sent about the country to inventory stockpiles of military vehicles and airplanes. While it was still being said that there could never be another world war, the accounting of the nation's defenses was taking place. Oscar's tasks took him to Atlanta and Washington, D.C., from New York to Florida, and as far west as Pittsburgh and New Orleans.

In all Oscar had been away from Camden almost two years and had traveled a good bit by the time he hung up his uniform and came back home in spring of 1919. He had enjoyed sightseeing and socializing during assignment intervals. Now it was time to think of settling down. He would turn twenty-five before long. With postwar job shortages, he felt lucky to find a job in Camden, but his new employer, a life insurance company, promptly transferred him out of town with duties he disliked. In the fall Oscar paid a visit to family in Camden to check on a different job prospect, and a chance bit of news caught his interest.

A pretty new schoolteacher, he heard at the supper table, had come from North Carolina to teach at Flint Hill's recently built Piedmont School. She was Miss Mary Ann Davis, boarding for the school term with the family of her uncle Bob McDowell, right up the road from the Smyrl place. The new teacher was the grown-up baby of Bob's sister who had died before her daughter was a year old.

It had been many years since young Oscar had been teased for saying he would marry an unknown little girl in a photo sent his mother. Others by then had forgotten the incident, but he had not. Without saying a word, he realized that the new teacher must have been that girl in the photo. Bemused curiosity piqued him, and he quietly determined to meet her. He wondered how she had turned out and expected to laugh at himself for how foolish his boyish notion had been.

On Sunday Oscar arrived early at Flint Hill Baptist Church, where he had been elected a deacon when he was only seventeen. He knew that the McDowells, faithful in attendance like the Smyrls, would be there. He was already seated when they arrived, Miss Davis with them. As they made their way to a pew, he could see only glimpses of a small, slight girl with dark hair who nodded pleasantly to others. Oscar's mind wandered during the sermon, thinking he had not seen enough of Miss Davis to tell anything about her.

After church he worked his way through familiar well-wishers over to the McDowells for an introduction. He looked into Miss Davis's dark eyes and forgot his expectation of finding her flaws. "May I," he blurted politely, "be introduced to you? I would like to invite you to take a ride with me sometime." She looked into his blue eyes and paused a moment. "I would be pleased to be introduced. Perhaps I would like to take a ride sometime."

In 1919 a ride in the countryside was an adventure. Most roads of the rural community were not improved enough for easy passage of automobiles, and by necessity horse-drawn vehicles were common transportation. Life at Flint Hill moved at a slow pace. Mae, a stranger, was curious to see the places native to the mother she had never known.

On their first ride together Oscar and Mae traveled by a buggy down the main-traveled country road and in conversation discovered a mutual interest in modern gadgetry. When they rode again, they followed side roads and took photos with Oscar's folding bellows Kodak, although they had trouble figuring out the exposures and almost none of the images turned out. On their rides Oscar delighted in showing Mae spectacular views from the steep hills. The winding glimmer of the Wateree River threaded through them. The young couple saw woods and fields, some of them beautifully cultivated, others abandoned and scarred by erosion and neglect.

Only two and one-half rugged miles by straight-line reckoning from the Smyrl home, Oscar and Mae felt very small looking down from a precipitous clay-and-stone ledge the locals called Eagle's Nest. Below them the broad top of a mammoth new dam more than eighty feet high stretched across the Wateree River. The raw concrete barrier, with ant-like workers and distant echoes of heavy machines, gave startling contradiction to nearby areas of quiet natural isolation. Building of the dam had begun before America joined the World War and had continued despite it. All the time Oscar had been away, the dam had been rising higher and higher. Hundreds of able-bodied workers were exempted from the draft to keep up the steady construction pace. Only recently, on September 13, according to the news report of the Southern Power Company, water had risen high enough behind the yet-unfinished dam to begin turning wheels on its five twenty-thousand-horsepower turbines. Behind the dam the impounded waters of the Wateree River were rising into a muddy body spreading over twenty miles back.

Along with the old river banks now submerged in the waters below where Oscar and Mae stood, rising waters had swallowed the fishery there that had belonged to the Smyrls from antebellum days. Before the dam huge ocean sturgeon had swum seasonally this far to spawn. Covered with water too were cornfields Oscar's family planted when he was a boy, including a plateau they called the Indian mound, where plows had turned up arrowheads and pottery. Also sunken under the waters for miles back were former farms and cemeteries with graves of folks, white and black. Like the native dwellers, they too had made the river valley home. As the young couple spoke of times past, it was also amazing to them to imagine the effect of the new dam once it began to generate the promises of electrical power. Ways of life were changing. What would the new world be like? Oscar and Mae talked readily on such subjects.

It was through writing, too, that the couple grew closer. Letters that Oscar wrote to her, Mae kept. He too tucked away for safekeeping letters she wrote him. They came from families of similar traditions, of similar values—people who kept mementos and correspondence. Letters from their courtship would outlast the long lives of them both.

Though for some time they were "Miss Davis" and "Mr. Smyrl" in their correspondence, the young couple grew comfortable in their friendship. Oscar took Mae home to visit his parents. She already knew them, Mr. and Mrs. Robert Love Smyrl, since Oscar's father was on the school board that employed her. The Smyrls were pleased with their son's new interest.

When Oscar first wrote a letter addressing "May" by her preferred nickname, he mistakenly spelled it "Mae." She liked his spelling, however, and soon adopted it, keeping it as her preference the rest of her life. The couple grew devoted, and by the time the school year ended, they had pledged one another that they would marry when she completed her teaching contract. Married women were not favored as teachers in rural classrooms.

Oscar meanwhile tackled with zest his new work in Camden. He was determined to get ahead in his position as a cotton broker for the local firm of Frank M. Wooten. Mae understood Oscar's ambition to support his family more securely than the way afforded by farming the earth, the only way of life open to his father in the Reconstruction South of his early manhood. Oscar was pleased to learn that Mae's fashionable, neat, and tidy clothing was the result of her own needlecraft, in which she took great pride. "A woman of gumption need never be out of style," she would say, "as long as she applies her needle." Mae was a woman of gumption.

Socially Oscar followed similar steps as his father, his grandfather, and his great-grandfather by completing initiation into the rites of Masonry. He was drawn to the fraternal organization, he said, for character-building advantages. On May 6, 1920, he was "raised to the Sublime Degree of Master Mason" in Camden's Kershaw Lodge No. 29, Ancient Free Masons of South Carolina, and remained a lifelong member. Mae approved of Oscar's interest, for the men of her family too were Masons. She and her family, like Oscar and his, were also active Southern Baptists, so there was no question between the two of them which denominational church they would attend. Like the women of her family and his, Mae throughout her life would teach Sunday school and work with devotion in women's missionary activities.

At the end of her school contract in May 1920, Mae left on the train for her home in Clinton, North Carolina, not to remain there but to arrange her wedding. Oscar followed her in a few days. They were married, as they wished, in a simple ceremony on Sunday, May 30, at the home of the grandmother who had reared her like a mother, with her father, John Nathan McDonald Davis, to give her away and with close kin as witnesses. Officiating was the Reverend Claudius D. Peterson, Mae's uncle. In 1898 in South Carolina he had married her parents in Flint Hill Baptist Church. Mae had grown up like a sister to her cousins, Reverend Peterson's children, since his family shared the Davis household. In Mae's adolescence her father remarried so she also had a young half sister and an infant half brother at the time of her wedding.

Mae was amused when Oscar related to her the incident from his childhood when he said he would marry the unknown little girl in the photo. She recognized the image immediately when he described it to her, and she showed him a twin copy of it in her grandmother's home. She was amused, but she was not surprised, she said, for wasn't their union Divine Plan all along? It was a belief in destiny they both accepted.

One year later, on the day of the couple's first wedding anniversary, their first child was born in their Camden home. They named her Lottie Mary. Her first name was given for Oscar's mother, and the middle was not only Mae's given name, but also that of Mae's mother and of her grandmother Davis.

Two years later when Oscar and Mae's first son was born, he was given with pride his father's name. In his family such name giving seemed right and proper. Years later, however, Oscar Jackson, Jr., in adulthood reflected aloud on another effect of being a "junior." "Every time I spoke my name,"

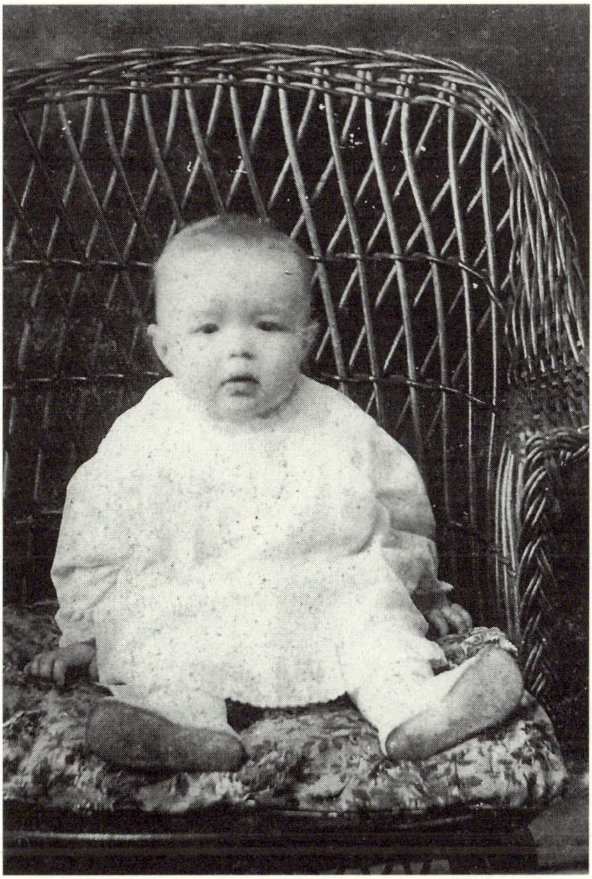

Oscar Jackson Smyrl, Jr., about one year old. Courtesy of the family.

he shook his head ruefully, "I was already marked with another man's deeds and reputation. Yes, I was lucky growing up that my father was a good man and no one to be ashamed of! But what a hard thing I felt it as a child to have to live up to a *good man,* to have to be responsible through *my* deeds and reputation to keep *his* name clean also!"

The parents had decided to call their infant son by his middle name. "Jackson" immediately evolved into "Jack," except for schoolroom rolls and military regimens that insisted on the first name "Oscar." The boy would resist efforts of those who would tag him "O.J." That was the business-like nickname of his father—and not an image he had of himself. Longing for his own name reflected youthful self-awareness and a desire for individuality in a family of long traditions and a world of conformity.

Jack's adult art career would be underway before he would humorously and professionally refine his name, at least its spelling, into "Jak." When asked the reason, he would chuckle one or another offhanded explanation. One favorite story he offered with an infectious grin. All his life, he said, he saw people struggle to spell correctly his frequently misspelled *last* name. Since "Smyrl" required all its letters to pronounce it right, he could at least help out by making his *first* name easier to spell. By the time the quirky humorist took a pen name, he had established an individual path in other ways as well.

Chapter 3

Community

"How quickly life can end"

He was born in the Roaring Twenties, grew up in the Great Depression, and reached manhood in World War II. That was the way that artist Jak Smyrl more than once condensed his biography. Indeed each of those distinctive periods of the 1920s, 1930s, and 1940s—when he was still "Jack"—influenced his character and his work. His own words and memoir notes, along with art, photos, correspondence, family memory, documents, interviews, and contemporary journalism, trace his journey through those decades. Initially a view of his surroundings in the first year of his life is a backdrop to the world that first nurtured him.

Friday, May 4, 1923, the day before Jack was born, the weekly *Camden Chronicle* appeared. Cheerily promoting the "city" of five thousand, the chamber of commerce praised its modern assets: "public utilities of every kind, schools, churches, parks, electric power facilities." Founded in colonial days, Camden blended old traditions with visible signs of progress. Not all citizens, however, were enthusiastic about some changes. Most of the streets had been laid out and named by 1798, and newcomer decisions in favor of renaming the east-west streets as numbered "avenues" were falling on deaf ears. *No,* local folk would *not* call a familiar street "Eleventh Avenue." It already had a good name—DeKalb Street for Revolutionary War hero Baron DeKalb, whose remains lay on that same street under a handsome monument.

When Jack was born at 213 DeKalb "Avenue," a compromise briefly in use, Camden's first paving program was underway. The first street to be hard coated its full length was Broad Street. The paving stretched from the front of "the colored church," Mount Moriah Baptist, through the main business section and residential neighborhood northward to the city limits. As the pavement laid its equally straight, equally smooth line through distinct areas of racial, economic, and social diversity, one letter to the local press worried that easier travel for "strangers" would jeopardize "privacy."

The Smyrls lived on the second street to be paved full length. DeKalb "Avenue" was hard coated from the depots of two railroads, the Southern and the Northwestern, at the town's eastern boundary, to the Seaboard Airline Railway's freight depot at its western boundary. Residential and business sections lay between. As the main east-west crossroad of Broad Street, DeKalb was the significant travel route that would later become part of U.S. Highway 1. Whatever it was called, sometimes it looked as deserted as a country road. At other times it brought into the town an interesting parade of horse-drawn and motorized vehicles of local and foreign travelers passing in front of the Smyrl home.

Since the late 1800s, Camden had been a social mecca for winter tourists. When northern temperatures grew uncomfortably cold, hundreds of persons privately referred to as "the Yankees" poured into town for extended stays. By springtime, the season when Jack was born, tourists departed. With the return of warm weather, they emptied Camden's large resort hotels, guest homes, and seasonal residences. Winter visitors were eager to escape the intensifying southern sun whose rays they had embraced in colder months. By May business and social life in the community resumed in the hands of the people visitors privately referred to as "the natives." Many natives found warm weather quite pleasant.

After the tourists left, a comfortable, folksy rhythm vibrated in community life and the local press. In May 1923, Jack's birth month, society columns that had thrived on elaborate balls and concerts were content to note that a local woman had "entertained at bridge complimenting her mother and sister." The annual May Day Festival featured a baby parade to select the prettiest baby. Nightly (except Sundays) at the downtown Majestic Theatre, black-and-white images of silent movies flickered across the screen, enhanced by music of a live orchestra. Sundays were cherished for going to church and for visiting family and friends. By custom and law, all stores, theaters, and other entertainments closed on Sundays.

During warm months evangelical revivals set up canvas tents in open fields and town lots for spirited gatherings day and night. Singing conventions brought together multiple church and community choirs to raise unified voices in hymns and old-time favorites. Some of the tents were pitched within sight and hearing of the Smyrl home. Colorful exhorters prayerfully admonished listeners to seek salvation and to stay away from wicked men, wayward women, and strong drink. Evangelist Billy Sunday had lately drawn crowds at the Camden Baptist Church, his national reputation preceding him for zingers such as "Whiskey and beer are all right in their place, but their place is in hell." Voices of Temperance rang strong in public settings.

On pleasant weekends Daughters of the American Revolution sold homemade ice cream at the public roller-skating rink beside the Carnegie Library and the Confederate memorial. Seven miles from town the DAR had marked the spot where Baron DeKalb fell wounded at the Battle of Camden, and the ladies were raising funds to mark other sites. Camden was a community that honored its military defenders. On Confederate Memorial Day, the United Daughters of the Confederacy annually served a dinner to veterans of the 1860s. In Kershaw County when Jack was born, fifty-three "boys in gray" were still living in the local area, and seventy-six widows survived those who were not. World War veterans were numerous and respectfully acknowledged.

Throughout town in early May 1923, posters heralded the upcoming live appearances of the Redpath Chautauqua. The annual traveling exhibition set up its enormous tent in the grove behind the public school a block off DeKalb. Flyers announced a full week of dramatic presentations and educational lectures for spiritual and cultural renewal. During their courtship Oscar had invited Mae to accompany him to a Chautauqua performance. She was pleased and thought that his choice of entertainment showed him to be serious minded and cultivated. Since then each year they looked forward to the Chautauqua as a special treat. This year its sponsors earmarked profits to benefit the Camden Hospital. Established ten years earlier but burned two years before, the rebuilt hospital was struggling to pay operating expenses.

Not yet two weeks after Jack's birth, while his mother was still staying close at home, horrifying tragedy devastated daily complacency. On the evening of May 17, five miles below Camden at the Cleveland School, families and friends gathered with pride to watch the children present a commencement play. Other visitors came as well, for school commencements were popular attractions, in effect pleasant community homecoming events.

The performance in the crowded, second-story auditorium was well underway when a burning oil lamp suddenly fell from its ceiling hook and crashed onstage. As flames caught stage curtains and spread steadily, the audience of three hundred began to panic. The only stairway down to the outside exit was an enclosed one, with an inward-opening door at the bottom. The rush down the unlit stairs pressed the door closed, however, and bodies jammed in the stairwell. The school burned to the ground, and with it perished seventy-seven men, women, and children who could not extricate themselves. Many more were injured jumping out of, or being thrown from, second-floor windows into the lurid darkness of night.

When word of the tragedy reached Camden in the still-dark hours of morning, Oscar's sister Mattie Creed spoke quickly to her eldest child, Alvin. It was a stunning moment etched in his memory, a tale he would retell decades later. "Look after the children," Mattie said sternly and briefly to Alvin, and she rushed from home with others to the scene of the fire. Alvin did not then know the details but knew something terrible must have happened for her to leave at such an hour and for him to be given such responsibility with his father away from home on business. Alvin had not quite turned eleven; his two sisters and brother were nine, five, and four.

During the World War, Mattie had joined the local Red Cross, raising funds, rolling bandages, and training for emergencies. Now amid the milling chaos of horrified sufferers and stunned witnesses at the Cleveland School, she gave what first aid she could. She stayed through the morning assigned to help direct families searching charred corpses in the dim hope of finding which unrecognizable body was a loved one.

Oscar reached the scene in early daylight. He described the agony of the bereaved as "unspeakable." The smell of burned flesh was so oppressive that he, like others, reported his appetite suppressed for weeks afterward. The sound of weeping was agonizing. He offered his help, but, he said, what could possibly help in such circumstances?

Among those lost in the flames were in-laws of Oscar and Mattie's sister Nannie Campbell—a twenty-year-old sister-in-law and a fourteen-year-old niece. Among others who died were a number, aged three to forty-two, whose surnames connected to Oscar or Mae by birth or marriage. The Hinson family, kin to Oscar, lost an eleven-year-old daughter, a nine-year-old son, and their nine-year-old cousin. Two Arrants youths and eight persons named Davis were distant connections to Mae's lines. So closely intertwined were the large families of Kershaw and its neighboring counties that few were the local families that did not have someone affected by the fire.

The shock of so many lives so suddenly and painfully lost or damaged traumatized the extended community and attracted national sympathy. Reflectively Mae looked at her family and held baby Jack close. "Had you not just been born," she realized then and told him later, "had your father not stayed home with me that night because of you, very possibly we would have gone to the Cleveland School play. We might even have taken Lottie with us." She shuttered and whispered, "In a way, little one, you saved our lives." Most important, Mae and Oscar would repeat, the terrible fire made them, like many people, realize how quickly life can end and how important it is for family members to cherish one another day by day.

Similar reflections continued for decades throughout the community and in an annual memorial service at Beulah Methodist Church, where most of the Cleveland School victims lie in a mass grave. Practical responses quickly followed the fire. Disaster relief poured in spontaneously from local and national donors. Safety laws were passed to benefit many—public requirements for more than one exit, for outward-opening exit doors, and for fire drill practice. Out of tragedy a positive note was reassuring—that lives of countless others would be spared in the future.

The terrible drama of the Cleveland School fire was well known to children growing up in Jack's generation. Cousin Luther Shaw, fourteen at the time of the tragedy, lived to age eighty-one. Though he had not been at the fire, for the rest of his life in any public gathering he carefully chose a seat at the end of an aisle and near an exit. Such became an ingrained habit of many whose lives were touched by the legacy of the fire.

Within the first year of Jack's birth, other changes also came to his family. When Jack was three months old, Oscar and brother-in-law Ted started a business together. The August 10 *Chronicle,* under "New Cotton Firm," announced that "Messrs. Frank D. Campbell and Oscar J. Smyrl," having worked several years for Frank M. Wooten, at midmonth were opening a cotton-buying and fertilizer business in the rear of the Army and Navy store. The pair moved on amicably and with good wishes on all sides, but they had seen handwriting on the wall. Between 1920 and 1922 the boll weevil had reduced the state's cotton production by 70 percent. Oscar and Ted in 1923 foresaw Mr. Wooten needing less help in the future.

They thought their best chance would be on their own. A brief rise in cotton prices due to scarcity gave them encouragement that prices would continue to improve. Cotton, the cash crop of southern agriculture, was a risky investment. As national opportunities and markets expanded elsewhere in the 1920s, Ted and Oscar banked on their savings and training. Cotton they knew from the ground up from boyhood on their family farms, and both had worked since in merchandizing and banking that relied on agriculture.

Oscar explained, "Ted and I planned to buy cotton directly from farmers, even contract it in the fields, then warehouse the bales and sell when prices went higher." From September to December of 1923, cotton ginned in Kershaw County increased significantly, and prices for a while also rose. "Camden," the *Chronicle* stated on September 21, "is said to be the leading interior cotton market of this state and pays the highest average market price." The business seemed underway in a hopeful time. In March 1924 Oscar took office as Camden city council alderman from his ward. He had run unopposed for the seat vacated by a long-serving member.

Both new responsibilities and a new baby delayed Oscar and Mae's involvement in the local chapter of the Order of the Eastern Star, constituted in April 1924 for Master Masons and female relatives. Soon they joined other Smyrl siblings and spouses already active. The Eastern Star was Camden's first fraternal group in which women and men served together. Social adjustments to female roles were coming gradually since 1920, when women achieved national voting rights equality.

In-town activities did not stop Oscar and his family from regular visits home to Flint Hill, however, nor did they draw him from lifelong outdoor interests. At the old country place, he had ample hunting partners with his father, uncles, brothers, brothers-in-law, and other kinsmen and neighbors. He thought often of the time to come when an older Jack would learn their traditions and join their parties. Oscar's father turned seventy the year Jack was born. His health was good, and he was still a dead-eye shot. Oscar hoped his father and his uncle Big Buddie would be around to teach and influence Jack.

Family sportsmen had grown up also skillful fishermen, drawn to the plentiful waters of the nearby Wateree River. Oscar's avid outdoor companion, his younger brother Willie, in the navy while he was in the army, kept dreaming aloud with him. From the hilltop porches of the old home place, they and older brother Henry were beckoned by distant glimpses of the waters submerging the riverbeds they had known as boys. They had

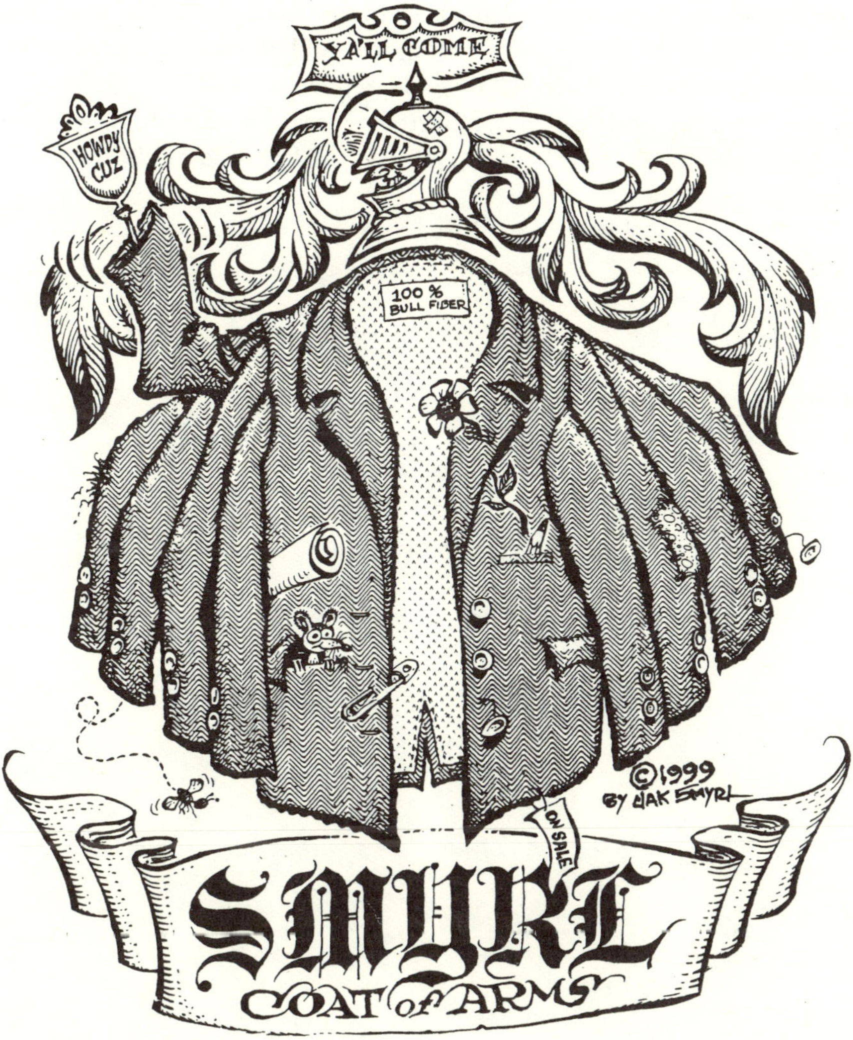

Artist Jak's humorous "coat of arms" for a Smyrl family reunion. Courtesy of the family.

hopes for that big body of water backing up for miles behind the Wateree Dam, which in 1924 was being raised six feet higher to impound even more. Close up the water looked unattractive, even alarming, to many people. Muddy and debris-filled, it was sometimes colored pink from unsettled clay. The dam that old people thought could never be built was holding strong. There was no going back to the way the river had been, but the "Big Pond," as people were calling it, could change. With time who knew what nature could do, what would happen next?

Such was the world of place, storytelling, and dreams into which Jack was born and in which he began to grow in the first year of his life.

Chapter 4

Camden Childhood

"Never lonesome, never bored"

Until Jack was almost ten years old, the DeKalb Street cottage remained the Smyrl family home. "It was an ideal location for a happy childhood," the future artist would later describe it. In his career he completed hundreds of illustrations of children in many capricious moods, sympathetic to thoughts, feelings, and actions of little people. In the last two decades or so of his long eighty-four years of life, he filled a small loose-leaf notebook with lists of incidents for an intended autobiography. The titled lists of memoir notes variously include chronological, topical, and thematic arrangements that suggest their relative importance to him. His bulleted references to childhood events were numerous, as significant to him in his retrospect as events of his lengthy professional career.

Jack was three years old and Lottie five when sister Lucy Love was born on October 1, 1926. Two years later brother Willie Alfred was born on September 16, 1928. Lottie, Lucy, and Alfred also often recounted memories of their early years and first home. Here they lived until late 1932.

On DeKalb Street the children grew close to a large extended family of young cousins and kin nearby. On their street Aunt Mattie and Uncle George Creed lived one block west with their family of four—two boys, two girls. Aunt Nannie and Uncle Ted Campbell lived not far northeastward on Mill Street with one boy and one girl. Next door to them were Aunt Hattie and Uncle Luther "Coleman" Shaw with three boys and four girls. All these children, except one, were older than Jack. He was a couple of years old when Uncle Henry and Aunt Ada Smyrl moved to Camden on newly developed Highland Avenue. They had one boy then and three girls, the youngest of them born a few months after Jack; a second son was born later. About the same time, Aunt Nettie and Uncle Fred Ogburn moved to Camden on Chesnut Street with their first child, a daughter a few months older than Jack, and afterward they added four boys to their family. Though Uncle Willie and Aunt Margaret Smyrl did not have children, they themselves also enlarged the family circle when they moved back to Camden during the same period. In all, in the time Jack lived in the DeKalb Street home with his parents and three siblings, he was living near six sets of aunts and uncles who during his childhood parented twenty-three of his first cousins.

Since kin special to all of them still lived at the old Smyrl home place, in seasons when dirt roads were passable for their autos, the Camden crowd regularly drove "up the country" to spend Sunday afternoons together "at home." They gathered under the shade of oak trees on the edge of the clean-swept front yard, beside the antebellum hand-dug well where cooling water was drawn up in a bucket by rope and windlass. From inside the house, they brought out handcrafted wooden tables on which to spread their basket lunches, and well-worn chairs on which to sit and talk. The children had plenty of space to run and explore. In Jack's early childhood, it was a working farm of about two hundred acres with fenced fields and pastures, and neat rows of outbuildings dedicated to specific tasks. The year before Jack was born, Oscar's mother, Lottie, died. The household continued smooth, familiar running, for his maiden sister Mamie gave up school teaching and moved back home to care for their father, Robert Love Smyrl, and their mother's bachelor brother, Alfred Love. Jak knew them as Mamie, "Grandpa Robert," and "Big Buddie."

Throughout Jack's adult life, many times while he slept he dreamed of Grandpa's house. The dreams varied but were literal views from memory, he a small boy walking safely from room to room with familiar glimpses and voices of people there in his childhood. They were always good dreams and comforting, he said. His brother, Alfred, summed up the feelings of them all: "All the cousins loved to be with Grandpa and Mamie. We always remembered those days and each other." When she was sixty-five, sister Lottie wrote a cousin: "The happiest days of my childhood were those at Grandpa's place rambling the woods. Even now—when stress and pressure get to me, I close my eyes and imagine I am sitting on the porch at

Grandpa's, listening to the crickets chirping and nothing but woods around us. I feel at peace again."

The heart-pine house built in 1853 with cedar-shake shingles remained proudly unpainted in Grandpa's lifetime. He had been a boy of twelve when he stood on that porch in 1865 to face the invading Union soldiers of Sherman's troops. Grandpa's whole life before and since then had been spent on that place, working hard to keep it productive. He was unreceptive to suggestions that he modernize it. Putting paint on his naturally weathered house, like owners of the fancy resort homes in Camden did year after year to look appealing to northern tourists, would be a foolish waste of money, Grandpa said. *He* had no interest in attracting Yankees. He had seen enough of them the *first* time they came by.

"I always think of [your father] as one of the most delightful natural humorists I have ever come in contact with," cousin Daisy Love Wade in Birmingham, Alabama, wrote Mamie on June 11, 1932. Recalling a visit in the 1920s, Daisy said, "Uncle Robert always saw the most amusing side of everything and kept me convulsed with laughter nearly all the time I was talking to him. I thoroughly enjoyed him." The reaction was typical of those who experienced the welcoming hospitality of sociable storytelling and good food at the old home. Visitors praised Mamie's cooking, whatever she served, with Daisy's enthusiasm: "You had the best hot biscuits, the best coffee and grits, the most delicious eggs, and oh, that jam and preserves! Fit for a king. And we all sat around and ate leisurely and chatted as long as we cared to."

Jack was among the children who loved extended visits to the home place. Especially throughout the summer, small groups of young cousins stayed together at Grandpa's without their parents for a few days or up to a week at the time. They easily mingled with other cousins and neighbors nearby. The Kelly cousins lived across the road on the home place of Grandpa's late sister Etta, now home to her son Blake and his wife, Ola, and their family. Jack was two years younger than Steve Kelly so they were special buddies. Jack thought Steve extra lucky to live so close that he could go to Grandpa's every day. Steve in adulthood said he grew up feeling as close to Uncle Robert as the Smyrl grandchildren felt. For the children who visited the farm, early hours and real chores had to be taken as seriously as they were by those who lived there, but there was time for companionship during work and for play after work. Jack and Steve also enjoyed tagging along after Big Buddie, an old-time trapper and fisherman. Jack later described Big Buddie as "more at home in the outdoors

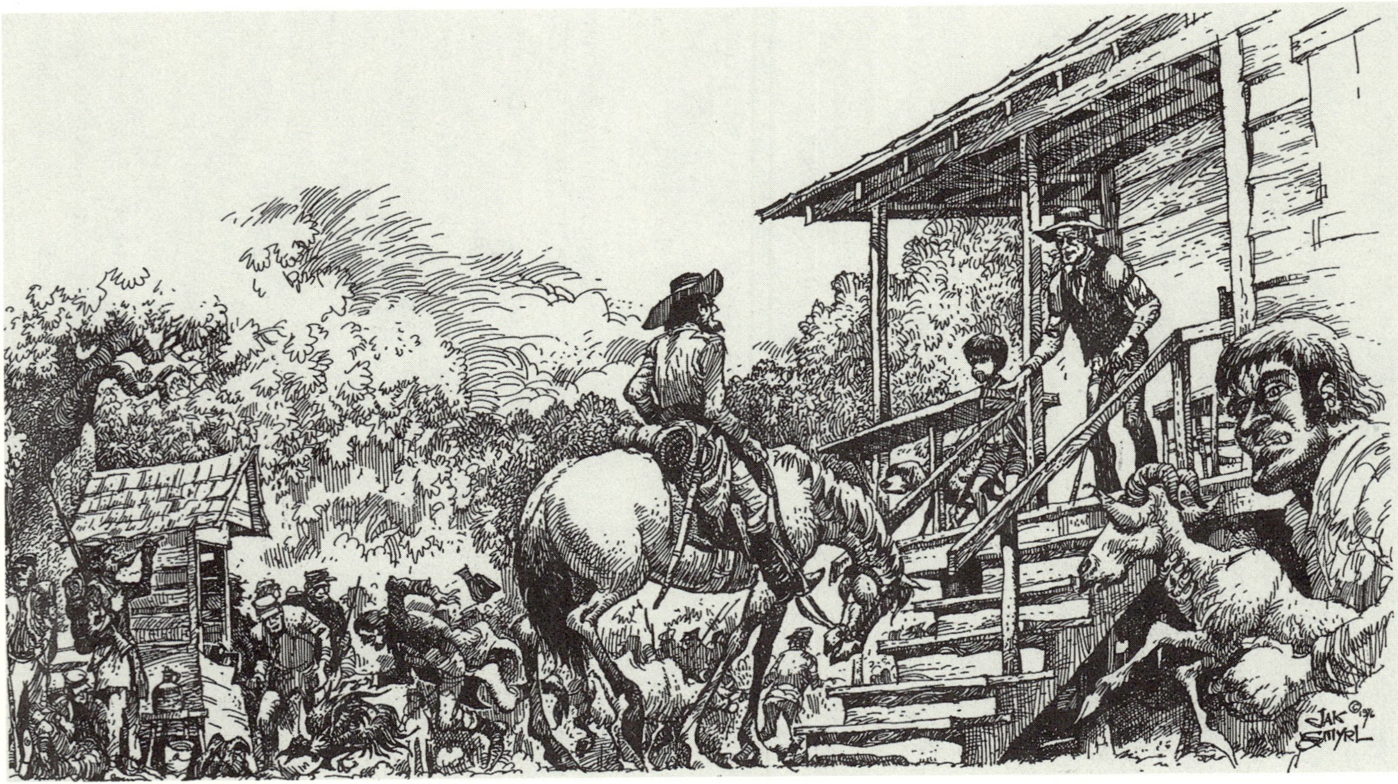

Artist Jak's sketch in 1976 (for *Kershaw County Legacy*), depicting Union troops at the Smyrl home in 1865, based on eyewitness details from his grandfather, the young boy on the porch. Courtesy of the family.

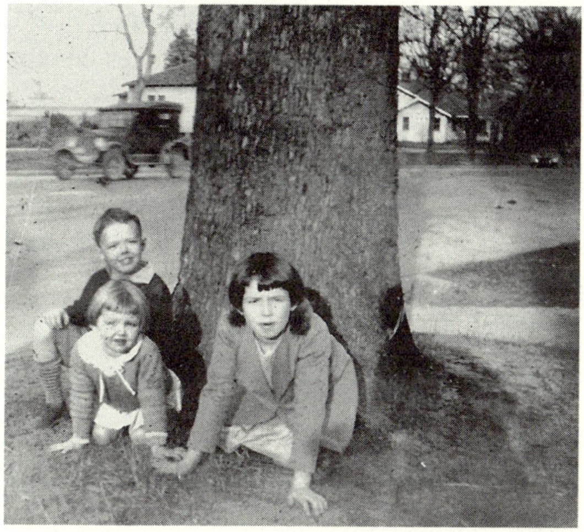

Jack, Lucy, and Lottie near their DeKalb Street home. Courtesy of the family.

than anyone I ever knew." Sometimes Jack and Steve just sat quietly beside Big Buddie and watched him silently carving a stick of wood while other people were talking.

Jack felt "never lonesome, never bored" as a child, he said, since there was always someone to play with, whether at the old home place or at his Camden home. With plenty of adults and older children around to keep an eye on the younger ones, he recalled feeling secure and not overly repressed. With so many young people around, cheerful spirits and even silliness dominated. There were general rules the families were all firm about when the children played together—older children were to look after younger ones, younger ones were to listen to older ones, and they were all to follow the golden rule: "Do unto others as you would have them do unto you." If squabbles arose among children, adults chided, "Hush. Work it out among yourselves. Be fair."

Among the youngsters of his family, Jack said that those rules and situations worked in his favor, but when he got old enough to venture out from his DeKalb Street home to play with neighborhood children, there were new lessons to learn. One he called his "first knowledge of dishonesty and theft" when "two street-wise kids down the block lured me into a game of marbles." Young Jack, on one of his first outings alone, carried with him his prized cigar box filled with marbles. When he came back, his mother noticed the box oddly rattling. "Mama looked inside and asked why I only had four or five marbles now. I was too naïve to conceive that the boys had stolen the others from me." Mama knew exactly who to ask for help. "Frank Campbell, my older cousin, went after the boys and retrieved my marbles."

Jack was delighted when Frank returned before long with his pockets stuffed with Jack's marbles. The older boy first helped him refill his cigar box, then elevated himself even further in Jack's eyes when he sat his young cousin down on the curb and told him some facts of life. The essence, as Jack recalled later, was that when you meet up with kids you don't know, you keep an eye on your stuff and you watch close what the others are doing. If they don't treat you right, you look in their eyes and glare (Frank demonstrated and made Jack practice). And if your look doesn't stop them, you tell them real loud and strong what Frank told the guys to get the marbles back: "There are more of *us* around here than *you*."

There was plenty of rough-and-tumble play in Jack's outdoor childhood. Adults thought it normal and healthy. There were also lessons to be learned from it. When Jack fractured his arm falling from his tricycle, his parents praised his persistence in learning to ride despite his accident.

Jack had another lesson after an exciting Saturday afternoon at the movies. His family had walked down the street to sit mesmerized in the Majestic Theatre before a silent screen of rapid black-and-white images, enlivened by local musicians. All the way home, Jack jabbered about the jungle adventures he had seen. His imagination fired, he ran into the backyard to play. The yelling came soon after—loud, startled, and pained. His parents rushed to the back door to see Jack limping toward them with a bloody knee and holding a bloody elbow. Broken blooms of purple wisteria scattered beneath a wide-limbed tree told the story. Like Tarzan Jack had grabbed a hanging vine and swung lustily forward. How shocking to be plunged midair to the ground and a moment later have a detached vine plop atop his head! "Jack," his parents said urgently, mopping his wounds with soapy water, "you cannot believe everything you see in the movies."

Jack's favorite play costume, a cowboy suit his mother made him, was inspired by his early fondness for western movies. While girls his age favored dolls, tea sets, and playing dress-up, boys all had cowboy hats and cowboy guns. Boys shot up smoky caps in noisy battles elaborately staged between good guys and bad guys. In Jack's eyes no one else had such a fine cowboy suit as he, with western-themed pants, fringed shirt, vest, and colorful neck scarf. One day he allowed a visiting playmate—familiarly known to everyone as "Piggy"—to wear the special costume. When his friend begged to run home so his mother could see it on him, Jack agreed.

True to his word, Piggy brought the cowboy suit back, but after he left, Jack was horrified to discover that the seam in the seat of the pants had been completely split by the chubby boy. Jack was in tears until his mother assured him her needle could repair the damage. "You don't want to hurt your friend's feelings, do you?" said Mae. The needle saved the friendship, and the split seam was never mentioned.

A freedom that DeKalb Street children enjoyed in early years was being legally allowed to roller-skate on the paved street. The Smyrls kept a wary eye on their children while they skated, allowing it only when traffic was sparse. They warned them against a practice of bolder youths—grabbing hold of an auto bumper, or a rope tied to one, and skating along behind, letting the car pull them. Sometimes a passing motorist or a passenger would extend an arm out of a window and let a skating child catch it to "ride" alongside the car. In later years grownup Jack reflected, "Imagine the danger of that! And there I was as a kid, being envious because my folks wouldn't let me try those tricks!"

One of Jack's favorite perches for watching the world go by was just down his street on Aunt Mattie's front porch, shaded by a huge and sweeping magnolia. Uncle George Creed was a building contractor, from time to time adding an embellishment here, changing a room there. Their front porch was grand. It overlooked Hampton Park across the street, a grove of towering longleaf pines named for fiery Governor Wade Hampton half a century past. The park was a primary gathering place for town events. From the Creed home, Jack and his cousins could watch crowds assembling for political speeches, band concerts, revivals, programs, ceremonies, picnics, and parades. The excitement and noisy crowds always seemed fun to him.

Jack was indeed a child susceptible to imagination, as he said, "always the one who really saw Santa Claus peering through the window." Once, walking home through Hampton Park, he encountered older schoolchildren who called to him, "Little boy, little boy, look out for the green man! He's in the treetops." They ran about shouting fearfully. "Ooo, look, look, there he is up there . . . Ohhh, noo, he's going to get us. You better run!" Jack ran. In following days Jack took prudent action. He began taking the long way home, walking down the sidewalk a block over to avoid the park. When his mother asked why he had started coming home so late, he told her truthfully—he didn't want the Green Man in the Treetops to catch him.

Jack's father took him by the hand and walked him back to the park. Together they peered up into all the tall, green treetops. "Jack," said his father. "Do you see anybody here?" The boy shook his head. "You and I see that there is no Green Man in the Treetops. Don't you think those big children were playing a game, making a joke?" Jack nodded happily. "Now," said his father, "remember how scared they made you feel, and don't *you* go playing mean tricks on other little people like they did you."

In 1926 Oscar was appointed by Governor Thomas McLeod to fill the unexpired elected term of a long-serving Kershaw County treasurer. Oscar served for three years in the position. One day in 1927 he was working at the courthouse when another job was offered. This one was for four-year-old Jack, invited by the clerk of court to fill a paying position unique for a child.

For two years, at the beginning of each court session, the small boy walked hand in hand with his father to work at the courthouse. There in the presence of the court officials, Jack stood on an upended wooden box and drew names from a hat to select jurors. All his earnings over the two years—nearly $75—his father deposited into a First National Bank account in his son's name. The job had just one requirement, that the person who drew the names must be illiterate so that an impartial selection of juror names was assured. In 1929 Jack started first grade. Thus, since he would now learn to read, he lost his job. "Education," the adult Jack liked to deadpan, "proved a detriment to my employment."

About the time Jack started first grade, he fell ill with measles. While he was in bed quarantined at home, itchy and miserable in his isolation, his mother gave him paper and a pencil so he could amuse himself by drawing. When he showed his parents his pictures—cowboys, and animals, and funny faces—they responded, "Oh, Jack, that's so good. You are a real *artist*." Over the years the adult Jack in various interviews would recall the experience with bemusement: "I was just a kid. I believed what my parents told me. They said I was an artist . . . so I believed I was an artist." He loved to take the story further. "That experience really helped me out in my life. Unlike other kids, I never had to worry what I'd be or go about searching for my identity. I already knew. I was an artist. I had it made, never wanted to be anything else." Laughing at himself became a hallmark of his humor, although he was serious that from childhood he felt destined to become an artist.

Some of the drawings Jack made in his childhood randomly survived. A few he compiled in later life when asked to supply samples of his early art. He labeled these in adult years "Jak Smyrl." Some are on a sheet of Oscar's letterhead stationery imprinted for the Kershaw County treasurer.

Some are on the backs of old calendars that Aunt Mamie recycled as scrap paper. Like his mother she saved samples of Jack's drawings, especially those done on visits to Flint Hill. The number of his sketches she kept in comparison to those of many other children in her life suggests her recognition of special promise in Jack's efforts.

At Camden Graded School Jack faced typical childhood challenges to conform and learn in set patterns. Of course he could very neatly draw that little circle with a stick on its side, the one the teacher called an "a," but what fun was it to keep doing that over and over exactly the same way and to make each one sit in a straight line? It was much more interesting to arrange them this way and that, to make one circle a funny face and another circle a fat puppy with a long tail. He could work quietly with much concentration on something like that.

For a time his long-experienced teacher was patient with the little daydreamer, expecting he would settle down, catch up, and do his work the right way like the other children. However the day she heard a giggle here and another there, she realized that Jack's sheet of pencil sketches was being passed around the room. "What's happening here?" she sternly questioned the little boy who concerned her because his academic progress lagged behind. He gave her a pleased smile. He was happy that his friends were amused by his drawings! "Oscar Jackson," she was only the first teacher to sigh, "what's to become of you?!"

Chapter 5

Rural Adventuring

"A paradise we had all to ourselves"

Many of the adventures that young Jack recalled of his childhood were powered by the same force that had Americans of all walks of life moving in the 1920s—the automobile engine. Improved roadways and more affordable, reliable vehicles opened access to distant places for many people. Oscar, Mae, and four small children at first bounced down the roads together in his well-worn Model T Ford. They fit more comfortably into the sturdy, roomy Chevrolet he replaced it with by the late 1920s. While their excursions were not as lengthy or distant as those of Camden's winter tourists, Mae said, paraphrasing Thoreau, whom she admired, "We travel widely in Concord."

During weekend visits to the hill country around Grandpa's, the family ventured off via improved sand-clay roads to view and picnic at scenic sites. Some lay farther than the ones that Oscar and Mae had visited by buggy during their courting days. Just over in Lancaster County were sites such as the once-productive Haile Gold Mine and two aptly named geological curiosities—Hanging Rock and Forty Acre Rock. Within the county line the family explored Cedar Rock and their favorite remote picnic place, an ancient shelter called Kelly Rock. Jack liked climbing around the boulders and inside the room-like overhang where Oscar said a man who did not want to be a soldier lived hidden during the Civil War. Jack wondered why a man would not want to be a soldier.

Only a little more than ten miles beyond Grandpa's, the children grew familiar with long views from the heights of the quaint village of Liberty

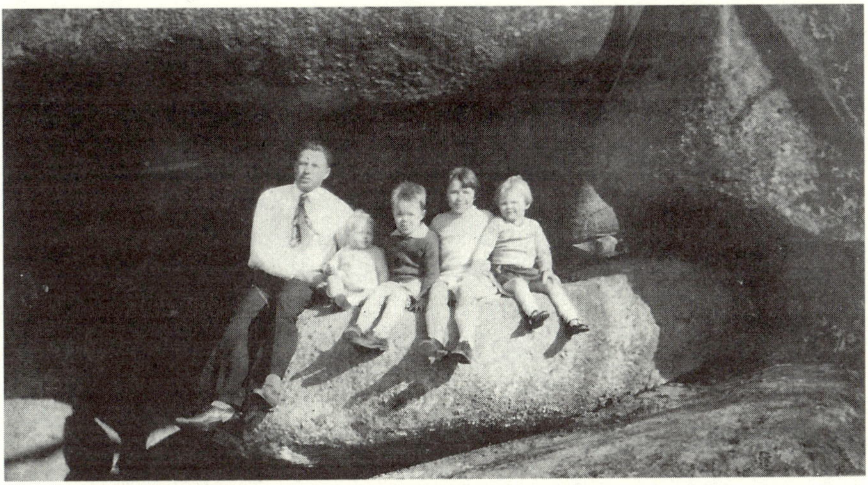

Oscar, Alfred, Jack, Lottie, and Lucy on family outing at a favorite picnic spot. Courtesy of the family.

Hill. One was the mountain-like vista in front of the home of their governor, John G. Richards. From that location the children learned to recognize the steep hill peak miles back that was topped by the old Smyrl Cemetery on a hill they sometimes climbed from Grandpa's house. Grandpa's big brother Jim was buried there. He had died in the Civil War. Jack felt sure that when Uncle Jim left home he had wanted to be a soldier.

From Eagle's Nest, where the family often drove on their way home from Grandpa's, the children viewed the Wateree Dam with its towers of steel and heavy tension wires stretching far distant from the concrete powerhouse below. Electricity from there and similar places, Oscar and Mae told them, made its way to homes such as theirs in Camden and to far more distant places. Someday it would also run to homes right there in Flint Hill. The children were too young for discussion of economic and political reasons why country people had not yet received benefits of the power that originated in their own neighborhood.

Jack may simply have assumed that electricity was just another new thing that Grandpa didn't want or need. He knew that years ago, when automobiles first came out, Grandpa had bought one, driven it briefly, then parked it permanently on blocks in his barn. Grandpa was afterward satisfied to keep getting himself about the rural countryside in his buggy.

His horse already knew where to pull the wheels on a rutted road and didn't have to be shown the way to get back and forth to town.

The family's rambles took them in other directions and much farther from home. There were day trips, overnight camping trips, and stays with distant kin. Very few roads were paved, and all were marked with desolate, isolated stretches. Any trip required packing a basket of food and supplies of water, extra gasoline, some spare parts, and tools. Jack was still very young when he was taken for the first time to the ocean. The Intracoastal Waterway was not yet completed, and coastal development was in its infancy. Jack's father held his small hand securely as they walked into the surf at Myrtle Beach. As the first briny waves splashed over the child's legs and sucked at the shifting sands under his toes, he quickly reached up to climb into his father's arms. "Daddy, Daddy," Jack said, urgently confident of his father's ability to fix all problems. "Make it stop *sloshing!*"

There were also trips to North Carolina. In Wilmington they visited Oscar's widowed Aunt Sallie Love "Lallie" Kohler and family, and they went together by trolley to Wrightsville Beach and its fabled old pavilion. In Clinton, where farms of Davises and kin lay along Beulah Road, they regularly visited Mae's extensive family connections. Mae's grandmother Mary Davis lived until 1931 so Jack knew among other elders a great-grandmother as well as his grandfather McDonald Davis. The hospitality and gatherings of North Carolina kin Jack likened to those at the Smyrl home place, although the farmers among them planted tobacco rather than cotton and the fishermen planned ocean rather than river jaunts. The same automotive advances and highway improvements that allowed the Smyrls to visit distant family also allowed those kin to pay return visits to Camden. "Come stay for a week or so," family members urged one another in letters back and forth.

The skillful hands that could always repair, improve, or replace a wayward engine or faulty part that might result in an auto breakdown were those of Oscar's younger brother Willie. He had first fallen in love with the power of movement as a boy riding his "wheel"—a heavy, two-wheeled, one-geared bicycle—to conquer rural roads with his same-age buddy Dewey Creed of nearby Cantey, the next hill over from Flint Hill. In their early teens the pair ordered and assembled kits to motorize their bikes. Always the family's free spirit, Willie was happy to be out of the classroom and resisted their urgings to continue his education. It was in the outdoors that he was at home, naturally drawn to the woods and water. Still in his teens, he took a job delivering messages and small packages by motorcycle for the Southern Express Company. Before long he was working for them in the railroad town of Hamlet, North Carolina, and driving long-distance delivery trucks to the mountains, the coast, and as far as Florida.

At age twenty-one in 1918, while Oscar was in the army, Willie joined the navy, serving as a fireman with mechanical duties on two ships that had been captured from the Germans and converted to American service under new names—the gunboat *USS Nashville* and the military cargo ship *USS Kittery*. At duty's end Willie came home with seasoned mechanical skills, cruising experience, a passion for broad expanses of water, and an impressively startling sailor's vocabulary. Wanderlust and adventure would always tug at him, even as home ties rooted him to family and familiar places.

In 1920 Willie was back in Camden, first near Oscar and Mae in the home of sister Mattie and brother-in-law George Creed, where Willie's childhood bike-riding buddy Dewey, George's half brother, also lived. Willie and Dewey worked as mechanics in downtown auto sales-and-service businesses, Willie at Kershaw Motor and Dewey at Carolina Motor. Less than one month after Oscar and Mae wed, Willie married another rural first-year schoolteacher, Margaret Cook, and the following year Dewey married Marie Williams. The interrelated circle of four energetic, friendly young couples with country roots remained actively connected for years, although at first Willie and Margaret moved about from town to town where his skills were sought for specialized engines and machinery. Dewey, like Oscar and George, settled in Camden.

By 1925 Willie and Margaret returned to Camden, where Willie owned and operated Smyrl's Garage. Jack would recall it from early childhood. On Market Street's northeastern corner near DeKalb, the garage was in a well-traveled location within sight of the monument to Baron DeKalb. Dewey, still at Carolina Motor while also pursuing rural business in timbering, soon owned and operated Creed's Gas Station and Garage, in which George was an investor.

Willie's garage quickly became a popular gathering spot for community menfolk who enjoyed tinkering, joking, and storytelling. In the yard out front, under the shade of trees, he set out a bench or two where the busy and the idle gathered for quick or lazy conversations. Neither customers nor visitors, and certainly not children, were readily welcomed very far inside through the wide doors of the shed-like work building where the serious work went on and equipment and parts were stored. Willie was stern and gruff about the dangers of anyone messing around with tools, motors, or electrical wires.

A natural prankster, he memorably reinforced his points with the curious. If anyone got too close to his tools, Willie would say, "While you're there, how about handing me my hammer at the edge of the table?" The unknowing curiosity seeker would willingly oblige, only quickly to drop it with startled oaths and rush out rubbing his strangely pained hand. "Oh, sorry," Willie would say, "it's mighty dangerous in here. That's why I have those signs up." Guffawing bench sitters kept quiet about what they knew—that Willie had a mild electric charge hooked up to the tools on his table, but they too were impressed with a lesson. Who knew what else he might have rigged in there? Cousin Steve Kelly recalled that Willie, not uncommon for customs of the time, always carried on him his .38 pistol, just not right out where everyone could see it.

Obediently watching at a distance, Jack remained fascinated by both Willie's work and his play. For several years at Christmastime Willie and his garage cohorts laid skyrockets on their sides in the middle of the paved street and shot them off horizontally down DeKalb Street, challenging themselves to see how far and straight the flaming rockets would travel. There was no law against it, and in fact a number of onlookers enjoyed the spectacle and remembered it years afterward. Noisy, even rowdy, celebrations were acceptable for Christmas then and almost always included fireworks for young and old.

It was far from town and the public eye, however, that a grand dream of the Smyrl brothers, with help of like-minded kin and friends, became reality on the Big Pond behind the Wateree Dam. The area was so unpopulated that Grandpa and Willie safely delighted in shooting rifle balls just above the water surface to make them skip like stones. The name Lake Wateree had yet to come into use. The men began simply, just wanting to stake out a fishing hole not far from Grandpa's that they could claim as their own, a camping spot where they could meet and conveniently stash basic gear from one trip to another. In November 1924 the holdings of Wateree Power Company had become part of Duke Power Company. It was from Duke that Dewey, with his timbering connections, leased a piece of property for them that they had scouted out as just right for what they wanted.

It was a small island that the men found, the largest one that lay within sight of an accessible shoreline familiar to them, but far enough out in the water for the privacy and protection they wanted. It was covered with the same wild vegetation and native trees that stretched inland from the banks of the lake. The men would need some kind of boat to get over to the island and back, but they were not thwarted. Generations of the family had grown up along the river and had always contrived various devices and conveyances to make use of its waters and to cross from side to side. What a natural duck-hunting blind they knew the island would make, providing an open view of waterfowl all the way down the big water! What access to the big fish they knew lay in those depths!

The islands that poked their rounded heads above the broad waters were stubborn survivors of the tallest hilltops that rose above the submerged river channel. They were yet little affected by the erosion, use, and time that would slowly diminish them to less than half in number and size. Most of the early islands were still forested, for their heights had thwarted the timber cutters working feverishly ahead of rising waters to make a final harvest from the future lakebed. Decaying debris of those operations, along with the natural litter of forest floors and uncut growth, darkened the waters of the early lake and collected in jams along its shores. Years would pass before the area in which the leased island lay would bear the name Clearwater Cove.

The old homemade hunting boat that the menfolk first adapted to get to and from their wild island had to move slowly and cautiously, carrying but one or two passengers and light gear. It was a beautiful and peaceful destination. They began to talk of ways to stay there longer and to have friends and family enjoy it with them. Willie, with aid of Henry, set to building a larger boat, a sailboat, broad and shallow bottomed.

By wind power when luck was with them and by manpower when it was not, the men sailed, poled, and paddled back and forth, pulling afloat behind them or balancing aboard the materials to raise an improvised shelter on the island. Vision carried them further. Cohorts aided along the way. Sometime beginning in the late 1920s, through sporadic but persistent efforts, a solid and comfortably sized camp house was raised on the island. One of the friends who helped with the building and shared in its use was Milton H. Deal, a county bridge engineer and supervisor. A wide and sheltering porch stretched across the front, overlooking the big water that reflected sunrises, sunsets, and moonlight. Open windows on the sides closed with solid shutters. Inside the men hammered together shelves, tables, and benches, as well as bunk beds and other flat surfaces for seating and spreading bedrolls for sleeping. Outside a patiently dug well provided water for household use.

Jack's family, like the kin and friends who shared time in the island house, enjoyed the simplicity of its arrangements. Vacationing there, they spent most of their time outdoors or on the porch. Relaxing, talking, fishing, swimming in summer or heading out to blinds for hunting in winter—their observations of nature were enhanced by peaceful views in all directions. Milton Deal's son, Jack Deal, in an interview in the *State* on September 1, 1983, recalled the time "when you could go a whole day on the lake without seeing another living soul." He stated, "In just a few minutes time you could catch enough crappie, bass and carp to fill a big burlap bag." The lake was so unpopulated then and so full of bounty that Jack Smyrl described those experiences as "living like kings in a paradise we had all to ourselves."

The sense of luxury increased when Willie rigged up a Delco generator to produce electricity for island camping. Since country homes still lacked electrification, the camp house seemed even more special. All cooking was done outside over open fire until with great effort a cast-iron, wood-burning stove was brought over and installed inside. It added comfort in cool weather and occasional convenience for cooking.

Meanwhile Willie and Dewey were adding motors to their boats. Willie was employed in Georgetown when he traded some labor in exchange for an old oceangoing dory and finagled a ride home for it on a flatbed truck. Then from a wrecked Chevrolet he salvaged a gasoline engine and rigged it with a shaft to power the dory. Steve Kelly laughed recalling that the first time Willie tried to run the motorized boat, it flew up almost out of the water. Willie made delicate adjustments, although he remained always "particular" about who he let run his motors. Jack remembered the flat-bottomed, high-sided boat as remarkably stable while transporting passengers and gear to and from the island.

Dewey later made a coastal purchase as well, a small oceangoing yacht with a blown engine. Willie repaired the damaged engine, and when weather and water conditions favored, he and Dewey embarked on the refitted vessel's maiden voyage—beginning by water homeward to the island. Leaving coastal Winyah Bay, they chugged against the natural flow of seaward-moving current to make their way up to the head of the Santee River and into the Wateree River. They handled together all navigational obstacles as far as the toll bridge at Camden, where Oscar recalled they pulled the craft ashore. With no water access around the dam six miles ahead, they sought heavy equipment and willing hands to haul out and truck the boat the rest of its journey.

Laboriously set afloat in Lake Wateree, the unfamiliarly designed boat was at once awkward and magnificent. Jack recalled that it could accommodate up to a dozen people aboard. Who had ever seen such a large craft afloat in that part of the country? At times the boat proved useful, such as ferrying the heavy cast-iron stove over to the island. Under the right water conditions, passengers enjoyed pleasant lake tours. At other times, especially when water was low, the deep-bottomed boat's use was clumsy although its sight remained a marvel. Gradually, from the early 1930s, motorboats and various other vessels became more common on the lake, making it "very interesting," Jack recalled. He added with nostalgia, "also less wild and private."

Hospitable gatherings and occasional vacation stays on the island were part of Jack's family life for two decades. The island being a recognizable river landmark, an increasing number of motorboaters dubbed it with a name derived from the "No Trespassing" signs posted there with names of "Creed Timber" and "Creed Construction." The site became Creed's Island, though to the family in the days of its early use, it was simply "the island." They knew which one they meant.

The experiences that Jack grew comfortable with as a child beyond his Camden home and his grandfather's Flint Hill farm nurtured in him an early belief that the world was a welcoming place of grand experiences. Acquiring a thirst for adventure while still in the companionship and protection of family, he developed also a gift for feeling at home wherever he found himself in the world. In particular the river adventures of Jack's early years stirred a sense of romance that he described as a lifelong "love affair" with islands and the waters surrounding them.

Chapter 6

The Depression

"The one choice you have"

The "happy years" that adult Jack titled his childhood were at times differently perceived by others around him. Letters and other documentation of his family and of the times reveal stresses and worries. Not all of them may have been comprehended in a child's world although they impacted it. Southern agriculture and thus the southern economy declined drastically in the latter years of the 1920s, prior to the 1929 stock market crash that signaled the Great Depression of the 1930s.

The boll weevil ate away at local cotton production. In 1927 agents surveying the Flat Rock section found only two bolls per five cotton plants. Grandpa's farm income was hard hit. So was Oscar and Ted's cotton-buying partnership. Despite crop shortages cotton prices fell. Despite low prices mills bought less and slowed production. What was happening?

Oscar took an additional job to tide him over. He and Ted had paid warehouse fees in Charlotte, Camden, and Charleston to store cotton they had bought, hoping to recoup when conditions got better. Alfred recalled that he and Jack liked his daddy's new work, selling fertilizer and running Swift and Company's cotton gin at the west end of DeKalb Street. The boys thought it fun to stand under the big funnel that sucked the bolls of loose cotton up into an overhead drying chamber. The vacuum above the boys pulled the hair on their heads straight up, and they each laughed at the other's silly appearance.

At the end of 1928 as business slowed, Willie closed his Camden garage, and he and Margaret moved to Orangeburg, where he worked as a mechanic with a large automobile dealer. Womenfolk sympathized with Margaret about her continued "female troubles" that resulted in miscarriages but not babies. The ladies worried that moving would be hard for her, although they also hoped maybe a fresh start would lift her spirits. Margaret was "getting along pretty good" but "homesick" when she wrote Mamie and Pa Robert on February 14, 1929. Health problems continued. Medications complicated them. On March 31, 1930, she wrote them: "I lost a good deal when I was sick, but have gained about 3 lbs since I came home from the hospital. I weigh exactly 100."

Health problems affected Grandpa's farm too. In October 1928 Mamie spent two weeks at the Baptist hospital in Columbia for a hysterectomy to treat a serious condition. The following year she needed her restored strength. "I am surely sorry to hear of Uncle Robert and Uncle Buddie's feebleness," cousin Bob Love wrote her from Birmingham on October 4, 1929. In the warm, exceptionally rainy season, the two elderly outdoorsmen had taken prevalent fevers. The week after Bob wrote, Big Buddie was found paralyzed. He lingered seventeen days unable to take any nourishment and died on October 29. The stock market crash on Wall Street that week slid by unnoticed on the farm.

During the bitter temperatures of early 1930 Grandpa suffered a long bout of pneumonia. On January 27 Bob's sister Daisy wrote Mamie inquiring about his progress and sympathizing, "You have certainly had a hard time this winter, and it has been such a cold winter, too." Snow and ice had come to the farm for the first time in years. Daisy revealed "a terrible shock" at their house that month too. Their kindly landlord, who lived downstairs with his family, had "shot himself straight through the heart." The death had upset them very much, she said, feeling it a "terrible thing for anyone to take his own life—usher himself unbidden into the presence of his Creator."

The Great Depression was underway. Willie's move for a new job was at the head of several economy-influenced changes in Jack's aunts and uncles' families in the early 1930s. By the middle of the decade the Ogburns and the Creeds were the only ones of the six siblings' families still living within the town of Camden. The Shaws moved to Columbia, the Campbells moved to Chester, and Henry moved his family to a house on Grandpa's place. Oscar's family moved outside the town limits of Camden. The families kept in touch, writing letters and spending time together at Grandpa's. Visits brought helpful hands and kept him cheered. It was encouraging to watch Grandpa rally from each spell of adversity.

Everyone was glad Henry's family was close by when others could not be. Even more than before, the old farm was their touchstone.

A tragedy in mid-1931 deeply affected the family. Jack, eight years old then, would remember it well. It was a sizzling Thursday afternoon, June 11, when his family, the Kellys with Steve, and some others casually gathered in Grandpa's shaded yard to cool off by eating spring-chilled watermelons. The same afternoon the teenaged Creed cousins, having made a churn of ice cream, drove up to share some with Grandpa. All visited a while, and then the carload of young people started home. Nineteen-year-old Alvin, who was spending his summer before college working construction with his father, was driving with sister Frances, sixteen, beside him. In the rear brother Otis, fourteen, and cousin Luther Shaw, sixteen, sat in the rumble seat. They cheerfully waved goodbye.

Conversation that had resumed in Grandpa's yard froze abruptly a few minutes later at the loud, horrifying sound of a collision. They knew the car that had just left must be involved. All began running in its direction, southward toward the Flint Hill church. Some prayed aloud, running. Some wept already. They saw black smoke rising before they crested the hill. Jack felt as if he were running in slow motion, breathless, his ears ringing. Two vehicles were in flames, twisted and unrecognizable. Through smoke Jack could see people moving. "Get back! Get back!" came an urgent cry. "The tanks may explode."

Women and children, Jack and Steve among them, were herded off to the front of the churchyard. They waited, huddled. A report was brought back to them. Everyone was being taken to the hospital by a road-construction worker who had heard the collision and immediately brought his truck. The driver of the second car, its only occupant, was another kinsman, John Henry McDowell, who had been on his way to the home of his parents. Someone ran to tell Uncle Bob and Aunt Sallie. Those left there began to pray for John Henry too.

Frances never regained consciousness and was pronounced "expired" on arrival at the hospital. All the others were admitted with "painful injuries" and afterward recovered. Alvin and John Henry, despite their injuries, had immediately removed Frances to the side and, while the twisted vehicles began burning, furiously pulled metal sections apart to extricate Otis and Luther, trapped inside. The dazed boys reported that the crushed auto top had made it impossible to get out on their own. It was learned the cars had collided because the drivers, approaching one another over opposite sides of the steep hill, had not seen one another in time to wrench out their wheels caught in the single set of deep ruts in the narrow road. The stretch here—deeply rutted from rains and hard-dried from heat—had not been scraped smooth for some time while work was underway nearby to build a newer and safer road, Highway 97, to Liberty Hill. When Alvin was ninety years old, he was asked how he had mentally endured such a deeply emotional trauma in his life. "You just do," he said simply. "You go on because it's the one choice you have."

In the early 1930s, Oscar and Ted dissolved their Campbell and Smyrl partnership. When the cost of warehousing their cotton exceeded its market price, they sold at deep loss. Oscar continued running the Swift gin, and Ted took a job in Chester, fifty-five miles distant, where the Campbells moved in 1932. Nannie's letters to her father and sister at Flint Hill confined themselves to reports of routine domesticity, with life in Chester continuing as in Camden. They made visits to Grandpa's, traveling straight there via Highway 97. Ted when not working went hunting and fishing with family and companions. Their one son, Frank, seventeen, had a job in a shop. Their one daughter, Laurie, and her husband, Sandy Woodbury, were living with the Campbells. Two years earlier the young couple had married in Damariscotta, Maine, an old New England coastal summer resort where he had a home and a gift shop business selling postcards and phonograph records. Laurie sent Grandpa cheerful cards from there, but resorts everywhere suffered in hard times. Nannie wrote in the fall of 1932 that Laurie had been helping that week in the cotton office in Chester and had a place promised in the office of one of the mills in a few weeks. There were no mentions of jobs for Sandy. After the middle of the decade, the Woodburys separated. Sandy joined his brother's family and worked in Massachusetts. Laurie stayed with her family. Eventually the couple would divorce, and Laurie would resume her maiden name. Depression years with job stresses brought similar separations in many households.

By early 1932 the Shaws, a family of nine, were living in Columbia. Fewer and fewer people could afford to take out the New York Life Insurance policies Coleman sold in Camden. Many had to discontinue paying premiums on old ones. He was glad to take a job in the company's capital city office, where paperwork was increasing from policies being surrendered for cash value. He also hoped to make real estate sales on the side, since many people currently wanted to liquidate properties. Hattie's letters to her father and sister chronicle the struggles of their household of seven teenaged and young adult children, variously trying to finish schooling and contribute what they could to the family. On April 11 Hattie was grateful that the children "seem to be all right about moving" and "talk very sweet about it." On March 7 she wrote, "Seems like we are tied up more than ever. Banks closed. Have no money in there, but what we do get comes through them." The young people pressed their clothes, stood in long lines, and applied again and again for positions. Despite concerns Hattie shared over the months, on October 3 she expressed hope: "Coleman seems to be in better spirits about business. . . . He said that nothing but the grace of God has pulled him this far. We had family prayer last night—& he gave the children such a good talk & Prayer is what we need[.] And he never forgets to bring you alls name in his prayer."

In 1933 the owner of the garage that employed Willie closed the business, putting him out of a job. When Willie suspected the probable closing, Margaret in early June accepted a job as a companion and driver for an elderly northern woman, "Mrs. Gillette," who had been wintering in the South and was to spend the summer at a northern resort. On June 23 Margaret wrote Mamie and Pa Robert from Sabbath Day Point, New York: "This is a beautiful place, and the folks here are very nice to me. They all laugh at my Southern brogue, and try to tease me about being a Democrat." She admitted, "I have been homesick a few times, when I stop to think of how far I am from Bill [Willie], & all of you." Margaret's August 29 letter reported deeper longing: "I can't realize hardly, that I've been here nearly three months. Here's hoping I can come home Oct 1st. That is when Mrs. Gillette closes this place. . . . She asked me could I possibly stay the month of Oct there in the city with her. I hate to refuse her, as she has been so very nice to me, but holy smoke I don't feel like I can stay away another two months." Willie found work again in Georgetown, where she joined him in the fall.

When the economy slowed construction work in Camden, Henry Smyrl, forty-five years old in 1932, decided to move his family back to a house he had built years earlier at the old home place. His father and Mamie did not hesitate to ask its present tenants to move to another house so that Henry could enlarge and update the home to accommodate his family of two sons, three daughters, and their mother. The youngest daughter, Cleo, interviewed seventy years later, recalled the move to the country as a very sad time in her childhood: "We had such a pretty little house in town. It had electric lights, running water, window screens, a bathroom, and polished floors. Very modern. We had to give up all our conveniences and all our friends when we left. It was the only home I had ever known in my life. I cried so hard."

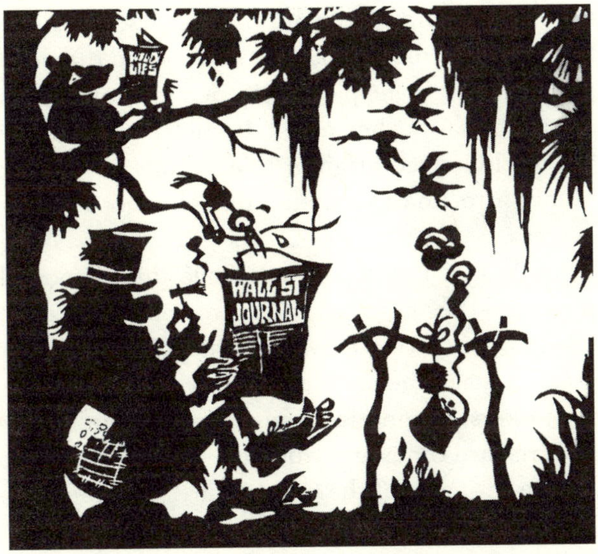

An amusing reflection on the Depression era, Jak Smyrl's silhouette illustrating "Hard Luck Harry" (*Random Rimes*).

Cleo remembered what a hard time her daddy had finishing the house. The carpentry work he did for hire took him away on crews for days, even a week or more, at a time. "We were so lonesome without him," Cleo said, "and when he came home, he was busy working on our house. He was tired all the time then." Henry and Ada had one absolute agreement. It was that the country house had to have its own usable water supply for them to stay there permanently. Ada and the children should not have to tote water like temporary tenants, carrying heavy bucketsful up the hill from the spring or down the road from Grandpa's well. "Get me water at the house," said Ada, "and I can make do with the rest."

There was much trouble over the well. The hired well diggers dug deep, hitting no water, just a layer of solid rock. There was frustrated consultation before a desperate decision to use dynamite. Water when reached was chemically tested and declared unsafe to drink, too high in lead or arsenic. The well was ordered sealed. "It was a terrible time for everyone," said Cleo. "Mama and Daddy were so worried. We had nowhere else to go." The family menfolk all put their heads together. The water in the abundant spring at the foot of the hill beyond Henry's house was noted for purity and sweetness. The problem was, how could they pipe it uphill through the woods to the house?

Alvin Creed, from engineering lessons in his classes at the Citadel, made the suggestion of an ancient solution—a hydraulic ram, powered by the free-flowing energy of the water itself. Willie, perhaps others, understood. The menfolk tinkered this way and that, experimenting and adjusting, until the principle was turned into reality, and finally water, by momentum, was pushed uphill through a pipe into Henry's house. Somehow the world looked brighter to everyone as the cold, clear liquid splashed boldly into Ada's kitchen sink. All were filled with a sense of mutual success.

Jack as a boy would not have understood the finer points of the physics—the angles, the pressure points, the distance calculations. However, from experiences watching people of different everyday talents cooperate to make the unorthodox workable, he formed a lifelong admiration for tinkers, visionaries, and craftsmen. Individuals helping one another endure hard times and troubles—such was the basis of survival for many during the years of the Great Depression and a lesson Jack took to heart. He applied it in his life and his art. Viewers of his characteristic cartoons in his mature years recognize that many of his characters sport functional patches and makeshift constructions unapologetically and even with pride.

Chapter 7

Country Life

"To work and do our part"

By 1932 Oscar faced a decision. Three years earlier, in spring of 1929, he had taken out a five-year mortgage to buy a small farm of twenty-five acres three miles outside of town and seven miles from Grandpa's. Intending the farmland as an investment, he had thus far used it only for recreation. Its abandoned fields provided good bird hunting. The family picnicked on the wide porch of the unpainted, single-story Victorian farmhouse. He and Mae took the children swimming in nearby Sanders Creek and at old Vaughans Mill Pond, for sale like many other rural properties.

Oscar and Mae talked the decision over with one another and then with their children. Jack stated in memoir notes: "Daddy was trying to buy house in town and farm simultaneously. Depression hit, forcing decision that one had to go. Family was ecstatic when he opted for the farm." Oscar decided that instead of two mortgaged properties, he would own one mortgage-free. The farm was more sensible because they could live more simply and grow their own food.

Young Jack thought living on the farm would be a great adventure. He had learned to swim in Sanders Creek, skinny-dipping when girls weren't around. He could fish too. Once at the creek Mama found a safety pin in her pocket and helped him bend it for a hook. He was excited catching a wiggly creek fish with makeshift gear. He was nine now, good at fishing and pretty good at swimming. Jack decided he would be very grown-up living on the farm.

Mama and Daddy told the children the farmhouse would differ from their home in town. Jack was not worried. He knew Grandpa got along fine without electricity and a telephone, and they could too. Jack was eager to try working a pump handle to get water. Sure, he could learn to milk a cow and plow the garden and chop wood. The big boys did things like that at Grandpa's, and he was ready to do so, too. He already knew how to pull up weeds and pick things in the garden. It didn't matter what they said about the house being a little shabby at first. Daddy said later they could paint it, and Jack thought it would be fun to help. Mama was always cheerfully sewing curtains and covers, and he figured she would be very happy fixing up a big empty house. Besides, with all that space, he just knew that when somebody found a litter of kitties or puppies, no one could say, "Oh, Jack, we *can't* keep them. We don't have *room* for any more."

When Mae brought out a little black book, Jack recognized her bankbook. She handed it to Oscar and told him to take it all to help buy the farm. She had started her savings with money from timber sales on forestland she owned at Flint Hill behind Grandpa's place. The ninety-two acres had been her mother's share of McDowell property, passed to Mae when she married. Mama spent her own money only for church and family. The children reacted quickly. They all ran for whatever savings they had. Jack was the first to come back. He had a bankbook too, started with the money he had earned long ago drawing names for jury duty, with bits of birthday and Christmas gifts added, collecting interest like Daddy taught the children. Jack's account totaled $98.32, a sum he pressed on his father to take. All his life Jack would remember that moment with pride. Among his memorabilia he kept the bankbook. He commented more than once, "In fourth grade I made my first investment in real estate. I helped my family buy a farm." It made him very proud and happy.

Once the decision was made, preparations began for the move to the farm late in the year. First there was the DeKalb Street house to sell, the farmhouse to repair, the yard to clear, the garden to lay out, and outbuildings and fences to fix or add. The farm would have livestock to house and feed, so preparations were as vital for animals as for people. Then extra visits were required to Flint Hill, for Grandpa was stricken by a bad spell that weakened his left side. This time he had fallen just after supervising the chopping of cotton he had insisted on planting as usual. No matter how low it sold, he said his black neighbors depended on making a little something from picking it for him every year. He held that keeping his land worked up in good order was a better benefit to all than just abandoning it. Grandpa believed he understood the role of his farm better than politicians and businessmen did.

The summer proved a hardworking one for Jack's family. Just before cotton-ginning season was to begin again for Oscar, they were pleased that he agreed to slow down for a few days' stay on the island. Jack was happy to hear that Dewey and Marie Creed and their children—Marjorie, James, and Tommy—would be staying there at the same time. Jack looked forward to riding in Dewey's motorboat.

Saturday, August 27, began as a beautiful day on the island. Adults and children enjoyed a playful swim together. As afternoon heat increased, parents headed the children out of the water for a rest in the cooling shade of the cottage porch. Jack and his siblings always recalled the heart-stopping moment soon after when someone asked, "Where's Tommy?" The four-year-old, who had been there playing on the porch just minutes before, was nowhere to be seen. In his memoir notes, Jack recorded, "The desperate search of Island left no doubt he was in water. We all searched, Daddy found him."

The *Camden Chronicle* reported on September 2, 1932: "A tragedy which brought sorrow to all of our townspeople as well as scores of friends throughout the county was that of the drowning of little Thomas Edward Creed, 4-year-old son of Mr. and Mrs. Dewey J. Creed, which occurred in the big pond of the Wateree Power Company about fifteen miles north of Camden Saturday afternoon." The article, headlined "Creed Baby Drowns in Wateree Pond," described the locale: "Mr. Creed and several associates have a nice cottage on a pretty island in the big lake. Numerous boats are at a beach near the lake and many townspeople have been guests for the week-end on the island."

As all searched for the missing child, Oscar waded into the swimming area, feeling its muddied bottom with his feet. In the roots of an old tree leaning in the edge of the water, he felt the soft limbs of the little body and pulled out Tommy. His lips were blue. The newspaper said: "First aid methods were applied but to no avail. A hurried trip was made to the Camden hospital with the lifeless form, where physicians worked to restore life. In the meantime a Pulmotor had been ordered from Columbia and two cars meeting near the county line had brought it here in around twenty-five minutes. But it was too late." For the second summer in a row, a tragic accidental death deeply touched Jack and his family.

Grandpa was feeling low when Hattie wrote encouragingly to Mamie and him on September 6: "I am so thankful he can walk. And he must not talk about being no account . . . for he is & we are so glad to have him here with us . . . & I know it was the providence of God to spare him to be with us. And I believe the hand of God so fixed it for Mamie to be constantly by his side." Grandpa's spirits lifted as his cotton picking began in early September. Life seemed familiar again. He supervised the weighing as Mamie carefully listed names and totaled the poundage of the bundled sheets of cotton brought in by neighborhood pickers. Paid day by day in cash and coin, a picker in that day earned pennies for pounds.

While Jack and other young cousins were allowed to help pick if they wanted, Grandpa was very strict that picking was not playtime. Cotton must be picked ready and dry, and it must be kept clean and free of dirt, sticks, and dried leaves. Jack recalled he was surprised by how hard cotton picking proved when it looked so easy. Somehow the rows got longer and longer, and everyone else moved away in lines farther and farther ahead of him, leaving him behind. The sun got hotter and hotter, and the swirling insects more and more annoying. His pricked fingers stung, his dusty legs itched, and his eyes blurred with trickling sweat. This was mighty dull work, over and over, and he decided that no, he was not afraid to go back right now and look anybody in the eye and say he had had enough.

A surviving list of Mamie's penciled totals of weighed cotton bags recorded up to 8,540 pounds harvested, perhaps or perhaps not a final total. Sold at six cents a pound that amount would have grossed $512.40 before labor costs of plowing, planting, chopping, picking, hauling—or for costs of fertilizers or boll weevil treatments—or for taxes and ginning. Grandpa, seventy-nine, said he was just glad he could keep on trying.

September greeted Jack's family still in their Camden home. It was a special time for Lucy, starting first grade. The first day walking to school between her big sixth-grade sister and her big fourth-grade brother, she squeezed their hands tightly. One part of Jack dreaded going back again. Just as when he had tried picking cotton, there would be dull work, over and over. Then another part of Jack thought about seeing his friends again, and he decided he would be glad to get back. "Don't worry," he assured Lucy. "You're going to like school."

Lottie saved her 1932–33 report card that showed her 213 DeKalb Street address changed at midterm to RFD #3, the rural route of the farm. Jack's bankbook was closed out on November 12, the same day the mortgage to the farm was marked "Paid in Full." The move took place shortly thereafter, probably by Thanksgiving. Driving away from the DeKalb Street home, Mae must have felt pangs of nostalgia leaving behind their first home, the house where all four of their children had been born. Yet, like Oscar, she turned her face forward. She was grateful to have a home when so many did not. She felt blessed, most of all, to be able to take all her children there with them. Her heart moved for the losses that Mattie and Marie had endured. No, she and Oscar would gratefully focus on the positive and encourage their children to do so also.

Others helped uplift family spirits, too. That first Christmas Eve in a different house the parents reassured anxious children that, yes, Santa knew they had moved, and, yes, he knew where. In fact Santa was going to like the bigger chimneys here. The children went to bed expecting a quiet morning the next day, far from the sounds of firecrackers and merry-making they had awakened to every Christmas in town. Just before day-break Oscar, Mae, and the children were startled from their beds. Autos with lights on and blaring horns roared up the driveway into their yard, full of whooping men and boys shouting "Merry Christmas!" Firecrackers popped in noisy crescendo, punctuated by hearty laughter.

"Quick! Get dressed! Fast as you can," Oscar directed the children.

"We caught you *sleeping* on Christmas Day?!" Uncle Fred Ogburn's voice boomed in triumphant query.

"Get up! Get up!" joined in Uncle George Creed.

"Did Santa get here yet?" town boys running up on the porch wanted to know.

The children, reassured by familiar faces, had not even looked under the tree yet. Mae immediately put on the big coffee pot and began stirring up biscuits for a crowd. It was holiday noise making and Christmas visiting rolled into a surprise housewarming—like a good-natured shivaree, not that they used the word for an old-time wedding custom, here altered for holiday festivities. Such a disruptive interruption intended as celebration would seem odd to many people, but high spirits were infectious and prevailed.

"Come out for sky rockets," the boys urged. Outside with Uncle Willie were more friends from town, and brightly spewing arches of light whizzed from their hill into the starry sky and into the just-coloring horizon of dawn. Jack was happily awed with the excitement and fun of the surprise. The celebration they thought they would miss in town had been brought to their door. They had been welcomed to a new home, and a long-standing tradition was begun of their place being a destination for early morning fireworks and breakfasting on a circuit of festive Christmas visitations.

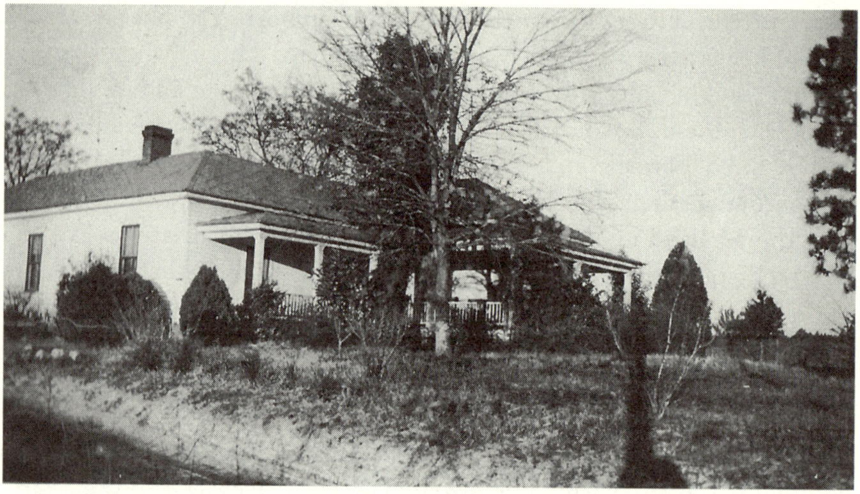

Smyrl family's farm home, Highway 97, north of Camden. Courtesy of the family.

The family's country home sat sturdily on a gently rising sand hill, beside a curve of the unpaved public road 97, which wound to Liberty Hill. The site on its deed was called Chinaberry Hill, and the children liked the broad-branched, flowering chinaberry trees that gave the hill its name although adults preferred the more useful pines and oaks. The chinaberry tree dropped bunches of inedible fruit like small, hard beads or bullets that provoked imaginative play and filled sling shots and pea shooters. In the rural custom of referring to properties simply and obviously, the family also called their dwelling "the sand hill house" and their farm "the sand hill place." Most distinctive was its loose, sandy soil, a distinct contrast to the red clay, dark loam, and rocky intrusions of Grandpa's soil in aptly named Flint Hill community.

It was well known that soil differences in Kershaw County appeared along the geographic fall line that divided it, with the sandy sections being closer to coastal plain conditions and the clay sections closer to piedmont conditions. Jack and the other children were interested when told that scientists believed that an ancient ocean once came far inland and the sand hills were its old sand dunes. Some areas on their sand hill were very white and fine, just like beach sand, they noted. Alfred said that once, walking far from habitation, he found a weathered, fossilized sea shell lying in a sandy field at home. Growing up the children spent a great deal of time in the outdoors, closely observant of natural characteristics and peculiarities. They wondered about that old-time ocean that had gone away and imagined how things would look if it were still there. Jack thought it would surely be fun to live with an ocean for a front yard. Their early years fostered appreciation for both reality and imagination.

Jack made several memoir notes describing his rural boyhood: "Moved to country in 4th grade . . . grew up on farm before rural electrification, plowed, milked, pumped water, raised hogs, chickens (the works, including horses, hunting dogs, etc.)." He continued, "Farm life included learning to plow with a mule, pick cotton, raise hogs, chickens, garden, etc. and care, feeding and milking the family cow." While Jack was part of such chores, the family was not burdened to the extent that survival depended solely on their own labors. Oscar continued working in Camden and hired some of the farm help. The benefits of rural living supplemented the family's well-being and encouraged a responsible lifestyle close to nature. The chores taught to the children under Mae's skillful organization were ones they saw as contributions to the family's smooth functioning. Filling a wood box and bringing in water on time meant Mama could have meals ready when they were hungry. Weeding the garden improved the quality and quantity of vegetables they grew and ate with relish. Collecting eggs from the chickens carefully meant a few extras could be saved for Mama to make her special custard or pound cake. Mucking the manure from the cow's stall before Daddy got home meant time for them to go down to the creek together. "We were very glad to work and do our part to help out. We were proud of our jobs," Jack and his siblings would assert, recalling those days. Historians mark the depth of the Great Depression in the winter of 1932–33.

When they made their move that winter, Mae and Oscar drew on their rural backgrounds as well as on scientific advice of government agricultural programs. In the January 27, 1933, *Camden Chronicle,* local farm agent Henry D. Green urged rural families to read, study, and work with the county agent, concluding: "Don't be downhearted in 1933. We are going right on living and we must make the best of things. Smile and keep your chin up. Depressions have come and gone before this. . . . Use your energy for thinking, not worrying."

Such too was the tone of the self-help and community-spirited programs that Mae became involved with through the Baron DeKalb Home Demonstration Club, which she joined in 1933. Mae was especially drawn to the "live at home" campaign of the time. At monthly meetings that rotated among members' homes, agricultural agents gave demonstrations on healthy family nutrition, on proper care of farm poultry, on clothing construction and remodeling, and on canning and preserving surpluses for savings and charity. Participants undertook projects that in concrete ways improved their families' lives and often extended into civic and religious activities. Mae was among the most active participants.

On the first Saturday in March 1933, a number of the family gathered at Grandpa's house. There they encircled his battery-powered radio, installed for him the previous year by Willie, a gift from the family to help Grandpa adjust to confinements of his increasing frailty. This time the listeners did not join him to hear his beloved *Grand Ole Opry*. They came to hear the broadcast of Franklin Delano Roosevelt as he was inaugurated U.S. president. Over the crackling and sputtering airway, they heard him pledge to pull America out of the Depression. "The only thing we have to fear," Roosevelt began, "is fear itself." Monday he closed all the banks in America to reorganize. The country was desperate enough to accept sweeping changes. The New Deal was beginning.

The period also marked another change for Jack's family. From later in 1933 to 1936 Oscar was locally employed in the New Deal as administrator of county relief work at the head of various government programs. In future years he modestly summarized that his job was "finding jobs for people out of work." He was head of Kershaw County's Emergency Relief Administration (ERA) in the fall when the Relief Council merged into the Civil Works Administration (CWA), a jobs project organized within the Public Works Administration (PWA). He administered the CWA, until it was phased out in 1934, and then headed other ongoing programs under the Federal Emergency Relief Administration (FERA).

The January 18, 1935, *Camden Chronicle* quoted Oscar's description of the local aim of emergency relief work: "not only [to] give relief but at the same time to accomplish something worthwhile." The newspaper detailed Oscar's report of a number of building construction projects completed as emergency relief in Kershaw County from November 1933 through September 1934: a new brick school, a hospital addition, and a dining hall and ten huts as community buildings. Playgrounds, parks, sidewalks, streets, highways, and several schools had been improved. Creek drainage to control malaria and installation of 750 sanitary toilets bettered health conditions. Several programs—a free community garden, surplus food canning, and hot school lunches—provided nutrition. A mattress factory and sewing rooms produced goods and clothing for the indigent. Some of these and other projects continued in later months. Old wills in the courthouse were copied and bound, and basic literacy was taught in seven adult schools. A major project was the renovation of the historic Camden Opera House from city offices to a modern auditorium seating seven hundred. The largest project, completed in 1935, rebuilt the dam destroyed several years earlier at Hermitage Lake to create an 825-acre lake for community recreation and residential development at the edge of Camden.

In adulthood Jack would realize that in his youth he had understood little of the significance of his father's work setting up and coordinating projects and completing paperwork during this period. The boy realized only that daily, after early morning farm chores, his father with bulging briefcase drove off to work in town, and he came home in time for afternoon chores. Regularly he brought back with him, strapped to the bumper of his auto, a huge chunk of ice to place, dripping, inside the icebox that kept their perishable foods cold and safe to eat. When his father was home in the afternoons and on weekends, he and Jack would do chores together. There was also seasonal hunting or fishing to add to the family larder. His parents would visit and entertain visitors, often for supper, and the adults would sometimes attend evening meetings. On Sundays the family went to church in Camden, then on to Grandpa's and sometimes to church at Flint Hill too. It was a busy schedule, and while Jack paid attention to what happened when he was with his father, he wondered little about his father's stacks of paperwork and frequent meetings. Jack would recall that his father took him a few times to observe the workmen's progress on replacing the blown-out dam at Hermitage Lake, which they both watched with great interest. They agreed that building a pond was a fine thing to do.

Jack's memoir notes on what was special about his country home reflect a child's point of view. He recalled good times exploring with his siblings. On Sanders Creek near them lay a small pond, an unfinished house foundation abandoned beside it. Neighbors called it "the Nettles place" for its owner, but Jack assumed it was for noxious "stinging nettles" he learned to avoid when walking there. Also nearby was a nearly finished, abandoned house belonging to a veteran schoolteacher who used it after her husband's death to store the contents of his law office. It had been vandalized before the children paid it a visit, and peeping through broken windows, they saw a floor covered with scattered papers, soaked with rain. It was creepy, they decided, and made up such entertaining ghost stories about the deserted house that they gave it wide berth.

On their own place, the children enjoyed imaginative play in the loft of their barn and in the sharecropper's house that Oscar would eventually fix up and rent. Lottie and Lucy played house with tea sets, brooms, and dolls while Jack and Alfred played cowboy, staging Indian raids and bank robberies. Part of the fun was fashioning costumes, weapons, and other props. The boys especially liked making "rubber guns" by carving a wooden stock and attaching a clothespin to release a twisted band of rubber cut from an inner tube. Anyone who needed a horse simply chose a greenwood stick cut to the length of his own legs.

The children devised elaborate hunts for buried treasures each hid for the others to find. They drew detailed "secret" maps of specific sites, noting directions and numbers of carefully counted steps with clues where to dig for treasure—a carefully buried jar or a cigar box of random trinkets or natural objects. The maps always included a distinctive tall tree that marked the farm's northwest corner, a landmark dubbed "the Lonesome Pine" from the title of a western movie. Alfred recalled that the pine was usually the site where the treasure was found. The fun, he said, was not so much in finding it as in taking the convoluted journey following the map to dig it up. Every map had to take a different route there when a new treasure was buried.

Jack's memoir notes also recall another distinctive tree on their place, a huge chinaberry shading the back door of the house. Here he once dramatically posed on a high branch to give a spirited yell before rapidly sliding down a swinging rope that he firmly secured to a strong upper limb. The rope held, for he had learned caution from playing Tarzan as a child in Camden. Yet, still believing too much of what he saw in the movies, he had not anticipated painful consequences of resulting "bad rope burns."

In addition to firing his imagination with movies and active play, Jack reveled in fascination for comic strips. "Reading the papers" was ritual in his family. His mother and father talked about news stories. His mother worked crosswords and clipped recipes and obituaries. His father studied the weather trends and prices, reading classifieds and legal notices. Everybody looked to see what movies were showing and what bargains were for sale. When a small child, Jack would crawl in his father's lap to see the "funny papers," which Oscar read aloud to him in silly voices that Jack mimicked. As he grew Jack spread the newspapers on the floor, and he and his father lay on their stomachs, side by side, to read them together. Because of the large number of comic strips in the Sunday *State* newspaper, it was Jack's favorite. Drop-in visitors would be greeted by Oscar and his children unselfconsciously sprawled on the living room floor reading the funny papers aloud.

One of the children's favorite indoor nighttime entertainments was sitting around the dining table, centered with an oil lamp for light, as Jack drew funny pictures to amuse them. Their reactions and attention were flattering, so he worked hard to keep his audience laughing. Sometimes they all drew pictures, and Jack eagerly praised them too. He liked seeing how others drew and what interested them.

In his long days in the classroom, schoolboy Jack continued to enliven the dullness of his lessons, especially math, by quietly withdrawing into his favorite world and filling pages with lively sketches, carefully concealed from his teachers' eyes. Along the way a teacher thought perhaps his slowly completed schoolwork was the result of a vision problem, and soon Mama and Daddy got him fixed up with glasses. Yes, he could see the board better, but he could also see farther out the big windows in his classroom, so Jack liked the new glasses. He did not work any faster looking out the window. Another teacher thought maybe he was shy wearing glasses and encouraged him to take roles in classroom dramas. He was so good at mimicking funny voices that his classmates applauded him. That made him work harder to read and learn his roles, so the teacher let him draw backdrops too. Jack felt having people like him was a fine achievement in school. At the end of fifth grade, art was the only subject in which he received a top grade of "1." He felt glad that his teachers knew, as he did, what he was good at.

Jack was eleven years old and in sixth grade in the fall of 1934 when his cousin Otis Creed wrote him from Charleston. A freshman at South Carolina's military college, the Citadel, Otis began with familiar teasing. "Have you learned to shoot your rifle any better, yet," he asked, "or have you left it out in the rain and sand and let it rust?" He was referring to the air rifle Jack used to practice marksmanship to be ready to handle a shotgun when he was taken to hunt birds with his father. Otis continued, "You should see the one I have to drill with twice a week and on parades every Fri. afternoon. . . . They are very strict about you and your rifles. I have had it ever since I have been down here and I haven't had my hand on a bullet or seen one." Otis included pointed advice: "You sure had better learn that math. You will need it in every grade in school and college. . . . You had better learn that English too because that is plenty hard here the freshman year." Jack was more interested in advice on rifles than books.

Living in the country, the Smyrl children followed a different routine to attend Camden Graded School, usually riding the school bus there and back. Area adults walking along the roadside could hail and catch rides on the school bus if seats were available. Sometimes walking on the road were other people the children knew they must never call black, Negro, or that other word. It was polite to call them "colored." Colored people never hailed the bus. If it had occurred to any young passengers to ask why the bus did not pick up colored students, someone older would have said "their" schools at Knights Hill and at Dusty Bend were close enough to walk to so they did not need a bus like students going as far as Camden. Children would not have asked why there were different places for people of different colors to go, since everywhere they saw that was just the way things were, with schools, churches, stores, and movies.

After school and when chores were done, sometimes colored children would come over to the Smyrl house and politely say that they could play if anybody there wanted them to. Jack for one was always glad for companionship. The children played outside on the Smyrls' place. The colored children had been living in the country a long time and knew a lot of good ways to pass the time, some of which the Smyrl children knew too. Together they strung green chinaberry necklaces and let them dry into dark, withered beads. They wove long grasses into plaited ropes, gathered browned broomsedge for play brooms, poked sticks into maypops and made animals and people, drew hopscotch squares in the sand, jumped rope with tricks that dazzled, blew over bottle necks to make music, sang songs, and told stories. The country children showed the newcomers where to find wild plums and pears and berries, where the best places were to hide the rabbit boxes the boys built together, and which of the pecan trees in the field had the best limbs to climb to shake down the nuts.

The family had not been living there long before one day the children and playmates ignored their pastimes to linger in a row atop the edge of the Smyrls' hill. From here, over a period of days, they watched intently as highway crews in powerful mechanical concert raised clouds of dust and acrid fumes, paving Highway 97 into a smooth, firm line all the way from Camden. Slowly the line extended past view of their eyes, northward to Liberty Hill and beyond. Maybe some of the children wondered about places where such roads led.

From January 1, 1935, through the month of January 1936, Lottie kept a diary that reflected some of the adult world as well as her youthful one. However, like Jack's recollections in his memoir notes, her main focus was on a young person's special interests. She was thirteen, going on fourteen, when she began the diary, midway through the eighth grade and thus a freshman at Camden High School. Graduation in South Carolina came at the end of the eleventh grade. Lottie's entries continued midway through her ninth-grade sophomore year. At her diary's beginning Jack was eleven and in sixth grade.

On March 16 Lottie described some improvements to the Smyrl place: "We have finished painting the house. The floors are being painted now and the sheds also." On April 1 she said, "Got fence up for flower garden and planted some flowers. Had fields terraced to-day." Between the two dates, another entry on March 23 reported that Oscar had squeezed in a fishing trip to Georgetown. He had visited Willie, who was working there in the garage for Stamper Chevrolet and running a motorboat for his employer. Georgetown was on a boom, according to coastal newspapers at the time, with a new bridge nearing completion in a few months, the last link in Highway 17 "from Maine to Miami." Oscar had enjoyed a fine trip fishing with Willie in beautiful, unspoiled Winyah Bay, the confluence of four rivers with the Atlantic.

Lottie's diary referred to Jack always as "Brother," her name for him since his infancy and a name that remained special between them. On Sunday, May 5, she wrote: "Brother's Birthday. He is 12 years old. I gave him a belt, Mama and Daddy pants, Lucy air rifle shots, Alfred 5¢." Cousins Freddie and Gary Ogburn, his frequent playmates, gave him a ball and clay and spent the night. Another visitor Lottie mentioned who came to the house that evening with his wife was the head of local recreation, likely conferring with Oscar on the playground projects that were part of government relief work.

Among adult friends mentioned several times in the diary were Mr. and Mrs. Ben DeLoache. Lottie's diary recorded that on Sunday, April 7, her family took the DeLoaches on a picnic to the Smyrls' favorite remote spot at scenic Kelly Rock. Here young Margie DeLoache "broke her finger and sprang [her] ankle." The mishap must not have discouraged them, however. Shortly afterward in the May 10, 1935, *Camden Chronicle,* T. Kirkland Trotter wrote that Ben DeLoache "told me of a place known as 'Kelly's Rock,' about 20 miles northwest of Camden and the account was so interesting that on last Sunday afternoon we decided to visit this place."

Trotter's directions were to take newly paved Highway 97 from Camden until the turnoff to the old unpaved 97, then go eight miles past "Mr. Smyrl's residence . . . the R. A. McDowell place . . . former Piedmont school . . . about one quarter mile towards Stoneboro" and then ask directions to find a "stubby cedar tree about 20 inches in diameter [and] turn to right winding thru woods for one-half mile." The directions concluded: "This brings you right to 'Kelly's Rock' and incidentally to the most wonderful array of mountain laurel, now in full bloom that is to be found anywhere in this section and equal to what may be found in the mountains." Trotter added, "The rock formation is most interesting and underneath one of the largest is to be found the shelter, almost a room, in which Kelly is purported to have lived. The rocks overlook quite a ravine several hundred feet deep and as far as one can see there are the mountain laurel and also other interesting shrubs and trees." Despite the article's verbal map, it is unlikely that many readers were able to follow it to the treasured spot so long special to Oscar's family.

Lottie's diary overall revealed increasing maturity. Most of all she was pleased to be learning to drive the car, especially after she recorded on May 31, 1935, that the family "got a new Plymouth." That same day overall was a sad one, however, because of other news: "Heard that Uncle Claudie died. Poor man! My favorite uncle!" The family left for Clinton, North Carolina, the following morning and arrived just in time for the widely attended funeral of the Reverend Claudius Peterson, Mae's uncle and the children's great-uncle. Following other apparently positive events, the passing of the beloved seventy-two-year-old uncle who had married Mae and Oscar, and who had earlier married her parents, seemed to foreshadow a series of sadder experiences.

Lottie reported in her diary on June 28 a shocking event: "Ernest Shaw drowned to-day! My first cousin! He was staying at Uncle Willie's—Mama & Daddy have gone to Georgetown. We are staying at Grandpa's. Body has not been found." Ernest, aged twenty-four, had fallen into Winyah Bay off a boat returning from an all-day fishing trip. Jack's memoir note reads of his death, "Fell from Stampers boat run by Willie." On June 29 Lottie wrote, "Mama & Daddy still in Georgetown. We are still at Grandpa's. Ernest's body has not been recovered. Oh! What will poor Aunt Hattie & Uncle Coleman do. Poor Uncle Willie!" Willie had been the pilot for his employer's fishing party, which Ernest, who was staying on vacation with Willie and Margaret, had been asked to join. Working with his father in real estate, Ernest had been attracted to the excitement stirring in coastal development. On Sunday, June 30, the third day he was missing, Lottie reported that Ernest's body had been found. She added what must have echoed others' words as well: "If he had to go that way I'm so glad they found his body it will be such a comfort." The agony of sudden, accidental death saddened all. On July 1, the day of the funeral, Lottie noted,

"Aunt Hattie, Uncle Coleman & Uncle Willie are taking it very hard." The family rallied to comfort the bereaved and one another.

On Sunday, July 14, the family gathered as they did every year to hold Grandpa's birthday dinner at his home. It was an effort so soon after their loss, but their collective faith taught them acceptance and belief that the best way to overcome was to carry on. It was, after all, Grandpa's eighty-second birthday. They would remember those who had passed and celebrate those who lived. Lottie recorded in her diary, "Almost all of family there." The list of names signed to a register of guests that day confirms that fact. Signatures also reveal transitions: Lottie signed her name adding "Artist" and quick-sketching a comic face. One cousin signed, "Laurie Campbell now known as Mrs. Sands Sandford Woodbury 2nd (for now)," and another, "Mattie Pauline Shaw (now) Mrs. L. K. Montgomery (later)." Someone added two-year-old Onnie Gene Ogburn's name, and he attached scribbles. Anyone noting Grandpa's signature may have been bemused to see that he dated it "1925," ten years behind the times. Gatherings such as these brought tears and smiles.

The next day, Grandpa's actual birthday, Oscar's family was among those who went back in the afternoon to see him again. Lottie noted, "Suppose to be an eclipse of the moon tonight." Freddie and Gary were visiting overnight with Jack, and the children enjoyed looking for the eclipse from the porch of the sand hill house. Watching with them Oscar had much to reflect on. Friday's *Camden Chronicle* had reported two recent accidents he felt touched by. One involved a local fifteen-year-old youth, Arthur Robinson, a gifted baseball player everyone in Camden knew. Riding home with teammates after a game in Cheraw, the young boy had casually rested his arm out the open window. A passing vehicle cut his arm off above the elbow, though quick attention saved his life. "Oh, no," the children had said. "Now Artie can't play ball!" The second accident involved the drowning deaths of two young men at the newly opened and instantly popular recreation area at Hermitage Lake. They and a third man with them had been thrown out of a motorboat on a sharp turn, while the driverless boat continued "circling at them throwing wild waves," the paper said. Onlookers were helpless to intervene. Oscar must have reflected on the heavy responsibility of a parent guiding his growing children to recognize that activities which gave pleasure could also present danger.

Only two days after Grandpa's birthday, Mae and the children were sitting on the shaded porch of their house and peacefully shelling fresh peas for supper. Because of the crest of the hill in front of their house, they did not quite see the new Plymouth as Oscar approached their driveway. Yet the sing of tires and their softening hum near the entrance started Lucy and Alfred down the driveway in anticipation of catching a ride uphill on the car's running board. The others on the porch were talking of the good supper they would welcome Daddy with when suddenly there was a horrifying sound of a crash. Bowls of peas overturned, and everyone ran down the hill. Jack's notes recalled his father being "hit by drunk driver as we sat on porch shelling peas." Lottie's diary on July 17 recorded: "Daddy was in a wreck this afternoon. Oh! What a scare we had. Broke nose, hurt head and neck . . . Daddy at hospital." The July 19 *Camden Chronicle* reported him "painfully hurt" when his auto was struck from the rear and overturned. Lottie stated of his return home: "He is not feeling so good. Lots of company." In a later entry she said, "Daddy feeling better car *all* bummed up. Oh what a shame *but* we must not forget it (the new car) probably saved Daddys life."

Oscar was still recovering when the family reached out to comfort their friends, the DeLoaches. On July 30 Lottie wrote, "Went to Mrs DeLoaches yesterday. Her son, Arthur Harris was killed in aeroplane crash last week." According to the July 26 *Camden Chronicle,* twenty-three-year-old DeLoache, with several years of flying experience, had been piloting a light plane owned by Seldon Hunns, another Camden airman. The previous October 19 the newspaper had commented, "The young men of Camden are getting more and more air-minded," listing Hunns and DeLoache among a half dozen with planes or taking lessons at the Camden Airport, which had opened five years earlier. Flying was still thought a sport, one in which risk taking and daredevilry were admired. Most of the young leaders named, including Hunns, within a few years would become casualties of their fascination. Only two months before DeLoache's death, another of the young men, one whom the Smyrls knew well, Christopher "Crik" Vaughan, had survived a crash landing, standing his plane on its nose only a few miles from the Smyrl home. Jack and Alfred, like friends their age, shared fan enthusiasm for flight by building and playing with model airplanes. It had been only thirty-two years since the Wright brothers' historic 1903 flight at Kitty Hawk, North Carolina, and each airplane that flew over the Smyrl farm gave obvious evidence to the children of a modern world on the move.

"Oh, what next?" Lottie wrote at the end of her entry reporting young DeLoache's death. The comment reflected increased anxiety after so many recent accidents of all types. The following day, July 31, Lottie noted, "Mrs DeLoache ate dinner with us to-day. Mr. & Mrs DeLoache ate supper with us." Lottie concluded, "How I wish school would start again." She clearly desired a return to normalcy. However, two days later, on August 2, another horrific local accident occurred that she, her parents, and her siblings would refer to for years in warning others. The August 9 *Camden Chronicle* reported "one of the worst tragedies in Kershaw county since the Cleveland fire." At a Seaboard railroad crossing, which the family had to pass over every time they went to town and every time they came home, in the area called "Dusty Bend," a farm truck, in which nine local people were riding to town, had swerved too late at a crossroad to avoid an unseen oncoming train. All died, seven of them members of one family and two of another, as the train struck and dragged the truck under its wheels. Fearful details of a one-hundred-yard gruesome scene lingered in community memory.

Having recently asked, "Oh, what next?" and wishing for the return of school, Lottie made no diary comments at all for the full month of August. During the month when they customarily took a vacation, this year they must have escaped to it with deep need. Oscar, in their repaired Plymouth, drove them away from all familiar faces and places. Their respite this year was at an ancient and undisturbed site, a place new to them. For a week they camped at Lake Waccamaw, North Carolina, the largest natural lake in the chain of mysteriously formed Carolina bays nestled in the sand hills of the eastern coastline. The oval freshwater lake, roughly five miles in length, was fed by creeks and fringed at its edge by cypress trees. Here there were no man-made constructions, no modern developments or conveniences, no noisy distractions. The water above the shallow, flat, sandy bottom of the lake was so clear that many species of fish were easily seen swimming. The children enjoyed trying to catch them in their hands and were able to pick up many different mollusk shells they could see on the lake bottom. Calmness, beauty, and rest restored the family's spirits. Watching fireflies and looking up into wide vistas of starry skies inspired peaceful evening reflections.

Jack's memoir notes include his statement: "Joined Baptist Church while still a child (on inspirational call)." Alfred later recalled that Jack's age was "about eleven or twelve" when he took this step. It is reasonable that it occurred about this time when so many solemn circumstances would have drawn a youth into deep thinking. Alfred stated too that Jack made the decision on his own, following his heart, not previously informing even his parents, as young people sometimes first do, that he felt ready to make such a commitment. He simply stepped out of the pew at Camden Baptist Church, when the pastor, the Reverend J. B. Caston, gave an end-of-sermon invitation, and went forward to the front. Following the beliefs in which he had been brought up, Jack gave his hand to the preacher and his heart to Jesus. In accordance with belief that an individual makes a personal decision of faith by which he is "born again," Jack ever afterward felt himself assured of eternal salvation, whatever might befall him. The ceremony soon afterward baptizing him by complete immersion in the sanctuary pool symbolized his spiritual awakening. Jack's thoughtful journey in difficult times had directed him to what he accepted as the most important destination of all.

Chapter 8

Transitions

"What you *do* with what you have"

When school began again in the fall of 1935, familiar patterns resumed for the older Smyrl children, with significant change for the youngest. Lottie's diary entry for September 10 reveals excitement: "First Day of School. Oh, I am so glad. I am in 9A, Brother is 7B, Lucy is 4A, and Alfred is 1A. Oh, I'm so glad." Alfred was especially pleased to climb on the school bus for the first time. Last year his birthday had just missed the cut-off date, and he was eager to catch up with the older children. He did not need anyone to tell him he was going to like school. He was sure he would. Alfred's birthday fell only a few days later, September 16, celebrated with new-student enthusiasm for gifts of a sweater, a pair of shoes, and a book satchel. Lottie wrote, "He was very pleased with them all."

Starting back with classroom routines seemed less enticing to Jack, who had spent the late summer with his father, uncles, and older cousins seining in the Wateree. Such trips every year continued until the weather got too cold to stand going in the water, so Jack hoped he could keep his homework from interfering with them. In memoir notes headed "School Daze," Jack's notes summarize "the great seining days (me the bag man) and the cook-outs and cat fish stews," and on another list he recalled in fall "the cold days seining with shirts on."

Jack felt honored holding the bag, the position given a trusted youth who helped collect the catch of the more mature seiners who waded offshore and lowered a top-floating, bottom-weighted seine, a dragnet. It

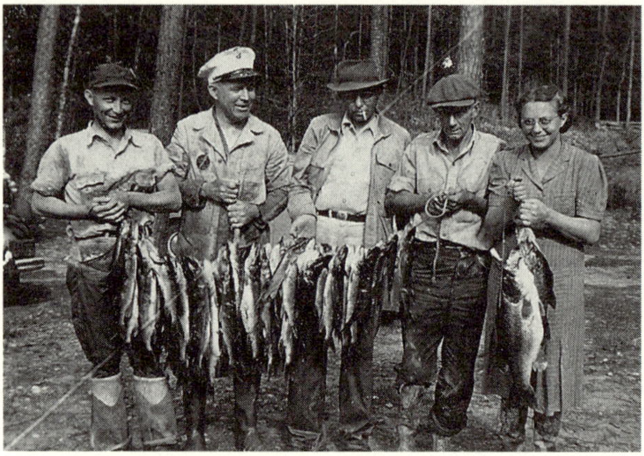

Muddy-legged seiners with catch: second from left, Willie Smyrl, still in work uniform; first, Buddy Denton; fourth, Pete Jeton. Courtesy of the family.

was attached at its ends to upright poles that the men held as flowing water arched the net outward, entrapping numbers of swimming fish that the seiners skillfully maneuvered ashore. Once the flopping fish were landed, everyone worked quickly to select the ones they wanted and to return to the water the ones they did not. Jack would in adulthood describe seining: "It was efficient fish *harvesting* and great fun to catch so many fish you could fry up or stew right there on the banks. You could easily feed a big crowd. You can't serve food fresher than that!" By September much of the talk at those lakeside cookouts focused on upcoming hunting season plans, and Jack's anticipation likewise turned toward cool weather activities.

His hunting interest also stirred higher from the first honks of their pet goose calling eagerly, his long black neck arching upward as he searched the sky and fanned his dark wings from his white body, strutting magnificently though unable to fly. Jack knew he was calling to a high-flying goose, perhaps a scout for the returning flocks that would soon follow in formation. Uncle Willie had given them the Canadian goose several years ago, a wild gosling he had found with a broken wing. The children had raised it among Mama's chickens, where it lorded the yard contently until kindred flocks winged overhead in seasonal migration. With one wing that could only half lift, the goose could only run along the ground and honk after his fellows that flew on, calling back to him.

Somehow the hunting dogs, aroused too and made eager by overhead flocks of birds, always viewed the single goose among them differently, never as prey, and tolerated its strutting with mere canine yawns. Jack, like

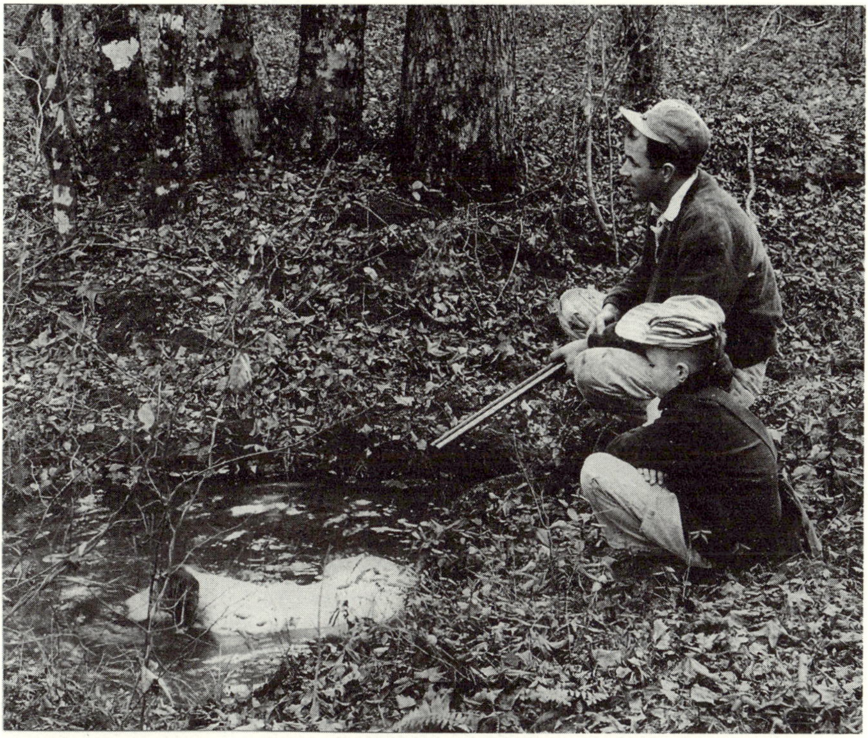

A hunting tradition being continued: the Smyrls' young Nell with Jak's young nephew Robbie Anderson and Robbie's father, Lewis. Courtesy of the family.

the hunting dogs that he and Alfred also treated as personal pets, viewed the goose affectionately but could not wait to go with Daddy and the dogs to target the winging flocks as soon as hunting season opened. There was sure a lot on a young fellow's mind when school opened in the fall.

This year there were additional distractions. During the winter of 1935 to 1936, Grandpa and Mamie noted dates of a record six snowfalls from December to February, each described in pencil on the back of the first calendar page of the new year. Sometimes the area saw no snow at all for a few years running, so even one appearance of flakes would have been worthy to note. Lottie in her diary described the first event on December 22: "Snowed to-day about 4 inches. Terribly cold." The next day she wrote, "Snow is very pretty. Hope to have a white Christmas." On December 28 Lottie noted "Sleeted and rained on top of what was left of snow," commenting the following day, "Every thing is beautiful with the sleet." Mamie observed that from these two events there was "snow on ground 13 days." It was indeed a rare and extended white Christmas season.

The weather extremes had inevitable consequences, as Lottie recorded December 30: "Cold as ice. Took a slight cold." January 4 she noted that "Mama & Daddy, Brother & Alfred went hunting. Lucy and I made candy, took down Christmas tree." It was rare that Mae really hunted, so that day it was likely more of a pleasant outing with the dogs and the boys as the ice was disappearing from the woods. Sometimes hunting was businesslike to gather game for the table, or sporting for the same reason with added pleasures of companionable competition. Sometimes "hunting" was just an excuse for sightseeing, for enjoying the outdoors, for letting the dogs have a good run. Good old Nell, everyone's favorite pointer, and her "pups," who in every litter quickly grew as long-legged and eager as she, were always ready to go. In any case Oscar was a real walker, one who could make his unhesitant way for steady miles through fields and brush and woodlands, up and down hills, without heavy breathing and without disturbance as he moved along carrying his shooting arms, ammunition, and equipment. Learning to keep up with Daddy in the outdoors was quite an exercise in athletic strength and endurance for even active young fellows such as Jack and Alfred.

In the dreary rain of Monday, January 6, 1936, all four of the Smyrl children boarded the school bus a bit downcast. As Lottie qualified Tuesday in her diary, she was "glad in a way to be back . . . to see friends" but found it "awful hard to get up so much earlier." The next day she lamented how hard it was to be back in school "after those good old holidays and the snow." Thursday she made a bored entry: "Ho, Hum went to school on the bus. Studied lessons came home. As usual." Friday she was glad the week was over for already the holidays seemed a long time past. Jack, had he taken a peek at her diary, as she sometimes scolded him for doing, would certainly have concurred with her thoughts.

Oscar met the new year with some trepidation. Passage of the Works Progress Act in 1935 had determined a new path for government relief programs he had been locally administering. Under the WPA earlier programs were to be phased out by 1936 or reorganized and administered not at the county level but through consolidated districts covering several counties. Oscar's position as county administrator was thus phased out, and Kershaw County was made part of a multicounty unit supervised elsewhere. The New Deal, in which Oscar had had an early part finding jobs for others, "had dealt *me* out of a job,' he would later wryly state. It had left him, he quipped, "jack of all trades and master of none."

Having known the change was coming, Oscar for past months had been directing transitions for local relief programs to the new administration. He had also been considering his own situation once his employment ended. The first of the year, however, must have been hectic and uncertain for him, as officially unemployed, he hammered out closing details of a new enterprise he undertook. Lottie, before she stopped her diary keeping at the end of January 1936, made one simple reference to the change. On January 24 she casually commented that her father was "going to make some soft drinks next week." The process was Oscar's trial run of equipment before he purchased a local bottling operation that he renamed and operated from February 1, 1936, as the Camden Bottling Company. The family business would have a major influence on Jack's life into his young adulthood, and more than once he would ponder the proposition that he might someday take over the bottling company.

The plant that Oscar bought in a leased building at 935 Broad Street, across from the old Camden Opera House, had been started in 1920 by William L. Jackson Sr. to bottle Chero-Cola. The popular brand that was developed in Columbus, Georgia, was later challenged in court by rival Coca-Cola and for a number of years was shut down by the lawsuit. At the time of Jackson's death, the Camden plant was bottling other fruit-flavored soft drinks under the supervision of his half brother Frank N. Mayer. Oscar hired Frank as his supervisor and with his advice set about upgrading some of the equipment. When he was running the Swift cotton gin, Oscar had overseen the upgrading of its equipment and understood the importance of efficient mechanization and operation, although he himself was not mechanically skillful. He could, however, hire and organize work for those who were. He would eventually hire his brother Henry, with his steady nerves and keen eye, to supervise the most precise operation, the machine that did the final clamping on of the metal cap.

Oscar researched new suppliers of fruit flavors and began actively to market soft drinks that his plant would produce. He had many civic contacts and knew the community and county well. Throughout the town and countryside there were grocery stores, service stations, eating places, and tourist spots where customers wanted soft drinks. He planned too on ball games, fairs, and big events such as the Carolina Cup. Meanwhile further down the street on South Broad in 1936, the Camden Coca-Cola plant purchased adjoining buildings and announced in the June *Camden Chronicle* that they were beautifying their grounds and building a large new warehouse. Soft-drink market competition was heating up.

Although one recent New Deal action had consolidated Oscar out of a job, another New Deal program resulted in an important improvement at the Smyrl home. Shortly after passage of the 1936 Rural Electrification Act, in Kershaw County power poles were being raised and electrical lines were being run down main rural roads within reach of developing electrical cooperatives. It would take much longer, even years, to complete the infrastructure and for services to reach all side roads and isolated individual homes in the county. However on Highway 97 just four miles from Camden and within reach of power expansions to the city system, the Smyrl home was connected relatively early in the process. A team of electricians installed a fuse box for the house with one overhead light fixture and one outlet in each room. The family was already dreaming about what new appliances they might someday add—an electric iron, a radio without batteries, an electric refrigerator in place of the leaky old icebox, maybe even an electric sewing machine?

"Children," Mae reminded them, "you older ones remember when we had lights in our DeKalb Street home, and you've all visited in Camden homes with electricity. We know this change for us is going to be wonderful. But don't ever forget we have still been very happy these years out here *without* this convenience. Remember. It's not what you *have* that is important. It's what you *do* with what you have."

"Yes, ma'am," they said, and paused respectfully as they knew they must. Then, "Can I turn on the lights?" "No, me, it's my turn," they jostled about excitedly. Alfred recalled after the electricity was installed they first appreciated the convenience of being rid of old routines tending to nighttime lamp lighting and fixtures. Certainly they enjoyed the brighter lights that made things easier to see at night. It was about that time, too, that Mama got very interested in repainting inside the house and touching up furniture finishes. The more direct light was making other things seem a bit shabbier than before.

Jack's seventh-grade year ended in 1936 with his finding a new interest in scholastic sports through tennis and intramural matches. The opportunity came as an outgrowth of programs developed to provide Depression jobs. In schoolyards, parks, and playgrounds built or improved by relief workers, volunteers developed and sometimes staffed recreation programs for schools and communities. Jack discovered that he liked dribbling and shooting basketball at the outside hoops set up for schoolyard practice, but his glasses and poor peripheral vision made him awkward in close-up, fast-moving team play. The competition of tennis with one or two opponents at a distance was also fast-moving and fun, as well as more comfortable for his vision. Besides, girls played tennis with boys, and Jack was definitely growing interested in girls.

In the summer Jack and his parents agreed on a good opportunity for him to advance his swimming skills, and he enrolled in the Red Cross Junior Lifesaving course taught at a popular local swimming area, Saddle 'n Paddle, on the west bank of Kendall Lake in Camden. Jack did well in the course and enjoyed socializing there. He did not mind one bit that his instructor ended the course telling all the graduates that they must practice frequently to keep up their new skills. Jack was always glad to go swimming with his friends and had no problem bringing up at home reminders of the importance of his need for continued practice.

It was also in 1936, when he was thirteen and before he started high school in the fall, that Jack approached his parents with a plan to pursue another interest. "Look, Mama," he said, "I found a home course of *art* lessons like the courses you get so much out of for home demonstration units." When he first exclaimed with excitement over art course advertisements he found in newspapers, magazines, and even his beloved comic books, his parents did not take him seriously. They knew his disdain for study. How could he handle an adult-targeted course on his own? His father told him, truthfully, that money was tight with starting and improving the new business, and the family could not afford more expense. Jack quickly beamed, "Then an art course will help out," and he showed them an ad proclaiming in heavy type: "CARTOONISTS MAKE BIG MONEY." Responses ranged from his mother's bemused "Jack, dear, you can't believe everything you read in a comic book," to his father's grim "Jack, trust me, there is a good reason for another phrase—*starving* artists."

In time, with continued persuasion, an agreement was negotiated. Jack would take on extra chores at home and help with odd jobs at the bottling plant to save some of the expense of other hired help. No one was going to remind him to do his art lessons, and if he lost interest in them he still had to do the extra chores and odd jobs. His father wrote a check, which Jack mailed promptly. With high hopes he had already ordered the free book and had sent in preliminary paperwork, so with payment his lessons arrived quickly from the Cartoonists' Exchange, Pleasant Hill, Ohio. Jack got started immediately.

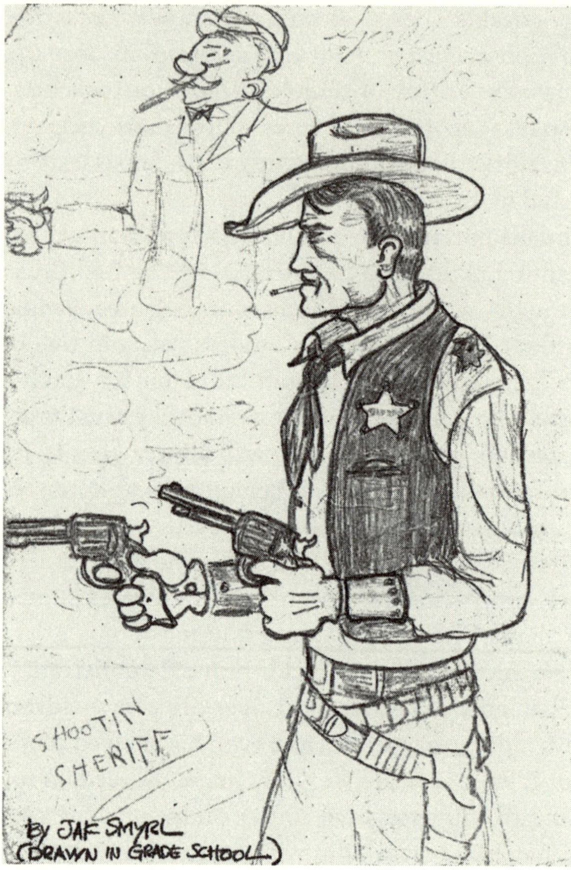

Sketch later signed by Jak when he was asked for a sample of his childhood art. Courtesy of the family.

Certainly the Cartoonists' Exchange advertising was appealing—an image of a happy artist at a drawing table with his work being admired by two cute and delighted girls leaning close to him, a blonde and a brunette whose hand lay casually on the artist's shoulder. The text enticed: "CARTOON Your Way to POPULARITY and PROFIT." The lessons of the course were, in fact, quite sound in art principles, and their basics continue to be admired in present times. Some of Jack's drawings that Aunt Mamie kept at the old Smyrl place were from the fall of 1936, when eighth-grade Jack was a high school freshman. These reflect stylistic influences of his art lesson exercises.

In a notepad headed "The Home Insurance Company New York," Jack penciled his sketches as he sat beside Grandpa, now often in a wheelchair though as active in mind and interests as always. The first scenes were some of Grandpa's favorite subjects, and Jack applied his art lessons to make his images more realistic and interesting, giving them dimensional rather than flat outline shapes. Grandpa enjoyed watching Jack draw and would suggest details to add. The first page they titled "Texas Cow Boy," a booted, big-hatted gunman on one knee in the act of firing a pistol in each hand. Detailed attention gave him a plaid shirt, polka-dot scarf and hanging gun belt with holster. As Jack drew, Grandpa talked, telling stories about people he knew who had gone west when he was a youth. On the second page, "Caravans" demonstrates perspective with a large covered wagon in the foreground and a smaller one in the distance, including busy subjects engaged in camping activities. A third page offers an even more complicated though well designed scene, a village of "Eskimose" amid well-rounded igloos, a dogsled in action, and ice floes and a paddler in the distance.

The next three pages in the notepad depict scenes from one of Jack's favorite interests at the time, Camden High football players in action. Grandpa too was keen on the subject, having closely followed the sport since grandson Alvin Creed played on the 1931 state championship team. Excitement was also high in 1936 when the Bulldogs took the state championship again. Jack was clearly caught up in closely watching the action that year. Two of his drawings depict a kicker with the ball in the air, the second of them more natural than the first in the positioning of the leg. The other drawing is a very active pileup about to happen with three players in action going down, the ball carrier still suspended in the air. Care is taken to keep subjects from looking flat and static although Jack was drawing quickly, not finalizing any of the sketches, and light preliminary lines are sometimes still visible.

At the time that Jack was drawing for Grandpa, Lottie and a usual crowd of girl cousins were visiting at his house too. Present with Lottie from Camden were Nettie Leese Ogburn and Alvin's sister Sophia, and from "next door," Uncle Henry's daughters—Alma, Eula, and Cleo. All the girls together were preparing a meal of seasonal homegrown foods according to their cooking skills. Alma took the notepad from Jack and wrote the menu they prepared for Grandpa and Mamie as guests of honor: collards, sweet potatoes, cornbread and biscuits, syrup and jelly, home-canned peaches, and milk. She listed next, with names, a program of playful entertainment the girls would provide with the meal. There were impressions, songs, and recitations, concluding with the whole group singing

"America." Mamie added a list of prompts for a game they could play afterward. Later Jack retrieved the sketchpad and added two more drawings after food and games. Both of the sketches depict horses and riders in pounding action, one of them a steeplechase rider going over a fence and the other a cowboy with lasso leaving a dust trail behind. Nothing was ever dull staying with Grandpa and Mamie.

Jack started high school that year on Laurens Street in a brick two-story and basement building completed in 1894. Student interest was high early in the 1936–37 term in watching work underway on the adjoining property to the west where WPA workers were constructing a modern new school for them. Noise and inconveniences were unavoidable interruptions until midyear when classes moved into the two-story, seventeen-classroom building. Jack's uncle George A. Creed was joint builder with R. E. Chewning, and they directed teams of government workers along with regular crews. Work continued during the year to finish the attached gymnasium that would become a community pride.

World and national events in 1937 must have seemed distant to young people experiencing exciting changes of a modern school with new opportunities so close at hand to them. Around them, however, there were hints of larger concerns. A lengthy article in the February 26 *Camden Chronicle* described a faraway man, Adolf Hitler, as "potentially one of the most dangerous men on earth," and May 19 reported, "The Nazi drive against Jews goes on in Germany." Few of the young people in Camden could have predicted the impact of such facts on them in the coming years.

In 1937 Jack's helping out with odd jobs at Oscar's bottling company introduced him to the inside life of his father's business. The search for additional flavors to compete for customers' tastes led to Oscar's bottling a cola drink, Pop Kola, from the Braser Company, Chattanooga, Tennessee. The cola soon became his single best-selling flavor and a competitor for Coca-Cola and Pepsi in area businesses. Priced to retail at a penny or two less per bottle than other colas, the new drink's sales grew steadily. Pop Kola advertised itself with a Depression-savvy slogan as "The Poor Man's Thirst-Quencher."

In Jack's extended family, too, change began in the spring of 1937. The Camden Chevrolet dealership changed hands, and Uncle Willie transferred home as service manager for new owner Perry R. Langston. Jack was especially pleased when his uncle and aunt moved only a short distance south of their home. On the opposite side of Highway 97 from the Smyrl place, Willie and Margaret rented a hilltop farmhouse where some years ago homeowners had operated a tea room for winter tourists. Neighbors, in fact, still referred to the house as "the tea-room place." Oscar and Willie, and Jack with them, looked forward to bird hunting the two properties. Willie felt that if the house worked out for him and Margaret, it and its attached forty-two acres might be a good place to settle permanently.

Old problems still troubled Margaret, however, and in time she was hospitalized again. She was home and ill in bed on February 9, 1939, when Mae and another neighbor visited with plates of food. They found Willie in the backyard, chopping wood. They were still talking with him beside the woodpile, inquiring about Margaret's health, when they heard the gunshot inside. All rushed in, Mae reaching her first. Margaret had discharged Willie's .45 into her heart. The shock and tragedy were wrenching to those hoping for recovery. Willie, stunned, moved in with his father and Mamie at the old home place. Jack saw up close the effects that acts of despair and desperation have on surviving loved ones. In the way that young people must adjust to adult sadness, Jack's daily life gradually returned his focus to the world in which he spent his time.

In lifelong references and memoir notes, Jack would recall his Camden High School years fondly, and his friends from that time would likewise remember him affectionately. He spoke highly of his teachers, veterans in a system that prided itself on the quality of the graduates they produced. The academic records that survive of Jack's years in high school show relatively dismal grades, but they are only part of the picture. There is also evidence that the teachers and administrators gave him vital encouragement and, in fact, sparked lifelong interests in him, for example, starting him on a journalistic career path. His artistic skills were recognized and used in ways to keep him learning when his interests in doing so lagged.

Big sister Lottie kept an eye on "Brother" the years they were in high school together, nudging and reminding him of assignments. She thought her talented brother would do well in the art class and club she had enjoyed, where she had taken up painting dogs and flowers and landscapes. However when Jack approached enthusiastic art teacher Mrs. Jo Little asking to take her class, she took a look at his work and told him she would not take him. "You already have your style set," she said, "and I must not interfere with that. Therefore, I have nothing I can teach you. Continue with the lessons you are taking. They are better suited to your natural talent." Briefly taken aback by Mrs. Little's reply, Jack quickly realized that her words confirmed his own assessment of his strengths. Her refusal strengthened his self-confidence.

Soon after the conversation with the art teacher, Jack was approached by a venerable English teacher spoken of with awe and affection by the upper-grade students whom she taught. Miss Henrietta Zemp told a surprised Jack that she had sought him out because she had heard that he was a clever artist and that was just what she, sponsor of the student newspaper the *Bull Dog,* was seeking to add to the staff. Thus only in eighth grade Jack began a long association with the prim and proper, gray-haired and lively, erudite and humorous, strict and long-suffering "Miss Etta."

Another faculty relationship began next year in ninth grade, 1937–38, with Jack's agriculture teacher, jolly young Hulan A. Small, also a baseball and girls' basketball coach who acquired the nickname "Pop." A country boy such as Jack didn't have much trouble in an agriculture class where he felt knowledgeable and could still learn useful information, especially since Mr. Small took his class on frequent outdoor field trips. Jack was one of the boys able to demonstrate to other students how to plow correctly with Mr. Small's mule. Jack also proved a patient and clear instructor helping other boys who wanted to give the plow a try. "You can do it. You just need to keep practicing," he encouraged their awkward efforts.

As an "ag" student, Jack became a member of the Future Farmers of America. At the end of the 1938 school year, he was pleased to accompany Mr. Small and other FFA boys to summer camp at Bluffton in lower coastal South Carolina. When the campers took a trip to Tybee Island, Georgia, and went in the ocean swimming, Jack learned an important lesson he often spoke of afterward as a warning to others. A strong swimmer, he was enjoying lengthy strokes beyond the breakers when he was caught in a riptide. His swimming lessons at home, having been given inland, had not addressed coastal conditions, and he did not remember warnings not to swim against the current. Jack was nearly exhausted trying to fight the undertow to reach the safety of shore where the others were swimming. He "almost did not make it," he said. He afterward learned and repeated to others that in such situations a swimmer must move with the current until freed of it and then swim ashore. Also a swimmer must be sure to swim close enough to companions to signal for help, he would add.

During summers Jack had extra time to help his father at the bottling plant, and his help became increasingly skilled on the days he worked. Although Jack was old enough to drive, his father continued to turn down suggestions related to his running errands with a vehicle. Jack had started out sweeping up, emptying trash cans, picking up litter out front. That was sort of dull, but he enjoying selling cold bottled drinks to walk-in customers near the front of the plant. Jack liked to talk to the people who stopped by. There were some interesting characters, black and white, who lived or worked in the sometimes teeming South Broad area, in the section of town affectionately called "Pot Likker" for the good southern-cooking smells emanating from its cafés and homes. In early 1938 Oscar added to the tasty quick bites that could be purchased there by installing a fryer to produce fresh-fried potato chips. Salt shakers were kept handy. Increased thirsts demanded more good cold drinks. Jack liked the chips so much that he had to be cautioned, "Hey, don't eat up the profits."

The January 7, 1938, *Camden Chronicle* described where crates of drinks from the plant went "to every section of Kershaw county and also to parts of Sumter, Chesterfield, Lancaster, Chester and Lee counties." Jack was not yet strong enough to load or unload the trucks on daily routes, but he wheeled carts of drink crates to stores and cafés along Broad Street. He hardly noticed the gradual strengthening of his muscles from bending, lifting, and swinging the crates.

For Jack's ninth-grade year, his second semester report card reflected higher achievement than any of those for the following years. His cumulative grades in spring 1938 included two B's (agriculture and history), two C's (biology and literature), and one D (English). It was in 1938 that Jack's big sister graduated from Camden High, and her advice, nudges, and overseeing reminders to him about school thereafter could be issued only at a distance. The next year, 1938–39, when Lottie was in her freshman year at Winthrop College, Jack's grades took a nosedive. In the tenth grade, Jack ended the year with two D's (literature and social studies) and three F's (English, French, and algebra).

It was a blow to Jack that he was to be required to repeat tenth grade. He appeared to have been quite surprised. When his teachers, who seemed to like him, had had long talks with him, he had felt appreciative that they were taking a personal interest in him. His parents were disappointed but supported the educators' position. They knew that Jack needed the skills and information in which he had not shown proficiency. It was not the outcome that Jack anticipated, for he had thoroughly enjoyed the year and was looking forward with high hopes to what he thought would be his senior year.

Only a few weeks earlier, the much anticipated Junior-Senior Banquet and Dance had started out with a bad scare that Jack would years later list in his memoir notes as "a brush with the Grim Reaper," and yet he had been able to enjoy the celebration with all his friends. Dressed in his formal "whites" and with a corsage on the seat beside him, Jack had been hurrying as he drove his father's freshly washed and shined car to pick up his date, Eby, whose home was on the other side of Camden from his house and farther into the countryside than he lived. Rounding a sandy road in the dusk dark, his headlights came head-on with a farm truck, which, like he did, wrenched away quickly. Jack's car plowed down into a ditch, but he was relieved when the other driver, his wife, and several children all piled out of the truck unharmed. They all stared at the crumpled front bumper that pressed against and around Jack's right tire. The truck driver offered to go home and get some tools to free the tire and pull him out. Thinking of the time, his date, and the big event awaiting them, Jack declined. Desperately he grabbed the bumper and, with mighty straining, straightened it with his hands. He did not worry that it had a peculiar bend now. He had surprised himself with his strength. Once his tire was free he sped on for Eby's house, where he delivered the corsage, washed his hands, and declined a sympathetic offer for a bandage on a small forehead scratch he had not noticed. They were then off to a fun-filled evening with an exciting tale to tell explaining their last-minute arrival. Perhaps Jack had expected a similar positive outcome on his final report card.

Examples remain of some of the activities Jack had enjoyed that year. A surviving May 30, 1939, issue of the mimeographed student newspaper the *Bull Dog* listed Jack and graduating senior Malcolm Anderson as "Ad Artists." Among the advertising they solicited to support the publication, each of the boys had sold ads to their fathers, respectively Oscar at Camden Bottling and L. P. Anderson at Camden Machine Works. This final issue of the year ended with Jack's caricatures of newspaper staff members. For example he included a play on Norman Baum's nickname "Peanut" and on Hugh "Shot" Cox's athletic prowess, and he depicted fellow artist "Mac" Anderson asleep under a tropical tree at the beach with an electrical fan blowing up a breeze. The last image is his caricature of himself as a simpleton in a turtleneck, with half-opened eyes, buckteeth, prominent ears, and an artist's pen behind one ear.

In a short, lighthearted rough draft of an autobiographical sketch titled "The Agony and Ecstacy [*sic*] of a Country Boy from Camden," Jack many years later described a contribution of his to the 1938–39 publication that attracted much attention: "The high school paper (the Bulldog), loaded with serious material like, 'Guess who was seen eating a hot dog with our star quarterback Tuesday,' decided to offer comic relief from this heavy stuff by featuring my cartoon creation, cleverly (or so I thought) called 'Wigwam News.'" Its playful Indian-history allusion was connected to a familiar, long-used logo for Camden, a downtown weathervane effigy of a feathered hunter with bow drawn, Catawba chief King Haiglar (historically Hagler), romantically "the patron saint of Camden."

That fact that Jack's cartoon feature and his other art were enjoyed by his fellow students may be seen in the autographs signed in the Camden High yearbook, or "annual," the *Gold and Black,* which appeared for the first time in 1939. The annual took the history of Camden as its theme and emblazoned the cover with an idealized King Haiglar riding a horse. Autograph messages to Jack include these:

> It has been a pleasure to know you (papose). Good Luck, and keep your chin up.
>
> *"Shot" Cox*

> May you learn to draw and what to draw—O you Chief—Love from a papose—
>
> *Ertel Lockee* [Jack's friend who was proudly Cherokee]

> Keep up the drawing and I'm sure you will make a famous man in art.
>
> *Nancy Sanders*

> The best of luck to the best cartoonist I've ever seen! Here's hoping!
>
> *Jane Trantham*

> Keep up your Cartooning but give Disney a chance!
>
> *Joe Rhame*

> The best of luck to *our* future cartoonist!
>
> *Dave* [*Wallnau*]

> "Wigwam News" was really good this year. Luck to you,
>
> *J. C. West* [John Carl West, class of 1938, had assisted the staff.]

An autograph intended as kindly reminder was this:

> May one of our most gifted artists realize that "genius is an infinite capacity for taking pains"—even in English!
>
> *Henrietta Zemp*

Chapter 9

Wartime Graduate

"Teach yourself to play in three easy lessons"

The blow of learning in May 1939 that he had to repeat tenth grade struck hard when Jack discovered that the failure rendered him ineligible to play football. To make the Camden High Bulldog team in the fall, Jack had gone out for Coach John M. Villepigue's spring tryouts and training. Despite his slight build, Jack's potential had impressed the coach. Jim Steinmiller in the October 28, 1981, *Chronicle-Independent* described the coach's style: "Finesse, speed, and timing—and not size—were the trademarks of his explosive 'Villepigue offense,' a variation on the single-wing." The coach used a metronome to teach his players timing. Jack was flexible and agile and caught on quickly. At the end of spring training, Villepigue told him he had "a natural sense of rhythm," and he wanted to play him at summer camp as spinback or wingback. Perhaps Jack's enthusiasm for football that spring had been the ultimate distraction dooming him in the courses he needed to pass for eligibility.

For a sixteen-year-old, it must have been bitter to remain in Camden in late summer working at his father's bottling plant when the Bulldog team was cheered on their way to football camp in the North Carolina mountains. The September 15 *Camden Chronicle* described a somber moment during camp when chaperones and boys were enjoying an outing at the peak of Mount Pisgah: "a clear, cool afternoon . . . 'on top of the world' [when] by radio we got the news that France and Britain had declared war on Germany." The message of retaliation after Hitler's invasion of Poland was heard in Camden also. Oscar felt its significance. In July he had been sworn in as commander of James Leroy Belk American Legion Post 17. At monthly meetings he listened to concerns of veterans. It had not yet been given a name, and America was not yet involved, but World War II had started.

Meanwhile Jack pursued athletic interests. In September Camden High principal L. W. McFadden wrote on his behalf to Coach Villepigue: "Smyrl did not pass enough work last year to be eligible to play this year. He is very anxious to practice this season in order to be in training for next year. If it is not against the rule for an ineligible student to practice, I hope you can grant his request." It is not clear if Jack was allowed to practice then, but he later recalled physical benefits of Mr. Villepigue's training. He found his own way of staying connected to the 1939 football team. Applying his correspondence lessons in portraiture, Jak earned his first dollar as an artist by sketching team members for "a fly-by-night Camden newspaper," probably an advertising supplement. The published small spread of sketches includes a dozen recognizable faces headed "Camden Football Personalities of '39" and depicts the season's star eleven and their coach in a few comic action scenes. Jack saved the dollar, which he marked and dated with its significance, and he saved a copy of the printed work. He wrote on it: "My 1st Cartoon Printed in Public Newspaper / 'Camden Sunday Graphic'—1939."

Jack's ongoing correspondence lessons having now racked up an art sale, he turned for success to another mail-order course. This time comic book ads lured him to Charles Atlas's body-building program, which promised: "I can make you a new man." It was twelve lessons, an expense Jack promised to pay back. "Yes," he told his parents. "I am keeping up with my schoolwork. No, the exercises won't interfere with my chores. In fact, I can do them better because I will be stronger." He smiled winningly. Jack was getting skillful in negotiating. In the way young people do, he had learned what arguments were effective, and in the way that parents of teenagers do, Oscar and Mae sighed and rolled their eyes thinking, "That *Jack!*"

There was, however, little quarrel with the benefits of exercise. In a time when large nations were engaging in conflict, who knew what young people must be prepared to face? When his box of materials arrived, Jack began immediately to follow instructions and to exercise seriously and regularly—push-ups, chin-ups, squats, and more—pushing muscle against muscle in Atlas's "dynamic-tension" method. Jack adapted exercise routines to everyday locations. His favorite spot for chin-ups was a limb of a backyard chinaberry tree. Every time he passed, coming and going, he grabbed the limb for as many sets as he could work in. Alfred said that as Jack built up strength, he experimented with variations, such as reversing hand positions and doing repeated one-arm chin-ups, which amazed watchers. The exercises and variations became a game he enjoyed, and he competed with himself and with friends he could entice to join his routines.

The football season was underway and Jack's exercise program beginning when a new interest rose on his horizon. In early October a school survey set students abuzz. A high school band was to be formed. Students were to be taught to play instruments. They would give concerts. Next year they would have uniforms and march on the field at football games! Who wanted to join? Jack was one of thirty-two promptly willing. Hadn't Coach Villepigue said he had a natural sense of rhythm? By late November the newspaper reported organization of the Camden High band "progressing nicely." In that interim before Jack even owned an instrument, he began listening more closely to the radio. Bypassing Grandpa's beloved *Grand Ole Opry* and the slow and relaxing strains Mama and Daddy liked, Jack's fingers twirled the radio dial to big-band swing and jazz. "Jack," his mother called from the kitchen, "turn down that volume! What's that jumping around I hear? Go outside to do your exercises!"

Across the highway from the Smyrls and near the tea-room place, a discrete dirt lane wound out of sight about a mile to the residence of seasonal neighbors on Chancefield plantation. The several thousand acres of farm and forest lands of widowed Mrs. Walton Ferguson, Jr., were managed by Dixie Boykin, a merrymaking local character. About this time Dixie and Mrs. Ferguson's son Matt, on a trip to the resort of Starke, Florida, impulsively purchased from Clyde Beatty's wintering circus an Indian elephant named Alice. Jack's cousins Charles and Jim McGuirt were boys at the time, living with their parents in the tea-room place by the Chancefield entrance.

In 2004 Charles W. McGuirt published *Alice the Elephant and Other Stories of Growing Up in Rural South Carolina.* In his title story, Jack (as "Jak" Smyrl) figures as a lead character. The story describes a bewildered Alice's unhappy arrival at Chancefield plantation after a long journey aboard a delivery truck. Coincidentally on the same day, "another neighboring farmer, Oscar Smyrl, had decided that his son, Jak Smyrl, was demonstrating enough musical talent that he would buy him a trumpet. Jak

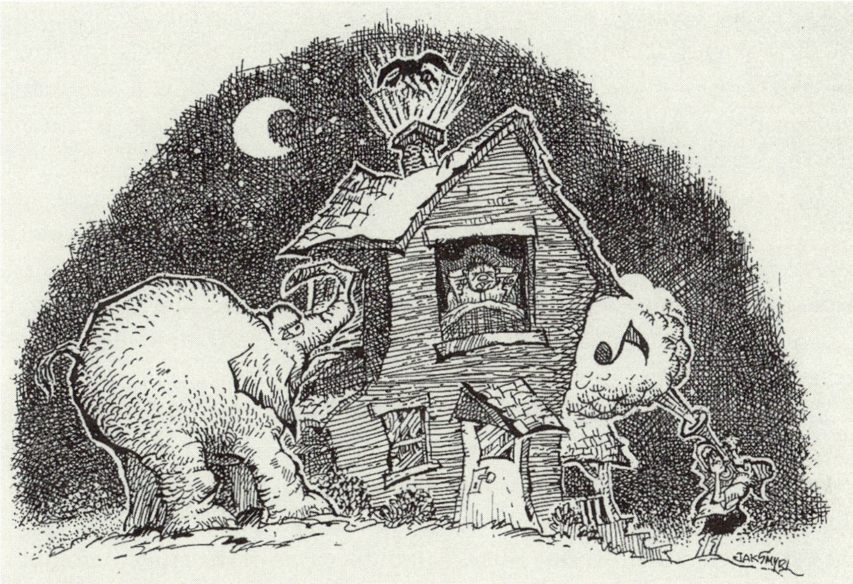

Illustration by Jak of his youthful trumpet playing, for Charles McGuirt's *Alice the Elephant*. Courtesy of Emily McGuirt.

arrived at home late Saturday afternoon with his new trumpet and instructions on how to teach yourself to play in three easy lessons."

McGuirt's story relates, "I heard the worst noise that a young kid can hear (later interpreted to be a trumpet, which sounded like an elephant). Shortly thereafter I heard the second worst noise ever (later interpreted to be an elephant, which sounded like a trumpet). Alice, apparently thinking that she had found her fellow elephants, began calling furiously. The dogs began howling. Our herd of cows, unaccustomed to either trumpets or elephants, started stampeding around the house along with our horses and pigs." Although the McGuirts heard the lonely pachyderm on a number of occasions trumpeting back when Jack practiced his horn, such incidents were overlooked in the flamboyant stories and newsreels of local and national media that playfully promoted Alice the Elephant as an agricultural laborer in the early 1940s.

Novice band music practice on a variety of instruments resounded across town and countryside for three to four months. Then on February 23, 1940, students performed their first public concert. In the Lyttleton

Street Graded School auditorium, the audience rose, applauding warmly for the amazing accomplishment of Fred Newell "Plute" Wimberly, director, and the new musicians. Names published that day included Jack Smyrl on trumpet, along with a number who would become and remain among lifelong friends through their band association.

By late winter Jack was busy with finishing touches on the 1940 annual. Miss Etta, stern disciplinarian and strict academician, had allowed him to remain on the journalism staffs during his make-up year. "You are expected to keep up your grades, young man," she told him firmly. To illustrate the "foundations of American democracy" theme she had selected, art editors Bill Major and Jack chose to sketch copies of heroic sculpture from books in Miss Etta's classroom. Jack's rendering of *The Thinker* was labeled "The Power of Real Thought," and Bill's discus thrower "Mens Sana in Sano Corpore." The careless mangling of the phrase traditionally "Capore Sano" was noticed by no one, not even Miss Etta when they submitted their work. "What?" mumbled one of the student staffers. "We're putting *naked pictures* in our annual?"

"Oh, no," said the artists, solemnly echoing words and tone teachers used to explain such photos in textbooks. "The *nude* statues are *classics.* They are *art.* They are intended to elevate the *mind.*" They added a final point. "Those Latin words mean 'A Sound Mind in a Sound Body.' Now, isn't that *deep?*" As Miss Etta and the staff pondered, Jack and Bill left quietly. Outside they grinned at each other: "Hey! We're putting naked pictures in our annual."

At the end of March, Jack's lettering skills earned him an interesting one-day job at the annual Camden steeplechase, the Carolina Cup. The bottling plant was well represented there, selling assorted drinks to the thirsty crowd—Pop Cola, Hy Up, and various flavors of lemon, orange, strawberry, root beer, and lime rickey. It would be a good day for a boy selling drinks to pick up tips, especially from happy folks wanting sodas for mixers. Jack preferred, however, to work at the choice grandstand area boldly painting race results on boards posted for all to see at the end of each event. The pay was generous for the work expended, and he was delighted to enjoy the sweeping view of races and spectators. Besides it was great fun to hold up his painted numbers to the attention of an appreciative crowd.

Delivering drinks, sometimes driving them himself in the plant truck, Jack visited numerous fairs and athletic events. In 1940 he eagerly followed the pitching season of Arthur Robinson for the Kendall Mills softball

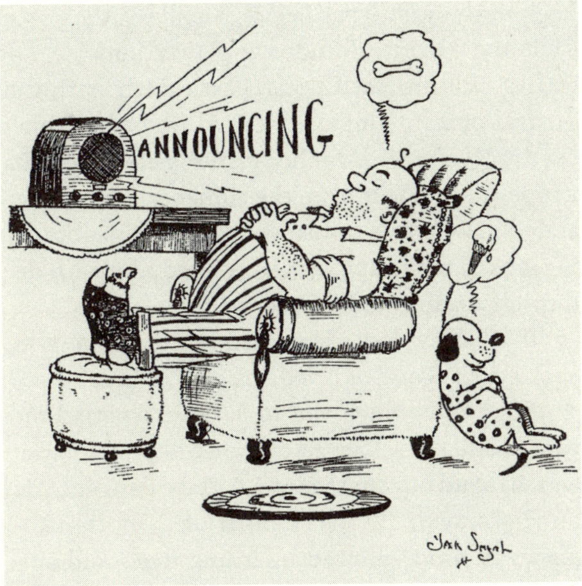

Cartoon for the 1940 *Gold and Black,* with his signature "a" and "c" so closely written that intended "Jack" appears "Jak"

team. A May 31 *Chronicle* article, "One-Armed Pitcher Struts His Stuff," largely credited the team's unbeaten record "to the pitching and fielding of Arthur Robinson who lost his left arm," cut off by "a drunken motorist," when as a youth he dangled it out the team bus window. One sports writer colorfully referred to the record-setting pitcher as "the one-flipper heaver." Jack was impressed that Artie had allowed nothing, not even terrible disaster, to stop his doing well what he loved best.

At the end of the school year, although still behind in specific units, Jack had earned enough credits to be a senior next year. The 1940 *Gold and Black* lay in the hands of an eager audience. Students ignored Jack's awkwardly executed sketch of a classical nude stature clearly copied from a textbook. He got appreciative chuckles, however, for seventeen small cartoons on two pages depicting "superlatives" and for his best work, the last sketch in the book. Heading the advertising section, his cartoon of a sleeping man and his sleeping dog, each dreaming unexpected dreams, is as whimsically humorous and skillful as his mature work years later.

At the beginning of summer vacation, Jack was off for a week to study government and politics with a group selected for the first Boys State to be held in South Carolina. The program for rising seniors ran June 16–22, 1940, at Columbia's Camp Jackson, soon to become Fort Jackson. Jack's "Palmetto Boys State" certificate identified its sponsor, the American

Legion, along with the Legion Auxiliary, the Forty Et Eight, and "All Other Civic and Patriotic Minded Organizations." Of all the activities of government, Jack returned home particularly enthusiastic about boxing demonstrations at Camp Jackson. At home he flipped his Charles Atlas book over to those lessons, filled a sturdy cloth flour bag with sand, tied it with a rope, and hung it from the chinaberry tree where he did his pull-ups. He added new moves to his workout routine, but when his repeated punching jabs to the heavy sandbag pelted him with dried chinaberries, he built himself a frame and moved the bag.

The family dogs, lean bird-hunting pointers, many white and liver-spotted like good old Nell, yawned in boredom. They were used to family comings and goings and to Jack's perpetual movements. Seeking backyard shade to escape the summer heat, they were simply waiting for cool weather and hunting season. A grave danger to dogs lay front of the house, on Highway 97. By the summer of 1940, traffic to and from the river and places beyond whizzed by in numbers and speeds unimaginable a few years earlier. Alfred recalled the day that he, Jack, and his father were getting ready for a fishing trip when they heard a screech, a thud, a yelp, and a cry at the highway. The vehicle had sped away by the time they found one of their young, half-grown dogs bleeding by the roadside. Jack and Oscar moved the injured animal carefully to the shelter of the garage, thinking his cries and his mangled leg indicated internal injuries as well. Alfred hurried to get him a pan of water. The dog was whimpering so painfully the menfolk looked at one another regretfully. There was only one thing to do.

"I'll get the gun," said Jack sadly, and Oscar nodded. Alfred ran in the house and covered his head with his pillow. Jack walked slowly outside with the gun. "Daddy," he said, "I helped feed him every day. I can't do this."

"I know," said Oscar and took the gun. He walked inside the garage and Jack waited, dreading the sound. None came. Oscar walked out. "Jack," he said, shaking his head. "I can't either."

Just then cousin Otis Creed drove in the yard, ready to go fishing. He saw their faces and heard the dog's cries. He peered into the garage. "Give me the gun," he said sympathetically. "I'll take care of this for you." Otis walked inside, and the others waited, dreading the sound. None came. Otis walked out, handing back the gun. "You know," he said. "I think I can fix this." A student at the Medical College of South Carolina, Otis was a summer intern at the Camden Hospital. "I'll be back," he said and sped off

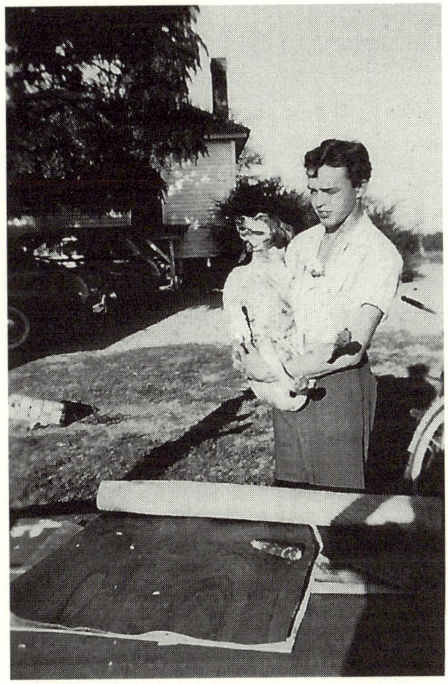

Jack with injured dog in body cast made with materials in foreground. Courtesy of the family.

to town. A tear-stained Alfred peeped out the back door, ready for a funeral at the Lonesome Pine.

Before long Otis returned. With an armload of hardware store supplies, he went back into the garage ahead of those who watched curiously. In a short while, before their eyes, he manufactured a plaster body cast for the dog he had quieted with pain-soothing medication. The cast started at the dog's front shoulder and ran down his side to circle his middle and to fit around his bottom like a diaper, with an exit for his tail, before encasing his broken back leg. It sure looked strange. "It has to be this way," Otis explained, "so that he can walk with it but with the leg steady for the bone to heal." Then Otis looked for something to make another vital part, an opening at the bottom. He found a corn cob to shape the necessary outlet. "There," Otis said. "He can take care of business. I think he is going to get along fine."

As the patient began to stir and lap from the water bowl, Oscar said, wonderingly, "Otis, I imagine you are going to make a fine doctor." In years to come, memories of the broken-legged bird dog, agreeably thumping about in a peculiar full-body cast until healed, may have played on the imagination of the artist to initiate countless cartoon variations of cheerfully oblivious "broke-tail" dogs. Jack admired the overcoming of adversity.

In July, when Oscar's term as commander ended, American Legion Post 17 had its largest membership to date. The outspoken group of veterans of the "first" world war shared President Roosevelt's concern that world domination was Hitler's goal. With France fallen and England standing alone against the Nazis after the evacuation of Dunkirk, the August 16 *Chronicle* reported that Post 17 had sent to Washington two unanimous petitions. One supported sending U.S. destroyers in aid of England, and the other "demanded support" for passage of a national compulsory draft act.

The Selective Training and Service Act, enacted September 16, 1940, called for America's first peacetime military conscription, and action followed quickly. The September 27 *Chronicle* reported eight men, including Oscar, appointed to the Kershaw County draft board. According to his certificate issued when the board expired, he served the full seven years of its operation. The board's first responsibility was to register all male citizens aged twenty-one to thirty-five. In October 3,375 men, black and white, registered in the county. The following month Roosevelt was reelected to an unprecedented third term as president. His emphasis on aviation immediately affected Camden. A "flying cadet school," part of a government plan for thirty-three pilot-training schools in the southeast, would be constructed at the Camden Airport, and the Southern Aviation School would soon change the look and spirit of Jack's hometown. Meanwhile a lottery inducted the first Camden men into the army, and all branches called for volunteers.

Lives altered quickly in the first semester of seventeen-year-old Jack's eleventh-grade senior year in 1940–41. In August he had pondered a perplexing matter. His cousin Nettie Leese Ogburn, barely older than him and a recent Camden High graduate, had married Henry Brown and moved to Georgetown with him, a plantation manager for one of the Baruch family he called "Miss Belle." Jack had admired Henry's gridiron exploits the year he graduated with Lottie, and he admitted the newlyweds appeared very happy. It was just that in no way could Jack visualize himself settled down and married. He had ambitions to go many places and meet many girls first.

Jack had been pleased, though, when Uncle Willie remarried, wedding congenial Elizabeth Denton, who quickly fit into the family. She and Uncle Willie were living in Camden, so Jack saw them often. It did not strike him odd for older people to be married. He sure hoped his sister Lottie, Nettie Leese's close companion, would not be in a hurry to marry. Lottie had a lot of friends around, including boys, when she came home on visits from college, but Jack had noticed his friend Mac Anderson's big brother Lewis spending a lot of time with her in their last year of high school. He worked at Southern Cotton Oil Company, taking breaks to go up to see Lottie at Winthrop too, and when she brought friends home to visit, he brought friends of his to date her friends. Mother and Daddy advised all their children not to focus real soon on just one sweetheart. Jack felt that best too. The family was just fine to him as it was.

On September 10 Jack started back to school. Daily the news told of people and places he had heard of in classrooms and Sunday school lessons. His parents seemed very concerned. Terrible things had been happening to Jews. Mama called them "the family of Jesus" and told her children to remember them in prayers. Jack had friends in local Jewish families, who sometimes sheltered relatives escaped from Europe. Last spring one of the refugees, Herbert Hecht, signed Jack's annual with a light poem in stilted English script and signed Norman Baum's in Hebrew, its message private. In French class Jack learned everyday vocabulary and thought of the people who used those words being under control of scary-looking Nazis. The radio told of Italy, now on Germany's side, sending troops toward Greece and Egypt. Jack visualized classic sculptures, pyramids, and bombs. Newspapers said Germany and Italy's next ally might be Japan, on the other side of the globe in every classroom. Three days previously the Germans had started bombing London. The English were the people Jack had studied about the most. He felt the war getting really close. He didn't like to visualize that, but there wasn't much someone his age could do about it—not yet.

Changes altered the Camden High curriculum. Mr. G. E. "Eugene" McGrew's basic shop classes expanded into adult-level carpentry as vocational classrooms added young adults eighteen to twenty-five in Defense Training programs he headed. At the rear of the gym, a machine shop was installed to open second semester for high school boys in the morning and for young adults afterward. Mr. James "Jimmy" Anderson, local machinist and older brother of Mac and Lewis, began teaching machine and welding classes.

Among staff changes, Jack's favorite history teacher, Mr. C. T. Baldwin, was acting principal as Mr. McFadden had been unwell since the previous spring. Professor Baldwin, or "Fessor" as he was familiarly called, was always tickled with the elaborate historical illustrations he let Jack draw on the chalkboard while he lectured. Any student who got in trouble with Mr. Baldwin would be assigned an essay to write. The more times the student got in trouble, the more words in length the assigned essay had to be. This year, Jack heard, Mr. Baldwin was assigning all his topics on world affairs. Fessor always kept up with what was going on. Physical fitness activities increased, and enthusiasm for sports, especially football, was encouraged as "patriotic" because of training benefits and the spirit it raised in participants and fans.

At halftime of the opening Bulldog football game at the densely packed Zemp Stadium on September 20, Jack and fellow band members, in natty uniforms and energetically performing patriotic songs, made their first on-field appearance. "Grandstand and bleachers gave a roar of applause," described the *Chronicle,* "when the Camden Schools Band, gay in their gold and black uniforms, paraded from the north end of the stadium. Down the field marched the several score musicians, doubling back at the south end and then sweeping with nice precision to face the grandstand." The article concluded that "drill formations and martial airs" would continue to add color to the football program. Not on the team but still on the field, Jack relished the band's "salvos of cheers."

A partial view of Jack's senior year, ending June 3, 1941, emerges from entries he began January 1, 1941, in the "Five Year Diary," probably a Christmas gift, that he filled faithfully until July 15, 1943. His first entry was on New Year's Day during a four-day family visit to Clinton, North Carolina, where Jack and cousin James Davis enjoyed a possum hunt, a picture show, basketball practice, and double-dating. At holidays' end Jack was back at Camden High when school reopened on January 6, but the next day he had a disciplinary infraction penalized by Mr. Baldwin: "got 300 word essay for being late to school." Jack's apparently rebellious reaction the day after the penalty appears to have gone undetected. He recorded that he "skipped a period of school, went riding with Sara Harvin, Grace, Betty, Bill—Rode bicycle to town—Went to picture show with Bill Burns and Bill Clyburn." He must have calmed down, for the next diary entry stated: "wrote 300 word essay for being late the other day." His diary mentioned no more cuts.

In the following week Jack helped carry out a solemn service. He was one of eight boys from Camden High who rode the football bus to Fort Lawn in Chester County to serve as pallbearers. The January 17 *Chronicle* reported Camden in sorrow following the death of L. W. McFadden, age forty-seven, for ten years high school principal: "His character was such as to endear him . . . particularly to the boys and girls." The school Glee Club sang at the graveside "My Faith Looks Up to Thee." On January 26 Jack noted another sad concern in his diary: "went to Grandpa's house he is in bad condition."

During January Jack recorded little about schoolwork and much about arts, sports, and socializing. At Lottie's request he drew for her and friends at Winthrop, decorating a radio for Bunny and making silhouettes for Iris. He made a poster for church and worked on two lessons in his correspondence art course. He bought a mute for his trumpet and ordered music and photo enlargements. He mentioned two times writing letters and three times receiving them.

On Saturdays Jack worked at the bottling plant. He hunted with his father and Alfred, acquiring a new interest in rabbit hunting. He skated, played hockey, and attended a basketball game. He went to a friend's house to listen via radio to the Joe Louis–Clarence Burman fight at Madison Square Garden. Heavyweight Louis, "the Brown Bomber," retained his championship.

Twice Jack went to friends' houses to listen or jitterbug to records. Seven times in January he went to movies, usually with friends, mostly band buddies. Five times he was at BTU, Baptist Training Union, and socialized with girls from that church youth group. One day Jack drove the school bus route. Often he rode his bicycle the four miles to school, or put his bike in the trunk of his father's car for after-school transportation. Twice that month he started walking home and hitched a ride with familiar drivers. One was cousin Lloyd Smyrl, chauffeuring Mrs. Ferguson's car for Chancefield plantation.

It was not until January 23 that Jack mentioned his schoolwork, stating vaguely "school is getting pretty tough," commenting immediately, "studied some on art course tonight—am getting myself in pretty good physical condition," thus focusing interest on both art and fitness correspondence courses. Exams began five days later, with no mention of study for them. The only other school activities Jack noted that month were an election for superlatives, a senior class meeting, and a meeting of the annual staff.

Contents of the diary the rest of his senior year reveal similar patterns of interests and activities, but also reveal scholastic intervention not fully appreciated by Jack at the time. On February 5, when report cards came out, he wrote in his diary what might be expected: "Mine is bad." The next day he reported: "late for school this morning," then "I am beginning to study harder." On February 7, after the band played for a school program, he "had a talk with Miss Etta about my lessons" and a few days later "stayed in for Miss Strother." From February 10, when Miss Etta showed him the artwork needed for the annual, Jack worked regularly and hard on his pictures, one night "until almost 2 o'clock." The following week he "started taking 10th Grade English that I failed last year," and recorded the next day in tone of resentment: "I am suspended from the band until I Improve my Studies." On February 24 he "had to stay in on History to-day" and added, "Practiced on my trumpet this evening—trying to keep my lips in shape while I am not in the band."

What he did not realize at the time was that Miss Etta, in collusion with the principal and other teachers, was using Jack's intense interest in art as a carrot-before-the-horse to entice him under her watchful tutelage to stay on academic track. The elderly, white-haired lady would not lower standards for him, but she would patiently use his interests to keep close tabs on him and push him forward to succeed in problem subjects. She saw that Jack lacked focus and confidence in academics. The more anxious he became in a subject, the more he avoided it. Encouragement made him less anxious. By the time Jack finished drawing his last picture for the annual on March 5 and the book was sent off the following day to be published, his other coursework had improved. One week later he recorded, "I was reinstated in the Band to-day—we played at Pine Tree school." The next day report cards went out, and it was with satisfaction that he wrote, "mine was pretty good."

Miss Etta did not let up keeping an eye on Jack. She gave work to keep him constantly involved on the *Bull Dog.* Jack's diary shows mimeograph stencil making began March 17, and the next day they worked "practically all day" to publish the hand-cranked newspaper before spring break. The next day, March 19, he wrote, "Got the paper out to-day—nearly rushed us to death." When Jack returned from spring break, he "started taking Literature at Miss Etta's to-night" and revealed that, "Miss Etta is coaching me." His personal tutoring continued through April 24, when he noted their lessons finished. Meanwhile Miss Etta assigned Jack to teach two younger students "how to work on [the] paper," that is, to do the mechanical and technical aspects he so precisely handled. She also selected Jack to attend the state student press convention in Charleston April 17 to 19, and he was pleased to accept the honor. "Had a big time," he wrote in his diary on his return and made a special trip to tell Miss Etta about the three days in Charleston with tours, meetings, a dance, a dress parade, and a banquet at the Citadel.

"Jack," said Miss Etta about his work on the staff, "you are very good at teaching. You are patient and don't embarrass people about what they don't know. You encourage them about what they do well, so they are able to learn from you." Jack was uncomfortable with her words. Did Miss Etta think he wanted to be a *schoolteacher?* He certainly did not. In time he would realize she herself had modeled those skills he continued to practice in his personal and professional life. "Miss Etta had faith in me," he stated. It was a gift he would pass on to encourage others.

In his family life a difficult time fell. "A sad day," Jack called March 7. "Grandpa Smyrl died to-day—he was 85 [actually eighty-seven] yrs. old, and a grand old man—and a true friend with a rich background." The next day he wrote, "Grandpa was buried at the old cemetery to-day—practically all his friends were there—the flowers were beautiful—It was a rainy day and very muddy." The obituary of Robert Love Smyrl, "one of Kershaw county's oldest citizens," appeared in the March 14 *Chronicle,* also with an item in the Liberty Hill column recalling "the venerable Robert L. Smyrl who rode with the Red Shirt riders" and was "always prominent in local affairs." From North Carolina, Mae's Uncle Arrie with other members of the Davis and Peterson families came to pay final respects. Jack's family took Uncle Arrie to view the Wateree Dam, which always impressed him and inspired stories of how different the area had looked in his youth.

During spring break Jack stayed with Aunt Mamie for several days at the old home place, left to her by Grandpa. Always special to her, Jack hoped to be helpful in a difficult time. On March 21 he recorded in his diary: "To-day was terribly sad at grandpa's—Mamie cried some because she is terribly lonesome since Grand-pa died—I drew some pictures to-day." His art was the only way he knew to comfort them. On March 23 Willie and Elizabeth as sympathetic diversion arrived at Mamie's to take them both to Chester to visit Aunt Nannie. Jack, overtired or overwrought emotionally, was "sick all day," even when he went to the airport with cousin Frank Campbell, who flew in a friend's airplane. Fascinated with aviation Jack would normally have been thrilled. He returned home the next day, still ill, and stayed home a day from school. In a short while, Mamie went to stay with an old friend, Mary Barratt Park, in Greenwood, South Carolina, and began seasonally working with her family at Park Seed Company, owned by Mary and husband George. Periodically when Mamie came back home, the family resumed Sunday picnics and visits in the yard of the old home place. Gradually in time laughter and memories helped soothe a deep loss.

Shortly before and after Grandpa died, Jack received two visits from "Mr. Barber" of the Federal Art School, offering instruction by mail. Having seen a magazine advertisement, Jack had entered their "Draw Me" competition and been selected as eligible. Mr. Barber's descriptions of commercial art careers enticed Jack, and later he ordered some lessons. On March 29 Jack painted numbers again at the 1941 Carolina Cup races, taking Lottie and her friend Bunny with him. The press reported special interest in some of the debut steeplechasers, "refugee horses" brought to America after the start of the war in Europe.

With Jack's schoolwork on even keel, he enjoyed more freedom, again driving his father's car socially and resuming band practices. A week before he left for the spring press convention, Jack reported in his diary on April 10: "We had the final band concert to-night it was a grand success—Mr. Wimberly, the band leader, has got to go to the army." Two days earlier the *State* had published a photograph of the seated Camden High orchestra, attired in monogrammed white sweaters. Jack proudly clipped the photo and on it penciled an arrow to a trumpeter he labeled "Me." The caption identified all the members. It was likely the first time Jack's name appeared in the *State*.

The April 18, 1941, *Chronicle* said of Jack's band leader that "Capt. F. N. Wimberly of Camden reports today for duty at Fort Jackson." It continued, "The captain is a graduate of the University of South Carolina, the organizer of the Gamecock orchestra, and the last two years—drum major of the university band." Furthermore the newspaper reported as good news that even in service "Captain Wimberly has arranged . . . to continue his direction of the Camden schools band." While at Fort Jackson, Captain Wimberly commuted twice monthly to hold nighttime band practices in Camden and to maintain musical enthusiasm awakened there. Jack and other students were deeply impressed by such dedication.

Musical interests of Jack and friends expanded beyond the school band. Early in 1941 the Kirkwood Hotel, a classy winter resort, installed a remote studio to broadcast live music of their orchestras and singers. On Sundays the Kirkwood also gave free public admission to concerts, some of which Jack attended with friends. At the homes of bandmates Bill Burns and Bill Clyburn, he often listened to records. The boys avidly collected popular songs and sheet music. Jack noted on February 8 that he "bought a blank record to try on Bill Clyburn's recordo," an early recording machine.

Music forged friendships with personable boys of varied ages. Bill Clyburn, like Jack a senior, was also a cousin. Younger Harry "Rock" Gandy and Francis "Mac" McCorkle had parents who were formally trained musicians. Jack's most obsessively music-driven friend was the youngest, Bill Burns, who also enjoyed art, and at Jack's encouragement he began a correspondence course in cartooning. Bill's father, a railroad agent, and his wife were avid fishermen and friends of Oscar and Mae. On May 5 Jack celebrated his eighteenth birthday at home with a group of friends of various interests and "sure had a big time."

The next day Jack was very pleased: "The long awaited annuals came to-day, they are fine." His artwork showed progress, with both cartoons and realistic sketches of student appeal, all lively with natural senses of movement. Head photos of football players attached to cartoon bodies were a hit. On May 7 he wrote in his diary, "I've been drawing pictures in people's annuals about all day—I made a date with Margaret Salmond for the Junior Senior banquet." He had been awaiting an answer for several days from the talented girl, a beautiful singer. On May 9, having been "still signing annuals," he went to the banquet and dance with Margaret, had "an exceptionally good time," got home at 2:30 A.M., and at the plant "was sleepy on the job all day." The May 16 *Chronicle* described patriotic decorations for the formal event—red, white, and blue ceiling streamers and American flags on tables with Uncle Sam hats for place cards.

With weather warming, drink sales were good. On Saturday, May 17, Jack sold $41.00 worth, but he was more excited about an invitation: "Bill Burns asked me to go to the beach with them tomorrow." Bill's family and a friend were going to North Carolina to fish for the day. On May 18 Jack recorded, "Went to Holden Beach today with the Burns. . . . We left at 4 A.M. and came back at 9:30 P.M. had a good time and got slightly blistered." The brief remarks belie the significance the day had for him, his first sight of a mostly undeveloped sea island that would remain strong in his memory and that would eventually become a very important place in his life. The single, long day at the beach was overshadowed Monday with a relief-filled realization: "It is getting very close to the end of school—I think I will graduate."

On Tuesday he took his English and literature exam, and afterward he and a friend went sailing on the river with shop teacher Mr. McGrew in

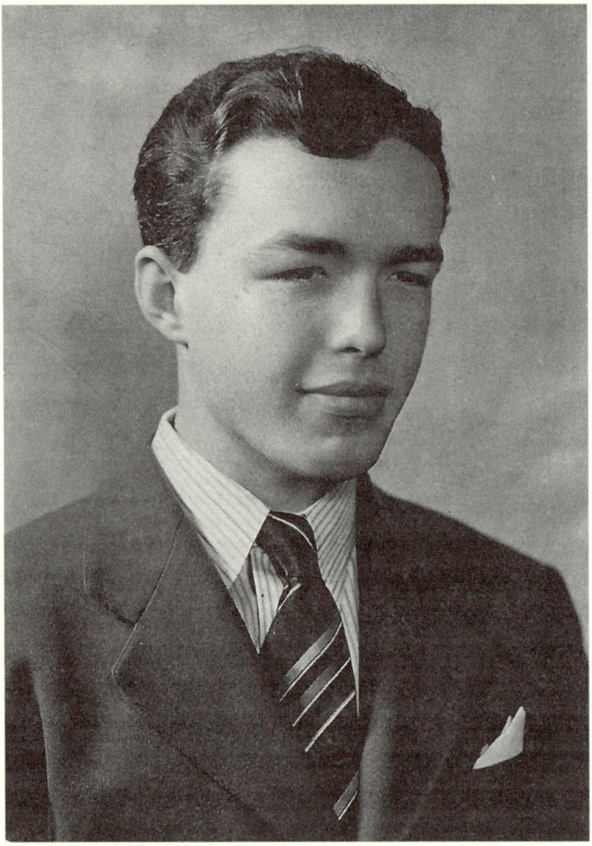

Jack Smyrl, high school senior, 1941. Courtesy of the family.

his sailboat. As exams continued so did practicing for the class play and socializing. Jack described a church hayride, bowling, riding around in cars, swimming, boating, eating meals at friends' homes, and writing graduation invitations. On May 27 he recorded in his diary an event in his honor: "The whole Smyrl Family had supper in our backyard tonight—am having a big time these days." Shortly afterward, however, exuberance may have carried him too far, for on May 31 Jack illegibly scratched out two lines and part of a third in his diary, and the next day, a Sunday, he had to stay home alone all day and write an essay for Mr. Baldwin. The length assigned was twenty-seven hundred words.

Whatever the cause or misdeed that prompted its assignment, the lengthy essay (assigned nine times longer than his previous punishment) apparently restored Jack to grace. That night he was at the baccalaureate sermon and the next evening performed in *The Pageant of America.* It was his dream role. He played a cowboy and loved every minute of it. He also enjoyed the attention given to the backdrops he had drawn for the pageant. On June 3 Jack went to one more practice and that date recorded in his diary: "Graduated from Camden High School." It was 4 A.M. before he came home from the dance that night, and he "slept about all day" before he awoke with a smile to face the future before him.

Oscar handed him a flat, wide brush he held by the handle, and Jack began an atonement that continued the next few weeks. He began painting the house.

Chapter 10

Time Ticking

"Hope I will have good luck"

On June 5 Jack worked on the house all day, painting outside shirtless and in shorts to work on his tan. On breaks he blew his trumpet, "to keep up my lips." As he painted he listened through open windows to the radio's mixed programming of music, comedy, and news. He concluded his diary that day soberly: "The war in Europe is getting bad." For some time his concerns had been the immediacy of school. Now world events of 1941 moved closer in his thoughts. Nine days earlier, while Jack's family was in the backyard enjoying his graduation dinner with the radio off, President Roosevelt had announced a state of national emergency and outlined actions for self-defense and war readiness.

In the coming three months, war preparation paralleled Jack's summer, the time he had to decide on his next educational step. By mid-June scores of British cadets arrived in Camden to begin flight training at the newly opened Southern Aviation School. With their homeland under steady Nazi bombardment, the English desperately needed pilots trained to fight off the attacks of German planes. The June 20 *Chronicle* described deep emotions at local Grace Episcopal Church when the previous Sunday a dozen English cadets in robes unexpectedly marched in with the church choir, and scores more joined the congregation for worship. Eyes brimmed with tears as the rector, Dr. Maurice Clarke, "gravely prayed for the safety of the British people." Voices rang loudly singing the recessional "Onward Christian Soldiers."

Jack's diary on June 29 reported his meeting some of the "English boys." In the coming months his family became acquainted with individual American cadets also training at the school. On occasion the Smyrls invited them for meals and took them on outings to the river. During the summer Jack worked extra hours at the plant when Oscar was away, busy with civil defense and war preparation assignments. Nationally World War veterans had been registered in February, and a number of local ones were helping prepare for upcoming military maneuvers. The nation's largest peacetime "war games" to date would encompass Kershaw County and far beyond. Oscar and brother-in-law Fred Ogburn were on a committee of five to obtain trespass rights from landowners of eighty thousand acres in Kershaw County. The Carolina Maneuvers, to last two months in the fall and cover large portions of North and South Carolina, required months of advance planning.

Jack stayed on the go. He exalted in his diary on June 13, "feels great to be out of school." When not at home or at the plant, he spent much time in the water, swimming at various places several times weekly with family and a string of friends. Once he drove cousin Sophia Creed and some girls twenty miles to swim in Denny's Pool in Bishopville. After sailing with Mr. McGrew, Jack and cousin William Watkins designed a sailboat and determined to build it. Mae sewed a sail, and Freddie Ogburn spent several days with Jack working on the boat. With various homemade rigs and other vessels, Jack and boys lazily navigated the river waters. Once Mr. McGrew sailed by, and everyone waved.

The Smyrl watermelons ripened, and Jack took juicy, red-hearted melons along on his river outings. He carved leftover rinds into funny shapes, especially comical teeth he made for anyone who wanted to wear them and join his silliness. After seining at the river with the menfolk, Jack ate fish fries and stews abundantly. The family spent July 4 on the island, invited a group there for dinner later in the month, and as usual stayed part of a week in August. One day Jack went to the island alone to help Otis Creed build a dock. It was a busy summer escaping the heat and the ever-moving passage of time.

In town Jack continued to practice with the high school band, performing with them on July 10 in a concert in front of the school gym. He finished lesson 25 of his art course and started reading a book about an old interest—*Tarzan, Lord of the Jungle.* Riding around to movies and church entertainments with friends and dates in the "beautiful sweet

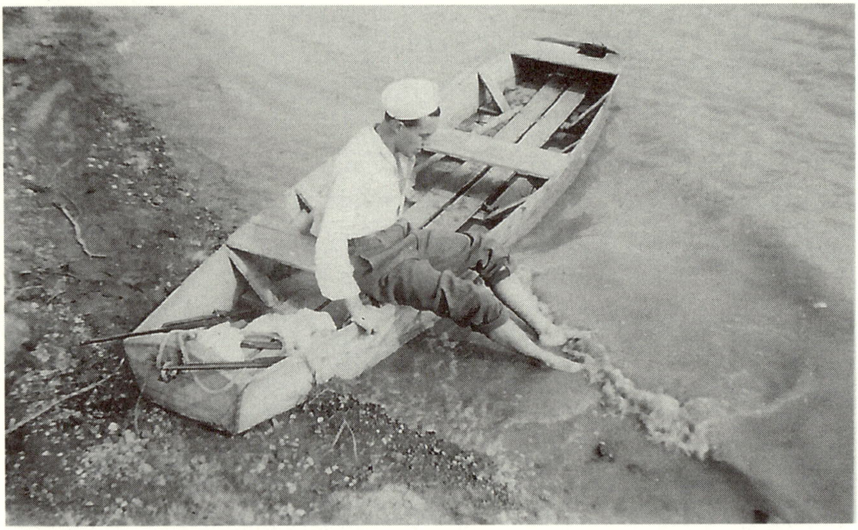

Jack at Lake Wateree with hunting arms in a wooden boat, possibly the one he helped build. Courtesy of the family.

running Buick" Oscar traded for in early June added to Jack's pleasure. Technicolor movies were a new hit, especially in "air-conditioned comfort" as theaters set up electric fans to blow across blocks of ice. One night when a church hayride got rained out, Jack and Lottie's friend Mareida Rector went to the movies with Lottie and Lewis. Next year would be his sister's senior year at Winthrop, and Jack hoped she wasn't making any serious plans.

Jack pondered decisions while appearing active in avoiding them. On July 1 he wrote in his diary, "Man came to see me about going to the University." Jack invited the visitor to the river to swim, and he stayed for supper. A week later the mail delivered a University of South Carolina catalogue. Jack had costs, courses, and his future to think of. Meanwhile he learned the final key production step at the plant, how to bottle. On June 25 he had recorded in his diary that "Russia and Germany are at war" and on July 13 stated that Alvin Creed had to go to the army. Since the Citadel graduate had civil engineering skills the army needed, he would enter as a first lieutenant. In August when Alvin, his wife, Nellie, and their toddler son, Bobby, took a brief vacation, Jack caught a ride with them far enough to meet up in North Carolina with cousin James Lodor and spend five days with him at Wrightsville Beach.

It was "a big week," Jack wrote in his diary. He went swimming and had dates with Blondie, Betty, and Mary, at times doubling with James and girlfriend Bunny. They went to the Watermelon Beach Party and an "excellent" big dance at Wrightsville Beach, where Cab Calloway and Orchestra played. Having come home by bus, Jack returned to work and reality, stating in his diary on August 16: "The war is getting pretty bad." Germans were defeating the Russians, and Japan had bombed China. It was hard to make decisions, not knowing what would happen next.

On August 25 Jack and Freddie took a bus to Georgetown for "a wonderful time" with newlyweds Nettie Leese and Henry Brown at Bellefield. Over the years Camden native Bernard Baruch, noted financier and "advisor to Presidents," had employed a number of people from his hometown on his Georgetown plantation preserves, and daughter Belle continued their contracts when she acquired part of his property. Bellefield was breathtaking, a natural and unspoiled coastal paradise. Jack was awed on arrival when Henry drove them around, especially pleased to see deer, which were extinct at home. On Wednesday Henry took them fishing in a saltwater creek. Also living at Bellefield, a Boykin family ate with them one night, and another evening Jack recorded, "We had supper at the Chamber with a lot of people . . . danced some at the Boykins—had a good time." He returned home and began to look around to see what jobs were available for him. Henry, he mused, had taken up very interesting employment after high school.

On September 1 Jack inquired at the airport about jobs at the new aviation school. Told to come back later, he drove back to town and "got a ticket for sign violation." Protesting the next day that the sign was peeling and illegible, Jack offered to paint a new one in waiver of a fine. He found himself quickly offered a job painting even more signs for the city. He was working on signs and at the bottling plant when public schools opened on September 9. Jack finished the signs and on September 11 "went up to the school this morning to look up credits—am trying to decide whether to work or go to school." The next day he wrote, "Made out my schedule for school today—Worked some at the Plant—went seining at the river, caught sixty fish, the weather was chilly." Clearly summer was ending.

On September 15 Jack reported, "Decided to go to school as a Post Graduate—started this morning—believe I am going to enjoy it this year—Hope I will have good luck." Camden High had long had a respectable postgraduate program, but this was the first mention of it in his diary. His memoir notes explain that with Lottie a senior at Winthrop this year, it made financial sense for Jack's family not to be paying for two students in college the same year.

For another year Jack would work with his father to save money and to earn additional useful credits. He selected practical typing and bookkeeping classes, as well as geometry to help in college math, and a new course being offered—journalism, which would allow him to work on both the newspaper and the annual. He would also continue in the band, though switching from trumpet to cornet. More mature and confident this year, Jack would avoid many of the snags of past years. Though mastery of algebra would remain ever elusive, geometry proved within his grasp, and Jack put new lessons to work by helping keep books at the bottling plant.

Jack's diary in his postgraduate year, 1941–42, provides a running account of a pivotal year in history. Jack at eighteen was not yet the age for conscription, then twenty-one, but he like everyone felt time ticking and winds of change. Even small decisions seemed of great momentum as choices grew fewer.

During October and November 1941, the Carolina Maneuvers stirred the sights and sounds of Camden, home of the official publicity headquarters for the war games that had been under preparation since spring. Jack watched a military band practice on October 2 and observed "a lot of soldiers" in town. Hampton Park ceremonies formally opened the exercises on October 7, when Jack reveled in the trip he took with the journalism club to observe the news headquarters at the Kirkwood Hotel. The army had taken over the entire resort to house military staff and communications. An impressive professional operation coordinated military and national press services. Print, broadcast, and film media buzzed actively. They utilized the latest publishing, recording, and broadcasting equipment from typewriters to teletypes, telephones to walkie-talkies, and darkroom labs to live studios. A specially equipped movie truck mobilized sound equipment and photographic technology to the field and even transferred them to airplanes. A glimpse of such a range of operations was rare exposure for high school journalists, an experience Jack would not forget. A few days later he was also impressed listening to "a soldier swing out on a clarinet," for military bands also included professional entertainers. Publicity aimed to present to nation and world a strong impression of America's military capability.

Jack was out of school a whole week from October 13, working full time on the truck to fill in for Oscar, treasurer of the Kershaw County

Agricultural Fair, cosponsored by the American Legion. Daily through Saturday crowds swollen with visitors filled the downtown midway and exhibit buildings for a highly successful and profitable week. Jack made numerous trips to the fairgrounds delivering drinks and peanuts from the plant. Following the final tough day, he spent most of Sunday sleeping in. The following week Jack marched with the high school band at the state fair, where they took eighth place in the band contest. For over two stimulating weeks, excitements of fairs, nightly fireworks, and patriotic brass bands played out against background rumblings of military convoys, overhead planes, and simulated explosions.

For a few days, Jack temporarily filled in at home for Lloyd Smyrl, who was sent to Connecticut to drive Mrs. Ferguson's car back to Chancefield. In his absence Jack stayed three nights at the plantation to work as station wagon driver, going into town early to pick up the house servants, groceries, and mail, and at the end of the day taking the servants home. "Staying at Chancefield didn't give me much time to work in town," he wrote, but he found staying there interesting. "They have horses, dogs, and fine plantation." He made no mention of Alice. The elephant, it turned out, had unknowingly been purchased pregnant and had been sent to live at the Atlanta zoo.

On November 7 Jack reported seeing "Army trucks from the maneuvers" and the next day "Army Convoy passing through town all day." Some thirty-five hundred soldiers poured in on weekend leave, according to the *Chronicle*. Entertainments arranged all over town greeted them with food, music, dancing, and local girls as dance partners. On November 22 Jack reported more crowds of men on maneuvers. In the intervals Jack and friends responded to the enticing and invigorating music all around them. They formed a dance band.

Jack's memoirs recall that the group formed at his instigation to compete in a talent contest. He recorded in his diary on November 11 that schoolmates Bill Burns, Bill Clyburn, Harry Gandy, Mac McCorkle, David Melton, Joe Tobin, and he had organized, and that night they "practiced again up at my house." The next day at after-school practice in the auditorium, they did not waste time figuring out what to play. They had learned only two songs. Practices continued while Jack also worked on the school paper, which came out on November 14. Three days later the musical group "had a fine practice" at Joe's house, aided by a soldier: "Wally, a professional clarinetist, helped us a lot, and played some for us." Jack began grandly calling the group "our orchestra."

School band and "orchestra" practice both continued, along with Jack's work and family life. The Smyrls went to Columbia for a combined birthday dinner for Aunt Hattie and Oscar, visiting Fort Jackson and the airfield for exhibits and demonstrations. At a fish stew at the river, Jack took a short swim in "awfully cold" water on November 18 "just for the novelty." Extended family shared "a big Thanksgiving dinner out in the yard at Grandpa's house," after which Jack and friends enjoyed a well-attended dance at the Court Inn, Camden's noted old-style grand hotel. After Oscar and Otis went hunting on November 21, they and Jack went seining "a little" in the chilly water. Everyone wanted to enjoy as much as possible before the confinements of winter.

Over the following days Jack noted soldiers "coming in by hundreds" and "packing into Camden." His orchestra had added a few more musicians to be ready for the November 25 talent contest, part of a junior class fund-raising beauty pageant. Before curtain time soldiers began filling seats to look at pretty girls. Some of the novice musicians, seeing so many uniformed strangers in the school auditorium, grew shy about performing. Backstage, in a last-minute decision, Jack and friends disguised themselves in blackface and went onstage under a new name. According to the *Chronicle,* it was as the "Harlem Jive Band" that Jack and his friends were awarded the judges' prize.

Jack in later years confessed that they secretly placed "a plant" in the audience. When polite applause began at the end of their performance of "Dipsy Doodle," the one song they were listed to play, the friend they had bribed jumped to his feet in the back of the auditorium. "Encore! Encore! Play 'Daddy'!" he cheered, applauding vigorously. The startled audience applauded louder along with him. The orchestra immediately launched into current hit "Daddy, I Want a Brand New Car," and the youthful audience wildly cheered in popular recognition. Elderly judges thus assumed the group was performing that perplexing modern music well to play anything spontaneously asked. The big prize awarded the winners was $3.00. With fifty cents paid as promised to the shill, the rest was divided among the original seven, plus James Creed, Mickey Langston, and Robert Thompson. "The shill," Jack chuckled, "made twice the money the rest of us did."

The emboldened new group began practicing every couple of days, determined to be good enough not to hide their faces the next time they performed. On December 6 Jack's diary noted "a good orchestra practice tonight." The next day after church, the family took a picnic to the river with Uncle Willie and Elizabeth, and two Southern Aviation cadets. In his diary Jack added the startling news they heard on their return home: "Japan attacked U.S. Islands, and declared war on U.S.A." On December 8 he stated solemnly, "The U.S. declared war on Japan today—Pres. Roosevelt made a wonderful speech stating that the U.S. is at War with Japan—Americans have been killed in Hawaii."

Jack presented jumbled thoughts on December 11: "The weather is beginning to get cold—Congress is talking of moving the Draft age down—I am on the annual staff—The U.S. is preparing for the War." The rest of the month was a fast-paced blur. Lewis had heard the Pearl Harbor announcement over the car radio Sunday on his way to visit Lottie at Winthrop. He turned around and telephoned her: "I'm enlisting." He quit his job the next day, signed up, and was in the army a week after the attack. One of the cadet friends with Jack's family on Sunday's picnic "washed out in flying school" and was sent on duty to Colorado. Alvin Creed received orders for the strategic Panama Canal Zone.

For Mae's birthday on December 18, North Carolina kin visited a few days. Jack's cousin Marion rode along with him when he drove Mrs. Ferguson's car to Starke, Florida. The two young men had much to talk about on the 350-mile trip. They returned home on a mail train, five hours late, and "got $10.00 for the job." On December 23 Otis Creed and Jack donned formal attire as groomsmen in cousin Frank Campbell's wedding in Aynor. Frank wore his military uniform. "It was a beautiful wedding," Jack noted. Driving home to Camden in the rain, Otis and Jack enjoyed the company of passengers, cousin Laurie Campbell, and her aunt "Jessell." Jack had known Uncle Ted's younger sister, Jessie L. Campbell, for years. Thirteen years older than Jack, Jessell liked to tease him about having babysat him. Jack liked her jolly sense of humor. Before long Jessell too would be in uniform, a nurse in the armed forces. "Surely had a big time at Frank's wedding," Jack wrote afterward in his diary. Appreciation of time with friends and family intensified with America now at war.

On December 25 Jack had a long but pleasant day. In his diary he wrote first, "Crowd came up early this morning for Christmas," and he finished, "Our orchestra was a success at the dance tonight." Jack and friends were excited to have been hired for their first dance, held at St. Mary's Hall of the Catholic Church. It was a favorite spot in town for such events, but probably few other groups were eager to work on Christmas Day. Jack thought their playing that night was sure to be remembered. They knew a lot more arrangements now. As "the Jive Bombers," which Jack said they soon called themselves, or "the Mighty Mites," as Mac McCorkle remembered them, the orchestra embraced other names and other musicians in addition to original organizers. Music practice continued as war worries intensified.

When his parents and younger siblings made their holiday visit to North Carolina in early 1942, Jack stayed home alone and worked at the plant. On January 2 he noted in his diary, "U.S. is having hard time with Japan." Four days later he was encouraged by a military repulse, but in two days he worried, "War in the Pacific is getting serious." Jack read with interest the January 9 *Camden Chronicle.* His friend Mac Anderson, twenty, had volunteered for the Marines with an explanation the paper quoted from him: to "give the Japs hell."

At times Jack's diary peppered news of war events with effects at home. When he observed on January 19, "The Americans are valiantly holding off the Japs in the Phillipines," he added a fallout of war in the islands where the world's rubber trees grew: "Tires are no longer available for automobiles." Transportation woes were spreading. On February 28 Jack noted that his father "had the tires switched around on the car to save them—the war situation is really serious." In March Americans withdrew from the Japanese-controlled Philippines, with General MacArthur promising to return.

Local efforts paralleled national ones to counter potential enemy attacks on the American homeland. Jack's role in civil defense was announced on February 13: "I am in the volunteer messenger service of Camden, in case of air-raid." His March 4 diary reported he "went to practice air-raid tonight," and next cited two headlines that day: "British Bomb Paris" and "Navy Fliers Shoot Down 16 Jap Planes." Jack's April 18 entry that "the American planes bombed Tokyo in daylight raid" referred to Doolittle's Raid, the first U.S. raid to strike the homeland of the Japanese, who had perceived themselves as invincible. On May 9 Jack wrote, "the American fleet has won a good sea battle over the Jap fleet." It was the Battle of the Coral Sea, the first major engagement with all firing between the pilots of ship-launched aircraft. The week of May 12–19, at request of Kershaw County chairman of defense Ralph Shannon, Jack drew a large poster map of Camden to pinpoint locations of air-raid and emergency stations. It had focal use in the main emergency station.

In Kershaw County's defense plans, practice air raids and blackouts were taken seriously. In rural areas out of earshot of the shrill, pulsating sirens that alerted Camden citizens, volunteer messengers such as Jack traveled from household to household to pass on an alert. Mae busily sewed blackout curtains to help neighbors without means of making their own. The possibility of air attack at home seemed real. Daily, planes from the aviation school and nearby airfields appeared in local skies, and recent maneuvers had given citizens a firsthand sense of invasion. Fines and public contempt fell on any household that did not cooperate with a defense drill.

As diversion from wartime worries, upbeat popular music unified young and old. The "big band" swing music favored by Jack and friends in their orchestra was the definitive sound of the time. "It was such energetic, happy music," classmate Meta Alexander (Beard) would recall years afterward. "Everybody danced then." The first 1942 appearance of Jack and friends in their improved dance band was at a chapel program for the school on January 16, with helpful soldiers dropping in to give advice during rehearsal. A number of other performances followed. On January 17 they played at St. Mary's Hall for an adult social group, the Horse Shoe Club. "We received $5.00—we are improving a lot," Jack wrote. They played on January 20 for a community Red Cross play, and more important on January 30 at a fashionable dining and dancing spot north of town, the Pines, for the annual adult social event, the President's Birthday Ball. Jack recorded in his diary, "We did well—had a big crowd." Mac McCorkle recalled years later, "We thought we had made the big time when we played the Pines. Tickets cost $3.00 each."

Some of the band members were inspired with further creativity. Jack's February 2 entry reveals that "Bill Clyburn, Bill Burns and I got Mr. Clyburn's mimeograph machine and started a little paper today—we call it *The Bugle Call*." Miss Etta had trained those three of her journalism students very competently, for they sold ads with spirit, wrote directly for a student audience, and produced a paper that they sold quickly at lunch. They had been taught "freedom of the press," and they exercised it. The independent *Bugle,* designed to be lively and "wake people up," sold well, according to Jack on February 10, bringing in $2.10 when it came out that day, selling at a nickel a copy.

After three weekly issues of free-wheeling production, Mr. Baldwin invited the entrepreneurs to his office. He praised them first for their interest, hard work, and initiative. "But, boys," he said, "there is one problem." As Jack wrote in his diary February 23, "We were giving the school paper too much competition." Mr. Baldwin explained that Miss Etta was having trouble keeping students interested in her journalism lessons since the student body wasn't buying their papers now. "Boys, I know you don't want Miss Etta to get her feelings hurt, and you don't want to stop your *Bull Dog* friends from enjoying journalism, too." No, they did not. Mr. Baldwin suggested that the boys wait until summer before selling any more of their newspapers. That seemed fair to the three. Jack wrote on February 23, "We are temporarily discontinuing *The Bugle Call.*"

Years later he would recognize and chuckle over the subtle censorship. Jack's enthusiasm for journalism was not dampened, and he completed writing a play he had begun for the class that was presented in chapel on April 3. He also enjoyed the tomfoolery of Miss Etta's allowing them to publish an April Fool's *Bull Dog* issue. The student journalists held a press banquet and dance at the Kirkwood, and Jack was among those who also attended the three-day Scholastic Press Convention in Florence. A highlight was dancing with Meta Alexander to the orchestra's special request rendition of "Stardust."

The orchestra begun by Jack and friends continued to be important, along with jams at informal gatherings. To improve their professional appearance, Mr. McGrew was helping them build music stands when he was called up for military service and had to leave the classroom. The boys finished the work in the Smyrl garage. They painted the box-like stands navy blue, and Jack decorated them with silhouettes of musicians in tropical settings. The more polished orchestra reorganized, pared mostly to original members, officially now "the Sentimental Southerners." Their first gig with new gear, a 4-H barbecue supper, earned them $15.00. The next week Jack wrote on March 27, "We played at the New Armory it sounded good." In April at their first dance at the Episcopal parish house since their new look, the crowd was small, and they took in only $6.00. On May 1, however, he wrote they played there again, and "It was good, the crowd was big—my lips are in good shape."

Jack's musical interests drew him to other performers. He and friends traveled to Columbia to hear top swing musicians Charlie Spivak, Tony Pastor, and Bobby Byrne, rated by him "wonderful" or "terrific." In Camden with Bill Clyburn, Bill Burns, and K. T. Price, Jack also "went to Colored dance at new armory . . . to hear the negro orchestra." Jack attended other local dances, met band leader Clarence Brazeale, and continued to play for the school band as well. On April 6 he played with them for the Army Day parade through town, at which time the Home Guard marched too. On May 10 he played with the band at Memorial Day exercises in Quaker Cemetery, and after the three-rifle volley, Jack blew "Taps."

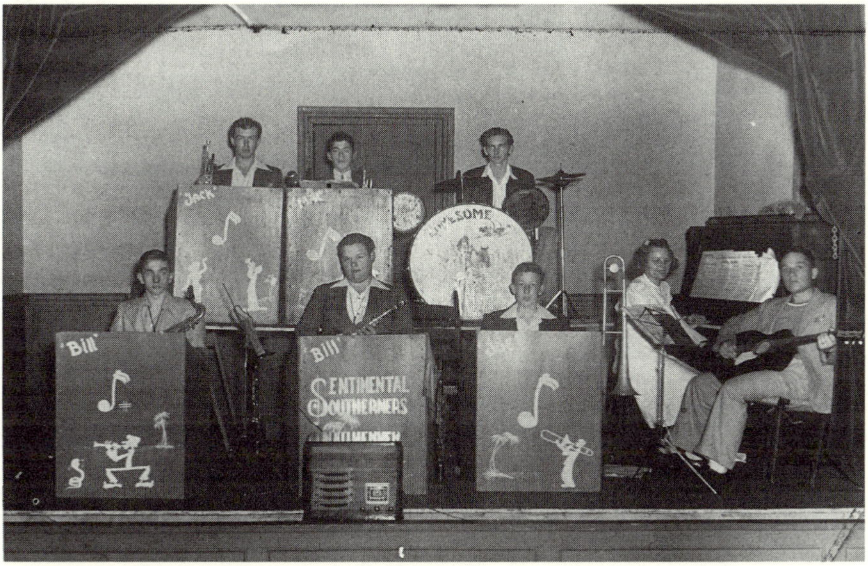

Sentimental Southerners at a 1942 dance at St. Mary's Hall, with Jack's art decorating the stands they built: back row, Jack Smyrl, Mac McCorkle, Dave Melton; front, Bill Burns, Bill Clyburn, Joe Tobin; piano, Mickey Langston; solo performer on guitar. Courtesy of the family.

Regarding his family life from early 1942, Jack made several sentimental observations suggesting awareness of a coming time he would be leaving home. On January 21, after he and Alfred went to the movies with Ogburn cousins Freddie, Gary, and Onnie, the three boys reflected on the date as the first birthday of Larry, their baby brother and Jack's youngest first cousin. Jack mused, "Freddie & I talked about old times." Jack also wrote sentimentally on February 19 after hunting with his father, "Old Nell is getting old but she's the best dog I've seen." On March 14 he commented about his community: "I went up in the town clock with some boys and looked over the town—It is a grand view." After working at the plant on April 30, he rode his bicycle home, noting "the moon is beautiful tonight." His comments about school were far different this semester. On March 5 he stated, "I am really enjoying School this year," and on May 8, "[I] am having a good time."

Major events reflected family changes. On March 29, when Jack's family picnicked with Uncle Willie and Aunt Elizabeth at next-door Nettles

Pond, it was not only because the nearby pool was "real pretty today." Just a week later, Aunt Elizabeth gave birth to Thomas Love "Tommy" Smyrl, another first cousin for Jack. Weddings were also distinctive. On March 15 Jack attended a double wedding at Camden Baptist Church, where cousin Sophia Creed married Richard Denny, and her brother Otis Creed married Jacqueline Daniels. On April 3 Cousin Cleo Smyrl married Allen Follin Watts. All three grooms in the weddings were bound for military service. Jack reflected nostalgically on May 26, "I sat up late tonight reading through some old letters of mine." On June 1 he "saw Lottie graduate from Winthrop College today—it was grand." She was considering a job teaching high school in Estill, South Carolina. The next day, June 2, Jack wrote that he "received my Post-Graduate certificate tonight at Graduating exercises of Camden High school—this finishes my High school days." Nineteen years old, he pondered, "Jack Smyrl, what's to become of you now?"

Chapter 11

Auburn

"All life is uncertain now, isn't it?"

Summer 1942 was a steppingstone for the Smyrl siblings. Alfred looked forward to his freshman year in the fall when he would join Lucy at Camden High School. Lottie was excited to be starting her first job, teaching English at a lower-state high school that hired her for her specialty in library science. Jack moved onward late in summer when he left his band, friends, and family to study art and life on the Plains of Auburn in Alabama.

Jack said a long good-bye from the beginning of the summer, without directly stating in his diary until the day before he left that he was leaving for college. He was already there before his diary named his specific destination. Until that time, except for reporting comparatively more time spent with family than with friends, Jack made diary entries that were typical of recent months. On June 15, for example, he wrote: "worked in the plant and on the truck—went seining in the river with Willie & crowd—we had fish supper on the river bank." With increased sugar shortages, the plant sold out of drinks as quickly as they could make them and at times had nothing left to sell. Shortages of tires and of metal for machine repairs frequently caused difficulties.

Family sadness fell in June with Uncle Ted Campbell's death. Aunt Nannie and Laurie would move back to Camden to live, and Laurie in time would marry again, wedding Herman Myers, who visited the Smyrls with her after her father's death. Several times the extended family gathered for picnics in the yard at Grandpa's house, which by late summer Jack began calling "Mamie's." Much of the time that Jack spent with older kinsmen involved seining or fishing. Much of the time that he spent with cousin Freddie involved rifle practice.

Music remained the main tie with friends. Early in June Jack played a couple of times with a few others onstage at the movie theater between pictures. He made trips to Columbia to help Bill Burns and Dave Melton buy instruments and to hear popular musicians. Jack and Bill hitchhiked to enjoy cornet and trumpet player Muggsy Spanier, band leader of hot jazz and swing. Jack was pleased when Aunt Mattie Creed offered him Otis's trumpet, left behind when his cousin headed for medical service in the military. Jack polished up the old horn, and their long-term relationship began. Like other metal items during wartime, instruments were in short supply as musical popularity increased. Jack blew sweet sounds with the Sentimental Southerners at the old armory for a July Fourth dance, and a week later at the Episcopal parish house for the aviation school's Cadet Dance. The following week he and Bill sat in with the army orchestra, and in August their band again played the armory. The night before Jack told everyone good-bye, he with the Sentimental Southerners played a posh venue, a dance at the swank Court Inn.

That Jack had many hidden feelings in the summer of silent farewells emerges in an episode in his diary. He described on August 20 an apparent send-off supper: "We had a big crowd up tonight for chicken stew, we ate outdoors, had a grand time." On August 21 Jack wrote: "went to walk this evening in the woods and got lost—had to go through swamp, yelled for help—Wm. Carter (negro) heard and brought me back, got scratched up bad." The next day he stated, "The scratches I got when lost in swamp are bothering me—it was quite an escapade." Some of Jack's memoir notes, headed "Traumatic Experiences," add dramatic details to the misadventure.

He described himself barefooted and wearing only shorts. Lost in the dark he panicked, yelled for help, and became "lacerated by briars," plunging through "snake-infested water and bog" to reach his rescuer who called him out from the opposite side of the woods. In a family history interview years later, he stated that in his panic he pictured his little drowned cousin Tommy and felt "afraid I was going to die in the swamp and my family would never know where I was."

Though Jack's scratches healed, panic apparently resurfaced in days ahead. His emotions intensified the night of September 3, just three days before he was to depart. Although he had made no diary reference to his plans or his destination, on the evening of September 4 he recorded that he "had a nervous breakdown last nite—Mama & Daddy brought me to the doctor—slept late this morning." Alfred, later reading the diary as part of an interview, recalled that after the swamp incident Jack experienced increasing difficulty sleeping and that one night he was so overwrought that his parents took him to the family doctor. Medication helped him sleep that night for a good long while, and he bounced back quickly. Jack added to his September 4 entry of the previous night's self-described "nervous breakdown" that he played at "Court Inn tonight—good dance." The next day he worked at the plant, "told most everybody good-bye," and stated for the first time, "I am leaving for college tomorrow."

Whatever Jack's dark thoughts had been, by the time of departure his optimism and ebullience were restored. Perhaps he was buoyed by his reason for having chosen the faraway college he had never visited, Alabama Polytechnic Institute, as Auburn University was then known. Several times he voiced what he stated in a 1978 *Sandlapper* interview: "It was the best military college I could find that offered art." Nineteen-year-old Jack believed like his father that he would be in service before the end of the war. He could get a head start on military training at Auburn, possibly qualifying for Officers Candidate School, and he could also pursue his first love—studying art. Jack's new love for music had blossomed in his belief that he had gone as far in art as he could go on his own. At Auburn there would be new opportunities.

Jack's diary on September 6 reported a trip of 450 miles with an "all-day ride" by train from Charlotte to Auburn. His father accompanied him, and both stayed at the boardinghouse where Jack would be rooming, "Mrs. Jackson's home." Travel in 1942—especially in hot weather—was harsh. Buses and trains were packed with uniformed men and traveling families. Through the open windows came track noise and hot air that offered little respite from a typical southern summer day. Windows invited in smoke from steam engines, and partly cushioned seats little mitigated the bumpy ride of frequent stops and starts.

Oscar stayed three days. Jack looked over the campus the first day, took tests, was photographed, and concluded, "I am going to like it here." The next day he took more tests, was fingerprinted, had a physical, and began "meeting people, getting settled." On September 9 his father went home, and Jack took more tests, registered for the freshman class, and got his cadet uniform. This fall, for the first time since 1918, all cadets including Jack were enrolled in the Enlisted Reserve Corps (ERC). He looked proudly at his course of study, "Applied Art," examining which art classes he could take in the three quarters of the academic year. Freehand drawing he would begin now, and he would choose others later. Art classes were taught in the Architecture Building, which Jack set out to find. He would be fully involved right away with what he had come to Auburn to study—art and the military.

Jack wrote home on September 9 from 330 Armstrong Street on stationery emblazoned "Auburn," with tiger logo and school seal. His letter reflected typical freshman experiences: "Have been busy every minute. Have had to stand in line for most everything." He was finding his way around campus—learning building names and library procedures, receiving a laundry tag, taking placement tests, and getting his "rat-cap." On September 12 Lottie wrote Jack from Estill. To aid national defense and pocketbooks, teachers were "being bold" in not wearing customary stockings to school. She urged her brother to attend Baptist Student Union (BSU) activities.

Auburn life quickly appealed to Jack. On September 15 he wrote in his diary that he had submitted a cartoon to the *Auburn Plainsman*. He added, "I am enjoying the class in free-hand drawing." A week later he wrote, "My cartoon came out in the "Plainsman" today (it's the college paper)." He settled in, attending church, Sunday school, BSU, and "friendship league" meetings, and involving himself in activities—attending the "Pep-rally at the stadium" and Auburn's 20–7 victory over Chattanooga. Jack easily developed friendships. His roommates Stanley Jenkins, Henry C. "Amy" Amerson, and Thurston Sumner became friends with whom he would correspond for years. Jack and Stanley shared a love for music and collaborated on compositions. Jack learned his way around the college town, finding grills and drugstore lunch counters and soda shops. There were six drugstores within walking distance of his boardinghouse. Among his favorites were Markle Drugs, where he could get a foot-long hot dog for a dime, guzzle a Coke for a nickel, or splurge for a fifteen-cent milkshake. He also favored popular Toomer's Drug Store, where patrons exchanged pleasantries with its founder Sheldon "Shel" Toomer, a star halfback on Auburn's first football team.

Oscar wrote Jack on September 15 on Camden Bottling Company stationery imprinted with a logo of new flavors: "Pop Kola—Califruit Orange, Polo Club Ginger Ale & Other Flavors." Oscar asked whether being in the Army Reserve would allow Jack to finish college before serving or enhance his chances of being called. "I hope that you can graduate first, if not I want you to later anyway," he said. "Always keep graduating in mind."

Subsequent letters to Jack caught him up on fast-moving changes. On September 26 Lottie observed to Jack about Estill: "Men are mighty scarce around here." She reported on her old crowd at home. Boyfriend Lewis was in New Mexico, and his buddies G. T. Hendrix and Bert Rush, who dated her college roommates Dot and Milwee, were in Texas and Kansas. Lewis, she said, had "received his wings, a staff sgt's rating and is to be an instructor at Ft Sumner . . . the largest advanced glider school in the U.S. Isn't that swell?"

Inevitably some of the news related to concerns, injuries, and losses. On September 29 Lucy wrote, "Cooley Hinson wounded in the leg . . . in California now." On November 12 Mae wrote, "Everybody around here was beginning to think that little Henry Carrison and Mac Anderson were dead like Jack Villepigue but the families have heard from them and they are ok." Lieutenant Carrison had been among survivors picked up after the Japanese sank his ship in the South Pacific, and Mac after the Battle of Guadalcanal had been shipped to a censored area in the Solomons from which word had been delayed. In the month before Jack left for Auburn, the community had been praying with Coach Villepigue for his eldest son, "missing in action" after his ship sunk in the Solomons. Realization that the bright and popular young man was lost and that his body would never be found came slowly.

Home folks offered letters and labors to support the war effort. Uncle George Creed in October wrote son Alvin: "I am proud that I have a son in the Army. I know you are going to do your part and do it right. . . . It is hard but what if we do not win this war. . . . Lets make this a better world to live in." Lucy wrote Jack about half-day schedules at Camden High while students helped in a scrap metal drive. Lottie's students too were collecting "scrap to slap the Jap." Home guards had been training Estill High boys to march, and "now they're training the girls too." Soon Lottie was helping with the girls. Meta Alexander, at St. Mary's in Raleigh, North Carolina, wrote Jack about the shortage of male laborers. In their place about 265 girls at her school spent several hours "raking the leaves on the campus."

In spite of war effects, Jack's letters and diary indicated an appreciation for college life: "am learning drill pretty good . . . am enjoying college life . . . getting to know some cute girls." Movies, dances, and socializing at times affected academics. His September 29 diary attests: "am having a hard time with Algebra." Always ready for travel and adventure, Jack went home with Stanley Jenkins to Montgomery the first weekend in October, and home with Thurston Sumner to Birmingham the end of the month. His comment "Met people, had a big time" could sum up a number of his recorded experiences.

Jack described Auburn in a letter to Freddie Ogburn on October 11. With forty-five hundred students, it was "supposed to be the friendliest college anywhere." His classes lasted about an hour, except for art class, which was three hours. He had physical education daily, some drilling but no regular drill, and he wore his ROTC uniform twice a week. They were training on 105 mm howitzers, "pretty big popguns."

A great contrast to Jack's usual upbeat diary entries came on October 15: "A terrible thing happened today; one of the boarders here committed suicide—He seemed to be such a nice boy." According to Jack's memoir notes, the young man in the room next to him "committed suicide by blowing brains out with shot gun." At the sound of the blast, Jack was among the first to observe the shocking scene. The incident had a profound and disturbing effect on him. The following day, Jack wrote that he "felt pretty shakey today—went to infirmary got prescription for some medicine." For weeks afterward, if his roommate was away, Jack either found excuses to spend the night with friends who lived elsewhere or invited them to stay with him.

Jack was bothered by an elderly boarder's reaction to the suicide. A veteran of the Spanish-American War, the kind of person Jack usually held in high regard, elderly boarder acted in contrast to others who were traumatized. The old man expressed indifference. Jack wondered if future experience with combat might make him, too, callous to death and suffering. In his memoir notes Jack recalled that the experience of physically confronting violent death "shook me emotionally." Writing to Lottie, he confided the disturbing suicide and its effects but did not mention them to Oscar or Mae. Lottie agreed with him that it was "better not to tell them, especially if it will only worry them." She wondered if the young man "might have been in some kind of trouble. Or was he worried about the draft?"

Mae, regarding ongoing debates about draft changes and enlistment options, urged Jack on November 4, "Make the very best of this year for 'Uncle Sam' may need you next year. I hope by next summer that things will look a lot brighter. I don't want you to have to go to the army but if you have to I am going to try and take it on the chin as so many other mothers are having to do, for I cant be a slacker no more than you can." Mae was no slacker. In a letter mentioning her work at the Red Cross center making surgical dressings, she mused, "Looks like the army will be needing a lot of them soon."

On November 10, taken aback by a decision of Jack's, Mae inquired, "Why did you decide that maybe you would join the Marines. That is the toughest branch of the force and the training is awful." Conscription changes lowering the draft to age eighteen also instituted a national lottery. On November 15 Mae urged Jack, "Maybe you had better not enlist in any branch of the service until you come home and talk it over with your Daddy. I sure hate to see you have to go, but it looks mighty like you will have to."

Jack had already decided, however, and two days later signed and filed the following document: "I desire to serve my county, when called to active duty, as a member of the Marine Corps Reserve, and I desire that I be discharged from the Army [Reserve] as soon as eligible for, and for the purpose of, enlistment in the Marine Corps Reserve." Jack felt pleased stating preference for volunteer service, although his choice could be preempted by draft lottery.

Four days later an event in Columbus, Georgia, temporarily set aside such concerns for Jack and friends, who enthusiastically attended Auburn football rallies and home games, giving a new cheer, "War Eagle!" At an out-of-town game on November 19, the Auburn team, with a 4–4–1 record, shocked the sports world with a 27–13 upset of the previously undefeated Georgia Bulldogs. Georgia would go on to capture the National Championship in the Rose Bowl, the loss to Auburn the only blemish on their record. In his memoir notes Jack recalled All-American Roy "Monk" Gafford, whose performance was outstanding in that monumental game. Jack and friends migrated to Toomer's Corner that evening to celebrate.

Jack's diary on Sunday, November 29, showed worries: "Slept till 1:30 today—It is rainey—One of the bluest days I've ever seen—worrying about my grades and stuff." The following day he seemed relieved, "Paid my fees for next quarter. . . . I think I may get in another quarter O.K.—I failed a couple, made A on Art / B on military." Apparently he could stay in school, perhaps feeling satisfied at least in his main priorities. Following Jack's enlistment decision, he diverted attention through December to a "cute" coed named Joy. "She showed me a lot about dancing," he said, and they enjoyed the Junior Prom to the music of the Alabama Cavaliers.

Letters from Jack's family and old friends continued to report changing situations. From Georgia Tech Bill Clyburn lamented, "That's hell!" on hearing his age group was to be drafted, but still in school in December, he grumbled graphically about uncertainties. From Camden High Bill Burns reported that "Miss Howard has joined the WAACs. . . . Everybody in high school was crazy about her." Winthrop graduate Louise Howard had been hired that year as Camden High band director following Mr. Wimberly's deployment. She was also playing piano for the Sentimental Southerners, still with Bill, Mac, Joe, and David, joined by Claude Lamoy, Jack's old friend Piggy. Mae wrote on December 1 about an older cousin of Jack's: "Margaret Shaw has joined the WAAC's and left Saturday." Two days later she wrote, "We heard that Henry Brown was about to be called up so he enlisted and that Nettie Leese is coming home to stay with Nettie and Fred."

The biggest news arrived on December 15 via Western Union telegram: "LOTTIE AND LEWIS GETTING MARRIED TODAY SEVEN PM EXPLAIN FURTHER WHEN YOU ARRIVE. MOTHER." Lewis's rare leave had come unexpectedly. Transportation from New Mexico was slow and difficult on trains loaded with soldiers. Learning he was on the way, Lottie left Estill early for Christmas vacation. Having for some time discussed marrying in the future, once together again Lottie and Lewis determined to marry immediately in the small window of time they had. The wedding was arranged in one day, and they married in the Smyrl home with pastor, family, a few friends, and many best wishes. After an overnight honeymoon in Columbia, Lewis returned to duty at Fort Sumner.

As his oldest sibling began a new life, Jack made plans for his first visit home. That month he had moved to another boardinghouse, Mrs. Monroe's at 224 South Gay Street, with "a big going-away-for-Christmas supper." He took Bill Clyburn's suggestion to save time and travel home by plane from Atlanta: "$20 for a round trip plus $2 tax." Jack left Auburn December 18 by bus to meet Bill at Georgia Tech. The next day they boarded a Delta airliner for Columbia. Lottie came home by bus and joined the family and Jack for Christmas.

Jack spent the holidays catching up with family and friends, cleaning guns and hunting with Oscar, going to movies, playing his horn with the orchestra, buying presents, and working at the bottling plant. On Christmas morning, he described traditional holiday jubilance: "The crowd came around by 6:00 this morning—went with them on their merrymaking rounds—we all had breakfast at Dewey's—Had a great time—ate Christmas supper at Mamie's—There was a big crowd." On December 26 Jack and Lottie "had the car in town all day—saw a lot of people" while Oscar and Willie went duck hunting. Jack enjoyed the comfort and familiarity of home despite shortages and rationing. As the New Year began, Jack spent his last days at home much like previous winter vacations. On January 1, 1943, he "worked some with Uncle Henry at the plant—went hunting with Daddy and Alfred—Had a good date with Grace tonight." The following day he "stayed with the family tonight. . . . Packed my clothes to go back to school."

On January 3 Lottie returned to Estill, and Jack "had a long train ride all day." Back at school, Jack learned from the *Plainsman* that "the reserves will get to finish the winter quarter before being taken in the army." Some fellow classmates had already left; others were exploring options. On January 6 Jack recorded in his diary, "Thurston quit school today to join the merchant marine—he is one grand fellow."

Letters of 1943 described changes at home. Mae wrote on January 10: "We will all stay at home now for we are not allowed to do one bit of driving for pleasure. Daddy & Willie had to get permission to go up to the river today to bring the boat home. The O.P.A. [Office of Price Administration] men are everywhere checking cars and I understand they have taken several people's ration books from them." The next day Bill Burns complained, "The gas thing is really terrible. I have to walk every where I go," and Harry Gandy bluntly stated in late January, "This new gas ban is hell aint it."

The insecurity of the times was evident. Back in Estill, Lottie rationalized January 11: "I realize that this is an uncertain time to be married in, but all life is uncertain now, isn't it? I am praying that all will be well, not only with us, but with the whole world, and soon this mad mess of war will be over, and people can begin to live again. War seems so useless and wasteful." On January 27 Mae wrote to Jack, "Got a letter from Lewis and the way he talked he must think he is going over seas." Four days later, Oscar offered Jack suggestions about a tuition aid application: "You can attach a note stating that we are in a small bottling business and have had our supply of sugar cut 30% that will work a hardship in meeting expenses for the coming year. Of course we may make it and we may not. During these times you cannot anticipate very far ahead in business."

During winter quarter at Auburn, Jack turned around his overall grades. Art, as always, remained his key interest. In Elements of Design, students were invited to take stints posing for others to draw. The professor explained that since an artist must look closely at his subject, it was helpful to understand how the subject felt being the object of such intense attention. Artists also needed to overcome shyness or self-consciousness observing models. The teacher stressed that drawing the human body was an academic endeavor not to be confused with prurience. Long an advocate of exercise and physical fitness, Jack was relatively comfortable posing minimally draped to expose muscle tone. Consequently, he was hired to model several times in figure-drawing classes. The log he kept in his diary recorded that he "posed for the art class" eight times between January 13 and February 8. On February 15 he recorded, "Got $7.00 for my posing—paid up my debts." The experiences of art modeling left him comfortable in appreciation of the human body, and likewise unconcerned in minimal attire.

With conscriptions pending, Mae informed Jack on February 6 that Bill Clyburn had not returned to Georgia Tech: "He is waiting to see what they will do with him about the service." She asked, "If you have to leave school in March will you be able to come home before you have to report for duty?" In the same envelope, Oscar revealed a business dilemma: "Got another fellow on the truck this week . . . and a boy to help Uncle Henry. Don't guess they will stay long, both subject to the draft." Oscar urged, "If you have to go to the Army try and get a few days home before you are inducted."

Although both parents used the word "if," military service seemed a certainty. Several people advised Jack on options once in service. Oscar wrote on February 7, "I want you to apply for the officers training school as they will permit you to do so. You will probably have to serve your three months basic training before you can get in." Alvin Creed echoed that counsel from the Canal Zone on January 27: "It's no fun as a private and you better remember that. Don't be a fool, get a commission—in any branch, rather than go in any as an enlisted man. You'll be sorry if you don't." Life as an officer, however, like so many other matters, proved beyond Jack's control. Mae wrote on March 29: "Got your letter yesterday and was so sorry that you could not get in the candidate school. I was so afraid about your eyes." Jack had passed all requirements but the vision test, being unable to see clearly enough without glasses.

Jack's friends at Camden High, not yet subject to conscription, saw advantages and disadvantages in the changes around them. On February 17 Harry Gandy referred to restrictions on travel: "Yeah! I'm out for basket-ball but we don't get to play any out-of-town games." That month Mac McCorkle described excitement that school was closing a week while the building was used for registration, and Bill Burns wrote about another week of closing while ration cards were issued. Mac also reported on

February 20, "The band is doing great in the *Happy Days of '43*." They were booked to play at the fashionable Sarsfield Club "if nothing happens to Piggy and the rest of us." A new feature, an obstacle course, was built on the high school grounds. From Alfred's descriptions of its ten stations, its design was to prepare students for military service.

On February 22, by Special Delivery Air Mail, Lottie sent word to Jack from Estill that she had resigned her job and was preparing to join Lewis in Victorville, California: "If you can't read this, don't be surprised as I have been rationing for the last 2 days (10 hours per day). . . . The school is having a holiday—but it's all work for the teachers." She cautioned Jack, "By the way, *be sure* to get your new [ration] book. Unless you do, you cant use your old one or get any food [without] the new one." Lottie mentioned that Richard Denny and Bert Rush were home on leave: "Everything seems to be happening at once, eh?" Jack in his diary on February 20–24 noted war effects on campus: "Ralph Thomas left for the air-corps today. . . . The girls in Quadrangle have to move to frat. houses, the frat. boys move to boarding house—this is to make room for soldiers."

By the time Jack wrote home on February 25, the day before exams ended, he had at last learned the date he was to be called up with the Marine Reserves—June 1943. He was eager for spring holidays March 6–10, "the last time I will get home before June." He had received their money order and paid fees for next quarter. "They were $66.50—I also just got my ration book, and just finished an English exam." Jack felt good "getting things done," stating, "The only worry I have in the world is Algebra," his last exam. After that, he was going to Birmingham to visit Thurston, leaving soon for the Merchant Marine Academy. Jack described his new room for next quarter at Garden Courts: "almost the same as a dormitory, except . . . privately owned. A nice 3 window room and everything." Should Jack be drafted before quarter's end, "the fees will be refunded."

Just before spring break, Jack received a March 2 letter from Lottie. She was not going to California. Lewis's orders had changed, and he was being sent instead to Fort Bragg, North Carolina. She hoped that Jack would be able to see Lewis when he came home. By train from Auburn and bus from Columbia, Jack arrived in Camden the morning of March 6. He worked that day at the bottling plant and "saw a lot of people," he noted in his diary, including Lottie and Lewis who were briefly at home. The next day the couple took a train to North Carolina, uncertain where they would find a place to stay. On Sunday Jack went to church and on Monday "had a swell time" visiting "the old school." On March 9 he rode the train back to Auburn. A postcard from his mother on March 15 reported that Lottie and Lewis were living in a camper trailer set up for them in the backyard of the Fayetteville home of cousin Thomas and Sarah Davis.

That month events that fell into place would eventually position both Lewis and Jack in combat on different sides of the globe. On March 26 "Oscar Jackson Smyrl, Jr.," finalized his pledge of intent made the previous November. Jack recorded in his diary, "I Joined the Marine Corps today," and he wrote home an undated letter: "I will be allowed to finish this quarter in school which ends May the 24th and will be called into active duty at the end of that time." He had asked advice from "all the men who could help me." Jack stated, "It was not a hasty decision and [not] a very hard one to make."

On March 28 Mae wrote, "[Lewis] thinks he is being sent over seas. They have issued him his overseas equipment and this is the last furlough he will have. He has been told to hold himself in readiness to go any time." For Lottie and Lewis, the reality of an uncertain future was tempered by happiness in being together and planning a postwar life. On April 12 Lottie wrote Jack from Fayetteville, "Lewis has been able to come in every night so far. We are still living in the trailer. They have clamped down on his squadron, and there are lots of rumors going around. We just live from day to day. It has been just gobs of fun. Even the simplest of things becomes the most wonderful in the world when you share them with someone you love."

The 1943 Auburn yearbook *Glomerata* summarized the year: "As each day passed we realized more completely what we would soon be losing and we were more determined to enjoy what time was left at Auburn." Jack too made the most of his final quarter. He juggled classes, drill, exercising, going out for track, working a part-time job in the Architecture Library, listening to and playing music, pledging a fraternity, and corresponding with family and friends. He found the ROTC drill and artillery training more intense, and now as relevant to his life as art and music. According to his diary, Jack "quit the track team" on March 29 but continued running on its course. He noted that his ROTC unit "paraded for Lord Halifax the English Ambassador" on April 9. He commented on May 3 on the blending of ROTC cadets and enlisted personnel then in training at Auburn: "We drilled with all the boys in khaki today—It was an odd sight—the war is doing funny things to the campus." Ten days later, he noted, "We Go to School with all Guys in Uniform now."

Jack doubled his art courses, taking two this quarter—Water Color and Art Structure. His water color assignments often featured local structures of special interest to the School of Architecture. Painting onsite outdoors was especially appealing in pleasant spring weather. In Jack's Art Structure class, at the end of the quarter he enjoyed three-dimensional clay modeling. Music drifted all about him through the open windows of spring, and he grabbed his horn for practice whenever possible.

From late March through the end of school in May, Jack's romantic interests focused on a fast-paced, fun-filled relationship with "cute" and "beautiful" coed named Caroline Robinson. He complimented her in a letter home on May 4, saying she "has really has got the old personality." From his first invitation to her for a "Saturday nite hay-ride" to a number of formal sorority and fraternity dances to casual times such as "a hike in the woods to pick flowers," Jack and Caroline were together every few days in a busy social whirl. Jack took roses to her and drew pictures for her, but a number of times he misspelled her name in his diary, sometimes correcting it afterward. Caroline appears also "Carolyn" and "Carolyne" in these entries, almost as if his relationship with one girl was subconsciously multiplied in making the most of the waning days of school.

Overall Jack's time at Auburn—if measured academically—was undistinguished. Fall quarter he made an A in Freehand Drawing, B in ROTC 101, F in College Algebra 101, and F in English Composition 101, the latter changed to D upon reexamination. He was placed on scholastic probation. Winter quarter he made B in Elements of Design, C's in ROTC 102 and English Composition 102, and D in a repeat of College Algebra 101. Spring quarter he earned OK on Physical Education 100, A in Water Color 205, B in Art Structure 214, C in ROTC 3, and E in Trigonometry 102, changed to D upon reexamination.

On the other hand, if measured by his gains in maturity, social skills, and self-confidence, Jack's Auburn experience was exceptional. It was those gains that in the immediate future would make him a better Marine. On May 22, 1943, the day Jack left Auburn, he saw Caroline for the last time, catching a ride with her and others to Atlanta on his way home. His mother had written him on May 3, "Lottie will be here [when you get home] for Lewis was sent over-seas."

In early summer of 1943 the Smyrl siblings and parents were reunited and all living for the last time under a single roof. Awaiting call-up, Jack's time home from May 23 was shortest. Lottie, expecting a child in December, would be living at home with her family while Lewis was flying gliders overseas. The family would not venture far, restricted by gas and tire rationing. While Jack appreciated comforts of familiar faces and places, he chafed that his call was not immediate. On May 27 in his diary he described himself: "waiting on my call to the Marines—am enjoying being home." A week later he "cleaned out all my Junk to pack up." Still his call did not come. On June 23 he "mailed letter to Marines requesting active duty," and on June 27 in his diary noted "Am getting anxious for the Marines to Call me."

Waiting, Jack corresponded with Auburn friends, most of them in training. His typical transportation was by bicycle, beneficial to his conditioning exercises. He fished, swam, tried out Oscar and Willie's new motor on the river, and explored with Freddie below the river bridge. Jack helped his father and Willie in their gardens, milked the cow, and worked at the bottling plant. He heard Bill Burns and the orchestra play, blew trumpet with them, and went to Columbia to hear Eddie Helms and Ina Rae Hutton. Jack practiced drawing, went to movies and to church, and enjoyed family gatherings at home and at Mamie's, where cousin Bobby Smyrl stayed overnight with him. North Carolina relatives came to visit. So did the Campbells, who brought Jessell with them, just back on furlough from Red Cross service in Hawaii. Jack grew more anxious to get his call.

On July 2 Jack wrote in his diary: "Bill & I dated Kitty Vinson & Anna Shuler from Rembert—We went over to Sumter—Had swell date—must do this again sometime." Five days later, he recorded, "I got my orders from the Marine Corps to report for active duty, July 16." It was what he had been waiting to hear. Jack would have to postpone a return visit to see Anna, a pretty teenager whose father owned a busy country store on the circuit of bottling plant customers. His last days home were busy ones. On July 14 he "went seining this evening with the crowd—Had good luck and good time—they all ate at the house." Jack wrote his last diary entry on July 15: "Bought some good steak in town. We had good supper at the river—Willie and Elizabeth were with us—Got my stuff ready to leave for 'Boot Camp,' Marine Training Base."

Jack snapped the latch closed. In the old trunk at the foot of his bed, he had put away his half-filled five-year diary, not on the list of items he was allowed to take with him. The navy-blue volume would remain closed for a very long time, and he would not write in it again. The next day Jack left home for Parris Island, South Carolina.

Chapter 12

Parris Island

"Most of my friends are overseas and I am still here"

A large number of letters to and from friends and family document the three-year military service of Marine Oscar Jackson Smyrl. These are supplemented by official records, photographs, artwork, news articles, his later memoir notes, and his comments in interviews and in conversations. As a lowly boot, a buck private, Jack began service on a coastal South Carolina sea island near Beaufort in the heat and humidity of midsummer. His acclimation to Parris Island went much smoother than for many, especially for more than half of his platoon who hailed from New York City. Accustomed to the climate, Jack actually liked hot weather. He had hiked the hills around Grandpa's home for years, had grown physically fit working on the farm and at the bottling plant, and had trained on his own and at Auburn. For more than a decade Oscar had taken him hunting, instructing him in proper care, cleaning, and handling of firearms. For one skilled in hitting a dove or quail on the fly, hitting targets at Parris Island was elementary.

Jack's first hurried letters from boot camp were undated as he lost track of dates. Basic training had "lightened up," he said in his initial letter. The Marine Corps for the first time included draftees along with volunteers, and men were being hurried to war assignments. Right away Jack had been appointed a squad leader in charge of eleven men, issued "rifles and everything." They were not allowed to keep diaries but were allowed musical instruments: "Please rush my horn will you?" He got plenty of food. He told the family not to send his watch, "any money, or any candy or sweets. *DO* send me some Baby Suntan lotion. The heat is terrific here." Jack's letter postmarked July 23 had been composed over several days, frequently interrupted. Training discouraged attention to any time but the moment. Recruits had been marched to the beach, "about 3½ miles" distant, for a picnic, and "had all the drinks, sandwiches, and ice-cream we could hold, then marched back." Effects of such exertions discouraged cravings. The recruits were always rushed, had "a thousand rules to go by," and wore "sun helmets all the time."

As a squad leader Jack was allowed to go to the PX but had seen no newspaper nor heard any radio. Boots were not permitted to leave the barracks area without permission. Daily they cleaned the Garand, or as they were required to call it, the "US cal. 30." Jack wrote Freddie Ogburn on August 16, "This M1 is the best damn rifle in the world. . . . We also throw dummy hand grenades, and get bayonet drill, and a little boxing instructions thrown in." Twice each day they had sick call, had mail call, and cleaned the barracks. They made their own beds and washed their own clothes. Mae wrote back on July 24, "Guess you are glad now that your Mama taught you to make beds and sweep and do things." Jack was glad too that Oscar had taught him to clean, care for, and use firearms.

In a later undated letter, Jack acknowledged receipt of "my horn, slippers, sun-juice, dark-glasses, the cookies, mutes, letter, chewing-gum and everything else. . . . We drill then we have a lecture, then we drill, then a lecture, and so on into the night. . . . We get lectures on gas, bayonet, first-aid, rifle, military courtesy and everything under the sun, and we have to learn it all." Drill instructors were extremely strict: "If they catch anybody scratching while at attention they make em scratch till it bleeds. If you don't shave, you'll get a dry shave in front of the platoon. If the D.I. walks through the Barracks after we fall out and he finds a bed out of order, he throws the mattress bedclothes and all off the second story on the ground." Jack had no trouble remembering his D.I.'s name—Jack Davis—but had the common sense not to ask a question he would have politely inquired in civilian life: was Sergeant Davis related to any of his mother's people?

The first of August Jack listed his mother as beneficiary on his $10,000 National Service Life Insurance application: "65¢ per thousand . . . $6.50 per mo." Expecting Jack to be sent to war immediately after training, the family was anxious to see him. Visitors were allowed on Sundays. In several letters from early August his family wrote of hopes to come down as soon as they could get new tires. Their present ones were too worn for the 350-mile round trip. Tire rationing restricted purchases to decisions of a "tire board," to which Oscar was making his request. Not long after arriving at Parris Island, Jack had been surprised by unexpected visitors. Cousin Luther Shaw and his wife, Jewell, drove in from nearby Charleston, where Luther was working for a wartime defense contractor. Their familiar smiles cheered Jack's isolation from home folks. It would be the end of the month before Jack's family could go to the camp.

When Jack wrote Lottie on August 2 he thanked her for cookies she sent although "we can't keep food in our locker-boxes," and he added more details about boot camp. Recruits got one or two shots every Monday, and haircuts cost a quarter. They had been issued dungarees, skivvies, field scarves, leggings, and cigarettes. They were wearing leggings "all day and every day." One boy "had to walk around all day today with his dungarees on backward for putting his leggings on wrong." Days started with "calisthenics at 5:30 A.M.," followed by numerous lectures. They received "boxing instructions, first-aid, water-discipline (this is training yourself to do without water), security on the march, bayonet . . . even History of the Marine Corps." He cautioned, "Don't Gripe about not having any tires, they use the rubber to go into gas-masks. We've had one gas-drill so far." That statement gave his family a different perspective.

Jack's August 5 letter named a few earned privileges. The boots now saw a movie once in a while and occasionally went to the PX. The previous night he had eaten "2 pints of Ice-Cream and one Coca-Cola." He was working for a private first class stripe which could now be earned in seven weeks but before the war had required four years. On August 8 he wrote from the rifle range, where they "rushed us up . . . 4 days early." Jack was pleased to be there "for 3 weeks of nothing but learning to shoot the rifle." They were living in sixty-four-man P.B. (personnel barracks) huts, prefabricated buildings hastily constructed after Pearl Harbor. "The corporal wants me to blow taps for our platoon every nite, and a couple of other calls," Jack said. He had received $15.00 advance pay and would be having $6.25 deducted for war bonds beginning October 1.

Not a smoker, Jack sold or bartered his issued cigarettes with buddies. He discovered another money maker: "I picked up a couple of bucks Friday, by ironing some of the guys shirts and pants for inspection. Most of the boys here have never ironed anything before, so it was a good chance for us who had, to make some extra dough." Mae smiled about the effects of another practical skill she had taught her son. On November 14 Jack sent a message to give Otis: "I've been using his trumpet to blow bugle calls for the platoon. The Corporal discovered that it is illegal for an unauthorized person to blow taps, hence the old jazz horn is now used only for making music, sweet & hot."

On August 17, the first day they fired the Reising submachine gun, the captain interviewed "boys who were 20, 5'9," and at least High School education" to learn who would like to remain at Parris Island as instructors should they be qualified. Jack wrote, "I don't believe I would especially like the job." On August 23 he stated, "We've been working in the Butts the last two days as well as firing. The Butts are where the targets are run up and down. I'm still kinda deaf from yesterday with those bullets flying over our heads all day and firing on top of that."

Disquieting news reached Jack when Mae wrote him on August 18 that cousin Marion Davis's family had received no word from him since the second day of the Allied invasion of Sicily, July 9 to August 17. More anxious time passed before they learned he was safe. Meanwhile Jack anticipated his family's visit on August 29. He asked them to bring a Kodak and a Pop Kola, and they did not disappoint him. Oscar, Mae, Alfred, and Lucy, with Lottie beaming roundly, arrived with a large picnic basket of fried chicken and goodies after an uneventful trip on new tires. The day was spent in feasting, hugging, and picture taking. Everyone was snapped with Jack, Lottie holding her purse discreetly in front of her expanding tummy and loose-fitting dress. Jack wrote afterward, "I sure hope you had a good trip home, and I hope you had as fine a time as me Sunday. I can't tell you how glad I was to see you, and how much it meant to me. I think I've got the best family in the World and I love you more than I can seem to show you."

About this time, Jack received an August 28 letter from Anna Shuler, whom he had finally been able to write to explain his long silence after their one date: "Well, I had almost decided that you had forgotten I even existed. . . . You didn't write for so long that I thought it was a closed chapter." She told him to come around or call when he got furlough in September. "Don't forget I want that picture you were supposed to draw for me," she told him.

On September 4 Jack reported: "We're all through with our training and we start mess duty tonight. I got a lucky break, the squad leaders will be room orderlies while the platoon is on mess duty." Since returning from the range, the recruits had been "treated swell." Jack explained, "We been going to the show every nite this week, and we went to the P.X. this

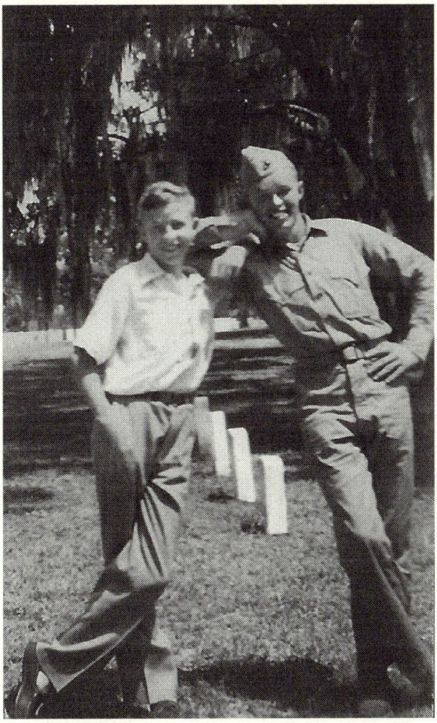

Alfred and uniformed brother Jack clowning as they pose during family's visit to Parris Island. Courtesy of the family.

afternoon and to the Smokeva last nite. (That's the prize-Fites)." Letters the next two days elaborated on orderly duties: "We clean up the Barracks twice a day and when we are through we have all this spare time to ourselves while the rest of the platoon is on Mess duty." While those guys had to be up at 3:30 A.M., Jack and the other four orderlies got to sleep until six. He commented, "We did the guys on Mess duty a favor this morning and cleaned their rifles for them. They really work hard."

Numerous correspondents reported home-front news to Jack. On August 25 Oscar's employee Murdock Graham described the bottling company running "all rite in the plant" although "we cant get much sugar But we hafter do the Best We Can." On September 8 Bill Burns wrote that Dixieland musician Bob Crosby was playing at Georgetown, where "a war bond, bought here, is the admission." The following day Caroline Robinson depicted transformations at Auburn: "I'm back to the ole' stomping grounds again and Jack . . . you wouldn't recognize the place. What few boys left are pushing 16 at the most and more girls are enrolled this year than ever before."

At the end of training, private first class Jack went home on September 10 on a ten-day furlough. He had made a decision about which he had earlier thought differently. He returned to Parris Island on September 19 as a rifle range instructor. The assignment would continue much longer than he expected, until September of the following year.

In an undated letter upon returning from furlough, Jack wrote home: "My, but things are different now. The Seargents [*sic*] who used to cuss us out now treat us like humans. . . . We got in around 7:00 P.M. Looked up our old D.I.'s They gave us a couple of blankets and some sheets and we slept in the D.I.'s room. We breezed into the P.X. last nite with our new stripes. Walks up to the counter and order what we want without having to stand in line." In closing, he added, "I needn't tell you what a fine time I had at home or how much I enjoyed being with you for 10 short days. You were surely wonderful to me. Mama the cake went over big with the D.I.'s and the other corporals and Pfc's."

Jack wrote on October 2 that he was in his permanent barracks, "the best place on the range. . . . I'm in a squad room with all men who have been in about a year, a lot of cpls. and sgts." He was in a large brick building only about two hundred or three hundred yards from the water and with a beautiful view: "You can see for miles from the 2d story across to the other side of the channel." His privileges had greatly improved: "I get to see free shows every night, and have been given a liberty card. I can leave the Island any night and have week-ends off if I want to." As an instructor, rather than a trainee, Jack had better access to the PX and purchased gum and candy bars, items not widely available on the civilian market, for family members and friends.

On October 4 Jack requested his green bathing suit be sent as he had recreational use of a large indoor pool about a hundred feet from the barracks. His only problem was that his mail delivery had not caught up with his current address. He was "working hard and learning a lot, and meeting a lot of fine guys." He repeated the prevailing rumor that "I will be on the range until Spring, and then . . . eligible to be shipped out on a moments notice." These two situations—mail delays in transience and rumors of impending change—would persist.

Jack concluded, "The Bugle is blowing outside. Everything goes by the Bugle out here. This time it is blowing for the lowering of the flag." He reflected on hopes for a Christmas leave: "I would rather be home Christmas than any other time." On October 10 Lottie wrote, "Say, I really am glad that you will be able to come home and see the new addition to our family which is to arrive sometime around the first of Dec." This was her first written reference to the impending event. A week later Jack replied, "Lottie, I am anxious to see my new nephew. He or she will be there at Christmas. I think that will be perfectly swell, and he or she won't know what a swell girl he has for a mother."

Jack continued to write prolifically, describing his life. On October 12 he was "doing fine and am crazy about the Marines. I have made some very good friends, and get to see free shows any night, but naturally I sometimes get lonesome for everybody." He was learning to disassemble and reassemble various weapons: "We take up the Thompson Submachine gun next. You should see these carbines (officers weapons mostly). I am going to try to get one after the war. They would be perfect for deer-hunting etc. They are light as a feather and shoot a small size 30 cal. bullet." He described the carbine to Freddie as a "wicked little weapon."

Frequent letters kept Jack informed about civilian life. Because his own tires were too worn, Willie borrowed Oscar's car to drive his wife to Georgia to visit her family. Lucy told Jack she was not going with the home economics girls to the state fair: "They can't get a school bus so they are going in a truck and you know Daddy, I can't go." Caroline wrote wistfully from Auburn on October 13: "A funny thing but I heard some one playing a horn at the Garden Courts the other day and for a minute—I thought it was you! I even catch myself looking to see if I don't see you strolling around this way."

Lottie expressed concern on October 10: "Daddy heard today that Bill McCoy is missing in action. I hope this isn't true. His wife, Edna Owens, who was a friend of mine at school, just had a baby. He was in India." Bill's parents, friends of Oscar and Mae, also had another son at Fort Jackson. Oscar, familiar with so many young men through draft board processing, had restless nights thinking of them, although lottery and not local decision selected the individuals to be drafted. Jack commented on October 23, "I hope the news of McCoy isn't true. I know him pretty well." He said as well, "You should see some of the kids that are coming through now. I feel sorry for some of them. Lots of them have never shaved yet and are mere boys."

Oscar wrote on October 10 about a letter received from Glenn McKenzie, going overseas soon and asking to buy Jack's hunting knife. Jack's old buddy and bottling plant employee told him "the government is short on trench knives . . . and asked the boys to secure them from home, friends or any source. . . . Officers assured them that they would need the knives."

Jack wrote back, "Give my white handle knife to Glenn. I know you won't be able to find a decent one anywhere. It is in the Gun Rack."

On October 27 Lottie told Jack that Lucy and Alfred were on a three-day holiday while teachers issued new ration books "which are to last for the duration." She referred to people close to Jack. Otis Creed was reporting to Miami. Frank Campbell was "waiting to be called in the Ferry Command of the air corps." Sophia and Richard Denny were in Durham. Henry Brown, expecting to be sent overseas, had returned to Rhode Island. Milwee Rush was fine but had not heard from Bert since he went overseas and did not know where he was. She said of the one closest to her, "Lewis has been moved again, but is still in Sicily."

Planning a weekend home in early November, Jack wrote ahead to inquire if there would be "enough room and ration points if I brought somebody with me. . . . I want to get home and get a real chicken dinner." His November 1 letter Jack humorously illustrated. On USMC stationery, he embellished the Marine in the logo at the top by drawing comical boots on his feet and a bullet bouncing off his helmet, adding "TWANG!!" He reported, "This afternoon I was on a detail that had to clear off a field for a new range. I was a bush-whacker and am nursing a few blisters tonight." He drew a cartoon of an axe-wielding muscular man. His letter stated that he and his buddy, with a forty-eight-hour pass, would leave Parris Island at 4:30 P.M. Friday and arrive in Columbia at 4:00 A.M. Saturday to connect with the Camden bus about five hours later. He commented that Bill Burns had "a regular booking at the 'Lookout Club' in Columbia now and is knocking down 45 per week. Not bad for a young guy like that huh?" Jack's own salary was $38.00 a month.

Bill Burns, seventeen years old, had indecisively enrolled in the University of South Carolina. He echoed thoughts of many youths in a letter to Jack: "This University life is really hard for me. I wish I had studied more in high school. I'd give anything if things were like they used to be and we were back in high school. Remember those good high-school days. After this war we're going to make up for all the lost time. We're going to get around. This war has really screwed up everything."

After his November leave home, Jack wrote, "Boy, I really had good Luck coming back to P.I. After we left you in Columbia they ran a special bus straight to Beaufort with a load of Marines & Sailors—with no stops except Walterboro for 15 minutes. We were in Beaufort at a quarter to 10 and caught a cab right on over to the Island. Man that was a quick trip There was a red headed school teacher going to Walterboro, and she happened to sit with me, so I had quite some interesting conversation on the way back, and bought her a cup of coffee in Walterboro. I'll probably go up to see her some weekend about February." He also made sure to tell his family: "Mama I can't thank you and Lottie and Lucy enough for fixing up those swell meals for us. . . . Daddy I certainly appreciate the trouble you go to for me, taking us up the river and over to Columbia and everything."

One wrinkle that had come up in Jack's weekend plans was later smoothed in a November 19 letter from Anna Shuler telling him that his letter asking for a date had been delayed in the mail, so she was unaware he had come home. She would be glad to reschedule, and regarding his friend, she said, "Why of course we'll 'fix' him up." In a later letter Anna said that she would not have known of Jack's visit home "if that colored man that helps your dad hadn't told me." Murdock Graham enjoyed matchmaking.

Jack did not go home on all furloughs. His memoir notes recall dating a girl who lived in "an oceanfront mansion in Beaufort," about ten miles from Parris Island. In November he wrote home that he was helping a friend find an apartment in Beaufort for his wife and child. Jack raved about the "ultra-modern" USO where "it only cost 25¢ to stay overnight and 25¢ for Breakfast. This is where the boys bring their families etc. to eat and chat. It is really nice." Mae replied with sober motherly caution on November 15: "So glad you had a nice time in Beaufort and helped your friend. . . . You spoke of meeting a girl friend of yours too. Where had you met her before. It is nice to meet people you know like that when you are away from home. You will have to be careful though about girls near the camps. Some are nice of course and some are not. You don't want to get mixed up with the ones that are not nice for believe me they are a bad lot."

On November 16 Jack described his work that day. "I've been one of the guys who give lectures on the weapons," he said. "The old professor himself." Jack was apparently a very good instructor, just as Miss Etta had told him in high school. In later years he spoke of how serious he felt the responsibility since a man's shooting skill could save his life, and the skill of many men was needed to win the war. Jack said he tried to use the kind of patience that others had shown him when he was a young boy learning to hunt. His memoir notes recall a "recruit with no right thumb I taught a new loading technique to."

The same letter also shed light on Jack's goals. "I am hoping to see action before this War is over. I would be ashamed of myself to let other guys do all the dirty work," he wrote. About long-range plans he said, "You meet some intensely interesting persons in the service. Some of which are artists. I am vaguely planning to go to N.Y. if I am still around after the War and make a stab at art maybe." As an alternate, he wrote, "I may want to remain in the service for a while after the War, but this is doubtful, however appealing it sounds. It's a cinch that this would be a racket in peacetime." In all, he summarized, "I am still nursing hopes of going back to college. . . . I have a thousand things planned that I want to do, which I probably won't, but nevertheless you can't blame a guy for dreaming."

In several letters Jack wrote of coincidental meetings. On November 20 he reported seeing Hugh "Shot" Cox in an OCS platoon: "He was really glad to see somebody from Home. . . . A South Carolina boy is pretty rare around here." This was the first of several times in his military service Jack would run into one the Cox brothers from Camden. Hugh, the eldest of four celebrated athletes, played football at Camden High from 1936 to 1940. Dickie, whom Jack would meet up with a few months later, played from 1939 to 1943 and was captain of the 1942 team.

When Jack wrote on November 24, he expected to get home for Thanksgiving, "at least by Saturday nite. . . . It sure is fine of you to wait for me like this." He mentioned, "I dropped the cotton out of my ear yesterday accidentally and my ears are still ringing." Years later Jack described lying on the ground at the range next to the recruits he was instructing as they fired. He experienced ringing in his ears the rest of his life, and in later years the Veterans Administration would fit him with hearing aids. He wrote briefly on Monday, November 29: "Mama I can't tell you how much I enjoyed the turkey dinner. It was worth coming home for." Letters for a time anticipated Christmas.

Caroline Robinson responded on December 3 to Jack's invitation to visit him during her Auburn holiday. "Jack," she said, "there's nothing I'd love better than visiting you. . . . It would be so good to see you again but I'm going to have to be disappointed. I wish that my Mother and Father knew you—then I'm sure they'd let me come. Some things they are rather stubborn about and I can do nothing." Later she would mail him a Christmas package.

Jack also heard from Bill Burns. "I have a lot of things to tell you, kiddo," he wrote on December 5. "I quit Carolina. I couldn't play and go to school so I stopped. I couldn't play til 1 and get up at 7:30. After the war I'll go to school with you if you go." Burns had a day job working at the A&P.

Jack next heard that one of Bill's key musicians, Piggy Lamoy, had left for service.

On December 5 Jack wrote Freddie Ogburn regarding his recent enlistment: "I know you feel good about being in uniform and will make as fine a soldier as your Daddy was in the last war." Uncle Fred was a Purple Heart veteran of World War I. Jack lamented, "There's a combat detail shipping out of here tomorrow and a lot of new bums coming in. I'm getting anxious to be transferred. I'm afraid the war's going to be over before I get a chance to see any of it." Jack received two letters written on December 7, one from former roommate "Amy" Amerson, in service in Jacksonville. Amy wrote, "I stayed in Auburn for a few days on my leave. The place is dead—no more spirit. I'm sort of doubtful whether I would like to be there. Kind of cuts to see those 4F's and Vets among all of those pretty girls."

Jack's other letter of December 7 was a reflective one from Lottie: "Well, this is the anniversary of Pearl Harbor—2 years ago. A lot has happened since then, hasn't it? Good and bad. Here's hoping that by next year this time, we'll all be back together again." The next day, December 8, Jack received a Western Union telegram: "HEY UNCLE. LOTTIE AND LITTLE JOAN FINE. MOTHER." Mae had also sent a congratulatory telegram that in a few days would be delivered by a Red Cross worker to her first grandchild's father, Lewis, living in a rain-soaked tent in Sicily with fellow glider pilots awaiting their next assignment.

Jack replied, "I got the message yesterday Mama. I see she has been christened Joan, and I think that is a swell name for her. I am expecting a letter soon giving me the details." He added, "I am going to try to get home Christmas nite. . . . Daddy I know I can get a ride if I could get some gas for a car. I was wondering if you could lend me about 5 gallons worth of gas stamps if you could spare them." Following the new-baby theme, he quipped, "I am anxious to see Nell's puppy and the new calf too, and how are the Guinea pigs?"

On December 15 Mae reflected on world conditions. "War is not beautiful," she said, "but the cause we are fighting for is right. We are fighting that men may be free to plan and live their own lives as they choose. To work, worship, speak & plan their lives, without any dictator or oppressor ordering them around like a drove of animals. It hurts me to see so many fine boys making such a sacrifice but it just seems that there is no other way." Strong faith was necessary to continue in dark hours.

Christmas season had deep spiritual significance for Oscar and Mae, who looked forward to sharing it with family and friends. Christmas 1943 was especially anticipated with their first grandchild, and they hoped Jack would be home too. Oscar was busy organizing the hunting plans the menfolk traditionally enjoyed then. He had written Jack on October 10, "Willie and I got a few shells, enough I think for the season, some 410's & 20's." Mae had written a week after, "Last Sunday . . . I was sitting on the porch at the camp house looking down the river and I saw a drove of ducks crossing the river. Daddy said there was over a hundred in the drove. I think it gave Daddy and Willie the duck-hunting fever when I showed the ducks to them." During the holidays, worries could be set aside with the pleasure of sporting companionship.

Six days before Christmas, on December 19, tragedy struck. Just at dawn Willie and longtime hunting companion Mose Jones were seated in Willie's boat in a duck blind they had prepared near a small island on the river at White Oak Creek. As they had done so many times before, they aimed their shotguns at a flock winging toward them as the sky began to color. Uncharacteristically and for no known reason, Willie suddenly stood up as his black friend discharged his gun, accidentally hitting Willie in the back of the head. He was probably killed instantly although Mose, grief-stricken, hurried frantically for help. In later interviews, Steve Kelly and Alfred recalled that Willie always ran the boat motor and Mose did not know how to restart it. Mose with great effort rowed the boat ashore, ran down the road to his house, mounted his mule, and rode to Henry's for help, arriving exhausted.

Oscar and some of the family were seated in church when word of the accident was brought down the aisle to him during the sermon. Lottie had stayed home with the new baby. Family, friends, and Mose were devastated, and all mourned together, especially sorrowful for Elizabeth and little Tommy. Jack came home for the funeral. On December 21 Willie was laid to rest on the hilltop of the old Smyrl family burying ground. Its peaceful panorama overlooked the Wateree River and the fields and forests of his birthplace. His World War I headstone would soon stand among the markers and stones of silent generations of kinsmen.

Unaware of the tragic loss, on December 19 Bill Burns wrote to "Uncle" Jack, updating him on band and girls. Likewise unaware, Anna sent a cheerfully chatty letter. His emergency leave at an end, Jack solemnly returned to Parris Island about 1 A.M. Christmas morning. He wrote the day after Christmas asking Lucy to have his negatives printed and Oscar to "give Murdoch the cigarettes for me."

Reflective after his return to duty, Jack observed in late December, "I sometimes wish I was a writer. I could write a lot of interesting things." He was pleased meeting "a guy up here doing some cartoons for the boot paper. He was an art teacher at Ohio State Univ." Jack was referring to the newspaper the *Boot* begun at Parris Island in 1943 by professional journalists recruited by the Marine Corps. He added, "I got a chance to draw some last nite, and am getting back in the mood. If you could ever get the right breaks, this would be a swell way to make a living." He thanked his family for subscription gifts to the *Camden Chronicle* and *Reader's Digest.* "I wouldn't trade families with anybody in the world," he emphasized. "Some of these other guys telling about the big time they had getting drunk makes me feel sorry for them to think what they are missing. They don't seem to realize what Christmas really is." As his elderly cousin Bob Love wrote Jack on January 12, 1944, "You had happiness mingled with sorrow for Christmas! That is the way it is all thru life. We should make the best of our time."

Rumors were everywhere in early 1944. Alfred, an infrequent correspondent but attentive to world news, wrote Jack on New Year's Day: "It looks like they are going to open a second front across the English Channel. The radio said they had been keeping up air raids along the coast for 36 hours straight. Invasions are preceded by big air assaults so they will probably send over our Marines soon. This will be dangerous because the Germans have the coast well fortified. So they had better keep up the bombings." Auburn buddy Amy wrote from his post, "I've got a feeling something big is going to happen soon that is going to involve all of us. Just pray that we are lucky." Jack reported home on January 12 of Parris Island rumors that "the U.S. will start a big drive this coming year. I believe I will get to see some of it. I am hoping so anyway."

Lottie proudly shared news on January 15: "Your little sister Lucy has been elected Editor-in-chief of 'The Bulldog.' . . . She is also Art editor of the Annual." Lottie commented too, "We really enjoy the 'Boot.' Thanks for sending them. It's a fine paper, and no kidding. The pictures are especially good." In return mail, Jack was eager to advise Lucy on her journalism appointments. "This is good stuff Lucy, and is good experience," he said, expressing confidence she would do well. "And don't forget to be considerate of Miss Etta's opinions. The old girl really knows what the score is—and will treat you right." Jack thought of Miss Etta's faith in him, and of her recognition of his instructional skills, among others. Yes, Miss Etta had known the score and had treated him right.

Jack was disappointed but probably not surprised by the January 17 letter he received from Caroline at Auburn: "I surely am sorry we can't get together on our little trip. Afraid Savannah is out of the question for me—too far!! I understand why you can't come to Atlanta, tho' so what'cha say we just leave it to fate and see what happens, huh?" A pleasant association that had survived for a time in letters dissolved in the miles between the letter writers.

On January 21 Jack received a letter from Anna in Rembert, closer in miles though younger in years. Level-headed Anna enjoyed Jack's letters: "very different . . . and definitely interesting." They would have fun on a handful of dates while he was on leave from Parris Island, regard one another with respect and friendship, and share many experiences with one another primarily through a lengthy wartime correspondence. They would exchange photographs, and he would draw for her. Anna wrote, "I think I'm a little young to think about any thing too-o-o serious. I'll probably go out and see a little of this terrible and wicked world and you go out and see how it is 'over there' and when it's all over then we can gather around the fireside one cold winter nite and discuss all of our foolish doings when we were young and very, very happy." The terms suited Jack, unable to promise serious commitment. In a 2011 interview, Anna Shuler Bynum recalled the war years for a young person as being "very romantic times. Lives changed so swiftly. Someone walking down a small town street could turn a corner, meet a stranger from a world away, and begin a relationship that changed lives forever. It was an exciting time, full of possibility. Danger, sadness, and possibility."

Opportunities to come home grew more infrequent and uncertain in 1944, and Jack often brought buddies with him. "I really don't have very many young friends in Camden now," he wrote February 6, thanking his family for recent hospitality. "All of my old friends are either married or in the service. . . . The ones who are there now have nothing in common with me, or for the most part are almost unaffected by the war." He observed further, "The war has completely changed my whole life and will probably cause a drastic change in all my plans that I had made—besides there is the possibility that I won't get back, but [that] does not bother me. I knew what I was getting into when I joined up and am hoping very much to be able to do my part."

Most of the men shipped out from Parris Island were being sent to "a tent camp" at New River, North Carolina, later to become Camp Lejeune. Jack was intrigued by a rumor that a detail would ship to California in the summer. That prospect appealed to him. Meanwhile he discovered "a sketch club down at the Main Station, free material," although he found "very little time though to do everything I want to." He had been making "a few sketches for some of the guys in their souvenier books to get a little practice. I enjoy it, and have made some good acquaintances through this."

On February 23 Jack wrote about his recent drawings. "How do you like the enclosed sketch of Walt Disney's Thumper?" Animated films had always fascinated him, and he was awed by Disney's artistry. Drawing did not make him forget his surroundings. Men were being shipped out every month. He would not mind when his time came, he said, but meanwhile he was longing for a forty-eight-hour pass: "I am going to take advantage of the fact that I am near home—especially when I've got such a swell home to come to." At Parris Island, there were few women Marines except for drivers. "Some of them are very attractive," he commented before joking, "Maybe it's because I haven't seen a good looking girl for so long."

Jack's March 5 letter provided a pleasant description of his "normal Sunday here." Getting up at 9 A.M., "a luxury," he "started painting a picture for one of the fellows," went to mail call, ate chow, went swimming in "the second largest indoor pool on the east coast," threw knives at a board, returned to finish the painting, had chow and another mail call, "and now I'm writing this letter. Not very exciting, but a wonderful day." On March 10 he wrote of military life that "I wouldn't be anywhere else now, but I don't believe I would want to make a career out of it." Rumor said they may be shipped out soon: "I am eligible to be transferred at anytime."

On March 12 Jack doubted he could get home soon. "I thought I had a ride all booked," he said. However, "this car is broken down." He requested stamps. On the bottom half of the back page, he drew a tropical scene with comic fish jumping out of the water. Such caricature fish would become a creative theme in Jack's future art. Another theme would be broken-down vehicles with bad tires, a reality then to be endured. After a weekend home, Jack wrote back On March 20, "We got back at 5:00 Monday morning. Had to change tires 4 times on the way."

After the annual requalification of weapons skills, Jack proudly reported on March 28 he had received the highest possible proficiency ratings. "This was quite a thrill to me finishing up with expert shooting on the Rifle and Pistol both in the same day," he said. His pistol score was 93 percent, expert being 86 percent or better. His rifle score was 314, expert being 306 or better. Expert designation increased his monthly pay another two dollars over the three dollars he received as sharpshooter, but more important "it's about the only important thing as far as your work on the range . . . and your status in the Marine Corps." In the same letter Jack praised his mother. Mae had been hired as assistant to home demonstration agent Margaret Fewell, leader in civic scenes and county homes. Civilian wartime needs enlarged responsibilities of government offices. "Congratulations," Jack said. "I know you will be busy. . . . Miss Fewell couldn't have picked a better person."

On March 31 Jack added a postscript: "The Americans hit the Phillipines this morning." The Marine camp faced increased demands for men and training, even as others including Jack awaited assignments with growing restlessness. In an April 4 letter he described meeting at his target a thirty-five-year-old from Camden, perhaps one of those he later recalled as "overage draftees (men badly needed)." At the main station in camp, "who should I run into but Dickie Cox. This is the 2d time I've seen him." On leaves traveling through the crowded Columbia bus station, Jack crossed paths with home folk. He wrote on April 11, "I saw Nancy Saunders you know her brother was killed recently." On April 24 he reported seeing "the Bradley boy who is stationed at Congaree Air base, the man who works in Burns and Barret, Arthur Robinson the one armed boy, and a couple of girls. One was a new girl in town that I had met at a dance last Christmas. . . . Also saw Lawton Truesdale." On his recent leave he had been accompanied by Stanley J. Law and William M. "Bill" Robinson, two Parris Island friends who made repeat visits to the Smyrl home.

On April 24 Jack was effusive about "the fine horse" his family had now: "I am crazy about horses and have always wanted one." Through Oscar's Clyburn cousins, local equestrian sportsmen and trainers, the Smyrls acquired a beautiful white thoroughbred, a retired polo pony who before the war had been a pace horse at the Carolina Cup. This year, for the second year in a row, like other public events the Cup would not be held. Steeplechase as a sport would not resume until after war's end, but beautiful, trained horses still required devoted attention and exercise to thrive in the interim. S. C. Clyburn begged Oscar to take ownership and care of a favorite mature horse with plenty of life and spirit. In a time of rationing and shortages, when so many fine horses languished in pastures, a loving farm family was a better option for a worthy thoroughbred retired by war.

Recent artwork and a decision were topics in Jack's May 1 letter: "This Sunday I painted a portrait for one fellow's girl friend and now I've been drafted by the first seargent to fix up one for some dame that is coming to see him soon. . . . We have only a few hours to ourselves at night now, and believe me we are working hard and long." Despite having scarce personal time, Jack enjoyed art at every opportunity. "I have already decided that my ambition is to be an ex-marine," he said. "That was certainly a true saying—whoever said that wars are fought by lonely men. However this is one of the greatest experiences that I ever hope to have—this place is certainly one mixture of personalities. Sometime I think I'll write a book."

On May 4 Jack was doubtful about getting home on the weekend. He had guard duty, "the worst thing that happens to you around here," every other week now instead of every other month. There were other causes for lamenting. The process for promotions had changed: "I stand a swell chance of losing everything I have waited for . . . about the unfairest thing that has happened to me yet. We on the list had already taken exams months ago, and now there is the chance that fellows who come in after us may get what we should have had." There was scuttlebutt that "they are shipping out a huge bunch, but so far nothing has happened to me but more work and stricter regulations. They even have started making [us] get into the uniform of the day to eat breakfast." He summarized, "Things are really miserable here now, and I dislike it more every day." He was also morose because, he said, "As far as this war is concerned, I feel as if I have not done my part. I know that I am doing valuable work here, but it gives me no satisfaction to know that most of my friends are overseas and I am still here."

"Well, enough of the complaining," Jack changed tone, reflecting on his birthday tomorrow. "It really feels good to be 21," he said. "I only hope I will be able to do something good with my life before it is too late." He expressed appreciation for good fortune: "In all my long life I believe I have been the happiest boy in the world. I have had everything that I could possibly want, and have the best family in the world, and love you more than I can say." He was thankful for education: "I am especially grateful for you sending me to school last year. This was indeed the most wonderful experience that I have ever had, and believe it was the most formative and progressive year I have ever known . . . the opportunity to become acquainted with almost every type of person and occupation imaginable. I have thoroughly enjoyed every minute of it, and am hoping to see the day when things will be back to normal."

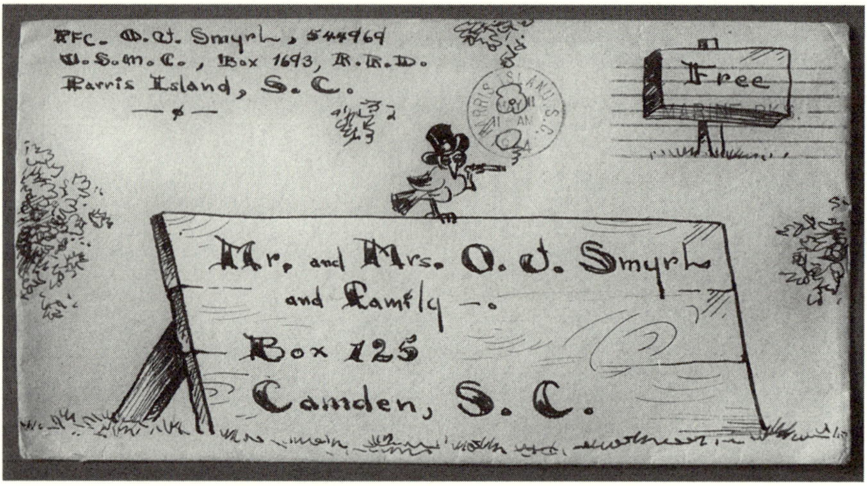

Art-embellished envelope from Parris Island, May 11, 1944.
Courtesy of the University of South Carolina.

On Sunday, May 7, Jack wrote home that he was studying for a test the next day that "has to do with making corporal." He embellished the envelope with art, depicting the address on a propped signboard on which perched a bird wearing a top hat and smoking a cigarette in a holder. The next weekend he went home alone and wrote back May 15, "I especially enjoyed the Mother's day services at Church, and the fine horseback ride Sunday morning." The family had been trying indecisively to choose a name for the latest farm resident. Jack suggested, echoing current slang for someone whose name was unknown, that they "call the horse 'MAC.' I think this would suit him fine, don't you?" He reflected, "The worst part about getting home is having to leave."

During Jack's visit, Lucy showed him layouts of the school annual on which she was working. A view of the finished production reflects the somber side of life young people knew at that time. A two-page spread appears at the beginning entitled "IN MEMORIAM—'They Shall Not Die in Vain.'" Featured are photographs of seventeen local men lost in service since the beginning of the war. Their youthful faces in a section followed by current student portraits silently reflects mature understanding of the challenges graduates faced in war and rebuilding.

In numerous letters Jack discussed his friends. On May 15 he expressed sympathy that one "who works next to me and lives with me" left on emergency furlough for the death of his father. "He is a big Pollock from the coal mine regions and is one of the finest boys I have ever known," Jack said. "I felt especially sorry for him. He will have his Mother and 3 or 4 sisters to take care of." On May 20 Jack reported meeting on the rifle range a recruit "who went to school with me at Auburn last year." He thought of Auburn roommate Stanley Jenkins, who had lately completed Army Air Corps training. At the end of May Jack wrote home that two friends he had brought home the previous week were shipping out: "I sure hate to see these boys leave here. That is always the tragic part of friendships . . . having to part."

Also lamenting what he missed being away from home, Jack regretted being unable to see Lucy graduate from high school. He promised her to be "thinking about you." Unable to go home the first Sunday in June, Jack went instead to the USO and wrote afterward, "They took a big crowd to Hunting Island Beach. It's exclusive for military personnel and friends—Very pretty." It would be Jack's first—but not last—experience with the beautiful, natural sea island. Meanwhile other news drew his attention almost immediately.

"We are getting all the news of the Invasion regularly," Jack reported on June 6 of the ongoing Normandy Invasion, D-Day, that began in the predawn hours of that day. He did not refer to what they all knew, that somehow Lewis was involved. He knew how concerned Lottie was, just as the rest of them were, just as the nation was. All anyone at home could do was pray and wait. It would be some time before Lottie would hear that Lewis was safe. He had flown into Normandy as copilot of a C-47 dropping paratroopers and then, as the invasion continued, flew a glider carrying men and supplies across enemy lines. Waiting and praying continued.

By mid-June Jack had received his corporal rank and was in charge of six targets on the range. Daily more and more men were being qualified for marksmanship and sent into combat. For a time the Pacific appeared on the backburner of the news, but as Allies fought their way toward Hitler, Marines were also battling the Japanese in the Pacific.

Jack decorated his USMC stationery with a sketch of exploding fireworks for a July 4 letter. Tomorrow was payday: "I've 35 bucks coming, so you can bet your life I will be home this week-end," he wrote home. He had been at Parris Island a year but did not expect to stay much longer. He had little time for art now, but he was "doing a portrait of one of the sgt's girl friends" and planning to charge him a dollar. "I'm tired of doing free work," Jack said. "I'm fixing up a couple of letter heads for a guy tonight for two-bits." He also reported that a recruit had shot himself in the foot: "It's amazing that no more happens here than it does with this extravagant expenditure of ammunition being fired here every day." In his memoir notes, Jack recalled being ordered at the range to bury leftover ammunition, a move that he considered wasteful and senseless, especially since it was rationed to civilians.

One condition did please him at the range. On July 11 he wrote, "I eat at a really fine spot now. We got the best food you ever saw, due to the fact that we got a swell cook out on the range. We eat under a clump of trees, and have been having music with our food lately. Swede, the field cook, got us a recruit who plays the accordion and he entertains us while we eat." At midmonth Jack got a furlough and on return wrote home, "Those 15 days really flew by, but . . . that was the best furlough anybody ever had." For the next two weeks, his family would be staying at Cheraw State Park, a relaxing vacation spot for them and other area families.

Having been recommended for the V-12 college training program, Jack requested Mae to obtain a copy of his birth certificate. However, on August 6 he wrote her not to bother sending it. His eyes had been checked, and "Just as I had feared my eyes do not come up to specifications." Jack required glasses, but candidates for officers were expected to see well without them. Jack continued, "So I have abandoned any hope of being an officer, and can now stop worrying about it. This simplifys things for me, and I can more easily make post-war plans."

He turned to the subject of his art. "I just made $5.00," he said. "I painted a portrait for one of the fellows here this afternoon and he was exceptionally well pleased. I did it from a photo. . . . If I had more time I could make a little on the side. Five bucks for about 4 hrs. work isn't too bad, besides I enjoyed doing it." Jack continued, "If I can ever get a good break after I get out of here maybe I could knock down a little dough. This art racket is just a gamble. Once you get something in a reputable publication, you're made."

Jack next offered advice to his sister about her upcoming freshman year in college. "Lucy, when do you leave for school? Have you got everything ready?" he asked. "I want you to do good at Winthrop. Don't study too hard, and don't be weak and fall under the influence of the wrong kind of girl." Her big brother sounded a lot like her father. Then he softened, "And don't forget if you need anything from me let me know. If you need any money just get Mama to take it out of my account at the bank. . . . I'll not be needing any money for quite a while."

On August 30 Jack wrote that he was coming home for the weekend: "Shall be in Columbia about 8:00 or 8:30 and follow the usual procedure of calling Aunt Hattie etc. As far as I know, I will be alone. Now Daddy don't come over if it is going to inconvenience you in any way. Bringing me back on Saturday nite is far too much in itself.—I really enjoyed last week-end more than I can say, and want to get back." He told Mae he wanted to talk to her about his birth certificate.

"I think they've got the wrong date," Jack said. He could not imagine why his birth certificate would say he was born May 4 and not May 5, as he knew he had been. He figured Mama could fill him in on the story.

Chapter 13

California

"Living in tents & really roughing it"

In the darkening afternoon the Western Union messenger quickly dropped his bicycle on the front walk at 311 DeKalb Street in Camden. With a dignified face, he hurried up the front porch steps of the big white house, its front window bearing a discrete card lettered "Geo. A. Creed, Contractor." These days there was no telling what news the envelope he carried would bear, and he had been carefully trained to be prepared. At his knock, the door opened promptly and Mattie Creed, composing her face also, reached out immediately for the envelope. "It's collect, please, M'am," he said politely, and she hurriedly complied with change on the table by the door. The message was addressed to Mr. and Mrs. O. J. Smyrl, care of George Creed. She quickly tore it open as she had been asked to do in such case: "TELL FOLKS AM LEAVING FOR SAN DIEGO AREA TOMORROW NOON AND TO RUSH ME ABOUT $25. BY MORNING THANKS WRITE LATER/ JACK." Mattie immediately reached for the telephone as she rushed George out the house with the telegram. "Drive down and catch Oscar if he's still in town. Give him this. I'll be trying to reach Mae and tell her."

Once Oscar and Mae got the message, they immediately wired money and began to check with railroad agent friends. Troop departures were not on regular schedules or openly publicized, but those who watched the trains recognized patterns, even for the special ones carrying only large groups of servicemen straight past usual station stops. After hurried arrangements, Oscar and Mae left home and traveled in a rainstorm, hoping to see their son one more time before he left, if only by waving at him as his train pulled through a station. Driving into Yemassee, two dozen miles before Beaufort, they were incredulous to spot the troop train stopped at the depot, unexpectedly delayed at that point.

Amid metallic clangor, swirling steam, and misty rain, there was a brief and happy reunion as parents and son embraced. In a tender farewell of loving words, Jack and his parents kissed good-bye. As the train pulled for California, their eyes streamed and their hearts were full, but they felt somewhat better for having had these moments. The impromptu reunion would be fondly recalled by parents and son. His first letter to them included that fact: "You don't know how glad I am that I got to see you before I left. That train holdup in Yemassee was really a break for me."

For four days Jack's train traveled across the country. On September 17 he wrote home: "We're passing through south Texas . . . and the scenery staggers the imagination. Mountains, prairies, etc. sage brush. Man it's beautiful. I wouldn't take a million dollars for this trip. . . . We don't get to see much of the cities, as we only pass through and stop for a short time. . . . Never saw so many mountains in my life. Passed a few ranches so far. You go for miles & miles & never see a person. . . . Wish you could see all this Beautiful country out here. We'll be in El Paso shortly, and I'll try to mail this from there. . . . I got some more staring out the window to do."

While he was crossing the country, as Jack would later learn from Lottie, at the same time in Europe Lewis was flying a gilder of paratroopers into German-occupied Holland in Operation Market Garden, the largest airborne action to date. In the Pacific, Mac was in a month-long battle on the island of Pelileu. Shortly Lewis and Mac's eighteen-year-old brother, Jack, would complete training and head for the western front and the Battle of the Bulge. In years to come, veteran friends, cousins, and other relations would put together similar scenarios of a time in history when the globe was encircled by small-town connections engaged in enormous purposes of survival and world improvement.

On September 19 Jack reported arrival at the destination to which the train had steadily progressed: "We're here!! Last nite we pulled into the main base. . . . We're way out in the California mountains getting squared away. We're living in tents & really roughing it. This is a brand new spot." The site was Camp Pendleton, a territory of about thirty miles. "It was formerly a huge ranch. We are here to go to school for about 8 weeks," Jack wrote. "Let me tell you kids its really beautiful here. Just a few miles from the Pacific. We're in one of many small tent camps scattered through the mountains. It's rugged country here & I'm getting a big kick out of it so far. There are 6 of us to a tent. We eat out of mess kits and have open-air showers. It's warm here in the day & freezing cold at night." Camp Pendleton at the time Jack arrived was still designated a temporary location. By the following month, it would be declared permanent and eventually gain status as the West Coast's largest Marine training center.

Jack's letter reviewed the route of over twenty-eight hundred miles his train had traveled: Savannah, Waycross, Montgomery, Mobile, New Orleans, Shreveport, Dallas, Fort Worth, Sweetwater, Columbus, Yuma, and "contrary to our expectations . . . to Los Angeles Calif, and down to Oceanside." The magnitude of the country he had passed through awed him, and he marveled that it "took us 2 days to cross Texas." Jack was excited now to be in a beautiful place where he would have liberty on weekends: "In a couple of weeks I'm planning to go visit Los Angeles & Hollywood." He closed his letter as dark began because "there're no lights in these tents as this camp has just been thrown up recently (I'm telling you, we're really roughing it.)."

On September 21 Jack wrote they had been issued "tin hats" (helmets), rifles, and gear, and had spent some time clearing the area about them. "We went about a mile from camp today & filled sand bags. I walked around a little and studied the terrain etc. ran up on a snake but he got away from me." Jack's one complaint was "waiting in that long line for chow. You really get hungry up in these mountains." He requested a sweater, a knife, and his camera, but only if they could send a roll of 120 film with it.

In his letters from Pendleton, Jack described extremes of desolate locations to liberty interludes bringing him face to face with dreams come true. Indicating no surprise but only pleasure, Jack reported meeting favorite movie stars and hearing top musicians. Facts of the time and place confirm that Hollywood openly and sincerely embraced the floods of uniformed men passing through on the way to unknown battles.

Jack's September 21 letter described his first weekend trip to Los Angeles, where he hitchhiked with three fellow Marines. Then he and a buddy took a bus to see Harry James play at Ocean Park, the Santa Monica seaside amusement. During intermission, Jack met Harry James and got his autograph. Later, walking along with a buddy, enjoying the kaleidoscope and cacophony of arcade games and players, Jack spotted another familiar

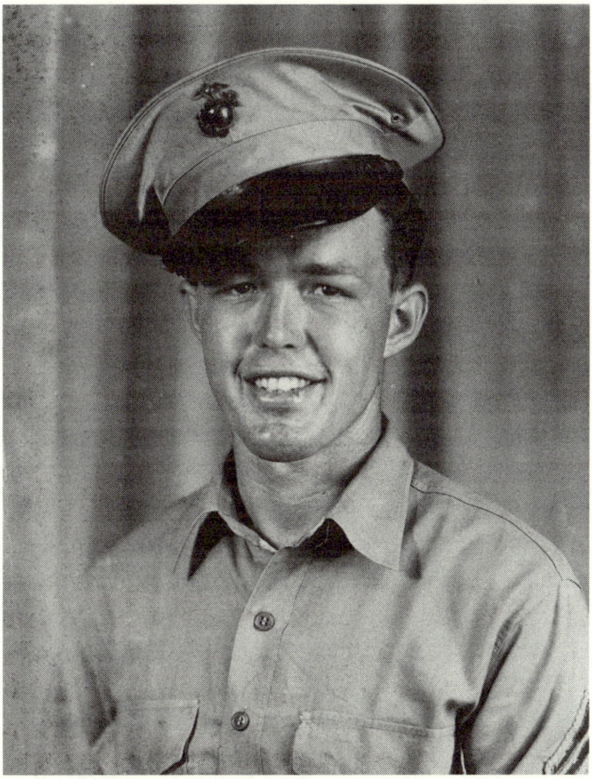

Jack, his cap at a jaunty angle while on leave, at Camp Pendleton, California, in 1944. Courtesy of the University of South Carolina.

face. Gary Cooper was among people throwing baseballs at milk jugs. The two Marines stopped to watch him. Jack said, "When he finished we started talking to him. He batted the breeze with us for quite a while. Asked him about the Movies, etc. and his U.S.O. trip to New Guinea. He was wearing glasses, and I asked him about them. He took 'em off and showed 'em to me. He was really swell and acted humble as anybody. Just the way he acts in pictures."

On September 25 Mae acknowledged Jack's letter: "Were we glad to know you were there at last and that maybe you would be there for a few weeks!" Lucy, soon to turn eighteen, was at Winthrop College now. No mail had reached Jack yet since Parris Island when he wrote on September 27, "We go to school all day from one lecture to another. . . . They are trying to teach us to be instructors. Just what or where we don't know and neither do they."

Jack had still received no mail when he wrote October 2 and again three days later describing more of the isolated camp with its dirt floors and lack of modern conveniences. "When that sun goes down behind the mountains it gets dark fast & early," he wrote. Lacking electricity, he wrote, "we got us a bottle and some oil, stuck a rag in it & have the original incandescent light." There was "a long line for the P.X. (a trailer on wheels)," and he could not buy air mail stamps, which he asked his family to send. On payday Jack "walked about a half mile to the pay office, stood in line for about a half-hour and then didn't get paid as the time was up, so I'll have to go through that again tomorrow." He was planning to see Tommy Dorsey in Los Angeles.

On October 8 Jack sent home a postcard designed for servicemen, an image of a school building preprinted "I ate breakfast at Hollywood High School this morning." Jack wrote, "Having swell time. Slept at High School here last night. Free to service men." A letter the next day described the trip, purchased in advance with bus fare, to hear "an old favorite of mine," Henry Busse, play at the Hollywood Palladium, "one of the biggest dance places in the country." Thousands of people were there, and there were also "over a thousand of us" put up at Hollywood High. Jack attended church Sunday morning and "met a girl who was a cousin of a friend of mine from Auburn." At the Palladium, he added, he met an Auburn friend of his. "He was an Army Lieutenant, and was dating the singer with Busse's Orchestra. He remembered me right off the bat, told me where I was from, and what I was taking at Auburn." Passes provided Jack opportunity not only to socialize with attractive party girls in a fast-moving society, but also to form at least one friendship with a local girl, Jessie Medrano, one of his future correspondents.

Jack was glad later that month when mail from home finally reached him at Camp Pendleton, a big bunch of letters catching him up on news back east. He wrote Lottie on October 25 "very relieved" about Lewis being back in England. He thought the "picture of Joan is terrific. . . . Mama tells me she can say a few words now." He mentioned that at one of the USOs in Hollywood he had made a voice recording, part of "an advertisement scheme put out by the Gem razor corp." He had heard Woody Herman at the Palladium Saturday night and gotten his autograph. He went to the Hollywood Canteen, with food, entertainment, and dancing for servicemen. On Sunday he attended the Hollywood Methodist Church. Summarizing his impressions of Hollywood, Jack stated: "90% of the people here are from somewhere else. You hardly ever run into a regular citizen. . . . People dress differently here as a rule, and it's a lot different from home. Big glamour town you know. It's flooded with 'would-be' movie stars. You know what I mean. The kind who wear dark-glasses everywhere in hopes that you will mistake them for some celebrity."

That same day Jack wrote Lucy at Winthrop. He mentioned that Dick Jurgens's orchestra was playing that night in their camp. Jurgens was now in the Marine Corps himself and performing for servicemen. He also wrote Lucy about someone she knew personally, stating, "I'm going down to Laguna Beach next week-end to meet Steve Kelly. He's out here you know." Thousands of miles from home, the paths of Jack and Steve, cousins from the same area, would cross numerous times over the coming months.

Jack wrote home on November 1 that he would be off Friday night until Monday for their first forty-eight-hour leave: "Should really have a big week-end." He conjectured they would be out of the States by the first of the year "if the dope is anywhere near correct." On November 8 Jack described his daily life: "We leave here in the morning before sun-up, and stay out in the hills all day till dark. When you get back you've got to shave, eat, go to mail call (long wait) everything means standing in line. If you want to take a shower after dark, its outdoors, and cold water, and the nights are cold. The chow line is half-mile away . . . up and down steep mountains with a heavy steel helmet, pack, and 9 lb rifle in heavy shoes. . . . K-rations for noon chow as we are too far to come back in, and K-rations are no luxury." He had given a lecture that afternoon: "I've really learned a lot about public speaking and stuff since I went to this school. It has been very instructive and interesting."

On November 12 Jack reported, "Big Storm came up last nite and blew a lot of the tents down. We had anchored ours pretty well, and she weathered the blow O.K." He thanked Mae for sending his sweater. He requested she send his social security number which he might need "if we get a few days off before we ship out." He explained, "Most of us are planning on working a day or two in Los Angeles and make a little liberty money. There's lots of places with openings for men on furlough, etc. who need cash. The Hollywood Guild also arranges these things for the men. The pay is excellent, any where from 85 [cents] per hr. up—places such as Lockheed aircraft, Bakeries (with all you can eat). Ranch-owners come in and pick up men who want to work a day or two on their ranches."

Jack declared the fruit cake the family had sent him "is the best yet. It made me think of Christmas at home, and brings it closer. I'm really going to miss you this year." His mother had recently attended the national meeting of the Home Demonstration Council to present the state report from South Carolina. He said to Mae, "I know you really enjoyed the trip to Chicago. It really sounded interesting—those letters you write are the best thing in the world, and you always tell me just what I want to hear, and all the latest most important news about everybody, and everything."

While Jack was living in the mountain tent camp, construction had been underway on more permanent facilities for the base. He was very pleased, especially with colder weather, to move to a new building at the main base camp, from which he wrote on November 15: "This place is Paradise after 7 weeks in that hole back in the mountains. You don't know how much a few little things mean until you have to do without them. We're in a swell barracks with real showers with hot water, good beds, a P.X., real movie-house (the one in Tent Camp #2 was on the side of a wall, no seats no nothing)." Calling the facilities "better than any hotel you could go to," he described the room he shared with only two other men: "Reminds me of school days. All you have to do to get heat is flick a switch on the wall. I'm telling you its heavenly."

Jack bought his family up to date on other news on November 17. "Steve Kelly and I are in the same Replacement, and live right next to each other," he wrote. "He's in Company 'A' and I'm in 'B.' How's that for a coincidence? We'll be going out together." Back home both Steve's and Jack's families were pleased to have their sons together, like old days at Grandpa's.

Jack's November 21 letter was airmailed the following day in an envelope bearing a sketch of a waiting man lounging with his hands in his pockets. With a scarcity of noncommissioned officers, Jack said he was now running the platoon: "I'm in complete charge in the absence of the Lt.s who are the platoon leaders in a normal setup. I call roll, give 'em exercises, march 'em to chow, to work, am the boss on the jobs, give 'em all the dope, nurse 'em, wake 'em up, help 'em out." They were told if they were not out by December 1, "we'll probably be here till Jan. 1." Oscar was already making plans to travel to California to see Jack if he was still there at Christmas. Jack proposed on November 22, "I'm going to figure us out a little code or something so I can let you know where I go, without the censor or anybody knowing."

On a forty-eight-hour pass in Los Angeles, Jack wrote on November 26 from the Rosslyn Hotel. A buddy had run into three friends from Meridian, Mississippi, "at the Southern Cal.-U.C.L.A. football game at the L.A. Coliseum," and the five of them were sharing a room. He had bought "a pretty Swiss made watch" for which purchase he earlier had requested money. After his leave he wrote Lucy November 28, first about her letter on the holiday he had missed with them at home: "Man, I'm telling you, the dope on the hunting was really what I wanted to hear. Tough luck about not finding too much game, but I was glad to hear that you got one of them. I wish I could see Old Nell now, and would have given anything to have been there Thanksgiving with you." He then told her about his forty-eight-hour pass. He and buddies had "picked up some females" and gone to the Palladium, where Woody Herman was playing. Lucy too was crazy about music.

Jack also mentioned to Lucy "a girl friend down at Rembert S.C." who thought she might go to Winthrop next year. He assured Lucy he was "not engaged or any thing, just better-than-average good friends, She's real sweet to me and a smart kid. Haven't known her long enough, as I've only seen her the few times I dated her. I'm not the marrying type you know. Not yet anyway. . . . You know I'm still mighty young, and had my life interrupted. Still got a lot of things to do and am pretty wild yet." He added that he had a date that night with a "W.R.," a Marine woman reservist.

Not mentioned in his letters, Jack also acted responsibly on a serious matter. On November 30 he signed his last will and testament, appointing Oscar his executor and beneficiary. On December 1 Jack wrote home that he expected only "about a couple more week ends." He commented on his niece, "I would give anything to see little Joan now that she is walking and talking." He still had "the old horn, and play it often. I've seen a million good bands and shows since I've been here." Jack wrote two letters December 5 and two more December 7 and 8. He had sent home a sea bag and a suitcase that included a green overcoat that he wanted Oscar to give to "Old Mose for Christmas from me." He received a box with Christmas gifts from them and told Lottie, "I wouldn't take a million dollars for the pictures of you and Joan, and I really appreciate it." He said, "If I ever get married I hope my children will be half as sweet, and have a mother as wonderful as Lottie. . . . I guess this must sound odd coming from me, but don't worry I haven't got any ideas about getting married and have no intentions of doing so. It'll really have to be some woman before I would make that fatal mistake."

He wrote Lucy December 10. At the letter's end was a sketch of a comic Marine seated on a comic horse labeled "Mac." In another letter that day, Jack wrote his folks that he was packed and expected to ship out at any time. He explained the involved code he had now worked out:

> When you get a letter from me that starts like this, "I'm Sorry I can't tell you where I am, etc etc.," you will know that is the one in which I will be telling you. That will be the key. (Got it?)—Immediately after the paragraph in which I say this, I will begin. (This may not be in the lst para. See?) Now after you read this key start deciphering. Here's how: All during the letter you will see dashes, like this (—). The sentences immediately following these dashes will contain one of the key letters. [It will be the first letter of the last word in the sentence.] When I say "I wish I could see Mac now" or a sentence in which I mention Mac, you will know I've finished the code. (understand)—Now one more thing—name of the place will be spelled backwards!!) Is this clear? Let me know by writing me back with a letter containing a paragraph which begins with a sentence saying "I know you can't tell us where you are etc. etc." this will mean "Got it! We understand, and know where you are" (this is after you know.) Answer this letter by saying "I know you can't tell us where you are <u>going</u> etc." This will mean We got the code, and understand it. If you don't understand it, say "Mac misses you and does not understand why you had to leave."

Many families privately devised correspondence code words undetectable to either censor or enemy eyes. However, it is doubtful many other codes were as convoluted. Jack seemed caught up in the spirit of devising a game.

"People are living in luxury out here," Jack commented on December 12 in one of his final observations on California. "Things are really booming. These big war plants seem to be making everybody rich." He reflected on "the same old story of 'Rich man's game and Poor man's fight.'" The same date Jack sent a telegram to Mattie and George Creed's address: "HELLO TELL DADDY NEED $25 IN MORNING. NO TROUBLE WANT EXTRA GLASSES. NO PAY LATELY. EXPLAIN LATER. PLEASE RUSH THANKS A MILLION=OJ SMYRL." The next day, he wrote explaining that servicemen there had "not been paid as usual since everything is fouled up and all my money is gone or lent out and I wanted to be sure and get an extra set of glasses before I shipped overseas. . . . I've got to get em right away.—We sent our sea-bags down to Diego this morning and are turning in our sheets and stuff in the morning." He mentioned that he and an artist friend from Parris Island, Hugo Schroeder, had found a quiet spot—upstairs in the officers' office—to write letters. Within the next few days, in a carefully guarded and clandestine operation, Jack's unit departed California.

Chapter 14

In the Pacific

"If I come back O.K. this will be one great experience"

In an undated letter late in 1944, Jack was allowed to reveal that he was in the Pacific. "I am aware of the fact that you don't know I've left the States yet," he wrote. "Right now I am at the place where Jessell Campbell was." However, his only view of Pearl Harbor would remain from aboard ship. The carrier had simply detoured to send ashore some seriously ill servicemen and sailed on without further pause. "It's hard to write a letter as all the news worth writing is illegal you know." He continued, "It will probably be after Christmas when you get this," and mused, "It would be great to take this trip on a luxury liner in Peacetime."

On December 17 Jack acknowledged he had been able to buy his spare glasses before he left. He also sent a message to his cousin's mother: "Tell Ola Steve is on the same ship with me." A week later he wrote, "This is Christmas eve on a transport. I have had you on my mind all morning and thought about you during the services on deck this morning. The singing of carols and everything made me think of Christmas at home." He noted it as his first away from home and commented, "The color of the Pacific is the most beautiful clear blue you could imagine and the foam is whiter than snow. It's extremely beautiful at times." Later a V-mail of December 30 groused, "I've been hot as the devil on this tub."

As 1945 began, Jack's letters told them what he could within censorship limitations. On January 3 (misdated the previous year), he wrote, "I'm sorry I can't tell you where I am but I'm doing O.K. and feeling great."

He followed with their private code to divulge he was in the Russell Islands. His family located it on a map within the Solomon Islands and less than fifty miles from Guadalcanal, where Marines had won a bitter battle two years earlier. The coconut palms, Jack said, were "really beautiful" but "especially so at sunset." In a sentiment shared by warriors over time, he conjectured, "If I come back O.K. this will be one great experience. This place is so beautiful it's hard to believe the world is at war."

Four days later (the year still misdated), Jack described to Lucy the "beautiful tropical island" where he was camped "in a coconut palm grove" with coral reefs in water "crystal clear and the most beautiful blue you ever saw." He had received no mail for over three weeks. His memoir notes identify the site as "a neighboring island off from Pavuvu," the largest island in the Russells. When a native appeared at Jack's tent offering "to trade grass skirts for our 'script' money to buy things at the PX," the notes state, "I tried communicating by grunts and sign language. He replied in perfect English, saying, 'I speak English very well sir.' He had learned it from the missionaries."

A letter Jack correctly dated 1945 but misdated "December" instead of January 10 he wrote home from his tent. Playfully he sketched himself as an island castaway with a Pop Kola at hand. He and "an artist friend," possibly Hugo Schroeder, had been to a Red Cross sketch club which served free coffee and tea. Daily the men were given fruit juice and a pill on doctor's orders. He liked the island's excellent food but not "the land crabs that crawl in the tent at night." He sent a message: "Tell Ola that Steve and I have been separated but he is on this same island." Jack also began a saga that dragged on for months, telling them that he had bought a grass skirt from one of the locals and was planning to send it to Lucy.

Sitting in his tent during a pouring rain on January 11, Jack read mail he received that day. Most of it had been written December 10. He wrote Lucy at Winthrop that he had found horses in a coconut grove and, after making a rope halter, had gone riding. In a practice he would often repeat, he wrote Mae a nearly identical letter the same day. He wanted her to ask Lottie to get him some colored pencils from an art store. Similar requests for art supplies would occur everywhere he went. Few of the pictures he made would be sent home or brought back. As he stated, he gave most of them to other Marines as souvenirs, or sold or bartered them—at times with locals—for other goods. Furthermore lost correspondence was commonplace in war zones.

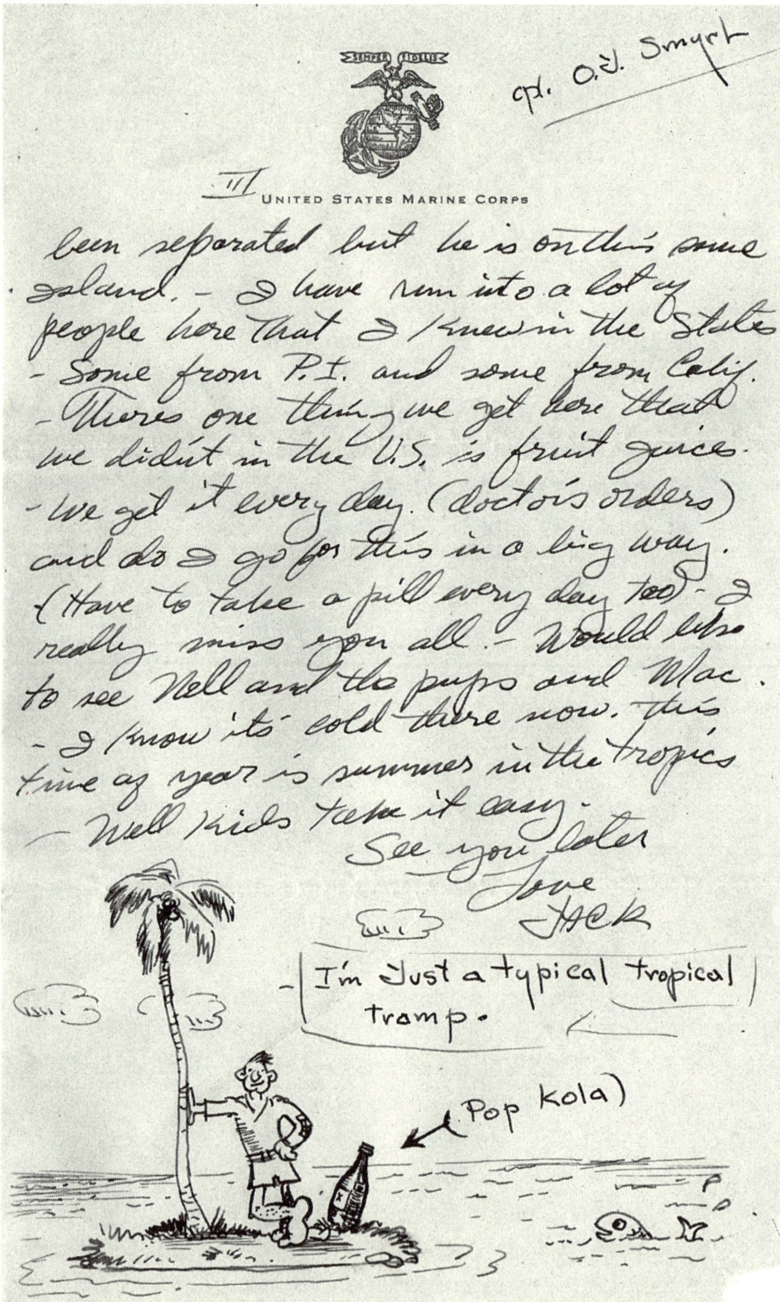

Cpl. O.J. Smyrl

SEMPER FIDELIS

III UNITED STATES MARINE CORPS

been separated but he is on this same island. - I have run into a lot of people here that I knew in the States - Some from P.I. and some from Calif. - Theres one thing we get here that we didn't in the U.S. is fruit juice. - We get it every day. (doctor's orders) and do I go for this in a big way. (Have to take a pill every day too) - I really miss you all. - Would like to see Nell and the pups and Mac. - I know it's cold there now. this time of year is summer in the tropics - Well kids take it easy.

See you later
Love
Jack

Sketch on last page of Jack's January 10, 1945, letter from Pavuvu.
Courtesy of the University of South Carolina.

On January 13 Jack's letter was typewritten. "It's been over two years since I've written on one of these things," he told Lucy, "so ignore the style." He asked his mother for some small watercolor brushes and sketching pencils. He sent a message: "Tell Ola I have located Steve. He is working just a short way from me, and I have seen him twice since we arrived." In spite of the rainy season, Jack wrote, "This is the best camp I've been in yet, even in the states, except Parris Island, and you know that was Paradise Island for me." He commented, "I like this running around in nothing but shorts all day," adding, "It's hard to believe that it's cold back home."

Jack called attention to his address in the First Division when he wrote on January 16, the same as Mac Anderson's division, he pointed out. It was all he was free to suggest about their mission. The only mail he had received since he left the states was "some that came over with us." He turned to casual details to entertain his family. He described the barter system: "A quart of liquor will sell for 50 bucks in this place—the beer we are rationed we pay 10¢ a can for will go for $1.00 a can. I trade mine off for Coca-colas. Ice is a rare item so you usually drink em warm." Memoir notes recall burying drinks in the sand to cool them a bit. "Outdoor movies (you sit on coconut logs), mail call, good food, all go to make life very bearable on this island," he wrote. "There are only 8 white women here (Red-Cross workers)."

Jack's January 21 letter reported he was attached to the First Service Battalion quartermaster. He knew Oscar would understand the kinds of work expected of him. He was surprised his mother had not seen any coconuts in the grocery stores this year: "They are all over the place here and are dangerous when they drop out of the trees (30 or 40 ft.)." Three days later he told Lucy he had mailed sketches home that included a hula girl picture for her. He was pleased once new mail began arriving and reported on January 31, "Mail is good now. Takes about 2 weeks to reach me." He was glad of news that Mac Anderson was getting home. Jack, having recently watched the movie *Casanova Brown* from a coconut log seat, remarked, "Gary Cooper himself had told me about it" when he met him in Hollywood.

On February 6 Jack complained about censorship preventing his writing "what I want to tell you" and about an annoying skin fungus that lingered in the damp climate. He had drawn his back pay, $135, and was sending home a money order for $100 and a little to Lucy as a gift: "I know how good those extra bucks come in when you're off at school." He reminisced that he "really had a big time on the West Coast" and "threw away a lot of dough there but I don't regret it, because it'll be one long time before I'll be in a liberty port again." Jack expressed an interesting desire: "I am secretly hoping we go to China from here—that would really be one experience."

On February 7 he had sent home "a coconut and some shells and stuff—and a small necklace to Mama." About the promised grass skirt, he told Lucy he let Steve Kelly have it to send his wife, but "I want you to have the best one I can find even if it takes a while." He explained, "You see it's a lot of red tape to getting one, then you have to have it sterilized (steam machine) then it has to be censored, and wrapped in front of the censor and you have to go to the P.O. to find out how much for the stamps, so you see it's no use to do this unless you've got a good one." Later that month he bought another skirt for Lucy but then confessed, "You know the grass skirt I had for you, well I sent it to a girl-friend, but I'm sending you one later," adding, "You know how it is with girl-friends." A grass skirt for Lucy would be discussed in many subsequent letters. It seemed that each time Jack found just the one for his sister, he sent it to another female.

In another February 7 letter Jack described a recreation spot or "rest camp," formerly a house for a plantation overseer, "like a pretty country house with all kinds of flowers" and "the prettiest place I've seen yet." Before the war, soap companies had managed the islands as coconut plantations to produce oils for their products. Jack's letter continued, "I'm seeing so many beautiful things that I only regret the time it is cutting out of my youth." He requested a pair of scissors and a fountain pen, "absolutely unobtainable over here," and explained, "I miss the smaller luxuries most of all, such as a pillow, cold drinks, candy (sometimes get a little), a little privacy, chairs, and a few other things you take for granted when you're in civilization." On the bottom of the page he sketched a bugler with his horn. Separately on Red Cross stationery, Jack wrote that he was "listening to the music, and taking it easy for a change. . . . These Red Cross women are really doing good over here."

Both Jack and Steve Kelly long recalled spare-time excursions together. On February 12 Jack wrote home that the previous day, a Sunday, he went with Steve "and a crowd on a visit to the neighboring islands. The most fun I've had since I've been here, and really saw some of the prettiest things I've seen yet." He continued, "We went by some of the native villages and went swimming. The natives are friendly and most of them use to work for the Palmolive [soap company] people and speak rough English. You should see their dugout canoes and stuff. The women are very immodest and only wear the [grass] skirts."

Jack, Steve, and buddies traveled to outlying islands by a DUKW, familiarly a "duck," an amphibious watercraft with six wheels for on-land travel. A later letter told of a trip they took to other islands, including a small, uninhabited one, and described beaches, jungle birds, and clear but treacherous water. Jack's memoir notes recall "the Melanesians in grass skirts, the native village on stilts." He described the people "of intense blackness to the point of having blue highlights." The military slang "gooks" for various native peoples that servicemen encountered was part of everyday language in the Pacific. Jack commented in one letter about them, "They are primitive people. Many speak English and work for the Govt. here. They have acquired a few Marine clothes and stuff, but still persist in going bare-footed and wearing little clothes."

In February Jack wrote also of other interests. He told Lucy he was "doing portrait sketches of guys for $5.00 each, and as I don't care for the beer I sell it to the heavy drinkers." He sent home a $10 money order on February 22 and told his mother, "Either put it in the bank or give it to Alfred as a gift from me if he needs it." His next letter mentioned Lottie's renting "that swell little house" in Camden. She had acted on scarce opportunity to ready a small home in anticipation of the windup of Lewis's European assignment.

On February 24 Jack reported rumors that "when you get out you can take either your mustering-out pay or a jeep. I may come riding home in a jeep after this war." He had earlier expressed enthusiasm for the tough and versatile vehicle. For the present he "would give 10 bucks for an ice cold Pop-Kola right now." He reported himself pleased to have been issued "a nice pair of Paratrooper boots the other day," commenting, "This beats the regular leggings a mile. Around this place we only wear a cap, pair of shorts, and shoes (I cut mine down for sandals). At night we have to wear long trousers and shirt if we go to the show or anything." By stating that boots had been issued, Jack may have hinted to Oscar a coming change.

Jack's picturesque and lighthearted letters, highlighting pleasant adventures, avoided subjects of military business. By assignment Jack was a combat Marine with duties in the organization, distribution, and transportation of the supplies and equipment supporting combat units. Daily he observed aspects of the buildup for the mission he and comrades heard rumored and felt coming. He slipped an innocuous opinion into a March 13 letter that made it past censors: "I would hate to be on the other side. Frankly I don't think they'll last but maybe another year or so." Jack's outfit in the Russells was among those helping to stage and about to participate in the looming final engagement between the armies of the United States and Japan—the Battle of Okinawa.

In March 1945 fifteen hundred ships and more than half a million men—the largest invasion force since D-Day—assembled in the Pacific to begin assault on the sixty-mile-long island of Okinawa, key to the homeland of Japan. Jack later related that to keep movements secret, the men before embarking via transport ships had been directed to write bland, postdated letters home as decoys to cover their whereabouts if the mail were intercepted.

Two of Jack's letters home may have been composed for this purpose. The one he dated March 19 he customized with cartoons. His content was "old news" and random trivia. He wrote that with hunting season over, he was gratified to hear the dogs did so well. He had gotten only a couple of *Chronicles,* both with old addresses. Cigarettes were plentiful, only a nickel a pack. He was glad Mose got the coat and it fit. Referring to the wedding of a high school friend, he said, "It will be sometime before you catch old Jack tying hisself to somebody's apron strings. Mama you're the only sweetheart I've got." In a letter dated March 24, he wrote, "Daddy . . . I am hoping to be with you on the next hunting season." If the worst came, he had worked into bland letters a special, loving message to each parent.

The March invasion began with United States ships commencing heavy shelling of Okinawa and its one hundred thousand well-hidden defenders. Troops aboard transports nervously awaited orders to go ashore. Jack's division was among them. Servicemen heard sultry "Tokyo Rose" tantalize via radio, "GIs, we know you are coming. Come on." The message gave them chills. Okinawa's defenders were entrenched, prepared to die for their emperor. Ready to sacrifice themselves, pilots of warplanes awaited at Japanese air fields. On other Pacific beachheads Marines had suffered horrific landings facing Japanese resistance. Heavy damage and loss of life were expected.

The first of April, Easter Sunday, two of the three Marine divisions in the Third Amphibious Corps, in coordination with two army divisions, began landing on the island's beaches. Jack, in the First Division, was among them. To their eerie surprise, they met little resistance. Americans had been prepared to lose eight of ten men taking the beach. They lost none. American tanks and infantry crossed the island, cutting it in two parts.

Jack's division had landed on the China Sea side. He was allowed to write home on April 3, still under censorship. "I am with Steve again," he told them simply. "We are bivouac[k]ed only about 300 yds. apart now.

Steve is in another outfit from me but luckily we have been together twice now." It would be some time before his family would receive that letter, but he knew they would be relieved to hear of both of them.

In the pattern of previous letters written under censorship, Jack seized on a topic from home. With almost fevered intensity, he addressed a proposed family project. On property his mother inherited behind Grandpa's old home place, Oscar was considering building a pond for family recreation. "I am very, very, excited about you and Alfred contemplating the pond," Jack said. "I want you to take my savings account, around $300 I believe, and put it into the project." Jack had another savings account with the Marine Corps: "My pay is riding up all the time with 20% extra for overseas, and my expenses for the last two months have been exactly nothing and will be for sometime." He continued encouragements. "I figure with the extra 300 you can swing the deal," he conjectured. "By the time I get home the fish should be multiplying in it and maybe the cabin will be up. This will be a terrific hide-a-way for us and when I get that jeep you won't have to worry about a road for it. Let's don't miss this chance." Familiar writing habits and plans at home countered tensions.

As Marines moved north and army troops moved south through Okinawa, opposition steadily increased from firmly entrenched Japanese. On April 6 Japanese defenders burst forth launching hundreds of kamikazes at a time. Suicide planes destroyed or damaged seventeen vessels, killing more than 350 men. Jack's and Steve's families had not heard from them in some time, not even that they had left the tropical island of coconut palms. Like families all over America, they followed the news closely. Wherever their sons were, they were in danger.

On April 14 Jack wrote home, "The censorship lid is off and I can tell you where I am. I am on the island of 'Okinawa Shima.' I imagine news of the Blitz here has reached the states by now." He reported they had heard (untrue) that Germany had surrendered and (true) that Roosevelt had died. The president had died two days earlier, and Americans mourned. Jack included a few battle specifics: "Have been strafed and in some air-raids. The first one was one night last week the bombs came close enough to throw sand and stuff on our fox-hole. It was so close to Steve Kelly that shrapnel fragments tore through his mosquito netting and under his cot. He was miraculously spared. We have an air-raid every night but it doesn't always come over us. We get to see 'em knock down the Planes often." In interviews Jack acknowledged that, even when at liberty to write freely, he left out much that would cause his family greater anxiety.

"Every night you can listen to the artillery duel that has been on a few days, and the bombs and flares and stuff," Jack continued. "If you want to see a firework display, you should see the sky when it's full of tracers and flak." He described his "hole" (foxhole) as "a "comfortable little shelter" and Okinawa itself as "some of the most beautiful farming land I've seen." He wrote that "the mail is coming through now as we have a couple airfields in our possession."

After that first factual letter, the eighty-two-day Battle of Okinawa would continue two more months through mid-June, the Pacific theater's longest campaign, costing its highest casualties. Contrary to elation about the lifting of censorship, Jack's April 20 letter arrived marked "censored for security reasons by USMC censor." One statement not censored read, "It's pretty spooky around here at night, I sleep pretty lightly."

Jack's family also slept lightly. Replying at the end of April, his mother expressed helpless feelings, unable to "do something" to protect him from dangers. The war in Europe was "almost over but as yet it is not." She packed the letter with family news: "Margaret McDowell Mullen has a new baby girl. . . . Johnny Mullen is on a ship somewhere in the Pacific. . . . Freddy made 20 missions and made Staff Sgt. . . . Gary [under age] was begging Nettie & Fred to sign for him to go in the Navy. It is about to worry Nettie to death." She continued, "Mr. Clyburn heard from Bill last Friday and he was OK. He is in Germany. I think I told you that Lewis was in Germany now. He said they were using a German Farm house for their head quarters." Mae added about a noted war correspondent, "I have read all of the articles that Ernie Pyle wrote about Okinawa. He was with the 1st Marine Division he said. That is one way I knew where you were. Don't you worry. I listen & read everything about that place."

Jack's April 27 letter, stating that things were beginning to quiet down, crossed in the mail. "The fighting is down on the southern end of the island now," he said. He had the "dug-out" all to himself since "the other two guys decided to move into tents." Writing on May 1 he expected to move "a couple miles from the front lines." He said, "This is a swell spot here—only worry is snipers and air-raids. They really put on the fireworks when ever a Jap plane comes over. The other night I was on the 10–2 watch—when they started prowling." Jack continued with a grimly poetic description: "It's one of the most spectacular sights to see the long finger of the spotlights reach up into the night and catch the plane in their beams and the sky is filled with great fountains of red as the tracers climb up after it from every direction just covering the sky and 90's have their flak bursting all around making a beautiful pattern that looks like Christmas. When the plane is hit the smoke streams out behind it in a long tail before it makes the death dive."

As combat increased, Jack grew less guarded in subject matter. One air raid he described comically, having dived into a foxhole only to find it filled with mud, but during another raid he nearly pulled the trigger on a fellow marine who crawled into his dugout. That occurred after Jack, returning from guard duty about 2:30 A.M., wrapped himself in his blanket and fell asleep. He described the danger of enemy prowlers, usually armed with knives and grenades: "They got one about 200 yds. from my shack last week." He added a postscript: "I check that cave every nite now like an old maid looking under the bed." Despite such harrowing events, Jack's memoir notes also recall "the beauty of the air raids at night, the tracers, the spotlights, the anti-aircraft explosions." Combat was a surreal existence. He endured in various ways.

On the night of May 3 Jack wrote by candlelight in his "shack," his self-fortified cave dugout, with "a couple of 'Hot-Boxes' lit to knock off the chill (it gets chilly here at night). Some of the guys call me 'the Hermit' now with my shack-in-the-wall. Even though it's crude and everything, I am in love with it; it's the first place I've ever had that was all mine. It's the first real studio I've had—one place I can lay stuff down and leave it. On the off time I'm getting to draw a little, and the guys like to pass the time here, joking, eating, playing my horn, etc, and posing for their portraits." He thanked Mae for sending photos for his twenty-second birthday: "They are too wonderful. I was just sitting here looking at everybody with tears in my eyes. It was almost like I was there with you. I would give anything if I were." He recognized that Alfred was wearing "my old white sweater" and "the old watch" in one photo and commented how good everyone looked. He mentioned that Steve Kelly was then about ten miles away, and "I was on a trip down to the beach the other day and got to see him."

Jack wrote on May 7 about rain every few days. "It's usually either muddy or dusty," he said. "It's the same kind of country as up at Grandpa's," hilly and rocky terrain, changing from sloppy to hardened. He described pines, horses, tomatoes, and people who were smaller than Americans. Jack later said that when he was away from home, he often dreamed of his Grandpa's house—the sights, sounds, and smells—just as it was when he was growing up and spending time there. He and Steve Kelly, whose family home was near the Smyrl house, shared similar memories. In the midst of the battle for control of Okinawa, his Grandpa's home was Jack's "comfort place" when he could sleep.

About the campaign, he reported, "Our division is back on the front, however I am not in any too dangerous zone right now—only worry is the air-raids occasionally now." He had it easy now, "just a little work on the trucks and a little guard every 3 nights or so." He "even had a chance to do a little drawing" with "a little box of pencils a red-cross lady gave me on the last island." He was still looking for the mailed boxes to catch up with him. He requested a flashlight and 120 film. As he did frequently, he asked about the pond project.

The next day, May 8, much of the world heralded the major milestone of V-E Day, Victory in Europe. Jubilation was widespread at home as spontaneous celebrations erupted. On May 12, when an elated Lottie wrote Jack, she was glad that news from Okinawa was good too. She was hopeful of discharge for Lewis, who was back in France. Lucy had four days left as a Winthrop freshman.

In Okinawa on May 12 Jack was far differently involved than his family knew. According to his later notes and interviews, he watched a kamikaze plane make a suicidal dive into a ship he thought was the *USS North Carolina* (it was actually the *USS New Mexico,* hit on May 12). He counted fifty bodies brought ashore for burial and saw the decapitated, de-legged body of the pilot tossed into an unmarked grave. He did not know at the time how many more were injured in the incident. Naval records exceeded 170. Jack may have served at times on burial details, as such responsibilities accounting for the dead fell to the quartermaster's battalion. The letters he wrote May 12 and 13 referred to the kamikaze attack, although at the time he omitted details. Some things, he would later admit when questioned, he never spoke of afterward. Some impressions too were later eclipsed or numbed by repeated or more intense experiences.

Mae also wrote on May 12, "We listen for all the news . . . over the radio about that place and what your Div. is doing. Today it said your outfit was near Naha." The fight to capture the capital city of Okinawa would continue for some time. Mae asked if Jack were rid of fleas bothering him. She rounded up local reports: a Laney boy was in the Pacific in the Navy, and Shot Cox was being sent to Okinawa. She commented, "Should you be sent to Saipan maybe you can see Jessell Campbell." At home the garden was doing well: "We have nearly 400 tomato plants living" and "want to have chicken, beans, tomatoes & fresh strawberries for you when you get here." Oscar added local reports on May 13 that Major Cullen Capehart

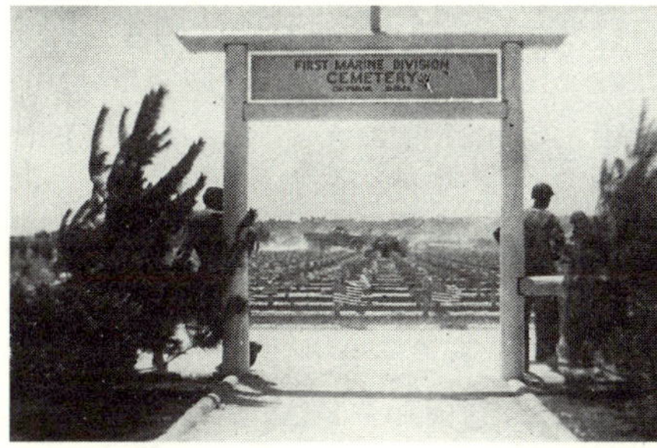

Jack's photograph of the First Marine Division Cemetery, Okinawa, 1945, with burial services in background. Courtesy of the family.

was on Okinawa, and Jack Nettles with an airfield ground crew near there. Construction had not yet begun on the pond. The contractor was in Georgia with his equipment and had yet to make a survey. Henry had bought fifteen yearlings to put in the pasture at Grandpa's and Mamie's "to fatten up and speculate on." Everyone asked about Jack. Oscar had secured a franchise to bottle a new drink, "Cheer Up," starting in summer with the availability of bottles. The peppy new name mirrored the times.

Jack's May 14 letter covered a range of emotions that showed his world far different from that of correspondents from home. He was jolly reporting, "I still have my old trumpet with me and blow reville for the company. The horn will rate a few campaign ribbons when it gets back. I gave the boys a little jive this morning, and was cutting the fool like we usually do. Some of them came out and threw clods of dirt at me. I'm with some pretty swell guys right now." Having just read a clipping of one of Ernie Pyle's last columns, Jack referred to the correspondent's death in an air raid the previous month: "He was killed in this blitz. Some of the fellows here were on his ship with him. I was in the same convoy."

Jack reported himself doing all right but losing sleep because some snipers had been loose. He was bunking now with Sergeant McIntyre from Shelby, North Carolina, who had been at Parris Island with him. Jack had learned that a rifle coach friend of theirs had died at Peleliu. However, Jack described in contrast a personal stroke of good luck. A two hundred-pound bomb had dropped next to him but did not detonate. It was a dud. "The bomb disposal boys dug it up," he said. "It buried itself over 15 feet in the ground." He left unspoken for the time how nerve-wracking that close call was.

Jack's letter then described a scene following a kamikaze attack. He saw six soldiers "standing together over the grave of one of their buddies and singing from some little hymn books and then I saw them pray before they left. It's the first time in a long time that tears have come to my eyes." Jack requested a flashlight and film and, from Oscar, a .38 or .45 pistol, adding, "a side-arm is the best fox-hole companion you can get." He said with irony, "I get all the big time news fast as it happens, in fact I get it as it happens here from sight." He listened last night "on a radio to the pilots talking while they were shooting down the Japs (they call 'em 'bogies'). They got 8 last night."

Letters from home also reflected a variety of conditions and emotions. Anna Shuler's May 14 letter described an effect of wartime rationing: "We got our annuals to-day. . . . We had to reduce our paper, material, cover, pictures, etc. until there's nothing to it. However, it will be a wonderful keepsake and I suppose I'm a little proud of it." She had been keeping up with Marine activity on Okinawa. She mentioned that one of her brothers in France would be in the army of occupation. Anna wrote of springtime, everything "green, alive, and very lovely . . . vegetables ready to eat in our garden and the plums and peaches are almost ripe." In a separate letter the same day, Anna contrasted last year when she was so eager to graduate with her present feelings of sadness and apprehension about postwar conditions.

The following day, Jack wrote home, "There were 4 Japs shot down about 300 yds. from my hole night before last, so don't be bashful about sending me a pistol. It's times like these that pistols were made for. They won't do any good laying on the shelf. I hope you can find me one. Is the colt that Grandpa used to show me still in the family? Don't worry about theft. Anybody with a side-arm here wears it everywhere like a wristwatch."

In a letter to Lucy on May 15, Jack reported, "The big battle is still raging in Naha. I am listening to the big guns right now. They rumble most of the time. The guards right up the road about 200 yds. got 4 more 'bogies' (Japs) night before last. I went up and looked 'em over. The sleep comes hard around here at night you can easy understand as the nips are up to no good. . . . I was down at the 27th Div. (Army) cemetery the other day and saw them bringing in a lot of guys that were killed when a zero made a suicide dive on one of our battlewagons. I saw the pilot but there wasn't much left of him. The going is pretty tough right now and this thing can't end too soon." He ended the war talk and turned to a topic familiar to both of them, asking Lucy to scope out record stores for some of the old songs such as "Stardust."

Mae reported May 15 that Calvin Sheorn recently returned from England. "He is in the air corps and his ship caught on fire and he had to jump to save himself and he came down in a Frenchman's chicken yard." The parents of John McCoy, who had been taken prisoner, "had not heard a word since from him until they received a cablegram from him for Mother's Day." They heard "that the boys who were in Africa will all be sent back. If so we know that Lewis will come home. Guess Marion Davis will also." Having been exposed to daily reports of deaths and POWs, Mae expressed the anxiety the family shared when she advised Jack, "Do take the best of care of yourself and trust no Jap as far as you can throw a mule by the tail." She said they asked God to take care of him, and she admonished him to seek God's care and guidance. She warned Jack, if he went hunting for souvenirs as many did, to beware of "mines & traps." She continued, "I understand the Japs are using a lot of them now. Wish I could ring a lot of their old yellow neck[s]." Mae, who had spent her life teaching her children kindness to others, could see that hardened sensitivities were necessary for her son to survive in a combat zone.

On May 15 Bill Burns, almost nineteen and in the navy, responded to a letter from Jack that had raved about Los Angeles: "We were in New York for a few days and if it beats that, well I know where I want to live." Bill gushed about New York's clubs and bands, "Man, I want to live and die on 52nd St." He was still playing but had little time for it aboard ship. His hands were full of calluses. It would take three or four months, he said, to get "where I can half-way move my fingers right again." He was doing "a little arranging now and am trying to develop some sort of original style to use after the war." He did not know what he would do if he couldn't play after the war was over. He regretted his hands must take such abuse. He wanted to have "a big dance with our old original band when we all get back and I want you in there playing that horn like you used to. Don't guess you have much time to play any where you are but don't dare give it up."

On May 16 it was a war-weary Jack who wrote home as he waited to go on guard: "I'm on the 10–2 watch—maybe I'll have some luck and get myself a bogie. They've been a lot around lately but I haven't been lucky enough for one to get on my post yet." He continued about "the ones that are loose in the hills and break through the lines. Most of them carry grenades. They're plenty sneaky you know and are up to no good. It was claimed that a few are looking for their families or food, cigarettes and stuff. I am anxious to get one. When I see the bastards laying out dead you have no more feeling than if it was a dog run over by a car or something. Don't worry about me, I'll be sure I get the first shot." Referring to a deceptive trick of enemy soldiers hiding their uniforms with civilian kimonos, he commented grimly: "They look good sprawled on the deck with holes through them." Hardened determination was vital to survival.

In the same letter Jack reported demands on his artistic talents. The captain wanted to submit some of his drawings to *Leatherneck:* "It's been a long time since I've had the thrill of seeing some of my stuff printed. . . . I've done a lot of drawing since I've been over here but it's always for somebody else and I never seem to get a chance to do anything for myself." He wrote that his "portraits have improved 100% and are beginning to get a professional touch. I do cartoons for a lot of people mostly as favors, but it has helped me in a million small ways to get things that were other-wise inaccessible." His musical talent also benefitted. The first sergeant offered to relieve him from standing guard duty if he would sound reveille. Facing war, as with other stresses in his life, Jack drew strength from his art and music to assure mental survival.

Mae wrote on May 19 that from newspaper and radio accounts and from Cousin Ola, who had just visited with a letter from Steve: "You boys over there sure must be having a tough time." She reported Alvin and Otis home for a few days, Freddie in England, and Bill Clyburn on his way back to England. Mae had claimed one of the cows Oscar had put in the new pasture to butcher and "put in our [freezer] locker box. I want some nice steak for you when you get here." It was in anticipation that returning troops would be hungry for fresh food, especially strengthening meat, that cattle raising was being urged on farmers. Mae referred to Jack's statement about being lucky when the bomb was a dud: "God must answer prayers for I ask Him daily to care for you, and keep you safe."

Jack remarked on May 20 to Lucy that, having completed her freshman year, she had had as much schooling as he had. He praised their parents for devoting time and resources to them, saying they "have given up more than we will ever know. I am quite sure Daddy would be rich now if it weren't for us. . . . Everything they did was for the benefit of our home and nothing else." On May 21 Mae sent the address of Frank Wooten on Okinawa and two days later reported, "Today I saw a very happy father. John McCoy came home from Europe. He has been a prisoner of the Germans for several months. He is in good health and said he did not fare too bad." She continued with the good news that Lewis had written from

England telling Lottie "to pack hers and Joan['s] things and be ready to come meet him" when he got to the states.

On May 21 Jack described his current setup: "I'm with a small detachment away from the outfit. We're set up in a captured Jap school-house. . . . I got a table to myself, a cot with a mattress, etc. and there are showers only about 50 feet away." Windows rattled all night "from the big guns over at Naha." He requested they send him Worcestershire sauce, pickles, "Heinz 57 Varieties Beefsteak Sauce (I don't get any steaks, but it would make this drystuff 10 times better)." He again urged Oscar "to locate me a pistol soon, so I will have it with me on the next blitz (That's good life insurance out here)." He continued, "Hope this will be over by next year. I can't complain when there are guys in the room here with me [who] have been away for 28 months, and even they can't complain when you think of the guys who aren't coming back at all."

Lucy wrote a week later that Lewis would be home in June. The wounded and liberated prisoners had first choice for transportation. She continued, "Speaking of prisoners they have heard from Hughey Tindal and Stevie McCrae. They're both in France. Stevie is in a hospital. I think he was almost starved to death." Despite lack of progress on the pond project, Lucy said, "Mama and Alfred have already started drawing plans for the house. Hope we can get it fixed soon and have it ready before you come back . . . and you can rest up. Just think you'll love your own private pond to go swimming in."

A letter from Mae the same day stated, "Two letters came from you today and did we have a feast. We devoured them like we were hungry." She continued, "So glad you can have time enough to draw some." She turned her focus to the enemy, "I could shoot one as quick as I could shoot a snake. Don't you spare a single one if you get the chance to put [him] out of business." She said if the "Japs" ever hurt him, "I would like to go over there and knock their old buck teeth down their throats." Mentioning news of a local serviceman marrying a native of mixed nationalities, Mae commented, "Guess that moonlight and music etc. got him. I think I would rather have a good old American daughter-in-law." Eight days earlier, Jack's Aunt Hattie had written him, "don't fall in love with any of those foreigners. Wait till you come home."

On May 29 Jack wrote of the enemy close by: "A bunch of us were cleaning up a spot next to our dump this morning and found fresh barefoot tracks where they had been prowling last nite. Hope you can find me a pistol. You see you can't always have a rifle with you but the hog-leg would be there like a wrist watch. I'm pretty well out of immediate danger at present. The old rainey season is on here and this is one mud hole." He wrote that he lost "a couple of very good buddies." He mentioned how lucky he had been, was proud of himself "so far in not getting too scared or excited." He reminded them of the experience from his past, in the swamp behind their house: "You know that little incident when I got lost taught me a lot about letting your imagin[ation] run away with you."

Jack's Auburn pal Thurston Sumner, a private at Fort Ord, California, wrote him on May 30, "Over here we hear that there is some mighty tough fighting going on—so fellow take care of old Smyrl, we want to get back to Auburn one of these days." On June 2 Mae exclaimed, "This morning the man [on the radio] said it was believed that the Campaign of Okinawa would be over in ten days. It won't be over too soon to suit me." In Jack's letter of May 30, his mood had lightened. He had time to provide a description of the local people and climate: "The little Okinawa kids are very cute and excite a lot of sympathy. The gooks as a rule are funny-looking, but I've seen a few young girls that are very attractive even by American standards (very few though, as the Japs took all they could with them). It rains every day here lately and the roads are quagmires." He reported other news. "Everything's swell with me lately and I have some stuff on its way to the 'Leatherneck' with a good chance of getting in," he said. "Also the captain got me an intro. with a Public Relations officer and he says maybe I can get into Pub. Rel. after the blitz. This would be right up my alley if I can swing it."

On June 1 Jack wrote, "Things are getting so good around here we had some ice-cream for chow, believe it or not. They say some of the sailors donated it from the ships." The following day he and a buddy from Brooklyn "took off to the hills today" and found a little deserted village, and, he wrote, "I made a few rough sketches. . . . I'm making a sort of scrapbook of sketches and stuff when I finish I'll send it home. I even got photographs of Jap soldiers, sailors, and Okinawa family pictures." He reported mail "coming through good now." Jack was elated on June 4 receiving news that Lewis would be coming home from Europe: "That's the best thing that's happened to the Smyrl family since Joan was born." On June 7 and 10 Mae updated reports of other local servicemen. Mac McCorkle was in Munich guarding German prisoners. Jiggs Watts expected to be sent to China. Robert McDowell was leaving for the Pacific as a navy pilot. Jasper Walden, at home on furlough, had been on a ship near Okinawa

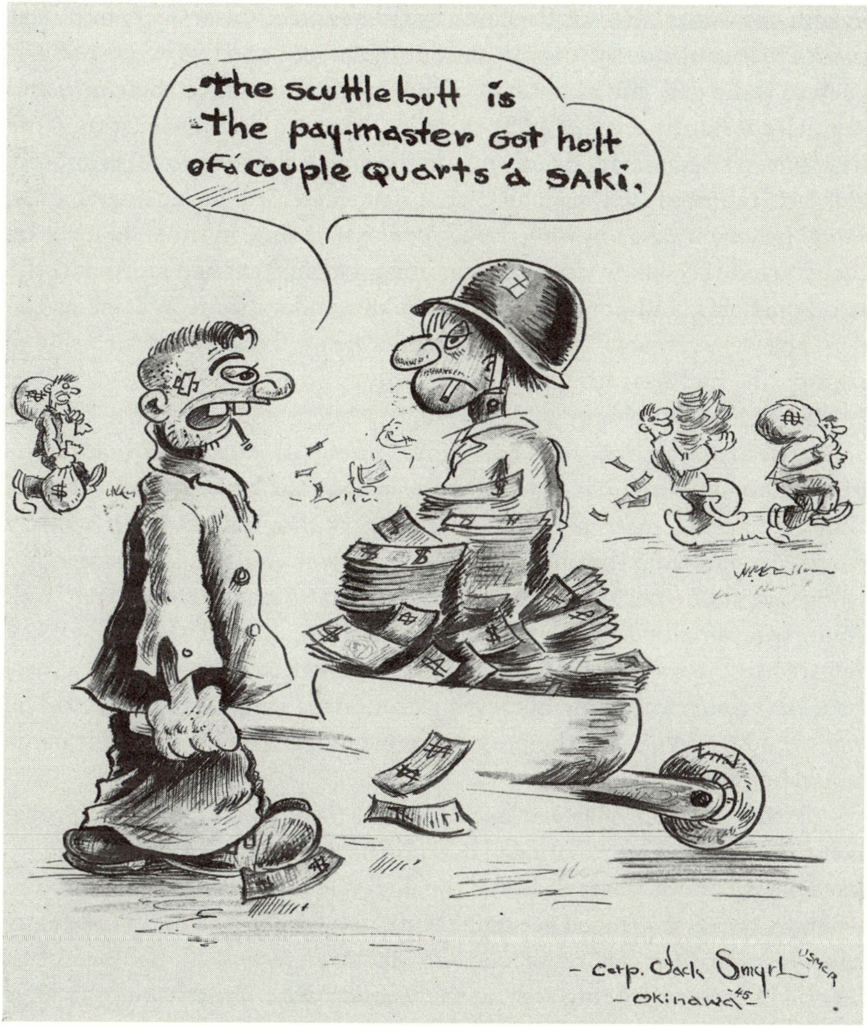

Cartoon from Okinawa, signed with Jack's rank, parodying rumors and mix-ups. Courtesy of the University of South Carolina.

and now in Charleston, which would be transporting troops home from Europe and the Pacific.

Jack explained on June 10 that he had not written lately "due to moving again. I left my place in the school-house, and now am living at the front door of a tomb under a tent." He drew an illustration of the tomb with an "X" marking his location. He conjectured, "I think this blitz will be over in a few days." He was bothered by the sound of the artillery unit next to him that continued firing on "the South end day and night." He had not been to Naha yet, "but about half of my bunch are camped there now and say there is hardly anything left standing." Jack said of his location: "The dead haven't been cleaned out yet, and the smell in some spot[s] is unbearable." He reported "only a small part of the island" still in Japanese hands, "and I believe it won't be long now." For the first time in three months, he had started receiving packages: "the map, pecans, canned stuff, and the two Pop-Colas, and powder. . . . The cookies and stuff are as fresh as the day they were canned." He asked Alfred to "be on the look-out for 2 sets of stamps" he had sent him for his collection and remarked, "The artillery is firing right over behind us now and the concussion shakes the candle."

Lottie also wrote on June 10, "Here I am—still waiting for that hubby of mine to get home. Since I heard 3 wks ago that he was coming home, time has passed more slowly than all the 25 months before. It's surely wonderful knowing that he's on his way. Now if you could just come too things would be perfect." Lottie reported that Richard Denny and Jack Anderson remained in the army of occupation. The following day Lucy referred to the waiting for Lewis, saying, "A week or so ago . . . he [wrote] he wasn't doing any thing but sitting around waiting to leave. He said he was afraid to even leave the post cause you never knew when your name would be called."

Writing June 12, Mae was excited to tell Jack about a home improvement. "We had an automatic, oil burning hot water tank installed and we have plenty of hot water 24 hrs of the day," she said. "We had you in mind when we did it. When you get home you can have a hot or cold shower any time you want it." She reported that Mac Anderson, who had been furloughed home, was being sent to the Pacific again. "Pretty tough to have to leave his new bride isn't it?" Mae continued reports on June 20, "Gary [Ogburn] is leaving for the Navy today. He did not finish high school. . . . Uncle Fred had to even sign for Gary to go, for he is not eighteen until December." Jack Nettles had been moved to Iwo Jima. McCain Richards was in the Pacific on the *St. Louis*. Included with the letter was an undated *Chronicle* clipping: "'Shot' and Dickie Cox Greet Each Other on Guam / Brothers Chance To Meet In Chow Line After 2 ½ Yrs. Separation."

On June 12 Jack wrote two letters. He asked Lucy to send her measurements. "I have some parachute shrouds of nylon and am going to make you a grass skirt that I failed to send you last time. It is beautiful stuff and will make a swell souvenier. I will make the skirt and bra top for you and send the rest home for you or Lottie or Mama to make a dress or something with." He commented, "The big guns next to us are shaking the old tent right now. I'm glad I'm on this end of the line. The Japs will be feeling those shells in a few minutes." He thanked them for the *State* with a wedding announcement of Meta Alexander, commenting, "She was one of my favorite high school friends. Don't you kids worry about old Jack getting hooked up anytime soon. I've got too much to do soon as I get out of this lock-up."

Jack described the hardworking, impoverished Okinawan people and the children to whom the Marines threw candy and cigarettes from the trucks. He continued, "I am living in a property-tent with a Jewish fellow name of Greenberg. He is excellent at comic poetry and he and I are collaborating. I am illustrating his poems." Reflecting on his own art, Jack said, "That's the only thing I really know how to do." Even if he were not to "get rich" as an artist, "it would be an extremely interesting life." He mentioned the pond and wanted a picture if it was completed before he got home. He asked Oscar whether he had been able to locate either a .45 or a .38. He had not seen Steve Kelly for three or four weeks but he was still on the island about fifteen miles north.

On June 17 Jack wrote that he had moved from the tomb to "the side of a hill overlooking the china sea. I can lay in my sack and have a beautiful view of the sea and our ships anchored there. It is now dry and dusty in contrast to the quagmire that exists during the rainy season." He predicted, "The island will soon be secured." He had received the pillow and was looking forward to the sauces. "I dreamed about the pond last night and imagined the men surveying it and everything," he said. He mentioned that one of the fellows there was a Gore from Clinton, North Carolina, who knew James and Marion Davis.

Jack began his June 21 letter with a statement that had been frequently made: "I guess you know the old island is almost secure now." The narratives he then related poured forth in bursts of strong descriptive detail. "I was up at the front lines day before yesterday and went out with a patrol to see what we could see," he wrote. One of the men, a "Mexican-Indian," noticed three Japanese about a mile away, and the patrol went after them. Jack continued, "I broke out across a field below the hill I was on. We opened up and cut them down as they reached the other side of the field. I emptied a clip in them myself."

He wrote on, "The countryside is full of caves and I ran across the hole of one (They mostly have two entrances). I called the guys over and one of the boys tossed in a phosphorus grenade. I was on one end of the cave but the Jap ran out the other end. The phosphorus had set his clothes afire and he was between me and the other boys. I was up on the hill and so I didn't get a shot at him for the smoke and everything. They cut him down when he charged out. One of the 1st two we got wasn't completely dead when this Indian took the butt of his pistol and started knocking out the gold teeth (Lots of guys save 'em but they don't appeal to me), so the Captain who was with us finished him off with his .45."

Jack next described a twelve- to fourteen-year-old private first class who came out of another cave with his hands up, and another enemy who was killed by men on the other side of the hill. "We ran across a lot of dead ones laying around. It was a very exciting day," he said. He reiterated wanting a pistol to sleep with. He had picked up some souvenirs, but since they were prohibited from sending such home, he traded them to a pilot friend for a quart of rum. He reminded his family of the value of alcohol in barter. He mentioned Mae's shell necklace and Lucy's grass skirt he planned to make, neither of which was yet underway. He asked if Alfred had received the stamps and if Lewis was home yet. He decorated the envelope with a cartoon and sent the letter on. Jack would not know it at the time he sealed his June 21 letter, but on that same day the commanding general would declare the Battle of Okinawa at an end.

Chapter 15

Okinawa Controlled

"Maybe it won't be long now"

"Now that Okinawa is under control," Oscar wrote on June 24, 1945, he hoped that Jack would have "some peace and quiet." He expected the Japanese would "continue to strike." Ultimately Jack would remain on Okinawa over three months longer. With the battle declared finished, the Army Air Forces positioned itself for assault on the mainland of Japan. Military casualties of some fifty thousand Americans and over one hundred thousand Japanese had amassed in the struggle for Okinawa, with similarly staggering casualties estimated among the island's civilian population. Yet on the mainland Japan stood ready to fight on, and though organized resistance on Okinawa had fallen, some hidden holdouts continued to harass American troops.

Oscar said he was still unable to find Jack a pistol: "They are hard to get." Likewise he was unable to find a replacement barrel for his damaged .45, the Colt Company being under government contract. He would keep trying.

Jack's family, jubilant at the battle's end, attempted to keep his spirits up with encouraging thoughts of postwar reunions to come with people, places, and activities he loved. The Smyrls, like other informed and thoughtful people, understood that trauma of war was more than a momentary experience, and that interrupted lives would not automatically resume an easy path at war's end. Such topics were seriously discussed in private conversations, and as well as in their veteran, civic, and church groups, though limited in frankness in a public press that was, like families,

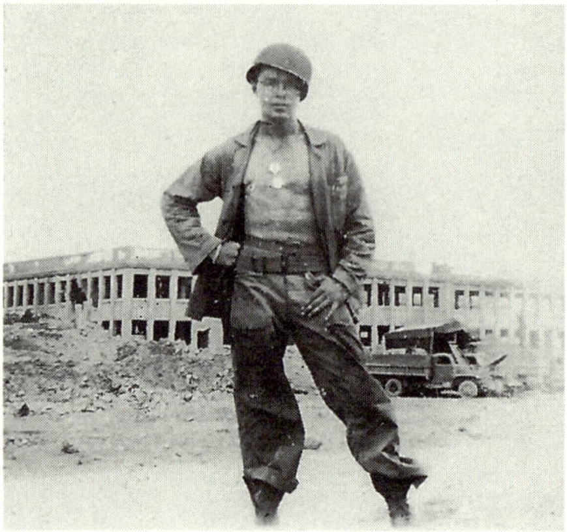

Jack and "grammar school" in bombed city of Naha. Courtesy of the family.

striving to keep up positive attitudes. At home and abroad, "keeping in touch" was vital.

Oscar reported that their cow was giving plenty of milk and that he was fattening a calf. They had rented two drawers in the community freezer locker to keep full of meat for Jack's homecoming. The family had mailed Jack a box "with pickles and Hines 57 Beefsteak sauce in it." There would be other food treats too, some home-canned in tins, as Mae had been teaching other families how to prepare. She encouraged Jack in another important way June 24. "So glad you have had the chance to do some drawing," she wrote, adding, "After the war I am sure you can do some real good stuff. I am hoping you can get more training to help you along the path to Success. Don't be satisfied to be a small fellow, be one of the top-notchers. You can do it with special training."

Jack wrote to them on June 25 using the pen he had just received from Lottie for his birthday. He appreciated the art supplies they sent him, and he had done two or three portraits with them. He would be "moving to another area soon for rehabilitation." Steve was still on Okinawa, but he had not seen him lately. Jack told Oscar there was "an army ordinance outfit" on the island now, so if Oscar could not locate a pistol, "send the old .45 and I am pretty sure I can get it fixed." He let him know, "I could use it." A postscript said to tell Lucy he had gotten some shells to decorate the skirt he was going to make for her.

When Jack wrote on June 28 from a Red Cross tent, he was "in the city of Naha, or at least what's left of it." Having looked though the decimated capital, he observed, "It is evident from the ruins that before she was hit this was once a thriving seaport. . . . It was very modern and most of the business bldgs are copied after Western Architecture and very impressive. The homes are oriental style. Of course there isn't a complete bldg. left in the city." Americans had taken over the Japanese hospital and were using it now as their own. Jack contrasted evidence of a former modern concrete and tile city using Ford automobiles to views elsewhere of traditional farms and villages with wooden buildings, ancient tools, and quaint horse-drawn carts. Jack had his captain's permission to roam the ruined city and make sketches.

On the Camden home front, the Smyrl household experienced relief with good news from Okinawa and from Lottie's long-awaited phone call from Lewis that he had reached Fort Bragg, North Carolina. The next day there, June 30, he processed out, and at Fayetteville he got happy hugs and kisses from Lottie and shy interest when he met his twenty-month-old daughter for the first time. Instead of a planned vacation reunion, the three instead left hurriedly the next morning to reach Camden in time for Lewis to say both hello and farewell to his furloughed brother Mac, leaving immediately to rejoin his unit for another Pacific call-up. Mae's July 2 letter to Jack reported that Lewis "is thin and looks real tired, but is not wounded or anything. Lottie is in the seventh heaven. Joan is already crazy about her Daddy."

With censorship lessened, Jack revealed information previously suppressed. On July 3 he clarified, "I was in the Russells which is part of the Solomons—I saw Guadalcanal, Tulagi, Ulithi, and lots of others. . . . The island I was on is 'PAVUVU.' . . . We visited a neighboring island of BANIKA . . . one of the most beautiful in the Solomon group." He also described the natives of Okinawa, whom he found "interesting" and with whom he communicated by hand signals since none knew English: "They are all small of stature, but very hardy, the little kids are cute. They are about a century behind us in their habits, with a few exceptions of the ones who were well-to-do, and you are never sure if they are as friendly as they seem having been under the Jap machine for ages and the young men in the Jap army." He felt, however, that most of them had started to realize they were benefiting from American control. He continued, "Most seem to be uncultured, simple souls, and by nature friendly. . . . They take such things as sex, bowel movements and such as a matter of course and the women as men think nothing of relieving themselves in public view."

Mae wrote on July 6, "Everybody at the post office gets a kick out of your letters that are all decorated up, Lloyd especially." Jack's cousin was now working in the post office. She added, "Alfred said he wanted to go with you to Auburn when you get back. This next winter is his last one in high school." When Jack wrote on July 10, he responded reflectively to his mother's references to church. He had not been attending services regularly, he admitted, owing to his being on duty or there being no service to attend, or sometimes, "I've just been negligent." He had been in "some very tempting situations that are hard to resist" but he tried to "do the best I know how, and live as I was brought up." He referred to her inspiration and values and verified the importance of religion, especially the concept of afterlife. "There would be no point in living if you expected to die and it would be all over," he asserted.

Jack said his experiences of the last few years had "all helped me to overcome self-consciousness which I secretly suffered from most of my life." He felt "more confident than ever and [I] have a better outlook on everything and am a better judge of what is right and what is wrong." He assured his mother, "When you see me again I'm sure there will be no visible change, but inside I am a more powerful man, if only to myself, and I am happier than I have ever been in my life in spite of the fact that I have been taken away from the life and people I love."

Meanwhile Mae's letters continued updating Jack on hometown news. On July 15 she told him Lottie and Lewis had moved to a larger rental, an annex to a winter resident's home, "the big Kendall house." Howard West had written home that "he could not tell them where he was but he was where Jack Smyrl was." Steve Kelly had written home that "he was sick in the hospital but that it was only a little stomach trouble." Jack had previously divulged to his parents that Steve had a stomach ulcer and was being fed through "a tube in his nose and in his veins." Mae also gave details about the canning demonstrations and assistance she was providing families. For her own family that week she had canned tomatoes and peaches and had put butterbeans, peas, butter, and beef in the freezer locker boxes this week. "Daddy and Alfred have been up the country stretching more wire today. Daddy has 16 beef cows up there," she told Jack. She did not want him to worry about his family now or a food shortage when he returned home.

Jack wrote on July 20 that he was in a temporary spot and expected to be moving in a few days. They were supposed to be in a "Rest Camp," but it had to be cut out of the wilderness and built from the bottom up. There was little danger now, things were more routine, and time dragged. Chow was improving: "I have eaten with the C.B.s [Sea Bees] a few times and they eat like kings—even ice-cold tea and plenty of fresh fruit that we seldom see. The navy really feeds their men, and on board the ships it's always excellent." He added, "I guess you know that the American fleet is only 6 miles from Japan. . . . Maybe it won't be long now."

On July 21 Jack wrote that the previous day he had traveled by truck on detail into the mountains. The forests were dense and impenetrable looking, "forlornly beautiful and wild-looking country," but "there are reputed to be roughly 2000 scattered Japs hiding out in these hills" so they could not let down their guard. He inquired whether Oscar had made progress finding him a pistol. Although his tent was "half sub-merged in a mud puddle," they were "too lazy to fix it as this is only temporary." They hoped to set up on one of the beaches.

Wartime prices and shortages compelled the Smyrls, in addition to growing and preserving food, also to make clothing. Still the skillful seamstress, Mae wrote on July 22 that, despite the summer heat, she was helping Lucy prepare her winter's wardrobe since "ready made things are so high." Alfred included a sketch he drew of the pasture that he, Oscar, and Uncle Henry had fenced with other help. He wanted Jack to see all the cattle-raising space they had added at Grandpa's old place.

Responding to Jack's recent letter on attending church, Oscar wrote encouragingly and seriously on July 22: "You always gain by going to church, if nothing else it puts you in good company and keeps you farther away from temptations. Hope that you are strong enough to resist all that you may be confronted with, most especially whiskey and beer. That is going to be the downfall of I would say eighty percent of the soldiers of this war. I see these young boys 18 to 25 coming home and spending their furloughs getting drunk [on] beer and whiskey." Oscar observed seriously, "They may have made good soldiers, but they will never make good citizens or family men, neither will they be the type that is going to keep the peace, and save the world from another and more terrible war. The present soldiers will soon be taking over the responsibility of running this country, and we should have it headed up with sober Godfearing men or we never will have a lasting peace."

On July 23 Jack wrote that censorship was stricter again and his letters would be monotonous. He surmised it would be at least two years before he could get home, but he was making the most of the experience "as there is so much to see and learn. . . . I could write a book that would be interesting." However, he assured his family, "The next time you see me I'll be the same old Jack that kissed you good-bye when the train pulled out of Yemassee one September morning in 1944." About female commitments, he had made no promises. "I'm just a normal guy," he said, "and if I play around with the women a little it's just because I find it fascinating. . . . I'm just having a little fun and there is nothing serious." He added, "I'm 22 now and have been thrown in pretty rough company most of the time, and live a lot under very im-moral conditions and trends of thought. I believe that I keep pretty straight and would rather do anything than have you ashamed of me."

"We all hope this thing will soon be over," Aunt Nannie declared in a V-mail July 23. Two days later Mae speculated, "If the news is true that we hear, about the bombing of the Jap home land, I don't see how they can hold out so much longer. You boys did a grand job when you secure[d] the island of Okinawa. They sure are using that place now for the Air Force." News reports about bombing flights from newly built American airfields made obvious to the public just how vital the control of Okinawa was in the strategy to defeat Japan. Such activity likely had prompted the tightening of censorship Jack had lamented.

When Jack wrote on July 27 he was expecting to move to a more permanent place. His friend Hugo Schroeder, who he reminded the family had come home with him from Parris Island, had drawn the map and "laid the plans for the set-up." Jack had already picked out their tent site on a terraced mountainside overlooking their battalion in the valley below: "There will be a panoramic view from the tent which I like very much, as I have come into the possession of an excellent pair of field-glasses that I got for a quart of wine that I received in exchange for some souveiners. With the glasses I'll have the sweep of the whole valley and the distant-hills and [an] excellent spot for gazing at the air-planes." He wrote that he was doing well selling and trading sketches, and that "ever since things cooled off I have always had money and even had some to lend—I am getting to be quite a trader."

Mae reported on July 29 that "Mac Anderson is stationed on the west coast for 3 months. . . . G. T. Hendrix and Dot were in Camden last week. He is stationed in Texas. He had a chance to get out of the service but would not take it. . . . Alvin is still in Calif, and Richard Denny is in Germany." She observed about an item Jack sent: "The Jap envelope looks funny. I try to save everything like that for you. Your trunk is pretty full now." Mae concluded this letter, "Sure don't see how Japan can hope to gain anything by keeping on resisting."

Jack wrote on August 6, "This is O. J. Smyrl, Jr., coming to you from hillside house over-looking the Yayhoo Valley, as a big transport is flying low over it, spraying the vicinity with some chemical. Yes, I'm finally moved, and set-up in my new spot I was telling you about." He mentioned either construction or planned construction of a chapel, mess hall, and other facilities. The place was called a "rest camp, but is just so much propaganda, as we dont even get Sunday off, and are early risers, and late workers." There was still an occasional air raid alarm, and "a Jap plane flew over us last night but didn't drop anything here." The last package he received "was really something. The fried chicken and everything in perfect condition. Lots of people are amazed by this shipping method and want to know if their folks can do it also."

Although on that same historic day of August 6, 1945, an American plane, *Enola Gay*, a B-29 Superfortress bomber, dropped an atomic bomb on Hiroshima, Japan, Jack's letter indicated no knowledge of any military activity other than usual. However, he also wrote a second August 6 letter inscribed at the left top: "Note: no more inside address—yippee!! . . . Hello, Hello, Hello, hello, hello!! Tonight marks a great and long looked-forward occasion. The yokes of bondage have been lifted! Tyranny has ceased to exist! The steel doors of censorship have flung open, and once again freedom of speech is the order of the day. Yessir, the dope is out and now we can write like U.S. citizens again."

There was indication of information about the bombing as he continued with news he had dreamed of: "The first thing I'll tell you, to take advantage of my new-found liberty . . . is where I am going. . . . Right now the old First Div., longest in the Pacific, is getting itself squared-away for a little *China* [double underlined] duty. Yes, that's the dope. Soon I'll be writing you from the land of chopsticks and Dragon-Seed. Just the exact date is unknown, but very soon." Suddenly, however, the next day censorship was back on.

On August 7 Mae, not having yet received his letter, was anxious about his whereabouts, asking "How about our code." She said next, "How about that Atomic bomb. We heard about it here yesterday for the first time. . . . This is the most amazing thing that I have ever heard of and it sure ought to shorten this war. . . . We heard a resume of what the 1st Marine Div had done since the war in the Pacific started. We heard it this afternoon on the radio. My you boys sure have had a tough job to do and you have done the job more than well. Bless your dear hearts. I am sure no outfit can beat your record."

On August 10, the day after the United States dropped a second atomic bomb and destroyed Nagasaki, Mae wrote from Cheraw State Park, where the family was vacationing: "Well today may be one of the most important days in our lives. The first thing I heard over the radio this morning was that the Japs had broadcast a surrender offer. I did not whoop or shout but just stood with tears running down my face saying over & over again 'Maybe Jack will be home for Xmas.' Oh my dear I do hope the news over the radio is true."

Jack's family—and the loved ones of servicemen across the country—had hopes that war had indeed finally ceased. Mae wrote from Cheraw on August 11, "The radio is saying now that the U.S and other allies accept the offer of peace from Japan and the Jap emperor will be allowed to stay on the throne and rule only as dictated by the allies. I am not sure that is such a good idea it seems to me that we can say that unconditional surrender is just what it means and stick to just that. How do you boys feel who have been fighting the Japs. I cant see why we would grant those Japs anything." Then she reconsidered, "Of course if we accept their offer it will mean the war is over and you will be coming home sooner and when I think of it that way I am softhearted. Oh! Jack wouldn't it be the most wonderful thing if you could eat next Xmas dinner with us or maybe be here long before that. I want to see you so very much."

Although the formal ceremony did not take place until September 2, the Japanese agreed to unconditional surrender August 14, 1945. Jack, his friends, and his family had varied reactions to the announcement of the ending of the war. Anna Shuler wrote on the day of surrender:

> *Today-is-the-day*—There's so little and yet so much to say—Nothing anyone could say could completely describe the greatness of this moment. The greatest in our short lives—you know, when you hear on the radio of all the rejoicing going on everywhere, it makes you feel good—I have no desire to join in with the 'whooping and hollowings' so to speak I only feel a greatness inside and sadness too—It's unbelievable—War, war, war has been as familiar a word in our everyday conversation as "Hi kid"—To become a peaceful nation and world overnight seems too good to be true—It's something we've prayed for four years and now, that it's here—well it's like the surprise of Dec. 7, '41. The radio is blasting forth

> with the good tidings from everywhere. If you were here, it would be perfect. I suppose that the relief you have seen on the faces of our boys with you has been wonderful.
>
> We went up to Camden for a few minutes. The town is wild, I've never seen anything like it in my life. The streets were crowded, horns blowing—everybody screaming "Peace, the war's over." A grand ole country. We didn't stay very long. Most of us had already seen the show. Besides you couldn't get anywhere near it. For some reason I wanted to get back home. I must have seemed crazy—not joining in the fun but my mind kept wandering over miles of ocean to a little island in the Pacific. I don't know why. I hardly know the place. In fact, I never had heard of it 'til several months ago. Now, it seems terribly important to thousands of people everywhere—what have you been doing tonight? Tell me about the effects the surrender had on the men around you. Today will be great in history. You've helped to make it and I've lived through all of it. In fact, I grew up during this last 4 years. The war has had its effect on all of us. It's been an education in itself. . . . This has been a most exciting day. Everyone is a little crazy including me.

The following day, Jack wrote his family: "It's twelve o'clock midnight and I [am] on guard, and the war is over. It always seems funny when something as big and important that you have been anticipating for so long finally happens you find that you are amazed that you don't behave as you had imagined you would under these circumstances. It is only a very sober feeling and very baffling. Suddenly everything is different you know, but still life is just going on in the same way. You find that you are more concerned with what you are having for breakfast or when are you going to get a little time to do nothing or more trivial matters than you are about the war and the world in general, although it controls your whole life and future. You secretly discover that you [are] not as ready to go back into civilian life as you had believed yourself to be and see that's it's more than just stepping in the harness."

He continued to wax eloquently about the futility and wastefulness of war and conjectured when he might be able to come home. He concluded, "Well kids let's drink a toast of Pop-Kola to a very, very bright future that's sure to come." The envelope was stamped "Passed by Naval Censor." In his memoir notes Jack noted that he "blew trumpet" in celebration. He also recalled that was the occasion when he took his first alcoholic drink—"grapefruit juice and 'sick bay' alcohol," the only choice at hand.

Lucy learned the news while visiting her high school friend and cousin Jackie Halsall in Florida. In an undated letter, she described the reaction there: "We were at the beach when victory was announced. Every body blew horns all night and got drunk. I've never seen so many drunk people in all my life. All the women & every body. And Gobs of Gobs [sailors]. There is a naval base there at Jacksonville. They weren't doing much at the beach but making lot of noise. But they said it was terrible in Jacksonville. Fighting and every thing. Every body there was drunk too."

The August 17 *Camden Chronicle* described frenzied celebration in Jack's hometown the night of August 14. When Mayor Francis McCorkle received the news at 7:00, he left his house for town and activated the siren at 7:10. In less than a half hour the business district had become "a seething mass of cheering people. Hundreds of cars roared back and forth, all loaded with cheering passengers and with horns wide open. The din was terrific." On August 15 Mayor McCorkle's son, Private First Class Mac McCorkle, wrote Jack from France, "I'll congradulate you boys for the fine work you've done. Yes Sir, you really put the *quietus* on the Japs." Mac had seen action himself, having taken part in the battle for Munich, after which his 180th Regiment was among the first Allied troops to liberate Dachau with its infamous concentration camp. Mac's unit, the Forty-Fifth Division, had been delayed leaving for home and were anxious to depart Rheims.

On August 18, back from vacation, Mae wrote of the war's end, first describing the suspense of waiting to hear from Japan when Allies sent terms of surrender. When President Truman announced their acceptance, "Americans just went wild. Every town celebrated in a big way. There were all kinds of celebrations that you could imagine. The Baptist Church had a special service just one hour after victory was declared at seven oclock E.W.T. Tuesday afternoon and the church was full and nearly all of the Sunday School room. We went down to that Service. There was so much noise on the street that we could hardly hear Mr. Caston. Next day all day was a holiday in Camden. . . . Oh! It is just wonderful that the war is over and you can come home. How I wish that you were coming soon." There were immediate impacts: "Gas rationing and the rationing of canned fruits & canned veg. and fuel oil was taken off the day after victory was announced. It sure seems funny to buy gas and not have to give a stamp. I am sure no other nation except America could do that the day after peace was declared." Looking ahead, Mae wrote, "I do so want you to get to go back to school now."

In letters home after the surrender, Jack addressed old topics rather than reflecting on recent ordeals. On August 22 he told Lucy to be on the lookout for the skirt, and he told Oscar not to worry about sending him a pistol, but to "lookout for a Jap rifle and bayonet (separate packages) that I have mailed to you. The rifle will need a little cleaning but is in perfect shape and working order. It is a .31 caliber sniper rifle, and will be a swell souveneir and look good in our gun rack, besides I hear that ammo will be available in the states so we can shoot it. . . . It was used by a Jap soldier in this campaign as you can tell from the stock etc. The bayonet is in perfect condition."

When Jack told his family about some work he was doing for "the captain" that allowed him to avoid "a lot of heavy work," he referred to artwork, as verbal comments and a memoir scrap confirm. Jack as usual had been entertaining buddies with cartooning when "one piece of satire on an unpopular colonel fell into the hands of a captain who hated him. The capt. considered the colonel a dud. Highly pleased, he 'appropriated' me as company artist to make unofficial combat zone sketches which was easier and more creative than shooting Japs."

In one of the few times he explained his regular job, Jack commented, "This is the service and supply Co. so we handle gear for the whole division. It is hard work but a good outfit to be in." The captain who was complimentary of his artwork had "sent in" some of it for publication. The captain was also trying to get some of the cartoons in the army magazine *Yank* "to be printed on this island." Jack was hoping for a chance to transfer into public relations, which had been impossible during the campaign.

Although before the surrender Jack had been told he was to be sent to Japanese-controlled China, "heavy scuttlebutt" kept them in suspense. "If we don't go home," he said, "I hope it will be Japan or China." On August 25 Jack sent home $360 for deposit, saying he needed no money there. Mostly he met his needs by bartering his pictures, and sometimes he was paid for them. He enclosed a photo clipping for Lucy that "shows them dropping the parachutes—the kind I made your skirt from." He had sent the garment by air mail so she could get it before she returned to school.

Steve Kelly wrote to Jack on August 28 that he had left Okinawa, saying, "I still have the same old trouble I can't say where I am at but it is in the Marianas. When you write send it to my old address. They wont let me put the address of the hospital." The same day Mae expressed the reality of all wars: "Oh I am so glad it is over so far as the fighting goes but it will be oh so long before the other part is over. There are so many homes that have vacant places and others with their service men coming back sick, wounded and maimed. My heart just goes out to them and it always reminds me how thankful I am that I still have my son and he is well & whole."

On a much lighter note, Mae provided the conclusion of *another* lengthy campaign: "The skirt that you made for her [Lucy] came Monday and it is beautiful. My you are the clever one to make a thing like that. She was tickled to death over it." In an undated letter, Lucy wrote, "I got the skirt yesterday and I love it. It is the prettiest thing I've ever seen. Thanks a million for it. I'll have some pictures made in it and send you. I'm taking the pieces of cloth you had it wrapped in and am making me a top piece to wear with it." On September 11 Jack's California friend Jessie Medrano wrote him, "I want to thank you for the beautiful skirt, I'm really crazy about it. I've never seen one like it. It must of taken you a long time to make, and a lot of work I bet?" With fabrics scarce, the fine silk of parachutes, when it could be obtained, was much desired for clothing construction.

Mae wrote of another sewing project for Lucy the same day Jessie wrote. "We made a real pretty white linen suit out of Daddy's old white linen suit today. He gave it to her for it was worn on the collar & sleeves so bad he could not wear it any more." Lucy returned to Winthrop on September 10. Anna Shuler too was leaving for college. She expressed great excitement in an illegibly dated letter. Her brother had returned from overseas, and she was preparing to enter her freshman year at Columbia College. She was anxious to know when Jack would get home. "Please write me often now," she said. "Mail will be one of the most important things at school. I *will* find time to write you as often as possible. It's been a year since I've even seen you. That's an awfully long time."

Mae sent Jack various reports. On September 3 she updated Jack's savings at $601.75 and reported Alfred would enter his senior year in high school the next day. On September 5 she said Alvin Creed had left for the Pacific. Five days later she reported that Bobby Smyrl was disappointed to have been rejected for service because of a punctured ear drum. Freddie had been sent to Georgia and looked "grown up." Dennis Coffey was on Okinawa, and Bill Burns was in the Pacific: "His letters [home] come in bunches, and some times it is weeks between them."

On September 5 Bill Burns wrote Jack, "We're due in Okinawa in the morning and I'm going to try to locate you. . . . We were in Tokyo Bay for the big day Sunday. I'd rather have been home." On Sunday, September 2, General Douglas MacArthur had accepted the surrender of the Japanese aboard the battleship *USS Missouri* in Tokyo Bay. Bill concluded: "Smyrl, are you going back to Auburn? Just what are your plans? Don't forget you've got to count me in on them. Also, we've got to finish seeing the world. You would have loved France—the place of artists galore also some fine musicians."

"It was one year ago today that we saw you last," Mae reminisced on September 14. (Her memory of the exact date would differ from Jack's.) "A lot of things have happened since then haven't they." She continued local reports. The Rush family had not yet heard from Alva Jr., but Robert McDowell was near Pearl Harbor, Joe Jenkins somewhere down below the equator, and William Watkins in India. Jack wrote the same day that they should expect a big box and a sea bag. He was sending a pair of army boots for Oscar and a pair of Marine boots for himself: "We can use them for hunting etc." Steve Kelly had been evacuated to the Marianas because of his stomach. "He may very soon be on the way to the States," Jack said. "You know John Henry McDowell was discharged for this reason." He reminisced that "tomorrow Sept. 15 is the day we parted a year ago in Yemassee—I shall never forget it—and then as never before I realized how much you meant to me."

Jack began to gripe that the Marines were like the "foreign legion" and got no breaks compared to army and navy personnel. He continued with ire over disparity between enlisted men and officers, and added "if the censorship were still on I would not be able to express myself this way." Clearly he was enjoying the exercise of free speech. Also everything was not bleak. They had a good cook and good food and were in a nice spot: "We're right at a cold mountain stream, plenty good water, P.X. handy, and P.O. right down the hill, and the weather is beautiful, the people are friendly, Mail-call every day etc." Of his duties in the quartermaster unit he said, "The work is heavy and the hours are long, I get up at 5 o'clock now for work—you see with the Division moving we handle all the gear and this is a gigantic job. Other outfits have rest camps, but this part of it has a work camp." He observed how time "flies by. It hardly seems possible that we have been on this Rock for 6 months." He had forty-five points in the point system that determined men with eighty-five points got to return "stateside."

On Alfred's seventeenth birthday, September 16, Mae wrote with news from kin and friends. They had just received Jack's first letter "that did not have a censors stamp on it." Referring to another shortage, Mae mentioned, "The prints of the last negatives you sent are not ready yet. Materials for making pictures have been a little scarce and sometimes it takes longer to get what you want done." The same day Anna Shuler expressed her exuberance: "College life is great! I'm crazy about 'C.C.' & the wonderful people." She had written Jack four times since she arrived there but had heard nothing from him. A day later Dennis Coffey, on Okinawa near Ichelou, having just learned that Jack was on the island, wrote, "Jack I wish I had time to look you up. But I will be going down to the harbor in about an hour to board the L.S.T. for Japan. Our Division left a couple weeks ago, and I was put in the rear echelon."

On September 21 Jack had "a little temperature, and a little headache . . . because of a little shot in the arm that we got the other day and it swoll up on me." He was "very busy getting ready" for the impending move. "A lot of the boys are leaving tonight, and I expect to leave in a few days. I know the ship I will be on, etc. and very excited about going." Where was not stated.

The same date Mae wrote that they finally received the scrapbook and were enjoying it but were "sure we can get a lot more out of it when you are here to tell us more about it." Marion Davis was back in the states and would be home in a few days. Mae concluded, "We are mailing you two boxes tomorrow and this is what is in them. A1 sauce, Worchestershire sauce, Anchovie paste olives, pecans, and 2 cans of Fried Chicken." September 22 Lucy wrote from Winthrop, describing classes, professors, and work load, as well as records she had purchased. She commented on end-of-war changes with electricity again available: "We have light privileges this year & we really take advantage of it. We stay up till all hours. Gotta stop that too."

Mae continued to tune in news that could tell her about Jack. On September 26 she wrote, "Wednesday morning over the radio we heard the broadcast from Okinawa and it said that two Marines Div. were leaving there that morning for China and would reach China by Sunday. It also said those men would only stay there until the Chinese could take over. We wondered if that was your outfit they were talking about." On September 28 she reported of others: "Heard today that Bert Rush would be home in Oct. . . . Saw Laurie today and she said they went up to Fort Bragg yesterday and brought Jessell back to Camden. I have not seen her but they say she looks grand. She is wearing her over seas bar with 1 battle star on her sleeve and 8 hash marks."

Mae was puzzled by some mail, the importance of which she could not determine. "Got a letter from Marine headquarters today from Brig. General Robert L. Denig 'Director of Public Information,'" she said. She made a copy of it for Jack, reading, "Dear Mrs Smyrl, Under separate cover we are mailing to you a folder containing sketches by Cpl O. J. Smyrl. These sketches have served their purpose in this office. We wish to thank Cpl. Smyrl for sending in this work." On September 30 she reported, "The sketches you sent to Washington came to us yesterday. They were grand and we enjoyed them so much. Of course we show them to all the family and friends. You are sure good and we want you to have your chance." She added that Jessell Campbell had come to see her and looked well. "She wanted to know all about you and raved over your sketches," Mae said. "She is the same old Jessell." Mae also reported that Ola had a letter from Steve, still on Guam and "waiting for a chance to come home. He is still sick, but not as bad as when you last saw him. Still cant keep very much food on his stomach." On October 2 in response to Jack's plight of having only forty-five points, Mae quipped, "My you are like Jolly Pitts. He said he had so few points to get him out that he was looking around for a widow with three or four kids. Seems to me he would be *in for life* then."

On October 8 Lucy wrote about social life at Winthrop, especially dances. "Freddie Mullen, Jimmie Gandy & Rock Gandy were up here this afternoon," she said. "I saw them down at the Blue Mirror. Freddie has a discharge. They asked about you." The previous day Mae had mused, "Little did you dream when you were in Camden High that by this time you would be a seasoned globe trotter. I am sure this traveling around will mean much to you in the years to come." Jack had already departed Okinawa for his next—and more exotic—assignment.

Chapter 16

China

"I am here and like it"

Jack began a letter aboard a ship anchored in a convoy fifteen to twenty miles off the coast of China in the Yellow Sea, the northern portion of the East China Sea between China and the Korean Peninsula. It was October 2, 1945, and he had received no mail for a week or two, nor had he had time to write much. He remained aboard ship four days before it was unloaded. As he wrote home, he was experiencing the first cold weather he had known since those cold California nights the past December.

The cargo-attack ship was "the best one I've ever been on," he said. "There are only about 150 of us and it's not crowded as the troop ships. . . . It is clean, the food is like a hotel. We sit down to eat on this one, and there's not too much work—a movie on deck every night, and everything is swell. The ship's store is open to us and you can get ice-cream, state-side candy, etc. I got a short hair-cut in the barber-shop this morning. These ships are each a little city in itself." There were more advantages: "It's a lot different traveling in peace-time with no darkened ship, etc. They are still cautious of these waters which were mined of course, and no more of this zig-zagging to avoid submarines. You take a straight course which knocks days off the journey, but now that we're on a good ship like this we don't want to leave it (Even have Heinz 57 sauce on the tables)."

Jack had nearly missed going to China. Beginning with mild discomfort, he experienced a recurrence of malaria, which he had suffered on Okinawa when reports of combat ailments were censored. Jack knew if

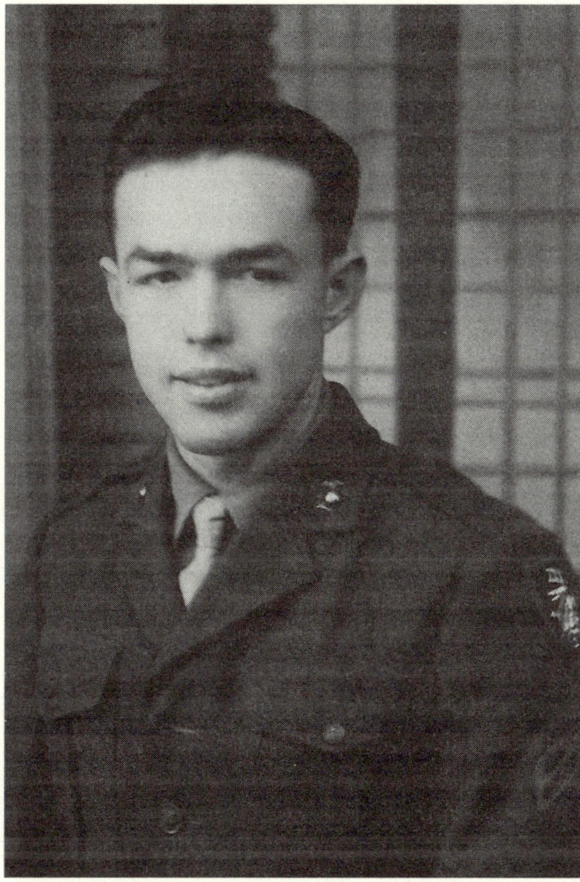

Jack in Tientsin, China, in autumn 1945. Courtesy of the family.

malarial symptoms were detected before or at time of departure, his orders would be changed and he would be detained for treatment, not sent to China. Marine buddy Paul Miller administered quinine he had received from home and covered Jack in blankets "to stave off chills." With Paul's help, Jack boarded ship without report or evidence of illness until the ship was underway to China. Although not physically fit, Jack enjoyed high spirits anticipating exotic adventure. The less stressful and much improved conditions aboard ship—good food, especially—were therapeutic. With temperatures cooling as their convoy approached China, Jack's health gradually improved. He felt more like himself.

When he wrote home on October 8, 1945, Jack colorfully revealed his whereabouts: "Today I was walking down the street and run into a chinaman, soon there were more of them. Evidently I am in China I sez to myself. Well kids, old Smyrl has hit a liberty port again. . . . At present we are working like dogs, living like pigs, eating like a cat, but hoping this won't last long. You see everything is well-fouled-up, we have no liberty uniforms, very little water, and have been eating C-rations for four days since we got in. And tonight was the first time I've washed in 4 days, and if I said what I think of the officers somebody might read this and lock me up."

He described the city of Tientsin (later Tianjin): "It is terrific, and I like it very much for many reasons. I have been on liberty once legally and illegally a few times to get something to eat. It is a very large city and it would be hard to find a more interesting place. It is a hodge-podge of rickshaws, Fords, large modern bldgs., street peddlers, carts with horses, (look like a mixture of horses & donkeys) and a million other things [memoir notes add "wood-burning trucks"], but the oddest feature of all are the Europeans who are living in this oriental city. The city has a Russian Concession, French, etc. . . . All this gives the city a strange flavor and is very cosmopolitan. . . . I wanted you to know I am here and like it."

An official U.S. Marine account, *The United States Marines in North China, 1945–1949* by Henry I. Shaw, Jr., described the "tumultuous welcome" the Chinese gave the first elements entering Tientsin, its streets "packed with Chinese of all classes and European expatriates." Shaw continued, "Trucks and marching troops literally had to force their way through the happy, flag-waving throngs to reach their assigned billets in the former International Concessions." Jack reported, "We received terrific welcome by the Chinese people and at present are still a novelty." His memoir notes recall "the fantastic 'reception' on entering Tientsin," the "accolades of the crowds," and "our 'hero' status."

According to Shaw, the mission of the Marines was "to disarm Japanese forces and to ensure an orderly environment for return of the Nationalist Government" and, on behalf of the Chinese Central Government, to accept the surrender of Japanese forces and billet them until repatriated. The two-decades-old conflict between the governing Chinese Nationalist Party and the Chinese Communist Party challenged the mission. Initially, tenuous cooperation existed between the Americans and the Communists, but in the first month of American presence, the Communists began to disrupt Tientsin's rail lines and to snipe at Marine units guarding trains.

Although mail exchange between China and home would be delayed, both Jack and his family continued writing. On October 10 Oscar wrote

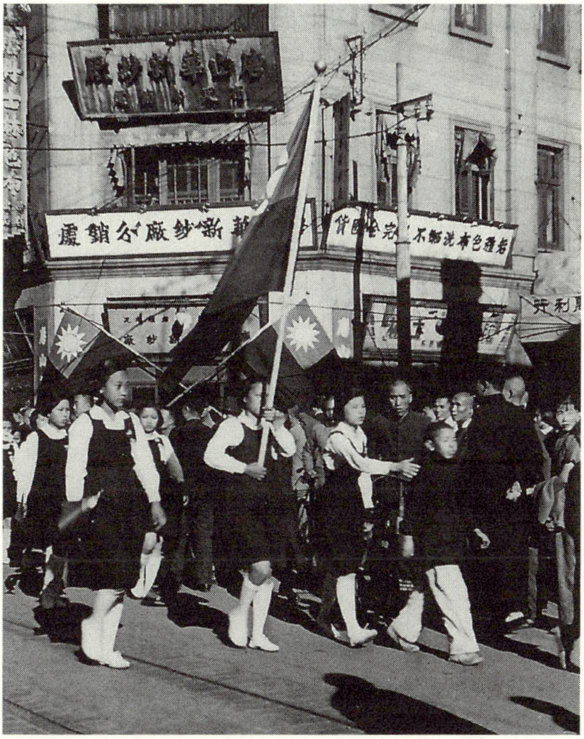

Jack's photograph of schoolgirls in a parade, Tientsin, China, 1945. Courtesy of the family.

that the sea bags sent from Okinawa had not yet arrived, but he had received the rifle "in perfect shape and I am going to clean it up and put it in the gun case with our other guns." Near their home Oscar had fixed up their tenant house, where guests were housed when Jack was in training, and was renting it to a man just out of the army who was working at the bottling plant, "a good helper so far."

When Jack wrote a detailed, six-page letter home on October 12, the only mail he had received yet was "from the church . . . a bulletin from the Marine Corps press, and 2 Camden Chronicles (dated May 4 and June 29)." He reported himself "really enjoying China" and things "better every day" since the mess hall had been squared away and showers fixed. There were movies at night, "old ones of course" since there had been no new ones there for eight years. Ironically, Jack continued, he found it easy to get some items presently not readily available at home: "cameras, film (plenty of it so don't send any more), radios, jewelry and silver-ware, to say nothing of the beautiful silk goods." He remarked, "It is a strange city, but we have been made so welcome that you can't help but like it . . . the next best thing to Stateside duty."

Although older servicemen and "70 point men" were leaving soon, Jack expected to remain three to six months, maybe longer: "it will be a Chinese Christmas for me this year." Prices were low compared to the States, but "high for China" with prices "jacked up to grab the 'Yankee Dollar.'" With an exchange rate of 1,800 to 1, "when you change your money into Chinese money you've got quite a wad." An ice cream sundae costing $200 Chinese was eight cents American. "If you've got $9000 in your pocket you've only got $5.00 in American money," Jack pointed out, "but 5 bucks will go a long way in China."

"The Rick-shaw runners are in their glory now," he continued, "and making more than they ever have before and want $100 to $200 at least for a ride depending on what you argue the price to. In China nothing has a definite price and everything is put up for a very high price, and it's up to you to argue them down (this is expected, and the Chinese way of doing business). Many times I see street peddlers demanding $10 (American) for a watch and settling for around $3.00 (American). Cameras and such are the same way." Jack summarized, "It's a strange country but very likeable and I'm getting used to it." Communication was not difficult, for "English is widely spoken, and finding someone who speaks English is easy."

The conquered Japanese were under control. "Jap soldiers . . . have been dis-armed and are now working for us," Jack stated. "There is a small detachment who come here each day . . . as laborers (they still wear the Jap Uniform). They are very submissive and the Chinese people get a bang out of seeing them work. There has been little friction as they of course can't afford to be cocky now." Jack related one exception when he was on guard. One of the Japanese left his work detail and tried to exit by an alley. He ignored the yells and motions of the Marine in charge by continuing to walk: "I was at the other end of the alley-way and barked at him and motioned for him to turn around and go back, but still he ignored me, until I jerked my rifle off my shoulder and threw it on him. This changed his mind fast and he made a hasty retreat."

From home Mae wrote of friends and relatives in service being released or reassigned and poignantly worried about Jack's whereabouts. On October 15 she reported Mac Anderson discharged and Richard Denny returned; Alvin Creed in Manila, but Otis still in Laurinburg and possibly not going overseas; Freddie Ogburn in Florida, and Gary in California; Robert McDowell on an island about fifteen miles from Pearl Harbor; and

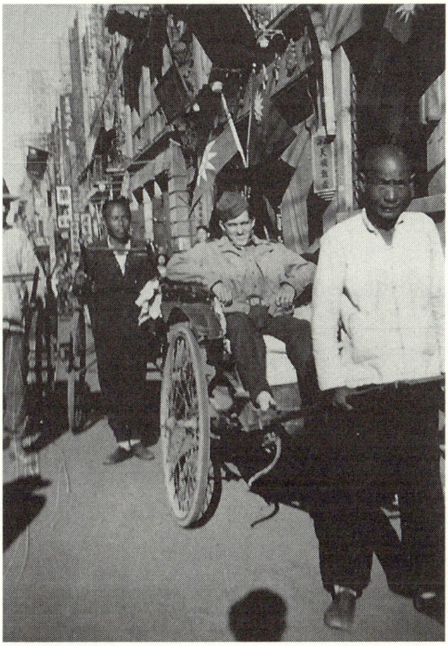

B. O. Smith in rickshaw, Tientsin, China, 1946, labeled by Jack. Courtesy of the family.

Dorothy Watts's husband, Dennis Coffey, gone to Japan. Mae mused, "Just think how you boys are stationed all over the world." In a second letter mailed the same day, she had been unable to get news of Jack's division on radio or in newspapers: "I don't know where you are (except that you were going to China) or any thing. Gives me such a funny feeling, like you have walked through a door and closed it behind you and I cant get it open or hear a sound."

Writing on October 18, Jack described unsettled conditions: "Everything has not been all quiet lately. The Chinese civilians have attacked the Japanese and the other day was a riotous one. The local police and detachments of Marines had to take over the town to get things under control. The Japs I saw were pretty badly beaten. They are being sent away now. No Marines have been hurt, but a Japanese in civilian clothes pulled a .25 pistol to shoot a Marine in the back, and the Chinese grabbed him. The gun went off and hit a woman in the leg."

He gave a lengthy description of an incident earlier that day demonstrating desperation and volatility. A small warehouse next to the Marines' billets contained "a large quantity of dried fish in long slabs" left by the Japanese. Civilian authorities had opened the warehouse to get rid of the fish. Starving people began "charging in and out of the gate with bundles of the fish." The authorities closed the gates, but an uncontrollable mob "started over the fences . . . and like a drove of cattle they broke through and were running over each other to get the fish." Reinforcements arrived to control the throng, "but 3 times they broke through and the street was Jammed with thousands of them. . . . When they came through the gate women, children, old men and young some fell and were trampled and covered up by the ones in back. (I was watching it all morning from my window and looked like a stampede)."

Marines "finally managed to clear everybody out, but up until late tonight we have been keeping them off the walls etc. to prevent mobbing. I was on guard 12 to 4 and was passing through the alley in back. Some of them inside were tossing the bundles of fish down over the wall to their friends, but they were like a bunch of dogs and the desperate mob would be on them and tear the fish from each other. It is pitiful indeed to see these dirty hungry people fighting over stinking dirty fish that we wouldn't even want to touch."

In contrast Jack stated: "There is [as] much wealth and well-to-do people as anywhere and the man with money can have anything—steaks, jewelry and such things are plentiful but the majority of the people are poor. All of the white people living here are well-dressed and doing all right for themselves. There is a heavy Jewish element that is obvious and they are here for business reasons of course, as the cost of living in China is ridiculously low to them."

He reassured his family about his own situation: "As for the set-up here for us, you couldn't ask for better duty, and the only thing you can really complain about is that you're not home. We have room-boys now who clean up for us, shine shoes, take care of your laundry, etc. The movies is right here in the bldg., the mess-halls are up and the food is good, very little work, and at present we get 50% liberty which means every other day. We haven't been paid yet but I haven't been short of money, and pay-day is in a day or so. Everything is really going fine." He was encouraged that mail was beginning to reach him.

On October 19 Bill Burns wrote from Okinawa that his ship had transported "a bunch of 3rd Marines to Tin Sin [Tientsin], China and there was a bunch of 1st Marines on the PA's in our convoy. Did you happen to be on that deal?" The night after the Marines disembarked, both of Bill's clarinets disappeared. He asked Jack to be on the lookout for cases bearing his name. Turning to the subject of going home, Bill jested about the point system: "If I have to wait till I get out on points, I'll probably be in for the next war."

The Smyrl family finally received its first mail from China, a letter that later proved not the first written from there. Mae on October 21 acknowledged Jack's descriptions. In positive tones, she revealed serious news. She was doing well but had undergone an operation, a hysterectomy, which she had not previously mentioned so as not to worry Jack. Five days later, she wrote, "My goodness I can hardly realize you are so far away from us. You write such interesting letters and make China seem nearer." Steve Kelly had arrived back in the States: "He wired his folks when he got to Calif. and asked to be sent to the hospital at New River." Bill Clyburn was expected home soon. Harold Rogers was on Okinawa as was Dr. Whitaker, who "tried to find you, but not having your address it was like looking for a needle in a hay stack."

On October 24 Jack wrote that mail was at last reaching him: "These letters from home mean more to me than anything else and you haven't let me down." He expected to write more regularly since things were settling down. He thanked them for forwarding a card from a Parris Island friend: "She is a Lady Marine that I knew there and thought she had forgotten me. She was on furlough and dropped me a card. I wrote her a letter last night." He commented again on the fluctuating monetary system: "Today I paid $100 for a bag of peanuts, $180 for 3 fried eggs, and $2400 for a yard of silk."

Four days later Jack described cold weather. China was snowy during the winter, but snow had not come yet. "We will be issued some heavy clothing soon—overcoats and stuff," he said. There was speculation that they would "be out of China by January if the disarming of the Japanese was complete but still a lot of things can happen between now and then." He planned to spend his time there "concentrating on enjoying China as much as I can."

Jack and artist friend Hugo Schroeder planned "to rent a room near the barracks here and set up a little studio where we can take our drawing stuff and leave it and go there in our spare time." Since barracks had to be kept tidy for inspections, they had no space for such projects there. "A Chinese friend," who ran a drugstore and lived across the street, was going to help them find a place: "Last night . . . he had me in for a little tea and talk. Has wife and 3 kids, speaks excellent English, educated in Peking, and wears European clothes. I have liberty tomorrow so he is taking me to a Chinese restaurant. This will be some experience. You see the places we inhabit serve American dishes, and I want to try out a place that is strictly Chinese—even to the chopsticks." Jack needed his family to send "canned stuff and films when you can get it. There was a lot of film when we came but it has been exhausted. I can buy anything here that you can get in any big city, but you never know if you're getting a bargain."

Lucy wrote on October 28 from Winthrop that she had been home the previous weekend: "Went to church Sun. and you should see all the boys home with discharges. It looked so funny to see them there in civilian clothes. Looked good too, just wish you were there." Cousin Edna Davis wrote October 30 from Greenville, North Carolina, at East Carolina Teachers College, where there were "about 800 girls and about 60 boys—'*Man shortage.*' Lots of fun here. A dance almost every Sat. night with lots of service men." Her brother Marion had a discharge, and brother James was at home.

On October 31 Jack's Auburn roommate Second Lieutenant Stanley Jenkins wrote from Gowen Field in Boise, Idaho. Since the Japanese surrender had canceled his orders for Hawaii, he had been able to get leave to be with his wife during the birth of their second child. Stanley still aspired to write music. He reminisced about times at Auburn when he and Jack had tried their hands at composing. Stanley had lately written and copyrighted, but not published, a song that had the same "break" that he and Jack used in a song they wrote together at Auburn: "You're #1 on my list of royalty sharers *if* anything should come of the song. I'll send you a copy of it soon—'Night Summer Sky.'"

Three weeks after Jack's first letter inside China had been written, Mae on October 31 acknowledged, "We just received your letter of the 8th of Oct. yesterday. Of course we got the maps down right away and looked it up. We thought you might be in Manchuria but we see you are in China proper. . . . You must be doing alright with someone to do your laundry, cleaning up and everything." Mae had come home from a two-week hospital stay only two days earlier and felt grateful to Oscar: "I still have to stay right in bed and Dr. West says I can't get up until next Saturday or Sunday," she said. "Daddy is taking real good care of me of course and seeing that the Drs. orders are obeyed to the letter." From Jack the family had received a box with a broken lock that "had been nailed up again. It had clothes in it, a pr. of field glasses, a compass, a box of drawing things and a pkg. of pictures. . . . Here are the things that have come so far. The scrap book, the bayonet, the rifle and this box last night."

Mae continued, "We are missing you more and more the longer you are gone. Some time my arms just ache to give you a good hug and I close my eyes and can see you smiling as the train pulled out of Yemassee. Are you brown and yellow like most of the boys I have seen back from the Pacific. It was the sun and medicine that did it they tell me. I think Alvin Christmas is the yellowest one I have seen." Mae described Joan trying to get her out of bed: "'Get up Gan-Mommie, Get up Gan-Mommie.' She is not used to seeing me in bed. She . . . is so crazy about your Daddy and me. She comes to the bed and hugs and hugs me around the neck. She is crazy about Alfred and calls him 'Al-poo' and calls Lucy, 'Lu Lu.' She can talk right good now and looks at your picture on the dresser and calls you 'Unka Jack.'"

On November 4 Mae wrote that Steve Kelly came "right over to see me the first day he got here. I think that was sweet of him. He talked a lot about you and told me what a fine fellow you were and how the other boys liked you. As he talked it seemed like you were nearer to us. He looked over your scrap book and explained a lot of it to us." Steve told Mae to ask Jack what he had done with "the mirrow [mirror]." In a 2000 interview, Steve was still laughing about an image he kept in his mind of Jack on Okinawa: each time they moved from place to place, Jack carried along with him, strapped on his back, a large, unbroken mirror with an intricately carved frame. Jack had found it miraculously unbroken in a combat-wrecked area and considered the antiquity so beautiful that he could not leave it behind. Mae said Steve was "still sick and is not out of service." He expected to return to the hospital after a thirty-day leave: "He looks pretty good and has gained a lot, but he has to live almost entirely on milk. He did not know where you were and when I showed him your picture taken in the rick shaw he laughed and said just look at 'Mr. Smyrl.'"

Mae commented, "We hear about a lot of unrest among the Chinese up in that part of the country. I wish those people would stop squabbling." Mae reported that Frank Campbell was being sent to Memphis and maybe overseas. She reported the death of a neighbor, Harry Porter. "His mother has moved back to town and is selling their place up here," she said. The Porter farm was about one-fourth mile south of Oscar and Mae.

Jack wrote on November 11 "from my private room across the street from the barracks." He had begun to receive packages from home. "The Cheer-up is the best thing I've gotten yet," he said. "You see there is some bottled drinks here, but no good, and not safe to drink." He said of China: "There are many disagreeable things, such as unsanitary conditions, lot of poverty, etc., but it also goes to both extremes. It is so unlike any place I have ever been." Despite the "thrill being here," he said. "It can't be too soon for me to see you again." He had been away over a year, but some of his fellows had been in Pacific service thirty months or more. He regretted not having been sent overseas sooner: "Maybe I would have gotten to see Australia." He enclosed for Alfred's collection some Japanese stamps used when China was under Japanese control. When he finished writing the letter, he was going to a movie. "You see we live in a large school bldg. and the Auditorium is for ball-games the movies and such."

Jack wrote that he expected the drawing table he had commissioned for his studio across the street to be ready the next day. He commented, "The family there is very nice. The name is 'Ho.' He runs a . . . drug store (very nice). His brother is the pharmacist. He was educated at Peking University. . . . His wife speaks English roughly. She was a nurse in an American Hospital for 8 yrs. and is a Christian. They have 3 children. . . . The other members of the household are two sisters of hers (very pretty) and an elderly lady who is the cook. All in all, it is an interesting set-up." Thus far, however, Jack said he had not had much time to spend there, "only a few hours every other day. The rent is $6.00 a month, which is split between Schroeder and myself, making $3.00 apiece for a month."

In his letters, Jack referred to "renting" the studio, but in references later in his life, he said they "bought" a house, possibly rough-English idiom for rental. His memoir notes refer to "the house my friend and I bought for $25." His notes also state that they "established a studio staffed with servants." Jack's letter described laborers: "A lot of the Jap soldiers are still kept here and are working as prisoners of war, and still in uniform. There is a detachment that works here in the yard. We also have Chinese coolies hired to work for us, so you can see the Marines have a pretty good racket here in China."

Oscar also wrote a letter that same day of November 11, Armistice Day, marking the day firing ceased in World War I. He mused that twenty-seven years ago on that day he was in the armed forces believing he was helping fight the last war ever and making "the world safe for democracy," never thinking he would have a son involved in another world war. "We never know what experiences life will bring us, nor where it will take us," he said.

He updated information closer home. He was installing an ice cream and frosted malted milk machine "in the little liquor store that Schlosburg used to run" in the same building with the bottling plant. He had purchased ninety acres of land from Uncle Bob and Aunt Sallie McDowell and family adjoining the old Smyrl home place and in front of the Flint Hill church. Oscar soon expected to have Jack, Lucy, and Alfred "all in college at the same time and maybe in the same school." The next day Mae sent a clipping from the *State* that Jack's Camden High band director Colonel F. N. Wimberly had just returned from two years' service.

Nearly two weeks after his last letter, Jack wrote from Tientsin on November 24 following a five-day leave to Peiping (previously Peking, later Beijing). When he returned he had "a slight touch of Malaria fever that I picked up on Okinawa, but took a lot of atabrine and am now O.K. I am on liberty tonight and over at my room." How Jack had met the first "Chinese friend" in the Ho family from whom he and Schroeder acquired the space to set up their "studio" is unclear, but gradually the lives of the Marine artists and the family and neighbors had been growing more familiar and homelike. At one point of the letter he comments, "Right now I am drinking a little hot tea that the lady of the house brings in to me every night I am here." He described a young street urchin, "a little Chinese girl that lives where I work who was in rags and dirty as a pig when we came that since I have been here I have been taking care of her. First thing I did was buy her some clothes, shoes, sweater, underwear, socks, and few knick-knacks, then I took her to a bath house and washed her good including her head. Then I dressed her up and had the barber fix up her hair and then took her out to dinner. She is a poor kid and lives with an old man." A photograph he saved of her he labeled "Sho-Roong."

Jack described his liberty trip, which did much to deepen his interest in understanding Chinese culture. "Peiping is really Old China at it's best," he said. "You see Tientsin is more or less a modern city with up to date bldgs . . . but Peiping has all the grandeur of the old days of emperors with all its palaces, temples, and beautiful Chinese architecture. The city of Peiping . . . is really 3 cities in one. Each one surrounded by a high thick wall. There is the Forbidden city, the Tartar city and the Chinese city. I have never seen anything more exquisite and beautiful than the spots in Peiping." Jack bought and took a lot of pictures to put in a souvenir book. He continued, "There were 500 men on the train in the liberty party with me. We stayed at Hostel no. 4 which is the W.A.S.C. (war area service corps) which is the same thing to the Chinese as our U.S.O. The place was an ex-prince's Hangout. You could get lost in it till you learned it. It was beautiful with its hand-painted paneled ceilings and chandelier."

The servicemen had been taken by truck on tours to see temples and other tourist sites such as "the Winter palace, the Forbidden city, Coal hill,

Llama Temple, Temple of Heaven, etc." Jack said there was too much to attempt to describe, so he would tell them more on return home: "I thought the Summer Palace was the most beautiful of all, but that is taking in a lot. The Forbidden City is a small city in a city walled in and worth Millions of Dollars. It is where the emperors lived with their families and servants. No one else was ever allowed in and no foreigner ever saw the inside up until the Chinese National government was established. It contains all the old splendor and things that were kept there, and pieces of art works made in jade, gold etc. and furniture studded with pearls etc., golden exquisite fantastic clocks, and large golden Buddhas each one worth a small fortune."

The serious side of the American occupation in China he also described. "The closest I came to 'great wall of China' is at the Summer palace about 10 miles out of the city, you can see the ridge of mountains that it is on," he said. "That is where the Communists are and we are not allowed there." He continued, "This place is a powder keg now and we may get mixed in it yet as a few Marines have been fired on. During the time I was in Peiping some of the Communists derailed a train track and wrecked a train. We passed it on the way back. We are all hoping we won't be called on to get in this thing which seems to be none of our business anyway." He stated overall, "The Marine Corps is a helluva life but I have gotten a few benefits by it."

Mae wrote on November 29, slowly returning to normal from her surgery, but concerned because they had not heard from Jack in a month. Bill Burns was "in the yellow sea and not so far from you." He had recovered one of his lost instruments. Dickie Cox was on Guam, and Shot Cox was on a ship. On December 1 Mae reported, "Your letters of Nov. 11 came last night and we were thrilled to death to hear from you. We had not heard in a little over a month and we were afraid you might be sick or something." She provided a health report that Aunt Nannie Campbell had leukemia, and it was "only a matter of time with her." The following day Mae attended Sunday school and church for the first time since her surgery.

In a guarded manner Mae commented on Jack's letter about acquiring a house and meeting females: "Sure glad you can have an extra space to draw and work in. The Chinese family you were telling us about sounds interesting. Some Chinese girls are very pretty and I know it seemed nice to find a Christian lady in a strange place like that." About Jack's visit to Peiping, Mae wrote on December 11, "I had heard of the Forbidden city & it must have been thrilling to see it and all of the other things." About the little girl he aided, she commented, "You have always had a soft heart for anybody in need. It was mighty kind of you to take your money and use it to buy things for that little Chinese girl. Hope you always stay that kind and thoughtful of others. I am awfully proud of you in a million ways." At the same time, she cautioned, "Chinese customs are so different from ours, that maybe you had better consult your drugstore friend about what to do for this child and how to go about it. I would hate for her folks to misunderstand your good intentions. . . . Maybe I could send her something from America. What would you suggest?"

Regarding her surgery and the upcoming Christmas season, Mae commented, "We are not spending much this year, for my hospital Nurse's and Doctor's bill has amounted to over $600.00. . . . We had some hospital insurance and that paid about a third of the bill and that was a real help. We could not stand too many of those kind of set backs." On December 2 Jack acknowledged the money order they sent as a gift: "You couldn't have sent me anything better at the time. You see my trip to Peiping set me back a bit . . . so the money was more than welcome." He thanked her also for other mailings: "Mama I have gotten about three packages from you now since I have been here with the food in it which has really been good. Please keep sending the fried chicken and sauces as I am about out again. I have just got back from over at my place where I have been drawing some stuff." He did not mind "the staying much [since] I am having it good here now, it's the not being home for Christmas that hurts."

He continued, describing other types of local people he had become acquainted with: "I was out to a Chinese General's wife's house with a friend of mine who knew her. . . . She took Post graduate work at Oregon University . . . in '36. She's really a swell personality. Later we went over to another home that was the wife of another Chinese General, her brothers, and quite a family, having 3 children an aunt and some other lady relation." Jack described the other general's wife as "very young and beautiful." They "had a big time talking and Dancing." The general's wife had tried to teach Jack to waltz: "Then we had a swell Chinese dinner, when we left we had a[n] invitation to come back. . . . They're really swell people. The Generals are away mixed up in the Communist business. Never thought I'd be dancing with a General's wife but it's true." In Jack's memoir notes he referenced the Chinese "general's wife's affair" with his friend. These enigmatic persons of the postwar Chinese community Jack documented in photographs posed individually and in groups alone and with the Americans as casually and comfortably as friend and family groups at home.

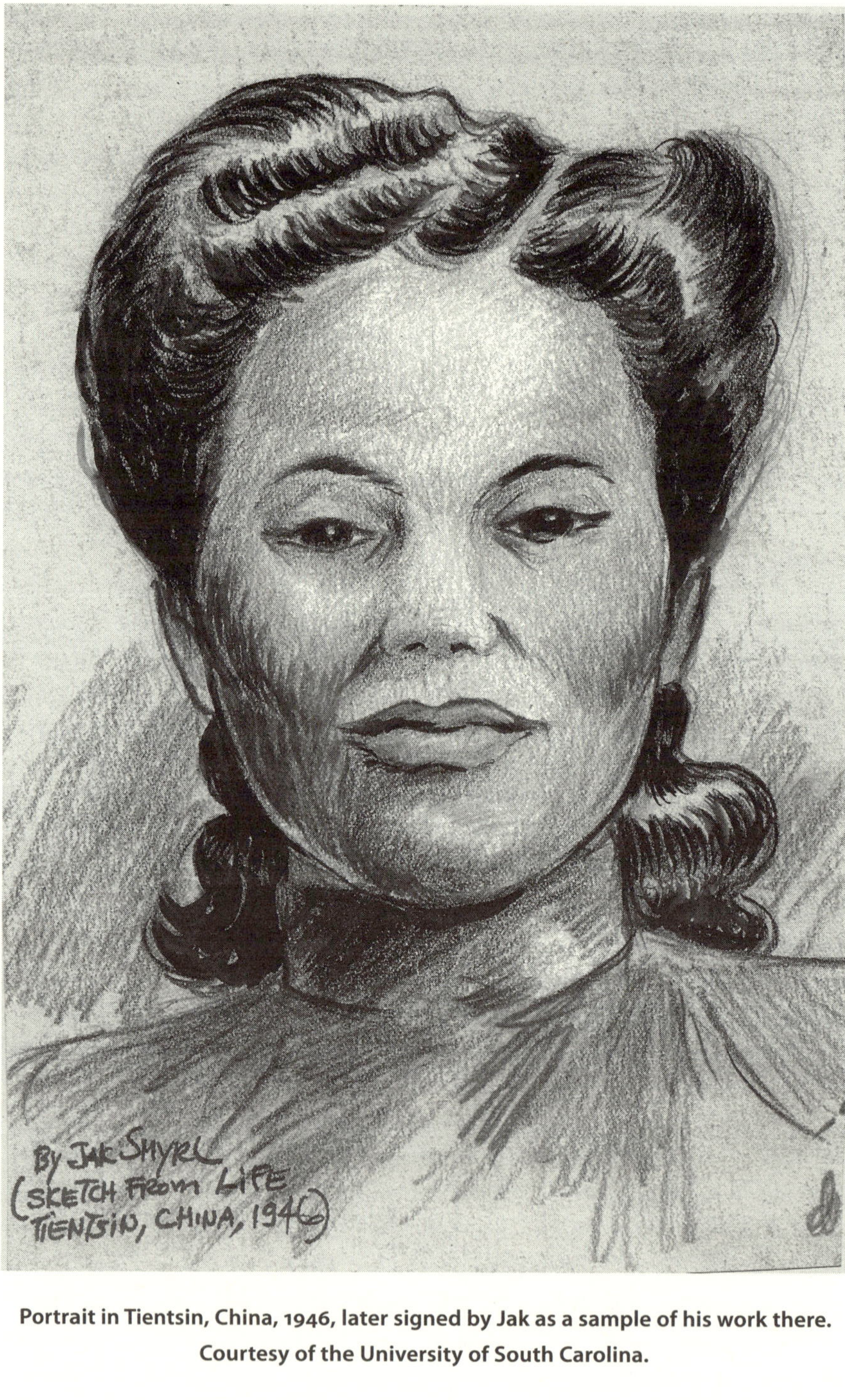

Portrait in Tientsin, China, 1946, later signed by Jak as a sample of his work there. Courtesy of the University of South Carolina.

Although China was not a wealthy country, Jack stated, "The houses where these people live are modern and up-to-date as the American homes. All the well-to-do people I know in China have servants." Jack described how cheap labor affected the servicemen: "We have coolies hired now that do all our work. This is one country where a common American G.I. is like a wealthy man and you can live like a king even though you're a Private. All I would need would be over-night liberty and I would live away from the barracks." He had "a swell job now for a change. All I have to do at present is take charge of the mail in our Company, and make a report down at the office every morning. Our Dump is about 8 blocks from here. After I finish there in the morning I usually catch a rick-shaw and come on back." He was fine and doing a lot of interesting things. He hoped to be out by next spring "so I can have a few months at home before I start back to school or anything."

On December 7 Jack wrote that fellow Marine Willie Gore, "from Clinton, N.C. and friend of Marion," and he had dates lined up "with a couple of Japanese women to have a little chow at the Tientsin Club today at 3:00." He described the club as "really a novelty . . . a modern place, but there they still wear the kimonos, sandals, etc. . . . You have to take off your shoes when you go in these little private rooms with the table about a foot off the deck and jap mats etc." This would be his first experience dating a Japanese woman, but "I know a little Japanese that I learned on Okinawa and I have a Jap-English book, so will be able to carry on a little conversation with the aid of a pencil and paper and a few pictures."

That Jack had learned those language bits in bitter combat with the Japanese only a few months earlier does not appear to have struck him as bizarre in that exotic land of contrasts shadowed with mixed motives and political intrigues. The Tientsin Club, he said, was "a very popular spot with the Americans, as well as the French soldiers, White Russians etc. who inhabit the place." While he seemed assimilating, perhaps naively, into a tenuous environment, he likewise remained grounded in art and communicated to his family about both influences.

Jack continued, "I met a Chinese artist yesterday whose work is on exhibition next week and Schroeder and myself are going down to see it. I was in his home before and met his sister. The one [who] studied in America and is the wife of the Chinese big-wigs whose job at present is sending the Japanese back to Japan." Jack discussed his own art as well. "At present I am painting a few Christmas cards for some people at $2.00 a card of scenes in Peiping (water colors) and week after next some of my stuff is coming out in the 'North China Marine.' Also I have been asked to contribute something for the Christmas issue, which I will start tonight. Sgt. James who is the artist for the Division in Public Relations and is a good friend of mine is slated to go home in a month and I may get transferred to there, having been recommended by Captain Diaz, but I am not as enthusiastic about the idea as I was before as I hope to be out of the Marines in a few months and now I have all my friends in this outfit and get to do all the drawing I want to anyway."

Jack alerted his family that he had mailed some items home for them—stamps for Alfred, a Japanese samurai sword for Oscar, "silk and stuff" for Mae, Lucy, and Lottie. He had a request for Mae. "The Chinese druggist that I rent our place from cannot get certain drugs now and has asked me if I could try to get the following for him if you can," he told her. "He wants it for his personal family use and will pay me whatever the cost is. I don't know if you can get it or not, but if you can please send it right away if you can in your next package. The enclosed slip is what he would like. I hope you can and it won't be too much trouble." Jack passed on the request seemingly without concern whether a darker motive lurked. At home his family had always helped those in need, so he was not skeptical of the Chinese people he thought were kindly to him.

On December 9 Jack reported a light snow, "enough to make things pretty." A local resident told him "the standard weather in china during the winter is three days cold and three hot, and seldom changes from that." Second-class mail had begun arriving, and he was receiving "the Camden Chronicle from as far back as August, just about four months late." Jack described the distribution of "captured Japanese stuff . . . the officers cleaned out most of the pistols and the best swords for themselves." By the time souvenir choices were offered the rest of them, "about the only thing left was bayonets and such which is not worth while anyway." He commented, "That's the way it always is the officers always get the gravy you know . . . not just with stuff like this but with the food, comforts, and everything else that's worth while." He added, "It's stuff like this make you want to get out where a man is not limited to the rank he holds." However, Jack acknowledged, his circumstances have been "just about as good as most any enlisted man could ask for" and "things have happened to me that never would have, and I am glad of the experiences."

Soon military discipline was being tightened. At present Jack was experiencing "a 3-day restriction for not folding my blanket right for a little inspection the other day." This was his second infraction of peacetime regulations. He also explained the first. He had brought to China a pair of "cut-down shoes" that he, like "everyone," wore in Okinawa. They were under his bunk to use for the showers. When the commanding officer saw them, "he blew-up, and so next month I will have $3.65 taken out of my pay to account for the shoes." Jack seemed irritated but ended the letter with light joking.

On December 13 Jack reflected on changes that had been taking place at home in his absence. He tried to visualize how Joan would look and Alfred too "because when I left for Auburn he was in grammar school." He was also amazed to think that "my kid sister Lucy is ahead of me in college as she is a sophomore, and I a lowly freshman. And Lottie is all grown up and married, and I am an uncle, and here I sit at 22 years old and haven't even started out in life it seems." When Mae wrote December 16, mentioning snow and a three-week span between Jack's writing and their receiving his letters, she also related another change: "Sure hate to tell you this but old Nell died night before last. . . . Mose helped Daddy bury her out by the Pine tree like you asked him to do." It would be December 31 before Jack received this word and responded with an expression of sorrow over the death of the beloved dog that he had grown up with and that meant "as much to me as a real person." He was comforted by thoughts of her burial at the tree that had figured in much of the real and imaginative life of his childhood: "It will be a memorial to the best dog that ever lived."

Jack's letter home of December 16 was reflective, contrasting American and Chinese "interpretations of how a life should be lived and one's philosophy of it." Especially "exasperating" at times was the Chinese tenet that "the time element is not necessarily of any significance," but he admitted, "Often when you think it over you see how right they often are, and wonder what's the object [of] getting nowhere fast anyway." He commented on the Chinese "seeming indifference to the man who is down and needs help." He wondered if the trait might be particular to the area where he was living "that has been under the iron hand of the Japs for 8 years." Yet he countered his feelings of empathy: "When I first came to China I was told by a Russian resident that if you are kind to the Chinese they will cheat you and I have learned the hard way that this is nearly always true and the best way to deal in business matters is to be very harsh or you will be taken for a ride every time. You must be just but firm." Jack's attitudes at age 22 are consistent with later ones. Interviews with

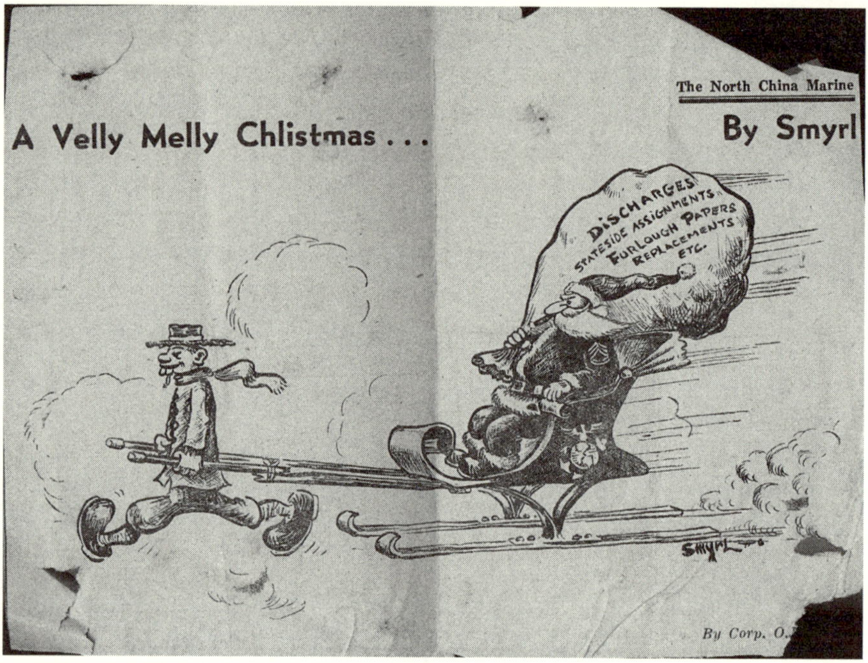

Cartoon by Smyrl in the *North China Marine,* December 1945. Courtesy of the University of South Carolina.

persons who knew him throughout life reveal examples of his lifelong humanitarian gestures, as well as his concerns in business dealings that others might be taking advantage of him.

Jack concluded that he liked China very much but was "beginning to think long thoughts of getting back at least for a while to see the people who are first in my heart and always will be—the ones I can go to no matter what I do, or whether I am bad or good. I am often bad, but the desire to please you and be at least a part of what you wish me to be often keeps me from slipping at times when other wise I am sure I would as that is my nature to try anything once and usually do and I always think how wrong I am and how right you are." He included his drawing of a Chinese Santa holding a sign that said, "A Merry Christmas and a Happy New Year."

Jack was serving as the duty NCO when he wrote home on December 23, sad to be away from his family. He was waiting until Christmas Day to open their package marked "gift" in order to "make it seem more like Christmas and I will seem closer home." He, Paul Miller, and several others were going to a party Christmas Eve at the home of some Chinese friends. He had other news: "It has been requested that I be transferred to the III'd amphibious Corps to work for the Marine newspaper here, and I expect to move there next week as I am quite sure the transfer will be effective." He felt a bit apprehensive but had been told that "it would not necessarily affect my going-home status. If this is true I believe it is going to be O.K. as I will be learning something at least and may get in a good outfit."

On Christmas Day Jack reported it was snowing. The party he had attended the night before was "really swell" and "just like any social party at home—Playing games and stuff." The Americans took "a load of Coca-colas, candy and stuff" with them. He reported a "funny thing" that happened there. All the houses in Tientsin were walled in because of rampant thievery. Nevertheless "somebody broke in and stole two of the Ladies coats," although a policeman recovered them before the thieves got out the gate. One of the coats belonged to Ellis, "a pretty young Chinese schoolteacher" with whom Jack made a date for the following Sunday.

In response to Jack's request for medicine for his Chinese friend, Mae wrote on Christmas Day, "Will try and get the medicine your friend asked for this week and mail it to you. I don't know whether I can get it or not but will try real hard." About his dating Japanese girls, she commented, "Well, anyway just so you remember you are an American, Christian, gentleman always you are ok. I am proud of you, have utmost faith in you and know that you have plenty sense and judgement and by getting around like you do you can see a lot more and learn a lot more of the various ways and customs of other peoples." She inquired if he was still playing his trumpet and asked for a copy of his work in the *North China Marine.* Regarding the home-front economy, she stated: "Nothing is rationed now in the good old U.S.A. except sugar." Prices were high during Christmas shopping, however, and not all items were back on the market yet. Tires were available without much trouble.

On December 27 Jack requested a money order of $50 from his account as soon as possible. He had missed the last payday there waiting to be transferred and would not be paid again until his records were straight, perhaps a month or more. He had borrowed some money from friends, but with his transfer "will not be able to pay them back for some time and I do not wish to get a bad name for credit. . . . You see I can do without the money very well but when I owe some money it is embarrassing to [put] people off and gives you a bad credit."

Jack drew a caricature face on the top of the Marine Corps stationery in his December 31 letter. He had opened his gift box on Christmas morning, kept what he wanted, and "put the rest in a box I fixed up for the little Chinese girl's family and took it to them. I just had to play Santa Claus." Jack described the abject poverty that produced street urchins who "become ragged little beggars and sleep on the street like animals." He acknowledged "he had as much fun dressing her up as she—and she is a far-cry now from the little beggar that she was. I am seriously thinking of putting her in school that is located right on the next block as soon as I investigate and see if it is not expensive or other obstacles that arise in the Chinese social system. She is a very intelligent child born like so many millions into rank poverty and will never have a chance in a dog-eat-dog society such as this. Most of the young girls who grow up under these circumstances later become prostitutes."

Jack described a contrast of wealth and extravagance, using as an example the Japanese house where that evening he was to attend a New Year's party hosted by his company's first sergeant. The house "is as nice inside as any expensive American home, with plush furniture, pianos, radio, rugs, beautiful paintings, etc." He had painted some big posters for decoration. The Chinese government had taken the property from the Japanese who were awaiting repatriation. In his memoir notes Jack mentioned "the Japanese invitation to their home seeking our influence to stay in China" and also cited "the party where I played 'St. Louis Blues' while the dancer from Shanghai performed." His letter divulged, "I have a Chinese girl friend now who is a school-teacher and is teaching me a little Chinese as she speaks English well. She is from a beautiful home, and is very pretty and interesting. I met her at a party recently and was with her last nite. It is really interesting the funny Chinese customs they have about dating and stuff."

His interesting experiences had Jack thinking about writing a novel "if I only knew how. There is plenty material here for that sort of thing." In fact Jack's papers include several pages in which he seemed to have attempted creative embellishments to begin a short story or a play. It was unclear whether he wrote these sketches in China or later. In what might have been intended as the beginning of a short story, the setting was a night club in Tientsin the night after New Years. In Mickey Spillane style, he described the beautiful wife of a Chinese general who was away in a northern province where the Communists were causing trouble: "You didn't have to be a jeweler to know that the rock she was wearing was a small fortune in itself. It sparkled with every movement of her hand."

At the beginning of 1946, news from home painted expectations for Jack's return. Lottie on January 2 lamented that Jack's education had been interrupted but stressed that his experiences would be to his advantage. "When you get back, the gov. will pay for the rest of your education," she pointed out. Lewis and "his brother Jimmy have bought out their Dad's [machine] shop, and officially took over yesterday. They've bought some new property too, but aren't going to move quite yet. Their brother Mac is going to work for them, so it will really be the 'Anderson Brothers,' and possibly even [their brother] Jack may work with them too when he comes home [from service]." On January 6 Oscar wrote that he had enjoyed Jack's cartoons in the "little division newspaper." He reported that "all family boys" were out of service but Jack, Otis, and Steve, who was hospitalized in Charleston. He wrote news that Jack had long awaited: "Having pond surveyed, 2–3 acres."

A second letter from Mae made the observation that there did not "seem to be enough trains to move the returned soldiers fast enough so they just have to wait turns." Mae's January 10 letter bore a Myrtle Beach postmark as they had been attending a bottlers' convention. "Sugar and machinery situation here is no better yet & I thought he [Oscar] might find out what the out look for bottlers was," she said. "Everything else but sugar has been taken off the rationed list." Oscar was moving his business office to the plant and putting her on the payroll. Mae for some time had been helping keep books for him from home. She quipped that she would be "glad to have my own money."

On January 7 (misdated December 7) Jack provided his new address: "As you will notice on the envelope I am not in the First Division now and 2 days ago I was transferred to the III Amphibious Corps, and now have the job of artist on the North China Marine newspaper here in Tientsin. I have been extremely busy with all the red-tape of getting transferred, moving, and a million other details." He summarized that it was "wonderful duty" and "things are running plenty smoothly. . . . I may leave China in 2 or 3 months or before. In the meantime I am making the best of it and having a very swell time." In a 1978 *Sandlapper* interview, Jack recalled of his newspaper work in China that most of the staff had been newsmen before the war. "It was my first real contact with professional journalists," he said, and the experience "greatly influenced my later decision to work for a newspaper."

A week after his last letter Jack wrote, "At present I am very busy all day on my new job, which I like very much, and every night I have been taking liberty with my friend Paul Miller who has been on a 1-hour stand-by to go home for the last two weeks." In his own case, "the points have dropped to 45 now for the next eligibility-for-discharge bunch, and I have 44 points so I just miss this one, so I believe I will leave perhaps around the first of March." He said of his new assignment that "I'm in a nice set-up now, and all I have to do is draw pictures. (I will be sending you some copies of the paper soon). I get paid regularly now, eat good, learning a little Chinese on the side and have a very swell Chinese girl-friend which makes the time fly by."

On January 17 Mae observed that the view from her window "looks like the picture of a beautiful snow scene." She and Oscar were setting up the office at the bottling plant, but "sugar is still scarce and daddy cant make many drinks." He had, however, "fixed you up as a member of the [American] Legion post here and is sending you your membership card. Freddie, Robert McDowell, John Henry McDowell and a lot of the boys in Camden who served in this war have joined. This is a good organization and does a lot of good and has a lot of influence on things of the Gov." She had mailed Jack the medicine he requested for his Chinese friend, although she could get penicillin only in tablet form and had sent the liquid with which to mix it: "The entire amt cost me $27.50." A doctor's prescription and pharmacy order had been necessary since "this stuff is still scarce here." Aunt Nannie was "a little stronger but whatever they do for her is just temporary for there is no cure for her."

Jack wrote on January 19 from the hospital in Tientsin, "I'm in for a few days to take a little atabrine for Malaria. You see I've had a couple attacks before but this is the first time I've been treated. I'm O.K. now just taking it easy for a few days. You see the way it affects you is you don't feel so good for a few days then you get the chills and shake like a bowl of jelly for 2–3 hrs. under some blankets which fail to keep you warm, then you get hot and start sweating like a steam boiler. I got it the other day and turned in at the hosp. and the Medics say they'll keep me here a while. I feel o.k. now, but my temperature goes up and down like the tide any where from 104 to 96 today. Anyhoo I'll be out shortly and O.k."

In another letter the same day (inaccurately dated 1945) he hoped to be out of the hospital the following day. "I am feeling great, just been laying around taking atabrine tablets. The weather was beautiful and warm today so I went outside awhile this evening . . . and played with some dogs that were romping around. This hosp. life is boring and depressing." He described his regular habitation: "The new place I live now is almost in the heart of town. There is a big Red-cross building across the street. It's really nice there and luxurious, as it was formerly a club. . . . They have almost everything there, restaurant, showers, classes in different subjects, art classes, Dancing, etc. The regular Red Cross women are supplemented by Russian, French, German etc. girls. There are some nice-looking numbers here, but they haven't got the old American pep." He inquired, "Has the man begun on the pond yet? Maybe I'll be there before it starts." He also inquired about Aunt Nannie's health. He signed off with the comment, "I can't wait to get some really fried chicken." He was released from the hospital January 21.

Mae's January 24 letter reported the receipt of a box "with the swords the drawing outfit the idols etc." She referred to the news that he would be home in "in 2 or 3 months. That is the grandest news I ever received. I am so thrilled over it I can hardly write this letter." She referred to his January 7 letter about his new job and social life, commenting, "You sound like you are happy and having a swell time and I am so glad. Always try to get all that life has to offer you in the proper way." Mae reported, "Yesterday Daddy went over to Columbia to receive a medal for his five years service on the draft board, service without 1 cent of pay. So you see he has done a fine job of serving his country too."

On February 13 on Camden Bottling Company stationery, Mae apologized for neglecting Jack. She had been "up to my neck in our annual reports as usual this time of the year. I have been having a time. You know Daddy during hunting season. He has the fever and I don't know that I blame him so much. After all this business of making a living and being always under a strain gets a person down." She also commented, "It has been pretty hard for me this year for it is impossible to get any help for me at the house so I have all the work there and have to try to do this other work too." She reported that Shot Cox was in Tientsien with the FBI and that Steve Kelly was getting a medical discharge and would "be a papa in Aug."

Mae continued with a business decision: "We have bought the building we are in. Mr [Joseph] Sheheen had several people wanting to buy it but he gave us the chance to buy if we wanted to. We knew if any one else bought it, we would either have to get out or pay a lot more rent so we did not want to do either so we just bought it ourselves. This property is going up in value so we feel like it will be a good investment even if we do not use it for a bottling plant. It is so hard to get any kind of a building put up now on account of the lack of material of all kinds right now. Any way we are property owners now on Main St."

On February 15 Paul Miller, back at home in New Jersey, acknowledged having received a letter and photos from Jack. Paul explained he had not written sooner because he thought Jack was also home: "Aboard the Wakefield [transport ship] they kept announcing over the speaker for Cpl. O. J. Smyrl to report to the troop office immediately with his special orders so I thought that you were aboard the Wakefield too so I went and checked and I told them that you had been transferred and that I didn't think it was the same name. They showed me your name, however, and I noticed your serial so then I knew it was you. I figured out later, after they gave up trying to locate you that maybe you were transferred again to the "Leatherneck" in Wash. and you probably flew home." Apparently, by paperwork crossovers, Jack had unknowingly missed going home in January, but consequently he had been able to join the *North China Marine* staff. Paul said he had written their Chinese friends Mrs. Hoo and Mrs. Tai, and he inquired if Jack were still visiting their homes. He and fiancée Jane were engaged and expected to marry in the spring. Jack was invited to the wedding if home by then.

Postmarks on several letters that arrived home from Jack in February and March need to be considered unreliable in actual date of events. Jack later stated that he had hoped to surprise his parents with his arrival back in county, so upon departing he left behind undated letters with friends to be mailed along to this family. An undated letter in an envelope stamped March 5, 1946, contains factual information he also later spoke of or made note of, although the incidents occurred earlier than the postmark suggests. He wrote, "Here's the latest big news. Doc Williford [a high school friend] is here (Looks as if my replacement has come straight from Camden). The other night I went to a movie and when I sat down, there was Doc right next to me—some coincidence, eh. We've been out together a few times since then. Next news is I saw Shot Cox go by in a Jeep today, I yelled but he was almost past and didn't recognize me." In another undated letter, he mentioned that Williford was trying to persuade him to go to Carolina next year.

Aboard the *USS Devosa,* Jack left China around February 9, 1946, according to calculation of information in his written notes. In a letter January 23, 1948, Jack would state that "it took me 20 days coming back over that big Pacific without any stops." According to his memoir notes, about the first of March 1946 "we marines were alerted to prepare to disembark in San Diego. My friend [B. O.] Smith and myself decided to get up extra early and get our sea bags up on deck before daylight in order to be free to watch the decking of our ship. As we worked our way across the dark, slick deck in the rain, with the heavy sea bag on my shoulder I stumbled on a cable that ran across the deck. (unlike pleasure ships, with uncluttered decks, troop ships were rigged for utilitarian purposes). As I fell quick and hard, the rolling deck came up to meet me and as my face [hit] the deck my front upper teeth were driven up into my sinus bone."

Smith helped injured Jack to the ship's dentist, catching him as he was leaving. The dentist "who was anxious to disembark also, did emergency procedures and extracted the broken teeth." The dentist gave Jack a "temporary wad of gauze . . . to be held between jaws & upper [lip] until ashore" and instructed him to report to sick bay at their base on land. Because the dentist was also in a hurry to go home, he either did not complete medical records or they were later lost. Jack, in a state of shock, "was led to the sick bay by Smith." He was given pain medication and joined other servicemen at the railroad depot. This was not the arrival home or the surprise for his family that Jack had been visualizing.

Chapter 17

University and Beach

"To make a living as an artist"

Unlike the train trip he had taken westward across America eighteen months earlier, a grand adventure of wide-eyed anticipation, Jack's 1946 eastward train trip home passed as a blur. Anxious moments and adrenaline rushes mingled with disorientation from pain, medication, and travel fatigue. The cars on military rails the last miles to Camp Lejeune, North Carolina, proved especially crowded and uncomfortable. Under other circumstances, Jack would have been interested to see the base. The New River Tent City, to which so many of his Parris Island buddies had been sent, was now a sprawling installation with permanent wooden barracks. But fatigued and numb with pain, he wanted only to get his discharge and to go home.

NCOs at the base depot barked orders to fall in ranks and come to attention. As surnames were called from a clipboard, Jack fell in alphabetically. The line moved methodically through various stations, checklists at each. Finally, a medical check: "Any injury or medical condition to report?" Jack nodded, opening his mouth to reveal the cotton mass. The officer in charge responded that it was Saturday. Therefore, according to Jack's memoir note, he would need to remain at the base over the weekend and report to a dentist on Monday, or he could finish processing out now and at his convenience "go to the V.A. to have my teeth repaired." Jack without hesitation fell in line and completed the process. His official Report of Separation was dated March 9, 1946.

Jack had come halfway around the world at the end of three years in the Marines. He had no strength or desire at the moment to begin another battle—one of bureaucratic red tape. He had no way of knowing that pursuing his medical claim at a postponed date was going to take longer than it took America to defeat the Japanese. He shouldered his sea bag and headed out the door. He was going home.

Boarding a nearly full bus to town, Jack reached the Atlantic Coast Line station and purchased a train ticket to Sumter, South Carolina. It was the arrival closest to Camden, about thirty miles away, predicted in evening hours. He had planned to surprise his family, but not to walk in and shock them with a swollen mouth and missing teeth. Contrary to plans, he dropped coins into the pay phone and called home. Mae was overcome with joy and eager to talk, but Jack had limited change and was unable to speak clearly. He hoped Mae had comprehended his mumbling. Jack boarded and napped restlessly as the train rattled along the tracks. When he heard the conductor announce "Sumter," he clutched his sea bag and carefully made his way from the train. There on the platform, huddled together against the night chill, was a sight he had longed to see. His mother and father rushed to embrace him.

Jack greeted his mother with "a wad of cotton" in his mouth, she would recall. In spite of Jack's swollen face, Mae thought he looked wonderful. She could not stop hugging him. With his hand firmly grasping his son's shoulder, Oscar beamed, waiting his opportunity to hug his son. Jack could barely speak. He was content to listen to familiar voices.

The drive through the countryside seemed short. Oscar's gray 1940 Buick moved smoothly through the darkness. His parents took turns telling him news since their last letters. Alfred had gone off with friends before Jack's call and did not yet know of his brother's arrival, but he would be home after the movie. As Oscar slowed entering Camden, Jack gazed out the window. Memories flashed as headlights fell on familiar sights, darkened but silhouetted against the moonlit sky. Oscar slowly crossed the railroad tracks at Dusty Bend, made a left turn onto Highway 97, and had picked up speed again before they passed the Carolina Cup race track. Shortly, Oscar made a left turn into the familiar sandy drive of home. It was 11:30, but in contrast to the dark houses in town, Mae had left her house lit and cheerful. Everything seemed much as it had been on his last leave from Parris Island, Jack saw as he entered his home. Would he be the same old Jack?

Inside, in the light as Oscar removed his hat and Mae her sweater, Jack noticed facial lines, traced by age and anxiety, and wisps of gray blending into darker hair colors. His mother seemed a little stooped, his father a bit stouter than Jack remembered. He heard a car in the driveway, some playful banter as a door slammed, and the acceleration of a vehicle leaving. When the door opened, Jack could hardly believe his eyes. His little brother had grown up. Glancing at Jack's bloated face, Alfred grinned and made a playful remark that a Chinaman must have taken offense at his cartoons. Jack could see Alfred's quip was a ruse to conceal emotion as his brother strode across the room to embrace him. It was too late at night and Jack was too tired to notify his sisters. That would come tomorrow, on Sunday.

Jack had often imagined his first Sunday back at home, walking into church in his uniform, Oscar's friends patting his back—"job well done, Marine"—Mae's friends hugging him and leaving traces of lipstick on his face. And the girls! Who would be there, and how would they react? But he was too tired, and he did not want to be seen in his condition. His mother, father, and brother would attend church as usual, leaving Jack home to rest. They would discretely tell a few relatives and close friends of Jack's return and injury, and that he would love to see them later. They would telephone Lucy at Winthrop and invite Lottie, Lewis, and Joan for dinner and a reunion. When all of them were together again, "Unka Jack" would be at home.

In the days that followed, the swelling subsided, and Jack made the rounds to catch up with family and friends. His old room somehow seemed smaller than he had remembered, but he had not slept on so comfortable a mattress since he left home. Sometimes in the dark nights he would abruptly awaken just before a bogie sneaked into his tent, or his slumber would be interrupted by the big guns shelling Naha. He would wipe the sweat from his face and neck, take in the comforting sights and smells around him, and usually fall back asleep.

Besides filing the routine paperwork of a returning serviceman, it was most important that Jack visit the Veterans Administration and get his mouth fixed. He made the trip to Columbia and waited quite a while to be seen. The words stunned him: his basic medical records had been lost during a hurricane on Okinawa, and no documentation existed of his emergency surgery aboard ship in San Diego. The VA authorized temporary bridgework, but without documentation the "operation to remove bone bits left inside from the emergency work" and permanent bridgework would be his responsibility to pay for. Jack had surgery the following week so the VA-authorized bridge could be fitted. The appliance, he recalled, was "adequate to get by but never fit exactly right." Later, he reasoned that had he postponed the fitting until all the swelling subsided, the bridge might have fit better.

With his mouth somewhat repaired, Jack concentrated on catching up with his past and preparing for his future. Recreation gradually resumed with going to movies, fishing with Oscar, and boating to Creed's Island at the river, now also being called Wateree Lake and sometimes Lake Wateree. Most of his old friends were scattered, back in college or off to new jobs, but familiar faces still at home were good to recognize. There were trips to see aunts, uncles, and cousins, some living in modernized homes. When Aunt Mattie visited and Jack mentioned the old horn that he had borrowed from Otis and played throughout the war, she blithely took the instrument back, presuming him done with it and treating it as a favor to return it for him to Otis. Jack was speechless, crushed by the departure of his old friend, and long told the story with wry nostalgia.

The old home place was one place Jack could go that was unchanged. Aunt Mamie had maintained everything in the house as it was when Grandpa Robert died, and neither electricity nor indoor plumbing had yet reached the Flint Hill home place. Uncle Henry talked of painting the outside of the house and adding improvements for comfort when power lines came their way. Jack helped his father and uncle with their new pastures and livestock at the old place, worked some at the bottling plant, assisted Mae with her chickens, and helped put in a spring garden at home. Lucy's semester at Winthrop ended in May, just in time to join the family at home for Alfred's high school graduation. Life resumed and moved forward.

Thoughts turned to the future. As much as Jack had loved Auburn, his friends once there had scattered. Applying for GI Bill college benefits, he chose to enroll in the fall at the University of South Carolina, only forty miles away in the capital city of Columbia. That decided, Jack determined to live in the moment and enjoy the summer. He moved his belongings into the basement at home, converting it into a studio apartment. There he had room for both his barbells and his drawing table. He could come and go and stay up as late drawing as he desired without concern that he was disturbing others.

Jack resumed working at the bottling plant, its physical labor helping keep him in shape. That fact was especially important as Mae's home-cooked meals were irresistible. Helping Oscar with his cattle, Mae with her chickens, and both with the garden also provided exercise, as did frequent long rides through the woods and fields on Mac. Jack sought out quiet paths as well for his own running, avoiding the busy highway. He rarely rode a bicycle to town, however, traveling there now by "wheels" instead of his old "wheel." His nights grew less often interrupted by dreams of sneaking bogies and startling explosions.

Autumn 1946 was a whirlwind for the Smyrls. Their neighbors the J. B. McGuirt family moved to the nearby Proctor farm and sold Lottie and Lewis the old tea-room place and its forty-two acres to make their home. Trying to garden its sandy soil, the couple jokingly gave the old farm a private name, "Sandspur Hill," for the prickly invader that stubbornly thrived there. Lucy returned to Winthrop for her junior year, majoring in home economics and early childhood education. With the draft still in place, Alfred, turning eighteen, enlisted in the army on September 18 for an eighteen-month hitch, chuckling over the numerical coincidence. Oscar had hoped to send him to college a year before service, but Alfred opted to enlist in time to qualify for soon-to-expire GI Bill benefits. On October 14 the family was saddened for Lewis when his twenty-year-old brother, Jack Anderson, a recently returned war veteran, died in downtown Camden, a passenger in a midnight auto accident. The end of war had not banished loss and sorrow nor assured certainty of life.

Among the swirl of changes, Jack left home once again, this time for Columbia. Moving into a rooming house at 1221 Pickens Street, he found the University of South Carolina campus teeming with an overflow of students. Many of them were veterans, and officials scrambled to adjust to a large and diverse population. Jack immersed himself immediately in active university life on and off campus. He had four interests to juggle—art, physical fitness, music, and the fairer sex.

The previous year artist Edmund Yaghjian had arrived at the University of South Carolina to become the first chairman of the Art Department, then boasting only 167 students. Born in Armenia in 1905, Yaghjian at age two had immigrated with his parents to Providence, Rhode Island. Showing early art promise, he studied in the Providence School of Design and the New York Art Students League. Considered an important rising artist, he dismayed those colleagues with his move to Columbia, South Carolina, then characterized as devoid of museums, art community, and artistic opportunity. Yaghjian's influence in promoting changes to that reputation was just beginning in 1946.

Jack, one of Yaghjian's earliest students, developed great respect for his professor's art and teaching but lamented to him that the USC curriculum included no classes in "how to *make a living* as an artist." The VA, administering GI education benefits Jack was depending on, required that students enroll in a career program leading to employment. He had ongoing discussions with Professor Yaghjian, who understood the difficulties and commitments of being an artist. He himself supplemented his creative earnings with his teaching salary and suggested that Jack pursue "art education" as a career major. Jack had been told before that he was good at teaching, but training to be a teacher was not what he wanted.

Seeking additional art involvement, Jack gravitated again toward student publications. He initially submitted cartoons to the long-established student newspaper the *Gamecock* but found art positions there already filled. He then offered samples to the student literary magazine begun the previous year and became art editor of the *Carolina Review.* In his first illustration, in volume 1, number 4, Jack seriously interpreted the rising conflict in which the State of Israel was established two years later. The black-and-white illustration labeled "Palestine" depicted stark images of starving people, skulls, and barbed wire. Perhaps the unrelieved dark view, not typical of his work in general, past or future, was prompted by wartime memories.

Jack also tried out but was not selected for the university boxing team, although he continued on occasion to spar with team members. As an enthusiastic Gamecock football fan, he gladly participated in pep rally excitement. In addition he followed both active and passive interests in music. For a time Jack played with a college dance band at local social events. The groups he had called "orchestras" were more typically being called "bands." To enjoy swing music and new sounds, he frequented clubs and venues in Columbia and cited in his memoir list of "USC Escapades" at places such as Joe Patrone's Hang Out. And everywhere Jack found girls, girls, girls.

Professor Yaghjian approved of social life for art students and encouraged them to involve themselves in the community about them. Jack would later relate that Yaghjian had advised that "an artist has an obligation to his art to saturate his senses and emotions with all he encounters so that he can better interpret and communicate the world he sees to others." At times Jack pondered the advice and its limits, or lack of limits, in application. It was a way he was still determining.

Bill Burns, discharged and back home, resumed his rollicking friendship with Jack. Together they purchased an aged but glamorous Ford Phaeton touring convertible they dubbed "G.J." for "Gulley Jumper." Eventually Jack finished the payments and ended up its owner. Bill quickly reestablished a band and urged Jack to play with them when he could. During December school vacation, the Bill Burns Orchestra asked Jack for a ride to the depot where they were taking the train for Starke, Florida, for a nightclub contract. At the station Jack, at their urging, impetuously got on the train at the last minute and without luggage left with them. In his memoir notes, he "bought stuff there. Had great trip, etc." He left the group behind in Florida and returned home to celebrate holidays with his family. Christmas 1946 was a mixture of homecoming and emptiness. Jack was home, but on Christmas Eve, Alfred departed with the U.S. Army in the occupation of Japan, where he would serve the next year.

Second semester Jack moved nearer campus to another rooming house at 1012 Marion Street, near the central Horseshoe, the historic U-shaped heart of the university. He resumed classes and his work as art editor of the *Carolina Review.* A moody piece he had created in early fall became the cover of volume 1, number 5. The blue-tone illustration of a jazz combo was more typical of subject matter for which he would afterward become known, although later executions would be livelier. Editorial notes in that issue stated, "Our 'winter' cover is a copy of an original painting by Art major Jack Smyrl, which might be called 'Jam Session.' The original painting was on display for some time in the Delta Zeta room. When members of the editorial board saw Jack's original painting, we convinced him that he should do a copy from the original for us."

Jack used cartooning features to create a bright and quirkily suggestive image for the cover of the *Carolina Review,* volume 1, number 6, spring 1947. That semester he began (and dropped) a psychology course, which possibly prompted his subject matter. The green-and-yellow illustration teased Freudian interpretation of a familiar campus icon, depicting a phallic Maxcy Monument on the Horseshoe being restrained by a gigantic, grasping (gamecock) spur while a lady's hat with coy eyes hovered, only partially concealing the globe at the top of the displaced monument. With seasonal attention to where thoughts of youthful fancies turned, the cover elicited chuckles among the visually perceptive. Widely known to USC students at the time was a mock fable regarding the stalwart memorial obelisk that was a focal point of the Horseshoe green. The fall 1951

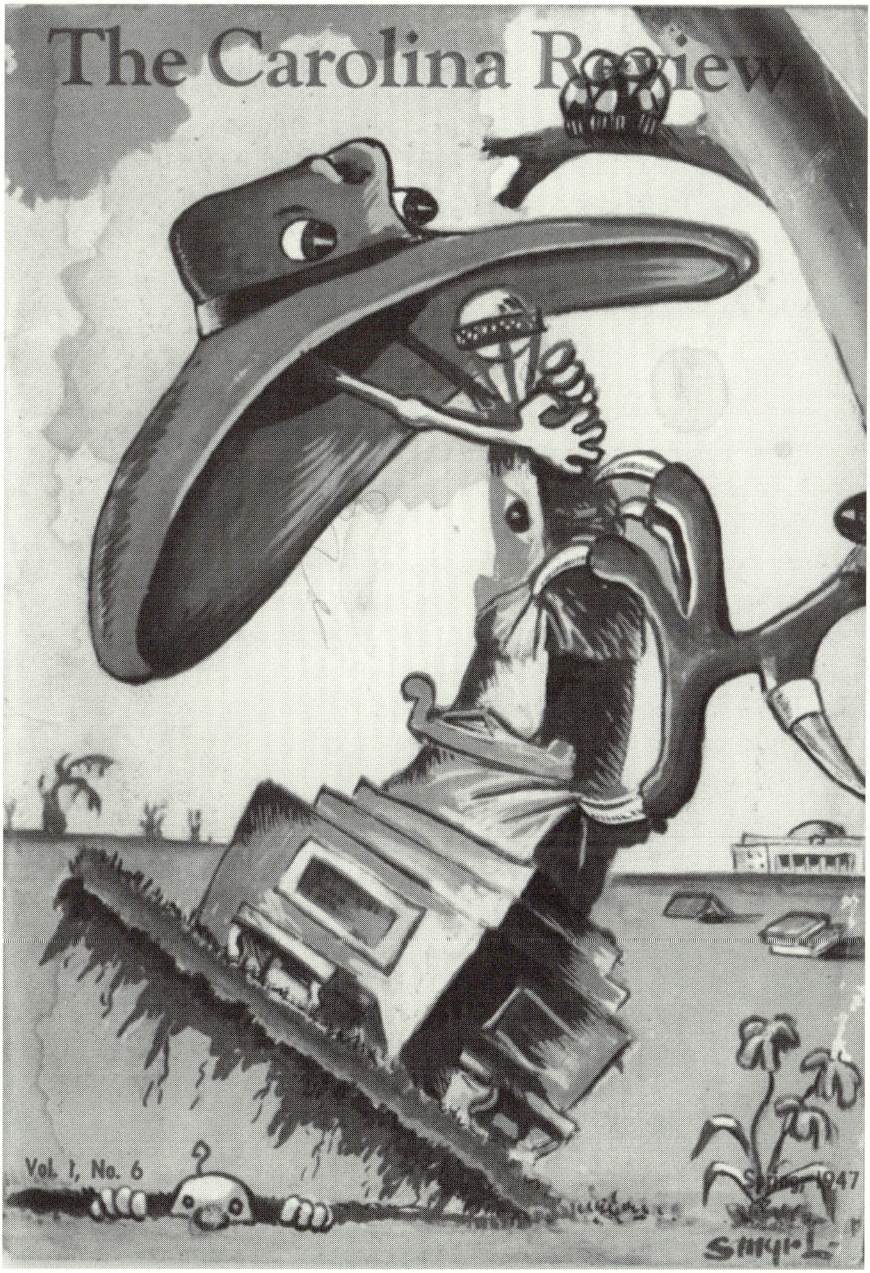

Cover by Smyrl, the *Carolina Review,* spring 1947.
Courtesy of the University of South Carolina.

Carolina Review directly stated a popular racy "legend" of the Maxcy monument: "The ball at the top of the monument spins around when a virgin walks past; but then who ever sees it spin?"

During his first semester at USC, upon selection by Professor Yaghjian, Jack submitted one of his paintings to an art show at North Carolina State College. Winning second place Jack's oil painting, a fashionable still-life canvas in the studio-admired style but with objects that suggested decaying of former beauty, was chosen to represent both North and South Carolina in a New York showing in the spring. The prestigious show, under the direction of Jacques Seligman, was titled "25 and Under," identifying ages of the participants. During spring holidays in 1947, Bill Burns accompanied Jack to New York to view the exhibit and to visit swinging clubs with hot music. An article in the June 20, 1947, *Camden Chronicle,* reported about the exhibit that Jack was the "only painter in the Palmetto State to be so honored."

After Jack's return from service, by the time he saw Anna Shuler again, she was exclusively dating another young man, so she and Jack did not resume dating one another. She did get him occasional dates with Columbia College friends, and a few times they double-dated. Anna recalled that Jack on his return was "as gentlemanly as ever" but appeared to her much older and more serious than when he was at Parris Island. During his year at USC, Jack's memoir notes recall "forays to Winthrop" and "weekends at Winthrop" to socialize at his sister's school, the South Carolina College for Women. Jack and other friends often double-dated at Winthrop, and he continued to maintain female relationships at USC. He believed himself open with young women about not being ready to settle down, a fact some found attractive and some did not. In memoir notes Jack recalled a romance with a much-adored Winthrop sweetheart that he considered on his part a "five-year love affair." In a March 28 letter, she wrote Jack: "I'm kinda disappointed in you. I always gave you credit for using your own head and not listening to everybody else. I've found out a few things lately and I don't wanta believe them. . . . I'm just waiting for you to tell me yourself tho' what's going on." She concluded a May 24 letter: "I think it's about time for another one of our serious talks. . . . You needn't try to spare my feelings. I've never tried to spare yours, have I?"

In spite of various social engagements, including trips to Rock Hill and romantic ups and downs that would continue, Jack's academic grade report for the spring 1947 semester tallied a B–/C+ average. He made a worksheet of requirements and education courses for future years should he pursue Professor Yaghjian's suggested art education major. The 1947 *Garnet and Black* pictured the portrait of "O. J. Smyrl" in the sophomore section, as well as in the group photo of the *Carolina Review* staff in their "modern-equipped office" on the third floor of McKissick Library. Jack as art editor had a staff of three. Despite enjoying his year at USC and realizing progress in his art, Jack felt himself far from prepared for self-sufficiency in a working art career. Professor Yaghjian made suggestions. With art education courses lined up as possibilities, Jack also wrote to commercial art schools. Over the summer he would consider his options.

Summer 1947 was busy, with lives of the Smyrl family pulled in different directions. Alfred in Japan was the most distant. Oscar's new endeavor, the Camden Ice Cream Company, was bringing heavy foot traffic into his bottling plant for cones and cups of the popular sweet treat, manufactured there of the "very finest of ingredients," said the May 9 *Camden Chronicle*. Jack set about painting the walls of the ice cream shop and "attractively furnished" it with "funny paper pictures," as the September 5 newspaper called them. Mae was busy with meetings and preparations for an upcoming adventure at the end of the summer. As state president of the South Carolina Council of Farm Women, she was to leave for Amsterdam, Holland, to attend the first postwar triennial conference of the Associated Country Women of the World. The American delegates including Mae were going as "goodwill ambassadors" to encourage the women of countries that had been decimated by war. Everyone was proud that Mae would be among the delegates.

Lucy came home briefly but returned to Winthrop for summer school, starry-eyed with plans to marry Rhonda Paul Brown, a high school friend who had returned from the navy and entered USC. Summer school attendance would assure Lucy of enough units to graduate with both her home economics major and a teaching certificate in early childhood education. Oscar and Mae were prevailing on Lucy and Rhonda to wait until she finished her upcoming senior year before they married. Oscar listed practical reasons a young couple needed a steady income. Mae described to Lucy the lovely formal wedding she would help her plan after her trip. Meanwhile on July 22 Lottie gave birth to a second child, Robert Randolph Anderson, warmly welcomed to family circles. His first name honored Grandpa Robert, and his second was the middle name of Lewis's recently deceased brother. In Rock Hill four days after the baby's birth, Rhonda and Lucy traveled to nearby Chester and quietly married. They would keep their elopement secret for several months during a flurry of family activities

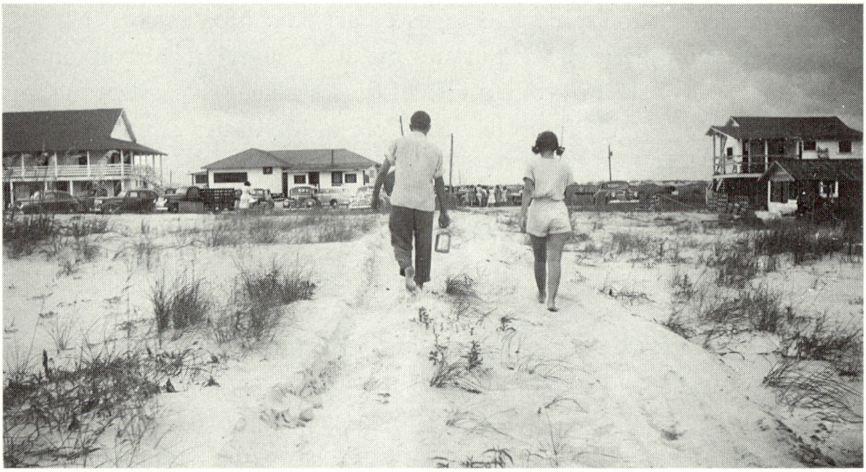

Holden Beach, 1947, photographed by Jack, with hotel at left. Courtesy of the University of South Carolina.

while Rhonda found a job working in Rock Hill and Lucy continued her senior year.

As much as possible Jack spent his summer near the water. His memoir notes recall "moonlight crossings to Creed's Island for romance." For the first time since his one trip in high school, he returned to Holden Beach, North Carolina, again with the Burns family and others. In memoir notes Jack viewed the postwar visit significantly: "Me and Edna, Bill and Margaret, Mama, Mrs. Burns, U.G. [Bill's father] start the Holden Beach Era." Photographs he identified as "Holden Beach 1947" picture a rustic cottage and a conventionally chaperoned house party from Camden composed of Mr. and Mrs. Burns, Mae, Jack and girlfriend Edna Team, and Bill and girlfriend Margaret Van Landingham, whom he later married. Jack listed details of "the first house party at Okie-Jima," a nickname coined from war references for what became his favorite rental: "the outhouse, the kerosene lanterns, the live chickens, fresh eggs, tomatoes, etc." Jack loved home-grown tomatoes, especially juicy slices with slathers of Dukes mayonnaise between slices of bread. He took his trumpet and long recalled music of Bill's "clarinet by the beach fire."

In a 1981 *Brunswick (N.C.) Beacon* interview, Jack described his irresistible attraction to Holden Beach. "A friend and I found out we could rent a place from (the late) John Holden for $25 a week—that was $12.50 apiece,"

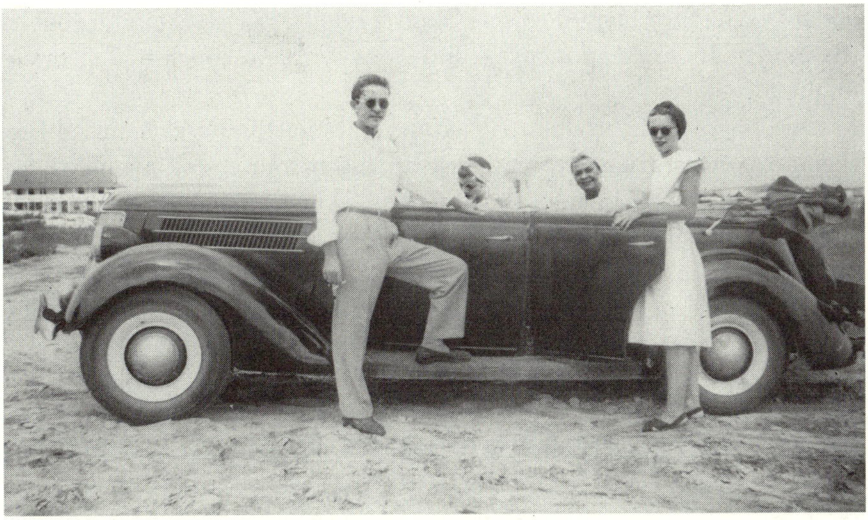

Ford Phaeton "Gulley Jumper" with Bill Burns and female friends at Holden Beach, 1947, photographed by Jack. Courtesy of the University of South Carolina.

he said. "We fell in love with the place." In 1947 the road from Highway 17 to Holden Beach was still unpaved. Only in the past year had postwar building commenced. John F. Holden and brother Kemp, returning veterans, enlarged the old pavilion to attract day visitors and entertain overnight guests. A bathhouse, café, grocery, and recreation area made up the "J&K," a simple, rustic wooden structure. Guest cottages were small and likewise rustic, as was the old hotel constructed in 1939. Other photos of Jack's summer coastal visits show him with friends, sometimes with his family, staying at small, simple waterway cabins and enjoying seaside sun and surf. Various poses feature him in a bathing suit with art supplies and easel, trumpet, and the binoculars he brought home from the Pacific. Carefree travels are evoked by photos of a loaded trailer behind the Phaeton convertible, in which are seated smiling girls in sundresses, sunglasses, and head-scarf turbans.

Driving the convertible always top-down, Jack traveled to Holden Beach often that summer. Working for John Holden, he spent part of his time painting signs at the beach, trading his labor for a place to stay, sometimes with meals thrown in. Jack also painted and sold seascapes to tourists to earn money, dreaming of purchasing his own property on the island. The first beach lots had sold at Holden Beach in 1935 for fifty dollars each. They were now one hundred dollars. Jack thought double-the-money an amazing increase and wondered how much higher prices might go.

One opportunity that intrigued Jack at the time and haunted him thereafter was a chance to purchase an oceanfront chunk of the island, then divided in two by inlet tides. Franda Pedlow recounted the incident in her autobiographical *Sand and Sea Fever.* In the 1940s nothing had been built on "Robinson Beach," lying across a tidal inlet that would later be filled to join the western end to modern Holden Beach. The isolated acreage had become a tax burden to its elderly owner, who offered to sell it to Jack for $2,000. Pedlow quoted Jack, speaking years later: "I didn't know anything, was just a kid. So I went home and got my father and a friend who was a real estate agent [J. B. McGuirt] and brought them down here. We all sat on the porch and Mr. Robinson offered it again. They [Oscar and McGuirt] said it was a wasteland, but I would have bought it for the beauty of the land. I had no money or the sense to borrow it. I didn't have the $2,000, or a job. If I had bought it, I would be so rich now it would be scary."

In a handwritten memoir note, Jack stated Mr. Robinson's offer was for "1 mile," although a length of three or more miles is in another reference. Logical business reasoning deterred Jack's older advisers from backing the purchase of uninhabited and unstable sand, inaccessible at high tide from an island itself reached only by a hand-cranked ferry after a lengthy and uncomfortable ride. In the postwar economy $2,000 was a fortune to risk, and had jobless Jack approached other lenders, similar responses were probable.

At the end of the summer Jack completed sign painting and returned home with resolve. He might not be able to own a long chunk, but he vowed to find a way to own some part of the island. Painting cartoon art on store walls or signs on beach amusements might earn a few bucks, but Jack had been giving serious thought to long-term goals. He enjoyed Columbia and USC, but for stability of gainful employment he needed commercial art training not taught there. His serious courtship was in a state of flux. The thought of leaving home again was unappealing, but his research discovered that commercial art classes being taught at the Art Institute of Pittsburgh, Pennsylvania, promised the training he wanted. He contacted admissions there, arranged for fall entrance, and informed USC and the VA of his plans.

Chapter 18

North and South

"I hope that I am improving"

On August 31, 1947, when a sun-browned Jack took the bus from Camden and headed to Pennsylvania, his family was far-flung. His brother was in Japan and his mother in Amsterdam. Oscar's September 7 letter abroad to Mae reported Jack's safe departure. The Art Institute of Pittsburgh, established in the 1920s, teemed with students in the postwar years. While Jack was there, the school at 635 Smithfield Street served more than eight hundred students on eight floors that included forty studios. He roomed in a boardinghouse "run by the Hughes," as he wrote on the back of a photograph of a roommate, Vern Milem, another art student. Jack recorded his experiences in letters, memorabilia, and later remarks. His convertible, exercise equipment, musical instruments, and records he left at home. His southern accent he took with him. Jack also kept South Carolina spelling patterns (such as "Orangeburg" and "Spartanburg"), almost without exception leaving off the final "h" and spelling the city he was in as "Pittsburg."

On October 14 Jack wrote to welcome Mae home from Europe, where women at the conference had united in favor of peaceful solutions to conflict and in support of the United Nations. He was anxious to hear about her trip and her meeting afterward in Washington, D.C. Writing four days later, Jack expressed pride in his mother's accomplishments in "making the speeches and for going to Europe." Very shortly after her return, Mae addressed a national meeting of farm women and began a circuit of civic

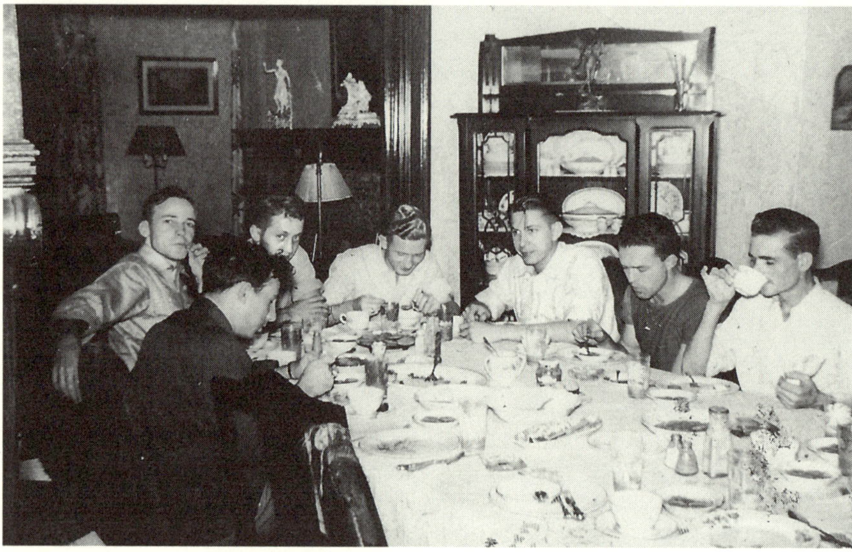

Jack (second from right), with other art students in boardinghouse dining room in Pittsburgh. Courtesy of the family.

speaking engagements describing postwar conditions in European countries her group had toured.

Jack's letter described himself as "real tired . . . I have been losing so much sleep working on the week-ends. As soon as my [VA] checks come in I am going to stop working and try to live off the checks. The work is cutting into my art work and holding me back. Maybe I will get a check next month. I hope so as I am continually broke and there's so much I have to spend money for." He added a bright spot: "A couple days ago I got a check from the University of S.C., an award that I won for my work there last year. It was $15.00." Jack at times worked at least three different part-time jobs to make ends meet. He worked the soda fountain at a drug store, parked cars, and washed dishes. He considered the dishwashing job the best one since the hot water and steam kept him warm in the cold climate, and he was allowed to eat leftovers in the kitchen where he worked.

For the first time in his life, Jack was completely on his own. In the Marines, the corps had made major decisions and mapped out his path. He had also lived away from home at Auburn and at USC, but in both cases, he was in the South in weather that was agreeable to him and among people his age and with whom, for the most part, he shared common speech patterns and cultural traditions. There he went to school to learn and to socialize, so that fun had been part of his education.

Pittsburgh was a large, soot-filled industrial city in a cold climate. Not everyone spoke English, and those who did had varied accents. People on the street did not readily give a quick smile and a friendly greeting. No one knew him as "Oscar and Mae's oldest son" or as "that Smyrl lad who likes to draw." No one knew him as a Marine who had held his own. Jack had no margin of buying power or control status that he had had in China. He felt himself instead on the edge of a poverty he had not known before. Students at the institute had little time for fun or socializing. Drawing well was nothing unusual. Students were highly competitive, there to learn a job, absorbed with learning skills for professional careers. Many were on the GI Bill and, like Jack, were struggling to make ends meet. Jack mentioned no experiences with music beyond attending one dance. All that he had for his comfort was his art, and he poured his focus into it.

Jack's letters home that fall ranged from exuberance over ideas for his art future to dismay over financial woes. His October 18 letter made a request about coins he had sent home: "If you can would you rush me back the $2.00. I am running very short and need a few extra dollars. My rent is all paid up until December 2 (this means rent and 2 meals a day), so if I can only rake up a few extra bucks I'll be straight." He continued, "I owe $3.00 . . . and it's 12 days till pay-day and I have $10.00 in cash to last till then. This is for car-fare, dinners, laundry, etc., almost enough to see me through but falls just a tiny bit short."

Jack's financial distress largely resulted from complications with VA paperwork, a frequent problem for veteran transfer students. He reported on October 24 that he "got a check for $62 from government . . . and was told by the Vets. Adm. that I am to receive at least $105.00. Soon as I do I'm going to quit work because it is hurting my school, and my health as I work at night and I have so much homework that I don't get enough sleep." He added, "After I quit work I am going to do those paintings for the Holden Beach people . . . and try to pick up extra money this way." Even with basic survival worries, Jack had to add, "Speaking of Holden Beach I am still hoping to take my [war] bonds and get us that Beach lot so we can build a shack and rent it out and use it ourselves."

Apparently Oscar wrote suggesting a sale of the Ford Phaeton in the garage at home to supplement Jack's Pittsburgh income rather than letting the vehicle lose value sitting unused. Jack exercised manipulative charm in his October 24 letter: "I was so glad to hear that Mama has started using the car. That will be so good for it. Daddy I want you to do what ever you want to with it, and even sell it if you need some quick money. You could sell it and pay for your new Buick Motor, or take both of our cars and trade in on a new Buick. It's yours to do with as you please. If you think it will do more good to keep it awhile then O.K. Of course I'm crazy about it, but I can always get another one later. I'm planning to pull some kind of a deal to get home this Summer and it will be good to have then. Also Alfred will be home in March and if you haven't sold it by then it will be nice for Alfred to have. When we all get home next Summer we can use an extra car." Clearly Jack was reluctant to give up the Phaeton.

Jack wrote a more optimistic letter on October 31. The weather, he said, was "still mild and everything is perfect with me." He had attended the institute's annual Halloween dance at the Fort Pitt Hotel. The dance "was a fine blow-off. The first good time I've had since I've been here. My woman for the night was a little doll from Maryland. I'm getting to know a few people now and it makes it better." He was "out of debt now as I sent the last check for the car and one to [Camden jeweler Des] Goodale for my watch, so all I owe is $2.00 I borrowed from a guy here so I am back on my feet."

His November 17 envelope Jack embellished with a sketch of the front half of a boney-sided dog with a large nose sniffing the address, explaining he had been busy with "school stuff" and other art. He had finished a picture for which he would receive $20.00. "After Xmas holidays I am going to get to work in my spare time on a few others that I have promised," Jack said. Some Camden people had asked him to do portraits, and "I intend to use the one I did of Edna [Team] for a sample of my work." He had been asked for a landscape to paint on the wall of Sheheen Brothers Grocery at home: "If good enough maybe others in town may want one." Other requests included painting the Camden trash cans for the Jaycees, which he could do "quicker this time as I am studying lettering." There had been numerous sign painting offers last summer, such as on the baseball fence. "I don't aspire to be a sign-painter," he wrote, "but when you need money in a hurry it's one way to make a few dollars."

Jack added a more ambitious proposal to his longing for a shack at the beach: "Maybe I could open up a Summer Art school down at Holden Beach or somewhere. Theres one of the teachers here who runs his own art school in the Summer at some resort around here for people who want to learn a little about painting and makes a killing at it. . . . My first concern is to get good myself first and try to keep from starving." He continued about the

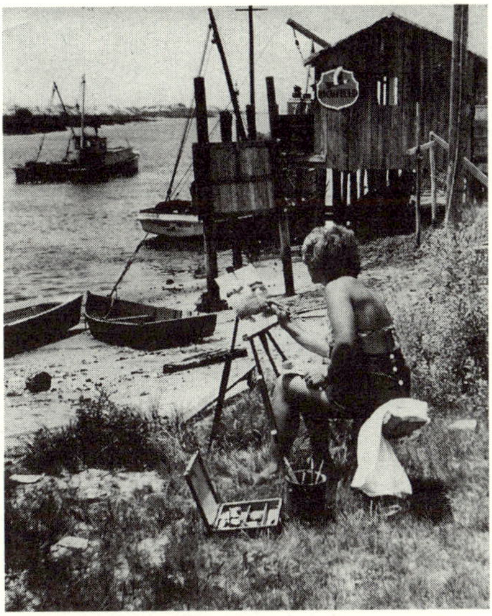

Photograph by Jack in 1947 of former army lieutenant Jessell Campbell (later Garrett) painting on the waterway at Holden Beach, where Jack envisioned an artists' colony. Courtesy of the family.

art school: "That would be a very pleasant way to earn a living. You and Daddy could be the managers and I could grow a beard and be the old professer. First we'd need a place. You know, build a studio, etc and do a little advertising etc." Jack also explained, "What gave me the idea about an art school is when I took Jessie [Jessell Campbell] down [to the beach] last Summer and besides a couple of ladies in Camden asked me about teaching their children and even over at Carolina the Professor there [Yaghjian] held a private art class at night for people in Columbia (Ladies business men, etc) who just wanted to paint. There are plenty of people like this and the idea is worth pondering."

At Christmas Jack returned home, anticipating details of his mother's trip to Europe and seeing her souvenirs. Other news awaited. With family gatherings approaching, Lucy and Rhonda presented their marriage certificate, to the surprise of all, and shared their plans for the future. They would live in Rock Hill, where Rhonda would work at a mechanic's job to support her through the rest of her last year at Winthrop. Then she would get a job in Columbia and supplement his veteran's benefits while he earned a degree. Oscar and Mae gave the young couple their blessings.

Frequently during his absences, Jack had written of his affection for his family and of his desire to spend time with them, especially during special seasons. Nevertheless he also had missed his friends and social life. As he had frequently done on holidays from Auburn, furloughs from

Parris Island, and breaks from USC, he spent a great deal of his December vacation away from his family socializing with his friends.

Returning to Pittsburgh, Jack wrote home on January 11, 1948, that "it really feels good to be back in school. The Christmas holidays was just what I needed to put me back on my feet—I am feeling wonderful and I'm sorry I spent so much time Christmas running around at night, but I was starving for a little social life and knew it would last only a few days so I wanted to get in all I could because when I'm up here, I don't have a car and money and things it takes to have a good time and practically all of my spare time is spent up here in the room." He seldom went out at night in Pittsburgh because of uncomfortable cold and expense. Streetcar fares that used to be 25¢ for three tokens were now 10¢ each. Jack also confessed to a habit of which his parents were likely already aware. He was an "extremely moderate" smoker and felt "deceitful for not telling you . . . but now that you know I'm glad it's over with. You don't have to worry about me on any other score because I am living a clean life."

He described himself that year in his memoir notes as "lovesick." Either before he left or when he was home for Christmas, he had offered an engagement ring and a marriage proposal to the young woman with whom he was deeply smitten. She had turned him down. He saved little of their apparently extensive correspondence, but he wrote his parents on January 11 not to think harshly of her: "She is the only girl I have ever loved. She perhaps seems to have given me a raw deal and all that but whatever happened was 70% of my fault and due to my own stupidity." He assured them, "She is of the highest character morally . . . in every respect every thing that a girl should be. . . . There is a quality about her that appeals to the artist in me and that quality makes her to me one of the most beautiful creatures that I could imagine." He continued, "To one of my temperament its what makes me very happy to be around her. . . . It's just that I think the world of her and can't help it any more than I can help loving you."

Having experienced negative effects of loving "very very intensely," Jack said he was "reverting back to my old casual self and waiting to let nature take its course." He continued, "Those kind of things are beyond our control and I am really just now beginning to grow up emotionally. Believe it or not I am a very high-strung person and am trying to be a sensible person and I hope that I am improving. Don't you think I am. Although I may be 24 yrs old I still feel like your little boy, and I hope I will

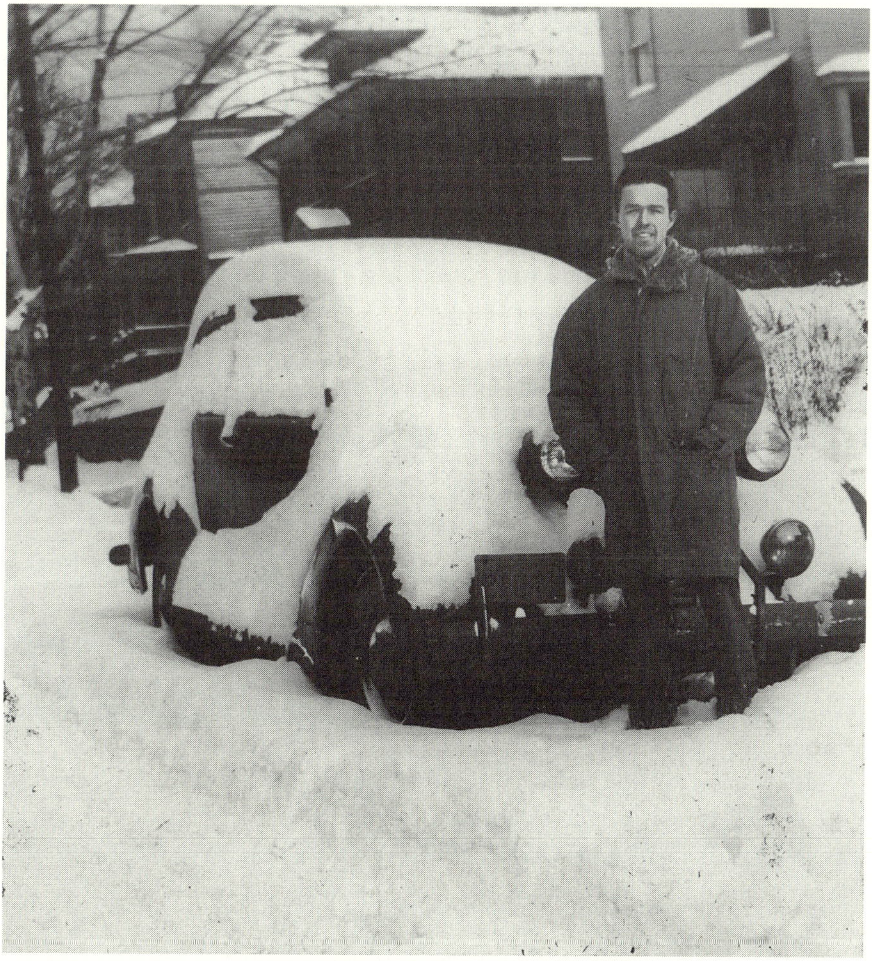

Jack in snowy Pittsburgh, himself not a car owner there.
Courtesy of the University of South Carolina.

always feel that way to you." Away from home, he analyzed himself in a way he had not done previously.

On January 15 Jack was discouraged by Pittsburgh's deep winter: "It's real cold here now and has been snowing lately a lot. . . . Theres snow laying everywhere but as its been there a couple of days, it is now dirty on top as the air here is always dirty from the smoke." His economic situation was likewise dismal: "I see that I'm going to run out of money in about a week as I had a lot to buy such as some dry cleaning & stuff you see it cost 50¢ to have one shirt cleaned to give an idea of the crazy prices here. It is important that I stay in a lot for a while and do all the work that I have to do. . . . If I take another job right now to get the extra money I need I can't get the work done." The problem with his education benefits was unresolved. He made a recurring request: "In the meantime I am going to have to ask you to see if you can let me have a few dollars if you can spare it. . . . One of these days I hope I can stop being a drain on the family budget."

Jack also expressed concerned about Oscar's business: "If anything develops about the plant or anything please let me know because I am very interested. I hope things will break right for you and the ice-cream business will hold its own till the warm weather." He stated that "my most important concern right now is passing here O.K. because I think I'll get credit for this at Carolina next year." Returning to his USC studies was an option he wanted to keep open. Jack commented on his training in Pittsburgh: "Every day I am becoming a better artist here and even if I never use it to make a living it is something I can fall back on at least."

The teacher at Pittsburgh who especially influenced Jack's art was Vincent Nesbert, at one time also dean of the institute. Born in Poland, Nesbert immigrated to the United States from Russia in 1914. He studied abroad for a year as a Joseph Pulitzer Prize recipient following his 1921 graduation from the National Academy of Design. When Jack studied under him, Nesbert, who spoke seven languages, had been a member of the institute's faculty for twenty years. Teaching that an understanding of human anatomy was essential for drawing or painting human art forms, he was especially gifted in training students in the close study and application of anatomy and movement in art. Life drawing, executed while observing a living model, is often considered the most difficult subject for an artist. Nesbert stressed that an artist must look at a subject from the inside out, not just on the surface, and that he had to understand what he was representing from the inside, not only the outside. Jack would often refer to these principles in explaining "an artist's way of seeing."

Nesbert could be blunt, especially in his life drawing class, reaching out and tearing a student's inaccurate work from the easel and demanding the task be begun again. Jack's memoir notes described Nesbert as "Russian art instructor, rigid disciplinarian . . . anatomist expert." Jack thrived under his tutelage, growing even more demanding of his own work and willing to continue refining it to meet his own standard of perfection. Live models were the subjects of figure studies, and Jack was paid for modeling at Pittsburgh as he had been at Auburn. Nesbert's classes were intensely focused with assignments for bone structure and musculature, for various poses and perspectives, for interplay of varied lighting. The subject matter of Nesbert's own work that remains especially admired includes human studies such as portraits and nudes, and a series of prominent public murals in the Alleghany County Courthouse, Pennsylvania.

In the midst of frozen northern weather, Jack was making warm summer plans when he wrote home on January 23. He had received a reply from John Holden about reservations at Holden Beach along with a job offer "to do some sign painting for him the first of June." John offered him free a place to sleep and dining room meals while he worked. Jack said, "I think I could do the work for him in a few days or a week. Of course I will go alone so that I can concentrate on the job and make a few bucks." He added, "I hope that sometime this Summer I can work for you and see if we can't fix it so you and Mama can take somebody and get in a week or so of fishing and resting. . . . I think you will need a break and that it will do you good." Jack enclosed Holden's letter: "We are expecting a good beach season. The state is to let the contract for the paved road the 29th of this month. As you know that will help us an awful lot. We hope it will be ready by June. . . . Due to the increase[d] expenses of everything I will have to get $40.00 per week this year for the Cottage. Let me know if you still want it." His postscript added, "We enjoyed having your Dad down last fall. He is a fine fellow."

Jack also enclosed a letter to hold for Alfred to welcome him home from Japan. Jack told his brother he looked forward to seeing him. Meanwhile "soon as the weather gets warm enough you can use my car. How do you like it Alfred? Ain't she a killer? The batteries may need a little recharging. All I ask is for you to take care of it for me Alfred. It's about all I've got left to show for my 3 yrs. in. Use it all you want to just don't let anybody mess it up. You will notice if you push the accellorator over to the left you will get more power." Jack expressed pleasure at the idea of both of them going to USC next semester: "I can't wait to get back. We can really save dough by going there Alfred."

In February Alfred reached the States and was discharged at Camp Stoneman, California. A stroke of bad luck had hit shortly before he left Japan. A barracks fire consumed all his possessions—letters, photographs, cameras, and souvenirs. Alfred arrived home with light luggage but eager to describe his experiences.

Still tangled in red tape with VA education claims and having "been re-assured here again that . . . I will start getting my money," Jack was apologetic writing home on February 1: "I feel bad about asking you for money when I know how rough the going is for you. I think about you often and pray that it will work out O.K." This was one of several times that Jack alluded to his father's financial difficulties. The bottling plant had never recovered from effects of the sugar shortage and the difficulty of obtaining glass bottles during and after the war. The ice cream business was naturally slow during winter months.

Jack turned to discuss his training and potential opportunities. He mentioned a classmate from Wilmington, North Carolina, assuming a job in a Charlotte studio and describing "an open market" down south for starting up similar studios. Jack stated his own intention: "I don't know what will become of me but I definitely want to finish school first and am planning big on living at home next year and finishing at Carolina. The school here is wonderful and I'm trying hard to catch completely up in my work. The work gets better and more interesting all the time and my time is definitely not being wasted."

On March 18 Jack reported having his hair cut free at the barber college and his shoes fixed at "a shoe repair school where you only pay for the leather." Of his training he said, "I feel as if I could be able to hold down [an art job] in case I find one, but for the time being I'm not looking for one as I want to finish school first. . . . I'd like to get started now but the older I get the more I see the value of this schooling and figure I better get all I can while the getting is good." On April 28 he wrote congratulating his mother for recent awards and thanked her too for "being the sweetest person in the world to me . . . and . . . the wonderful person you are."

With his Pittsburgh coursework ending May 22, Jack five days earlier wrote a lengthy letter home in a last-minute agony of decision making. "I want to finish my [college] education, but to be a commercial artist it would be smartest to stay here and practice," he debated. "If I go home I may regret it, and if I stay here I may regret it." However, another year in Pittsburgh would not guarantee a job he enjoyed or an agreeable place to live. Returning to South Carolina "may not be the best move, but then again it might be the smartest" because, he finally concluded, "its what I'd rather do." His decision wouldn't be hard "if I weren't trying to be an artist and still keep my contact at home."

He concluded the letter with self-analysis: "One reason I am happier than I've ever been before is because I'm not only a man physically, but I have finally become emotionally mature. It was a long hard fight for a person as extremely sensitive as I, but somehow fate has thrown me among some of the most intelligent of people who have helped me no end. . . . I want more than anything for you to know that I feel closer to you than I've been able to let you know, and I hope that you understand me better. I am a rather complex person who really wants to be simple."

In late May Jack returned home, especially eager to see Alfred and hear of his brother's adventures in Japan. Stories were all Alfred could share because of his losses in the barracks fire, but the brothers could joke that at least he got home with his front teeth. Jack gladly admired the Winthrop College diploma and teaching certificate that "Lucy Smyrl Brown" proudly displayed. She and Rhonda would remain in Rock Hill that summer, and he would keep his job until USC resumed in the fall. It seemed strange to Jack that his baby sister had finished her education ahead of him, and she and her husband were pursuing a clearly mapped plan for their future. Her big brother was still contemplating his future. For the meanwhile Jack anticipated pleasurable summer days at John Holden's beach cottage. He would paint signs, seascapes, and portraits, and spend time with friends "just for fun."

Amid pleasures of familiar home faces, comforting meals, socializing, and outside exercise without cold chills, Jack helped at the plant and with chores. He was nostalgic that Mac was gone. Reluctantly the family had recognized that the thoroughbred was too fine an animal to languish in a pasture without young folks there to groom and ride him, so shortly after Jack left for Pittsburgh, a new home with another family had been found for Mac.

Jack was glad, however, that his beloved Ford Phaeton was still there for both his and Alfred's use. That summer Jack enticed both family and friends to join him at old haunts, especially waterside retreats, but for stints of time he stayed alone at Holden Beach. He paid his way, working small jobs, turning out saleable art, exploring coastal life, and thinking. Idyllic dreams of someday establishing an art colony there stayed fresh in his mind.

In the way that returned veterans reflect, Jack was drawn back to thoughts of China. Newspapers reported ongoing struggles between Communists and Nationalists. What had become of his friends near his studio there, of the generals' wives, and of the waif Sho-roong? He wrote to Paul Miller to see if he had addresses of Chinese friends. In mid-June 1948 Jack received a reply, including a street guide and addresses of Mrs. Hoo

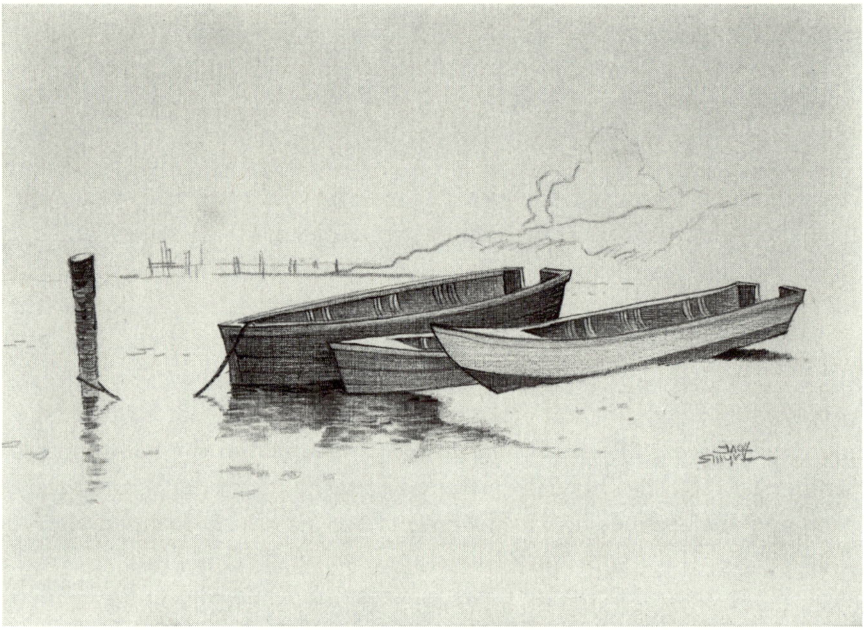

Boats moored on Lockwood Folly River, an original signed "Jack Smyrl" and kept by him from coastal art pieces marketed to tourists. Courtesy of the family.

and Mrs. Tai. Paul was realistic about concerns for the orphan Jack had aided: "I'm afraid you'll find her back in the condition that you first found her." Paul too wished to revisit China someday: "You said you'd give anything to visit there again; well that goes for me too. It seemed like leaving a second home with those good friends we left behind." Most of the letter focused on their current lives, however, and Paul ended with reference to a romantic interest Jack had confided to him. "Take it easy," he wrote, "and I hope you can accomplish that 'Certain One' into seeing it your way."

With all of Oscar's children emancipated adults, he felt freer at age fifty-three to seek less demanding business interests. Returning war veteran Ernest P. Sheheen, rejoining his father, Abe's, grocery business next to the bottling plant, asked to purchase Oscar's drink business. They agreed to terms, and in June Oscar sold Ernest the half of his building containing the bottling company. Oscar planned to continue his ice cream business in the other half, but soon afterward he also sold it and the rest of the building at modest terms to Ernest. Large national bottlers had promoted a costly sterilization process in new public health regulations, effectively putting smaller competitors out of business. Pop-Kola had lost in the local cola war. With the ice cream business, Ernest was able to have an income to make building payments.

Oscar afterward took a sales position at Smoak Motor Company, which sold autos and farm equipment in downtown Camden. Mae continued to lead the South Carolina Council of Farm Women, in October attending a national convention in Tulsa, Oklahoma. Shortly afterward she was named State Woman of the Year. Still active but with all their children moving out, Oscar and Mae began planning a smaller home. A couple of years would find them building a modern, comfortable brick home in a lovely natural setting only a few miles away on modern-named Colonial Lake, an old millpond fed by Sanders Creek.

By fall 1948 three Smyrl siblings were living in Columbia. Peacetime and the effects of the GI Bill had swelled enrollment at the University of South Carolina. Housing was in short supply. Rhonda reenrolled in mechanical engineering while Lucy took a full-time job teaching on campus in McMaster Nursery School. They first set up housekeeping in Columbia by moving down the same small trailer in which they had lived in Rock Hill. Later when the Carovet Apartments for married veterans were completed, they would move there. They would not dispose of the trailer but would later lease a lot for it at Lake Wateree, add a large screened porch, and use it for many years as a summer retreat, a place Jack would often frequent.

Alfred began his freshman year as a business administration student living in a USC dorm near the center of campus. Jack found lodging just off campus, at the southeast corner of Pendleton and Pickens Streets, where he moved in with acquaintances living in a partially finished basement rented as an apartment. It was a place he and Alfred memorably dubbed "the Mole Hole." When a roommate moved on, Alfred for a time lived there with Jack. They and others colorfully described the dreary space that stubble-faced Jack turned into an unforgettable "Bohemian pad." Fresh from an unconventional summer and determined to live an artist's life, Jack with flair and ingenuity restyled discarded furnishings. A humorous and quirky bachelor air of sensuous indulgence overcame the starkness and deprivation of the purely practical.

Jack in conversation and in memoir notes made numerous references to "mole hole days in Henry Green's cellar." The Smyrls had known the landlord, at one time the county farm agent in Camden. The Greens lived upstairs in the aging mansion that he, owner of a Columbia farm equipment business, had purchased in recent years. In future years the once stately property would be absorbed by the USC campus. Jack described it from local stories as the "ex-governor's mansion." Richard I. Manning, serving 1915 to 1919, lived there for a time while repairs were being made to the governor's mansion. As in many other aging housing units in postwar Columbia, the rambling basement with overhead pipes and exposed wiring was in primitive repair, dark and damp. Jack's notes described "spring flooding" when renters had to "walk on bricks" they laid on the floor to keep their feet dry. The basement was unheated in cold weather. Jack wrote of "embezelling heat from the duct pipes" by diverting some of the furnace air supposed to be going upstairs.

The fall semester in session, Jack was glad to rejoin art classes of Professor Yaghjian and Catharine Rembert, blending lessons from them with what he had learned in Pittsburgh, especially from Nesbert. Jack had taken a critical look at some of his earlier works and understood how to improve those efforts. Still captivated by active musical performance as an art subject and enjoying his return to southern music, Jack attended performances and hired models to pose for a new painting he began of a group of exuberant black jazz performers. Never formally titled by him but sometimes called *Jazz Combo,* the painting would become one of his signature works, full of feeling, always popular on exhibit.

Jack also resumed an active student social life. His name appears as art editor of the *Carolina Review,* volume 2, number 3. The publication had changed to a larger 8½ × 11 format, and both cover and interior designs focused on photography rather than art illustrations. Jack soon met a free-thinking and precocious freshman, up-and-coming writer Jane Gerard, whose short story "Apostate" appeared in that first issue. Her story, which ends with the suicide of a young protagonist struggling with a lack of faith, stirred controversy, but it received the South Carolina Student Press Association Award for the best short story of the year, with the *Carolina Review* being named "the Best College Literary Magazine in the State." As soon as she had graduated from Bishop England High School in Charleston, Gerard had talked her way into a summer job with the *News and Courier.* The spunky, ambitious writer was among other creative young people crossing Jack's path whom he would later claim as good friends.

Although the cost of living was cheaper in Columbia than in Pittsburgh, Jack found money "still tight." One dreary night in late October, he was attracted to a nearby church function because it advertised to students a supper of "free sandwiches." There he ran into an old friend from

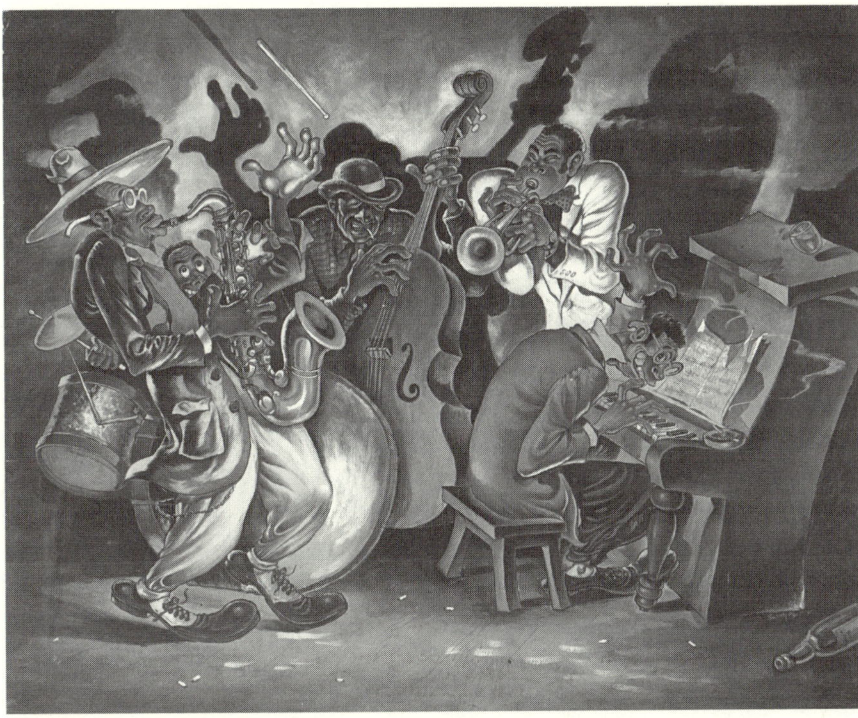

Exuberant oil painting Jack began as a University of South Carolina art student and afterward completed, referred to as *Jazz Combo*. The almost hidden drummer is observed by the prominent shadow of his hand and flying drumstick. Courtesy of the University of South Carolina.

Camden High, and they reunited with animated conversation. Sybil Drakeford, formerly a student journalist and a high school band member with him, had also for a time played piano for the Sentimental Southerners. She was excited about the hit Jack's front page cartoon of a tiger and gamecock facing off had been in the *Gamecock* October 21, day of the Big Thursday Carolina-Clemson football game. Now living in Columbia and working in an office at the *State* newspaper, Sybil happened to be privy to information of interest. As they ate their free sandwiches, she told Jack about a newly created position. The *State,* in publication for nearly six decades, for the first time ever was looking to employ a staff artist. "Jack," said Sybil, "you really should apply."

Chapter 19

A Career Beginning

"An adventure and a romance, not just a job"

Name, the form began. "Oscar Jackson Smyrl, Jr.," he wrote. *Date,* "November 12, 1948." He filled in his address, "1600 Pendleton Street."

He checked "never been employed," but in response to a question about employment by another publishing company, he said "Yes—1945, Marine Corps paper, Tientsin China, Cartoonist & artist." He was seeking the job because "It is the type of work that I have trained myself for." The position sought was "commercial artist." His qualifications were "3 yrs of art training plus practical experience free-lancing."

Newspaper sections that interested him most were: "story illustrations, and art work, photography and human interest articles, cartoons." He listed *present income:* GI subsistence $105 a month; *savings accounts:* First National of Camden and Commercial Bank of Camden; *real estate:* none; *insurance:* $5,000 (beneficiary mother). His health had been excellent for the last five years except for recurrent malaria attacks, with no attacks in the last two years. He wore glasses only "for viewing distant objects such as for movies." In addition to his studies at Pittsburgh Art Institute, he listed completion of a correspondence course in cartooning. He listed references: Edmund "Yagdjian" and Catharine Rembert, USC art instructors; C. T. Baldwin, Camden High principal; U. G. Burns, railroad agent; and L. P. Thompson, insurance salesman.

The application was handed in. A brief interview followed, and at its end a simple statement was typed on plain paper to the veterans adviser at the Veterans Administration at the University of South Carolina: "This is to notify you that we have employed Oscar Jackson Smyrl, Jr., as staff artist at a weekly salary of $60.00, effective Saturday, November 20, 1948. Mr. Smyrl requested us to advise you of this fact." It was signed "R. D. Haltiwanger, advertising director, The State–The Columbia Record." The letter evidenced that in a brief space of time a life-altering choice had been made: to abandon the pursuit of an academic degree to accept a position that required immediate occupancy. On November 20 the new hire for the *State* and the *Columbia Record* began work, and a long career was underway for the young man who soon became professional artist *Jak* Smyrl, "the same old Jack."

Jak felt from the beginning that he had found his "dream job," and he would still say the same at the end of his career. At that time, in sentimental retrospect, he claimed he had enjoyed his years so much that "I should have paid them to let me work there." In 1948 the State Company was overcrowded in its office and production building, a three-storied, granite-fronted structure built half a century earlier. At 1220–24 Main Street in downtown Columbia, its tall windows and balconies overlooked city bustle only one block from the imposing facade of the state capitol. Daily rolling out from the company's buildings were two formerly rival publications—the morning newspaper the *State,* begun in 1891, and the local afternoon newspaper it had purchased at the end of 1945, the *Columbia Record,* begun in 1897. Their corporate association evolved into the State-Record Company. Housing the staffs and press equipment of two daily publications resulted in noisy, cramped workspaces at all hours.

In later years Jak delighted in describing the beginning of his employment for the company, a tightly budgeted operation where fellow employees seemed initially baffled about what the job of an "art editor" was. His first day at work, he said, he asked for a pencil. Office manager Sam L. Latimer led him downstairs to a safe, bent over, and unlocked it. "Then he pulled out a box of pencils, opened it and handed me a pencil." Jak took it slowly and then asserted himself: "I told him I would need more." He was, he said, cautiously handed one more.

In a memoir draft, Jak described the beginning of his career when his "desk" was a piece of plywood supported by stacks of old newspapers. For his chair, "I sat on a pile of old papers in the corner of a run down old building and labored under 18th century conditions until I was finally transferred to the rotogravure mag. staff as layout artist. I soon established myself as editorial illustrator." In that position, he said, "I drew everything except a large paycheck."

Jak, at $60 a week, was in fact hired at a relatively higher salary than some other *State* employees in a profession not noted for high pay. In a 2012 interview, James "Jim" Holton and Robert "Bob" Kaminer recalled their experiences with Jak and early working conditions at the newspaper. Holton, with two years of college, had been hired a few months earlier at $45 per week. Kaminer, one of the first people Jak met, was making $35 at the time. He had started at the newspaper two years earlier as a copy boy making $20, a fresh graduate of Lexington High School. He recalled, "That was the dirtiest, nastiest building. . . . The production department was above us and that silt [from the press machinery] would come down through the wall" soiling the white shirts they wore daily. "We had 10 or 11 electric fans in there so you could put nothing on your desk without putting an anchor on it." Those fans wreaked havoc with Jak's art materials.

Sharing adversities bred comradeship. Jak found Kaminer and Holton congenial colleagues, and all became amiable personal friends as well. Years later, for Jim and Edna Holton's fiftieth wedding anniversary, Jak prepared remarks describing conditions when the men met in "the old State Co. building on Main St. that had seen the best of its days." Jak recalled, "The roof leaked badly and when it rained, the boss, Mr. Haltiwanger, had to put a bucket on his desk to catch it. . . . The old paint peeling off the walls would fall on my drawings." He nostalgically recalled good times as well, such as watching "the Main St. parades [that] passed right beneath our windows and all the big doin's across the street on the State House steps."

Holton in an interview spoke of frequent visits to the Mole Hole apartment where Jak continued living after leaving his USC studies. Affordable and only six easy-walking blocks from the State Building, Jak's pad was a convenient off-beat hangout and casual party space for convivial coworkers. It was, in fact, at a Mole Hole gathering, Holton said, that he proposed to his wife, although she in ladylike manner deferred her answer to a "more thoughtful" time.

When Jak joined the working world of daily news journalism, he entered a colorful world that its participants have described as fast paced, heavy smoking, hard drinking, womanizing, and frank speaking. In *Between*

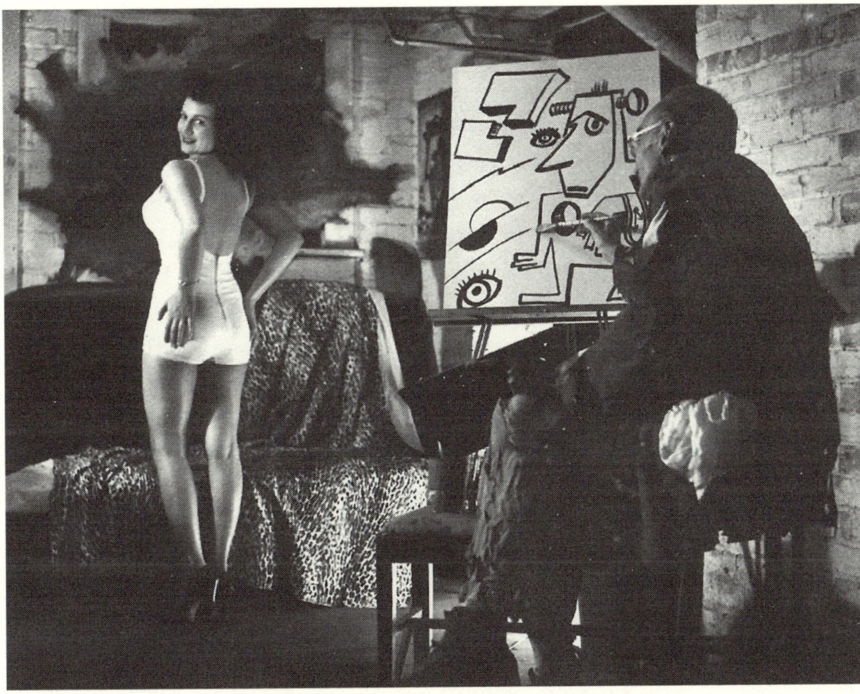

Poverty and glamour of the Mole Hole apartment, where Jak set up a photograph parody with roommate Russell Henderson as a modern artist painting a pinup model. Courtesy of the family.

the Sheets: The Journalist and His Lore, former *State* editor Robert A. "Bob" Pierce recalled it as "the days when journalists drank before noon . . . when journalism was an adventure and a romance, not just a job." Many of Jak's colleagues had backgrounds of mixed experiences, and most were war veterans. They worked late hours to meet deadlines. Many of their assignments dealt with tough issues and put them in contact with seamy sides of life. Cynicism mixed with sentimentality. Newsmen loved a good story, and every writer and photographer had stories to tell.

When the paper was put to bed, journalists dragged homeward via the Capitol Cafe, just doors away at 1210 Main Street. Politicians and legislators also frequented the popular twenty-four-hour hangout, rubbing elbows and sometimes speaking freely with journalists. The café had an important merit—it extended credit to newsmen. After work they made up for missed meals with comforting foods washed down with lots of beer. The later the hour, the thicker the smoke, and the greater the quantities of alcohol consumed, the more impressive the day's accomplishments, the more beguiling their female interests, and the more contemptible editors and other injustices grew in conversations. Some of the female employees were as adventurous and maverick as the males. In one flamboyant gesture of disgruntlement over office demands, two aggrieved employees working alone late engaged in sex on a boss's office desk after he went home, a fact afterward mutually shared. It was a favorite story embellished among coworkers, smug that the boss never knew.

When Jak was hired there was no artist's workspace "so they put him in the advertising department where I was, although he had nothing to do with advertising," said Bob Kaminer. He recalled of Jak's space, "He sat on a box with a bunch of newspapers on top of it. . . . Some of the windows had been knocked out and they had put cardboard in them." While the company worked out expectations, he began working on whatever assignments were handed him from the *Columbia Record* or the *State*. Eddie Finlay, *Record* sports editor and like Jak a war veteran, was one of the first eager to use the humor of the new artist to illustrate his sports column, frequently on hunting or fishing familiar to both of them. Kaminer explained that what the *State* had really hired Jak for was still in planning stages, "to work on that rotogravure magazine that we started putting out in 1949." He was referring to a significant financial and creative gamble the newspaper undertook.

On January 2, 1949, the *State* published its first issue of an innovative color tabloid, the *State Magazine,* distributed weekly inside the Sunday newspaper. Locally written, designed, and illustrated, roughly 11×15 inches and generally twenty pages on slick paper, the ambitious publication was a risk for a newspaper with such a small market. However, the *State* was seeking growth by increasing reader interest and enhancing its reputation as a major voice and advertising outlet throughout South Carolina and beyond. The magazine made an immediate splash with rare lavish use of color, sophisticated layouts, attractive illustrations, eye-catching ads, and well-written, insightful articles. Printed in Kentucky on a high-quality rotogravure press not available in South Carolina, the issues were expensive and labor-intensive to produce. Weekly there was a race to meet the train that carried the laid-out pages to the Kentucky publishers. Another anxious trip to the train followed to pick up the color-printed magazines to be inserted in locally printed black-and-white pages of Sunday newspapers in time for deliveries to homes and newsstands.

Working on the magazine with its high standards and deadline pressures, Jak developed a close professional and personal friendship with its editor, Eugene B. "Gene" Sloan. A veteran, he had been a navigator-bombardier with over forty missions in the Southwest Pacific. Like Jak, Sloan totally immersed himself in work that interested him. As a writer, historian, and photographer yearning to capture beauty, he found these in abundance in the mountains, forests, and coasts of his native South Carolina. After work Jak and Sloan, with much in common, escaped stresses with congenial beers and deep philosophical conversations. They were also companions on numerous statewide rambles that resulted in published stories and illustrations.

Jak's technical training and artistic skills enhanced Sloan's innovative concepts. Freelance writers found the magazine a prestigious place to have high-quality work accepted. Creative layouts enhanced text content with font variations, art lettering, spot color, and dedicated illustrations. Articles, art, and photographs focused on the well-known and little-known in South Carolina—its history, heritage, environment, arts, places, and people. Photography from different perspectives sported new techniques, such as aerial shots inspired by Sloan's aviation background. Jak tediously attended to layouts, hand-trimmed photos, touched up blemishes, and visually entertained. His reputation as an artist grew as he became known statewide for rib-tickling cartooning, for representative and interpretative illustrations, and for striking full-color covers on popular subjects. Annual events—such as the State Fair, the Carolina-Clemson football contest, and the Carolina Cup—received special treatment, along with local festivals, foods, customs, state symbols, historic events, holidays, and seasons of the year.

Recognizable cartoon traits caught the public eye. Some of Jak's early devices were slapstick ones, such as depicting surprise with bulging eyes literally popping from the head of a startled character. Developing variations of slapstick humor, he froze motion, depicting in a single view a surprised character jumping out of shoes, socks, even trousers. Some of Jak's tendencies endured as thematic. Lessons he found abounding in the natural world he translated in subtle comic messages to the human world. For example a hunter completely focused on gunning a bird fails to notice himself being stalked by a bear.

Dogs, Jak's lifelong companions, joined his artistic storytelling of human situations. The watching public as early as 1950 began to see his cartoons occasionally include a random hard-luck dog getting along cheerfully with a sloppy bandage around his tail. As the image pattern grew familiar, but always with a different dog, it evolved to more dramatic occurrences of a random dog with (ouch!) a completely broken-off tail tied back on and jauntily held high. A tale (excuse the pun) of optimism and endurance amid adversity inspired admiration even as it elicited chuckles.

An illustration of Jak's in the *State Magazine* on June 11, 1950, elicited an unexpected response sharpening his perspectives. An older reader slapped him on the back, "Great drawing Sunday! Funniest picture I ever saw of a little [racial slur] eating a watermelon." Jak was taken aback. He had not intended stereotyped humor based on race and disliked the misinterpretation. His quick reply, that he was illustrating the story beneath it, was interrupted by the man's guffaw, "Oh, I didn't *read* it. Picture was enough for a laugh."

Jak reexamined "Watermelon Waterloo," an account of a Greenwood County black youth baseball contest in which a disparaged rural team emerged victorious over a cocky city team. The rural team had welcomed their traveling opponents on a hot summer day by offering to share some thoroughly chilled watermelons. The visiting players greedily consumed all the melons without leaving any for their politely waiting hosts and thus scored debilitating bellyaches throughout the game. "While the nature of cartooning relies on exaggeration," Jak later explained, "I did not want humor to be hurtful." He understood country-city rivalry, ravenously loved watermelons, and thought he had depicted the characters sympathetically. Afterward he used perceptive caution in anticipating potential responses.

To avoid a dull appearance of sameness throughout the magazine pages, Jak at times produced feature illustrations deliberately using different art styles and techniques. He explained with a laugh, "The *State* did not want to look small-time, able to afford only one artist. Maybe that was true, but they did not want to *look* like it was." Depending on material to be illustrated, his sketches might employ architectural precision, photo-like realism, appealing sympathy, or outright comedy. The width or curvature of a pen or brush strokes could vary a look, as well as the openness or richness of background and detail. He even suppressed or varied his signatures to suggest a "big-time" working staff.

Jak's typical early signature was "Smyrl" or "Jack (or J.) Smyrl" in varied handwriting styles and locations, or even just his initials "JS" or "J.S." By late 1952 he had adopted the signature spelling "Jak Smyrl." That is, he spelled his name that way when he took time to sign his work. At times

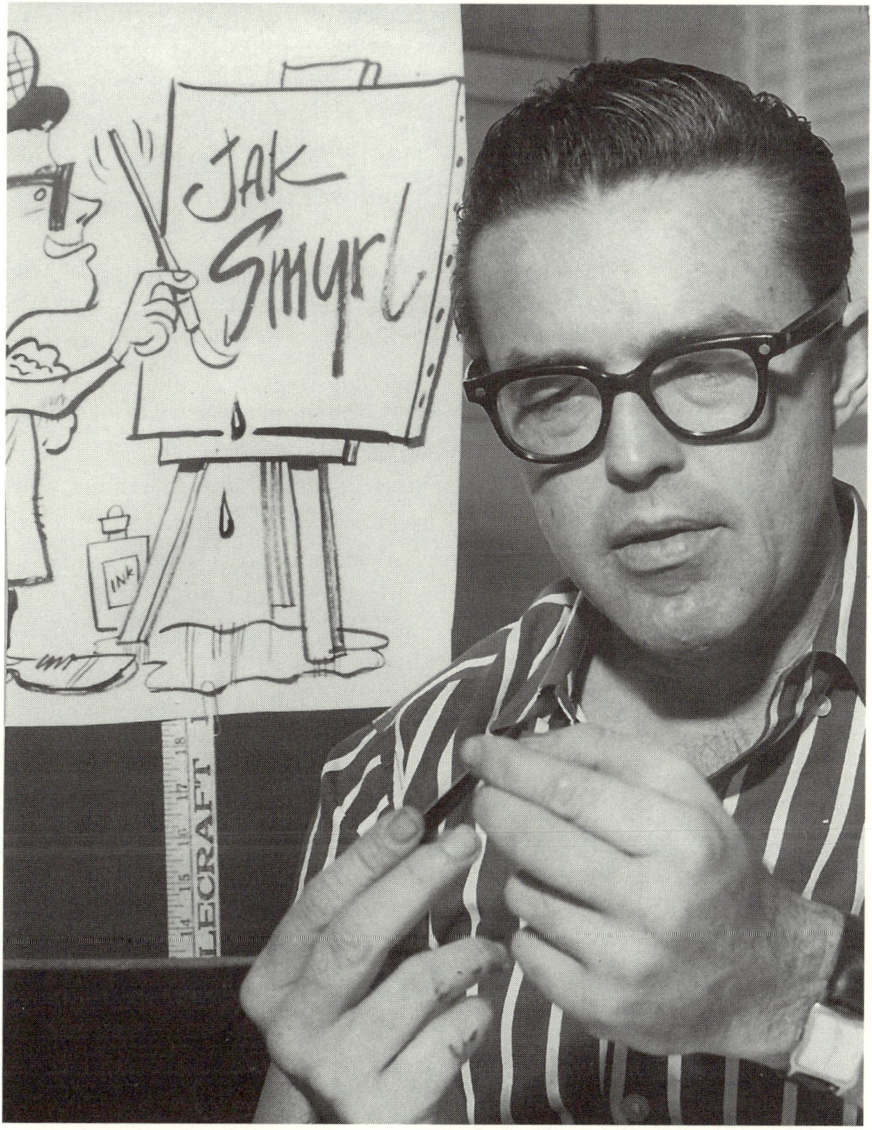

Image with self-portrait, Jak's professional "photograph card" for personal appearances in the late 1950s. Courtesy of the family.

because of deadline hurry he simply neglected to add any signature, or when producing several images on a page, he thought that signing each seemed "too big-headed." After all, he could recognize his own work, signed or not, and could claim his original to keep, as long as he got to the press room before it was thrown out. From the beginning of his employment, the company's agreement with him was that once his work was printed in either the *State* or the *Record,* it was his to do with as he chose. Any work he submitted that might be unused was likewise his to retrieve. The publications kept no originals and had no interest in reprints. What they marketed was the freshness and frequency of Jak's first-print art. Newspapers came and went, eagerly snatched and read one day, tossed out the next. The medium was disposable. The money was made in advertising; the more readers, the more advertisers paid.

The *State Magazine* went to great lengths to attract readership. One example was its April 3, 1949, cover updating South Carolina's historical past as a royal colony. The magazine had scored an American exclusive, arranging through the Associated Press for popular Princess (later Queen) Elizabeth of England to pose with her new baby, Prince Charles. The picture taken in Buckingham Palace, stated the issue, "is purported to be the first full color photograph of the Princess with her son released for publication. Prince Charles was born last November 14." Under influence of Jak's artistic eye, colors on inside pages of the magazine were elegantly coordinated in lighter tints, rose and teal, of the dominant burgundy, royal blue, and gold in the striking cover photograph. The princess afterward wrote a note of appreciation for the publication's interest and for copies sent her.

Other ploys to grab readers' attention included contests with cash prizes. "Can You Rhyme This" provided four lines of a staff-composed limerick, inviting readers for a two-dollar prize to supply the best ending. Jak had fun helping compose rhymes. Winners' names and hometowns were published, along with various responses. A one-dollar prize went to selected anecdotes submitted to "Home Grown Tales," true stories of fewer than two hundred words, again published with names and hometowns. Jak jazzed up entries of both contests by humorously illustrating them. In a later contest, Jak drew cartoons without words for which readers suggested witty captions or titles. The *State Magazine* indulged in both the serious and the silly, both the sophisticated and the folksy—something for everyone. As Sloan guided well-written subject matter to broad appeal, Jak delighted in being an "everyman's artist." He quipped that the magazine had a regular staff of "two persons—Gene and me," and for seven years they devoted their primary time to it.

Jak had begun his newspaper career at age twenty-five with a basic goal of becoming self-supporting as a working artist and with an ambition of enjoying life along the way. To afford both he sought from the beginning of his employment to supplement his salary by moonlighting as a freelancer. W-2 statements from 1948 and 1949 show Jak's earnings from the State Company and from another business it later purchased, Carolina Engraving Company. A small specialty print shop near the *State,* Carolina Engraving did some of the plate engraving for the newspaper. Going there frequently with his job, Jak became good friends with experienced graphic artist Ray Twork. Both were veterans with tales of adventure, both were creative artists, and both liked a good party.

In a later interview, Twork recalled his giving business advice to Jak about how to be a successful freelancer: keep a notepad handy, develop a client list, and build a portfolio. He also passed along moonlighting jobs to Jak. When Louis Arthur Searson wanted an illustration of a mule and wagon with driver for his book *The Town of Allendale,* published in 1949, Twork recommended "a country boy artist" he knew. Jak was hired, and Searson was pleased. Jak and Twork were soon collaborating on projects, and Jak began visiting Twork and his wife, Polly, at their Meadow Street home. She invited him to stay for home-cooked meals, invitations he always accepted. The Tworks hosted congenial parties where Jak brought friends and made new ones.

With a steady income and a supplement of freelance opportunities, in January 1949 Jak began payments toward the $1,600 purchase of more reliable wheels, this time a vehicle with a solid top, a working man's 1946 Ford sedan. Well-built and detailed, the model had been one of the first back in production at war's end, based on a 1942 design. With job transportation settled, Jak had a bigger dream to put into place. Lots for sale at Holden Beach had been redrawn to a larger scale, now priced at $500. He scraped up enough for a down payment, determined not to wait for prices to escalate further. He would not miss this opportunity.

When Jak met his late-night press deadline on August 26, 1949, he did not go out with the gang to celebrate as usual. Instead he headed home to the Mole Hole to grab a few hours' sleep. When the alarm sounded at 4:00 A.M., he sprang up, splashed cold water on his face, and quickly dressed. He had made all arrangements and fueled his Ford before going to work Friday. All he needed to do was drive to the beach and sign the papers. He stopped briefly at a familiar grill near Conway, leaving three quarters on the table—paying the fifty-cent bill and adding a 50 percent tip. He felt like Rockefeller! He would soon be the owner of property facing the Atlantic Ocean.

Just north of the sleepy village of Shallotte, North Carolina, he turned right onto a fresh ribbon of asphalt. The unmistakable fragrance of salt marshes invigorated him. The rest was an excited blur: friendly greetings, signatures, handshakes, then a sandy mile-and-a-half drive west down the Holden Beach island to lots 7 and 17, marked only with wooden stakes. Beach lots were end-to-end "double lots" that formed long, narrow parcels. Kicking off his shoes, he walked the 250 feet to the edge of his property. With the slip of paper tight in his hand and warm sand shifting between his toes, Jak stood there, gazing at the waves breaking before him, and smiled. He *did* feel like Rockefeller.

Monday morning Jak was pleased to share his good news. Although not blood kin, many of his coworkers were like family. They shared ups and downs and looked out for each other. Generosity was highly appreciated, and among some lending and paying back money seemed a regular pastime. Even the most practiced of them, however, thought Jak a "sucker for a pretty girl with a sob story."

Coworkers looked out for one another in other ways too. Managing editor John A. Montgomery, for example, proved a matchmaker, suggesting that Gene Sloan meet a certain writer on the Winnsboro newspaper, Kathleen "Kitty" Lewis, who frequently submitted material to the *State*. Montgomery thought the two a natural match owing to common interests. Basically shy by nature, Gene typed a letter to "Miss Lewis" on November 29, 1950, on newspaper letterhead, asking for a blind date and adding, "However, if you are unwilling to take the chance do not feel that you are being editorially coerced and please keep on sending us stories of interest, as you have done in the past." He signed it, "Hopefully, Eugene Sloan." They dated, discovered compatibility, and eventually formed not only a marital partnership but also a journalistic one. They collaborated on design, layout, composition, and photography, processing film and making prints in their home darkroom. Kitty's entry into Sloan's life enlarged Jak's circle of close friends.

During early years working on magazine or newspaper assignments, Jak traversed the state for unique stories. Sometimes he traveled alone, sometimes with Sloan or another reporter or photographer. Sometimes they camped or stayed overnight in order to get just the right lighting. Jak referred to a number of these trips in his memoir notes. He recalled, for example, a visit to deserted Dataw Island "to find the tabby ruins" of buildings from the 1700s for a magazine photo essay. On a "campout on Fripp Island before the bridge came" Jak saw wild hogs and sea turtles. Once when he was driving at night, a deer jumped into his headlights and was unavoidably killed. Jak stopped and dressed it before driving on, making use of hunting skills from boyhood.

One plus for Jak on his travels to scenic places was that he often invited a girlfriend along as a model to photograph or sketch. Jak casually called all his female friends "girlfriends," regardless of length of acquaintance or degree of intimacy. His companion's main prerequisite was a spirit of adventure. It was fearless Jane Gerard who accompanied Jak on one adventure he chronicled in his memoir notes: "I drove car down beach at Seabrook Island when it was still wild, collected drift boards on beach, made road up into dunes, drove car into dunes, waited for high tide to come in, spent night trapped in." Another memoir note alluded to danger the night that he and girlfriend Micki Inskeep drove across an old wooden bridge so rotten that "the front wheels broke through the bridge" and they escaped only by "ingenious, instinctive engineering employed to escape the trap."

Sometimes Rhonda and Lucy took Jak in their motorboat to places inaccessible by car. Once they traveled seven miles off the lowcountry coast to Cape Romaine, where Jak's memoir notes recall the lighthouse with "the great prisms vandalized." Several times he referred to another outing, a "moonlit night in abandoned lighthouse on Hunting Island" with Rhonda and Lucy, another couple, and an unnamed girlfriend. The other couple, "averse to the climb," stayed below and spent the night in the car "victimized by mosquito hoards." Rhonda, Lucy, Jak, and the unnamed girlfriend carried air mattresses to the top: "The view was fantastic, the wine was heady." The next morning, he said, "We threw mattresses off top, watched float down. Birds . . . flew below us." He long recalled "the euphoria of being in a strange, unique, romantic place elevated above the wilderness below."

Jak maintained contact for some time with adventurous Jane Gerard. He had met the "journalist extraordinaire," as he called her, in his last semester at the University of South Carolina. After Jak took his job at the *State,* Jane was hired part time in the sports department and wrote some features for the *State Magazine.* In 1949 she returned home to Charleston to attend school there. Jane wrote Jak on October 16, 1950, about her new job she got there in advertising: "Night before last I worked . . . on a sketch at the office and I declare I felt just like you—burning the midnight oil. But I'm so slow . . . I have to work day and night to finish what a real artist would dash off in an hour." A lively writer Jane was afterward employed at the Charleston *News and Courier,* where she wrote breezy and gutsy features based on firsthand research.

Jak and Jane explored several scenic lowcountry sea islands together. She wrote him on February 12, 1952, about her new assignment for the Charleston newspaper: "I love it . . . the first time that a woman has been on the waterfront beat." On March 4 Jane described going out "Fri, Sat & Mon . . . day and night with the tug boats trying to pull a freighter off a sand bar . . . had the time of my life . . . made page 1 for 4 days." She concluded, "After those days & nights at sea, life is intolerably dull anymore." Jane's thirst for excitement, danger, and challenge enticed her further. To write a story on a group of shipwreck survivors, Jane followed them to New York City and landed a job there as a feature writer for *Newsday.* She wrote Jak on April 14, 1953, urging him to visit her in New York. Later, as Jane Gerard Chekenian, she would become the Long Island correspondent for the Sunday *New York Times.*

Young women wandered in and out of Jak's bachelor existence, according to his acquaintances and to his own memoir notes. Keeping in good physical shape by running and lifting weights, staying naturally tanned by being outdoors, and with friendly good manners, Jak was very attractive to females. His family in Camden never knew who might arrive when Jak's car pulled up in their yard on impromptu visits. He dropped in with friends of all types, some of them looking quite startled on a first date to find themselves among sedate folks such as Oscar and Mae or active, curious young children. Some young women were models, or would-be models, since Jak kept with him release forms to be signed by attractive females he met and requested to photograph or sketch. Enjoying music he liked going with dates and friends to clubs, dancing and "night-hawking," as he referred to staying out late.

Among girlfriends were also a lounge singer, a Fort Jackson officer's daughter, a schoolteacher, a movie ticket taker, and friends of friends. Once a girlfriend inquired whether their relationship might become serious enough for marriage. Jak replied, yes, only there was another girl to whom he "owed" a proposal first since he had known her longer. The spunky inquirer gave him an abrupt good-bye. Apparently Jak had thought the reply a "polite" way to disentangle himself from commitment. Some young women played on his sympathies and sought his confidence. One, whose relationship with a mutual acquaintance had ended badly, left town and wrote Jak lengthy, anguishing letters detailing personal problems, divulging confidential details and private thoughts. As Jak approached his thirties, family members were shaking their heads, wondering when he was going to "settle down" with a nice steady girl. Jak still professed that he was not ready to settle down, that he had much he wanted to do first.

An experience Jak treasured from early days at the *State* was taking a VIP informational flight across the United States with the U.S. Air Force, which had become an independent military branch in 1947. The air force flew a group of artists and syndicated cartoonists to the West Coast and back, stopping at bases for banquets, flight demonstrations, and overnight stays. The complimentary trip was arranged by Milton Caniff, whose adventure comic strip *Steve Canyon* from 1947 to 1988 featured a World War II veteran who returned to service in the air force during the Korean War. At the end of Jak's trip, he excitedly offered to write an article for the *State* about his travel. Corporation president and general manager J. M. Blalock nixed the idea, advising him "not to bother doing any publicity report . . . for the Air Force." In Jak's memoir notes, under the heading, "Regretable Mistakes, Dumb Errors, By-passed Opportunities," he wrote that guests on the trip who had voluntarily written about it were the following year "treated to a flight to Japan." That was an adventure he missed and a time he regretted taking advice from a boss. Besides, Jak thought, writing about travel was a good idea.

In 1951 Jak was competitively selected by the South Carolina Forestry Commission to create a series of three posters advertising the state's participation in the USDA Forest Service's national campaign to prevent forest fires. The commission requested that one poster include Smokey Bear, whose image had been created for the Forest Service in 1944 to encourage protection of raw materials valuable as war supplies. Jak's fire-prevention posters, especially of Smokey, received popular reception. They were requested for distribution in other states as well and received special recognition from the Forest Service in the national campaign. The work brought Jak to the attention of other state agencies, and over the years he received freelance assignments from several of them for handbooks and public information announcements.

Jak began another grand venture. He had been making payments on his beach lot for two years and freelancing as much as possible to fulfill his dream of building a cottage at Holden Beach. With his lot paid for and a steady income, Jak wrangled a mortgage to build. In 1951, the same year that the coastal island got a post office, his cousin Alvin Creed began to construct a bungalow for him on his beachfront lot. Alvin had been in Camden overseeing the building of Oscar and Mae's new Colonial Lake home when Jak showed him plans he had sketched for his beach house. Alvin agreed to build it, sandwiching the work between commercial jobs to save money. Jak smiled. Things were falling into place.

During difficult days on Okinawa, Jak's mental refuge had included reflections on his grandfather's old home place and dreams of a getaway on a private pond. Now he was achieving a retreat on an unspoiled beach graced with seabirds, driftwood, and shells. This would be a family vacation house, a bachelor pad, a party shack, and an art studio—a place to sketch and photograph seascapes and models in a pristine setting. Here from a front sundeck he could watch and capture breathtaking sunrises and sunsets thanks to the island's orientation facing southward to the ocean. Once the cottage was usable, even before it was finished, Jak began to stay there, sometimes working on the house, sometimes bringing friends to enjoy the beach with him. Visitors recalled from its earliest days that, for the amusement of all, he kept the place always stocked with popular comics and well-thumbed issues of *Mad Magazine,* which began as a comic book in 1952. Jak thought laughter, like beauty, benefitted everyone.

Bob Kaminer recalled that at the office Jak would "borrow money from me all the time, although he never borrowed over about 50 cents a time." The money would be for a bowl of soup or a sandwich at the nearby café. "I used to kid him about that, here he's buying a beach house and I'm paying for it." Later Kaminer would come to work and find lying on the layout pad on his desk the repayment with "some great big cartoon Jak had drawn with a message like 'now I hope you can sleep at night.'" Coworkers liked ribbing one another.

Over the years Alfred had always enjoyed hearing Jak tell of his travels and experiences at Auburn, at Parris Island, in the Pacific, in China, at Pittsburgh, and along the coast. He was proud of the acclaim his older brother was garnering working for the newspaper. However in June 1952 it was Jak who beamed with pride at his younger brother's achievement when Alfred graduated from USC with a degree in business administration. That year too Jak was a smiling member of the wedding party on December 6 when Alfred married Princa McManus, whom he had met and dated during college.

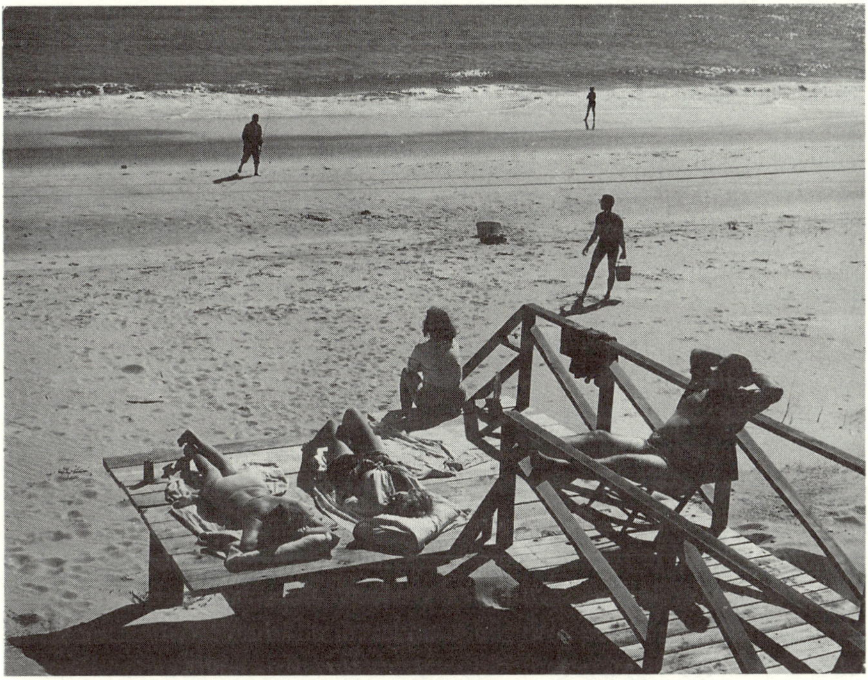

Sunbathers on Jak's Holden Beach deck, friends posing for his rental publicity photograph, with Jak on beach with pail. Courtesy of the family.

In 1953 Jak took freelance work with the new DuPont May Plant, which had opened in Camden three years earlier and which would soon employ his brother-in-law, newly graduated mechanical engineer Rhonda Brown. Former *State* coworker Dick Dunlap, now on the DuPont communication team, had contacted Jak seeking the creation of a graphic image around which to launch a safety incentives campaign. Jak drew a goofy character that in a plant contest was named "Moe Awards." Management was so pleased with Moe that they hired Jak for additional safety messages. Thus was born a motivational comic strip series with Dunlap, "The Misadventures of Moe," tagged "by Jick Smylap" to combine names of the collaborators. Jak's zany creativity taught safety by showing the results of Moe's doing all the wrong, unsafe things. The series ran for over a year in the plant publication *May Times*. Jak also illustrated several DuPont plant booklets.

Early in 1954 the magazine *South Carolina Wildlife* premiered. The publication's first issues included Jak's humorous cartoons, which attracted wide attention. Published by the State Department of Natural Resources, the magazine's educational mission was to create awareness of the conservation work of the newly founded Wildlife Resources Commission. For several years the magazine's first editor, Eddie Finlay, reran or updated relevant Carolina Sports columns he had written and Jak had illustrated for the *Columbia Record*. From its beginning as an attractive black-and-white quarterly, *South Carolina Wildlife* captured audience attention, growing to continue as a color monthly subscription magazine important to the Palmetto State.

With proceeds from salary and freelancing going into his house construction at Holden Beach, Jak enjoyed trips there at every opportunity, salvaging and collecting materials to suit his pocketbook and his taste. When he spotted an abandoned shrimp boat that others considered an eyesore, he visualized the ultimate guest house behind his cottage. Owners Bill and Susie Grady consented to give the wooden vessel to him if promptly removed. Jak worked out another deal. John Holden agreed to use his equipment and move the heavy discard to Jak's lot in exchange for Jak's painting a twenty-foot sign reading "Holden Beach Pavilion" on both sides of Holden's oceanfront establishment. Jak's memoir notes relate that John finished moving the boat onto the lot just ahead of arrival of the highway inspector, notified that a strange spectacle was moving along the road. No special permit had been issued, but the inspector saw no movement. The boat was settled and equipment gone when he passed by.

Although the beach house was finished in 1954 and being enjoyed by friends and family amid its decorating stages, Jak had no chance to transform the derelict vessel. On October 15 Hurricane Hazel, a category 4 storm, made landfall near the North Carolina–South Carolina border, roughly twenty miles south of Holden Beach. Jak's memoir notes state of the old boat that the great storm "picked her up and carried her away back across [the] island and waterway to [the] mainland for her last ride." More crucial, however, was the complete loss of the cottage itself. Builder Alvin Creed's May 4, 1955, statement to Jak for insurance records specified the total cost of $9,185 and stated that they did "the final work up there the week of April 2, 1954." Completion preceded the hurricane just over seven months.

Methods of predicting hurricanes were then unsophisticated. Two days prior to landfall, Hazel was in Haiti with no forecast that it might hit the Carolinas. Midday on October 14 Hazel had strengthened to 150-mile-per-hour winds and was moving at 20 miles per hour on a path headed

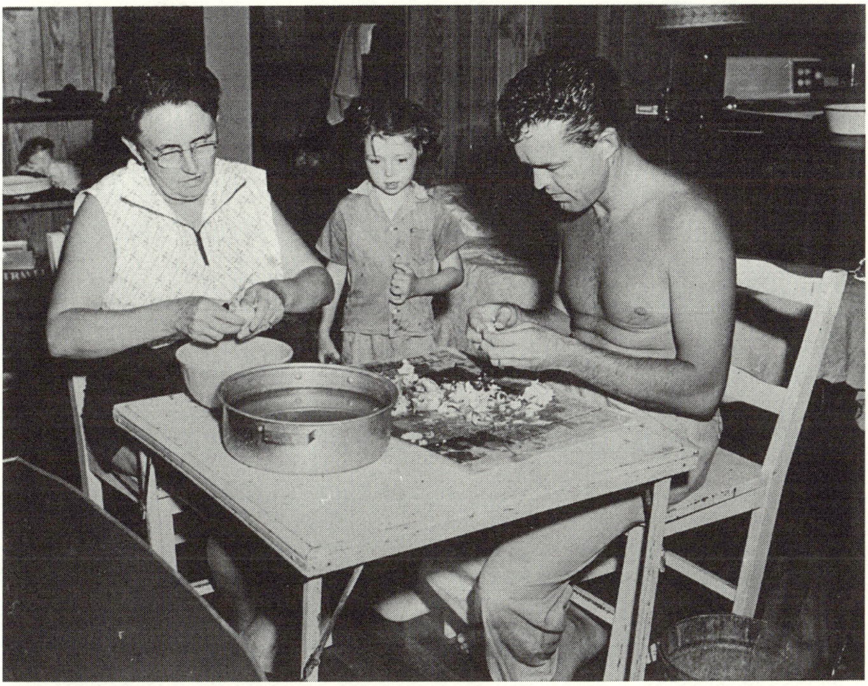

Inside his new beach cottage in 1954, Mae and Jak cleaning shrimp and crabs with niece Mary Ann Anderson watching. Courtesy of the family.

toward Cape Hatteras, considerably further north and west than the Brunswick Islands. Before midnight a surveillance airplane reported a change of course, predicting the hurricane would come ashore the next day between Wilmington and Myrtle Beach. Unaware most persons at Holden Beach had gone to sleep without trepidation and realized their predicament only upon awakening to heavy winds and rain and rapidly rising tides. They quickly collected what they could. A turn bridge that in February had replaced the old ferry was instrumental in allowing evacuation of the island. The hurricane's eye passed over Holden Beach around 10:30 the morning of October 15. Two of the three people who remained on the island were casualties. The third—John Holden's father, Luther—alone miraculously survived.

As John Holden related in his *Holden Beach History*, he was the only Holden Beach resident two days later at a disaster meeting in Wilmington on October 17 when he reported the hurricane's effect on the island. Of some three hundred cottages and businesses there before the hurricane, only twelve cottages afterward stood, themselves damaged. All oceanfront property the entire length of the island had lost a strip of beach sixty or seventy-five feet on the average. The hurricane had opened a new inlet dividing the island from the Intracoastal Waterway to the Atlantic Ocean, and the tide was rising and falling through the inlet. Electric power poles were heavily damaged, and of six miles of paved road, only one-quarter mile remained. John, himself, had lost everything—his home and his business—with no insurance.

As is typical of policies, Jak's insurance did not include flood damage. The company would pay only for damages he could prove had been caused by wind and not by water. Jak, Oscar, and Mae went to his place the day after the hurricane and scoured the beach and the area across the waterway. He took photographs from which, for a November 7, 1954, spread in the *State Magazine,* he created a series of sketches, one of which depicted his parents walking among the rubble. Continuing to scour the area in additional visits, he eventually located among debris on the mainland a nearly intact interior closet that had been in his house. Inside was indisputable evidence of ownership. An electric iron handed down to him from Lottie's Winthrop days, the one he had taken to Auburn and carved with his name "Smyrl," was inside, its handle flattened from impact. This convinced the insurance company that wind had blown his house across the waterway before the sea surge washed over the island area. The insurance settlement enabled him to pay off his mortgage and left him the balance of $1,018.97. The island, its infrastructure, and his lot lay ruined.

Chapter 20

Adjustments

"A Bohemian and a full-fledged member of the Establishment"

When Hurricane Hazel struck on October 15, 1954, Jak was in Columbia settling into new work quarters in Columbia. Only five days earlier, on undeveloped acreage off Stadium Road, next to USC's Carolina Stadium and opposite the State Fair grounds, the *State* and the *Columbia Record* took occupancy of a new building constructed as a modern newspaper plant. Promptly the next morning's and afternoon's issues rolled smoothly off newly installed Goss Headliner letterpress presses. It was widely jested about the move to the remote location, 2.6 miles southeast of the capitol, that most of the newsmen lamented the distance, as did owners of downtown bars who lost customers, but that Columbia politicians rejoiced to be further removed from journalistic scrutiny.

Ample new space and up-to-date equipment enabled reorganization and merging of *State* and *Record* duties and employees in modern corporate sharing. Clean white workspaces with air conditioning and efficient equipment changed the work environment. While some employees felt the surroundings "sterile" or regretted loss of the familiar, others responded, "About time!"

For Jak an exciting aspect of the move to the new building was the spacious addition of a photography department boasting a state-of-the-art darkroom. Even before the move, he had been using photographs as illustrations in a variety of creative ways. On January 3, 1954, the *State*

Magazine published his feature "Artist's Life," subtitled "one-act photo-comedy." Like comic strip panels, a series of farcical photos told a story parodying modern art and pinup poses. The unidentified setting was Jak's Mole Hole apartment, and modeling as a cubist painter was Russell Henderson, in real life an artist of far more realistic style. In the magazine on February 14, Jak repeated the format in "a short photo comedy" with artist friend Ray Twork, who the following year appeared in another strip captioned "photographic nonsense."

Jak hung around the new photography department often, picking up tips and becoming friends with professionals such as Vic Tutte and Tom Nebbia who were enticed to the *State* by its new facilities. They too were war veterans and passionate about the importance and art of photography. English-born and reared in Scotland, Tutte had been a POW of the Germans for five years and proudly adopted American citizenship. Nebbia, a war correspondent during the Korean War, had arrived at the *State* via Fort Jackson, his last military assignment. The appearance of one of his photos in a 1950 *Life* magazine had inspired him to seek a career in photography. The *State Magazine* on October 31, 1954, ran full page one of Nebbia's scenic photographs of the Wateree Dam, with a foreground perspective of two unidentified persons looking down from the vantage of Eagle's Nest. Seen from the back, in a place he had been many times in his life, Jak stands beside a young female. Jak eagerly shared favorite places with photographer friends.

Designed in the new office, a special technique cover of the *State Magazine* on January 2, 1955, announced the New Year with a locally photographed baby breaking through a graphic art calendar. An appealing magazine cover on February 20 resulted from Jak's prudently developed habit of keeping his camera handy. The smiling image of his five-year-old niece Mary Ann Anderson with a giant snowman had been snapped when the two of them happened to be visiting Oscar and Mae during a rare South Carolina snowfall. Jak had romped with sister Lottie's youngest child in the snow, helped build the snowman, and afterward grabbed his camera. On an inside page, a candid photo follows. On a rug before a warm open fire, a tired little girl lies asleep, along with Tommy the cat and Nell, the current dog with that family-favored name.

Photography added to but did not distract from art in Jak's bag of skills as illustrator, storyteller, and entertainer. New challenges in presenting both art and photography in the *State Magazine* resulted from another change in the company's process of modernizing and expanding. With the issue of September 25, 1955, the expensive outsourcing of slick color rotogravure printing ended. The next Sunday, October 2, premiered the magazine's appearance as a newsprint tabloid from the more economical in-house letterpress printing. While the new equipment was much improved over the old presses, the resolution and paper quality were not as fine as in the costlier process the company had been hiring. Jak worked hard to make his art for that first letterpress cover iconic and memorable with the South Carolina flag in indigo blue and white and the state seal in yellow and black, superimposed on a background of snowy clouds.

Tom McLean, who worked with Jak through many years of his career, remarked in a 2011 interview that, as an artist, Jak was always working at a disadvantage with his medium being the newspaper. Acidic newsprint and low screen resolution provided a harsh environment for display and preservation of illustrations. While Jak's creative efforts benefitted from higher-resolution printing and finer paper, McLean explained that the cost-effective letterpress process "used to churn out newspapers at 20,000 an hour or more—just ink on newsprint. If you had a simple black and white drawing, that was fine. But for color illustrations you had to make four separate plates that went on the press, as opposed to just one. Jak used to be frustrated, and we all got frustrated, because half of a press run would be like looking at a 3-D movie without glasses because it was difficult to keep it in register. In a lot of ways, some of Jak's best work was misplaced in the medium in which he was working." Jak continued to befriend pressroom operators, visiting them regularly to retrieve his originals and to keep a concerned eye on mechanical operations requiring their hand adjustments.

The *State Magazine* as a Sunday "supplement," in modernized lingo, continued its South Carolina focus, although subject matter would begin to broaden with the changing of times and staff assignments. Jak and Gene Sloan had desks in the busy newsroom, phones ringing, where Sloan tackled current news reporting as well as magazine topics. Jak's desk, labeled "Staff Artist," grew piled with art requests from various sections of both morning and afternoon newspapers. The *State Magazine,* after existing over thirteen years, would be discontinued in March 1962, replaced by a nationally syndicated slick supplement. By that time graphic and special effects, along with expanded feature writing, were appearing on regular pages of the daily *State* and *Record.* Jak's cartooning, various illustration styles, and photographs popped up variously on news, editorial, sports, feature, and advertising pages.

The newsroom bustle that Jak found interesting proved also a distraction from getting his work done, with onlookers hanging around his desk. On request an "office" was set up for him, a cubbyhole tucked behind the women's department. Tom McLean said it suited Jak just fine because he could think and work at his own pace, "sort of out of sight, out of mind" of his bosses. McLean described Jak as being "always torn between being a Bohemian and a full-fledged member of the Establishment." It was a statement that described his personal life as well.

The 1954 striking of Hurricane Hazel, coinciding with the *State*'s move to a new plant and subsequent changes, had more direct impact on Jak's personal life. Having lost his Holden Beach investment, he lapsed back into a lifestyle of enjoying money while he had it. Jak survived from paycheck to paycheck, often obtaining short-term small loans in the interim. In 1955 on borrowing, midway to payday, at a familiar loan company, he was attended by an employee he had never seen before. Captivated by the tall, attractive blonde with a quick smile and pleasant demeanor, Jak immediately determined to ask her out. Conversation revealed her name—Betty Spires, recently moved to Columbia from Edgefield, South Carolina. Betty was likewise attracted to the handsome, athletic man. Movie star James Dean might have inspired Jak's appearance, she said—slicked-back hair and tight black t-shirt, sleeves rolled up, one side conspicuously nestling a pack of Lucky Strikes.

Betty agreed to go out with him. On their first date Jak drove her to Camden to meet Oscar and Mae. Betty said one of the traits that early endeared Jak to her was the manner in which he interacted with his parents. He always greeted Oscar with a hug and Mae with a hug and a kiss, and he treated them with love and respect. When Betty first met them, Mae had just been named "Kershaw County Master Farm Woman of the Year," and Jak proudly told everyone of the accomplishment.

In time Betty took Jak to meet her family in Edgefield, and they too liked him on their first meeting. They were impressed, she said, that he was so comfortable with everyone and greeted their pet dog like a member of the family. A cousin of Betty's, Ann McCrickard, in 2013 recalled Jak's photographing her family in Georgia and taking a shot of her at twelve or thirteen that made her see herself "in a whole new way, expanding my thinking." Jak and Betty enjoyed one another's company and families, and they dated frequently but not exclusively. Later she took an office job with Sears on the corner of Rosewood Drive and Bluff Road, on the other side of the State Fairgrounds near Jak's office, and they met often for lunch, sometimes picnicking.

In summer 1955 Jak took Betty on a weekend outing to Lake Wateree, boating and skiing with Mac and Polly Sims and with Rhonda and Lucy, whose old trailer sat on their leased lot with their motorboat on Clearwater Cove, south of the public landing. Vestiges of the old islands Jak had known as a boy could be seen from there, where motorboat action had helped erode their beaches. Duke Power no longer leased island lots and had removed old structures on them. The lake, or "the river" as old-timers still called it, was popular for weekenders, summer vacationers, and even a few year-round folks. Jak thought that motorboating activities there would make an interesting photo spread for the *State Magazine*. That's why he had his camera along and was busy snapping shots. He was very pleased to see what a pretty picture Betty Spires took.

The spread appeared on August 21, 1955, identifying Rhonda Brown and Mac Sims as two Camden water sportsmen with outboard motors and "much dexterity at skiing such items as flying saucers, wonder boards, aquaplanes, water skiis." Stating that "the fun is shared by their wives and friends," captions primly identified Lucy and Polly simply as Mrs. Brown and Mrs. Sims and did not mention Betty's name at all. However, her mother wrote "Betty" beside the photograph of an unidentified pair agilely skiing double and put the page in her scrapbook. Mrs. Spires was already fond of Jak.

One week later, on August 28, a two-page spread entitled "Dream Trip" featured one central character appearing graceful, natural, and attractively attired in eleven cleverly posed photographs enhanced with background yellow. The playful introduction reads: "Miss Betty Spires of Edgefield, South Carolina, had always dreamed of traveling to distant and fascinating places. She came to work in Columbia and discovered that with a little imagination and a little trick photography she could achieve the effect of visiting distant places without leaving home." A key at the end of the spread identifies the real locations of postcard-like photos resembling worldwide travel shots, all in fact places in Columbia. Costumed Tom Nebbia, who helped Jak set up the shots, posed sheik-like with Betty in a "desert" scene, actually a local sand pit.

In the same issue another series of photos is headed with a sketch and art lettering by Jak: "Selections from a Beachcomber's Album." The photographer, sites, and persons in shots are unidentified, but photos are all old ones of Jak's taken at coastal locations that depicted but did not name Holden Beach and the inland waterway as early as 1947. Several different bathing-suited girls are pictured. A photo of a former special girlfriend, back turned, stands beside a waterway ferry stop sign and is captioned "End of the road." Even if the photo and caption in "Beachcomber's Album" was not intentionally Jak's farewell to a past relationship, he was in fact moving toward a future predicted in his "Dream Trip" feature.

For eight years Jak's Columbia home had remained the off-beat Pendleton Street basement apartment, close to downtown action. Colleague Bob Pierce wrote of him and his dwelling, "I considered him one of Columbia's first Bohemians, the predecessors of the beatniks and hippies." Once the State office moved to Stadium Road, however, the Mole Hole was less convenient to work, no longer mere blocks away. Jak's memoir notes reminisce about "models and photo sessions, the darkroom . . . the wild parties." Roommates, friends, and "transients" had come and gone. One roommate, a self-absorbed young man, perceived himself an aristocrat and spent his time there "writing his memoirs," according to Alfred, who said he and Jak wondered how so young a man had that much to remember. Another roommate, older artist Russell Henderson, worked for a time on assignments for the *State Magazine*. When Jak first met Betty he was living only three blocks from her apartment at modern Cornell Arms, a snazzy eighteen-floor high-rise advertised as "the tallest building between Richmond and Miami" and a far different atmosphere than the Mole Hole. Columbia housing authorities were pressuring landlords to end rentals of substandard units such as his.

In 1956 Jak moved to what he called a "rural bohemian place," a shack at Arcadia Lakes, which Alvin Creed's son Richard recalled "down below the dam and on the right hand side of the spillway." The house had a screened porch and a yard of longleaf pines. In memoir notes Jak detailed conditions he found: a rotten kitchen floor, big barn rats, and a possum picking at the window screen. When his landlords' kids' horse died, Jak was called on to help bury it. When adults dragged the horse's body into the hole they had dug, it was too shallow, and the legs from rigor mortis projected above the opening. Jak had to help saw off the legs and throw them in beside the body, then fill up the grave.

In this secluded setting Jak enjoyed "woodcarving, painting, swimming," and "nude bathing in back yard." Skinny-dipping in the lake was followed by showering with a garden hose. Jak continued to hone his photography. His memoir notes mention a makeshift darkroom and photography models. He threw parties with "champagne drunk from a mayonnaise jar" and referred to area "bootleggers who wanted to stash booze in the barn." One of the frequent partiers there was Dan Wall, with whom Jak traveled to Florida investigating a sign-painting job. Jak had always been attracted to that beautiful state with its wild natural swamps and beaches.

In wintry weather of early 1956, a lifelong fascination of Jak's stirred upon his overhearing that *State* reporter Joe Barnett owned a boat. Over weeks of dialogue, the two concocted an itinerary for a grand voyage. During their two-week vacation, they determined to follow the Intracoastal Waterway as far south as they could travel in seven days, then turn around and come back. Details of the trip were reconstructed from Betty's recollections and from a "ship's log" Jak kept in a small notebook.

On April 7, 1956, Jak and Joe trailered the eighteen-foot craft to a landing at Rice Hope plantation near Moncks Corner. Betty and her roommate went along to drive the car and trailer back. Despite extensive planning, Jak and Joe had omitted a trial run prior to the noonday launch in the Cooper River, and "severe winds drove the boat into rice fields against bad stumps." Rescued and towed back to the landing, the next morning they were led to the main channel by rescuers. Their odyssey began in earnest. They immediately remedied a "steering failure" two minutes from the dock, but the twenty-five-horsepower Johnson outboard made only slow progress against a strong headwind. Unfamiliar with channel markers, they discovered they were using the "wrong side." That fact they noticed in photos in a "waterway article in *Sports Illustrated,*" which they had brought along.

For fourteen days they endured small craft warnings and engine malfunctions and several times were stuck on mud flats. They found marinas still "closed for the winter" and exhausted their emergency gas. They ran short on money. Because Joe had an Esso gas card, they sought Esso marinas, difficult to find because there was "hardly anything but Gulf" on the waterway. At idle times they fired a .22 pistol at floating objects and once nearly collided with "a Canadian Destroyer in [the] Savannah River."

They were also befriended along the way by a variety of people. A Thunderbolt, Georgia, proprietor offered them a free room for a night and a free meal on the return trip. Jak reported that millionaire yachtsmen invited them aboard for meals and parties, and a Daytona Beach café owner, moved by their beards and shabby appearances, paid for their coffee. They were grateful too to a Savannah repair facility that expedited overhaul of their failing engine. All along the waterway, Jak and Joe saw beautiful scenery, waterfowl, and marine life, and in Florida they saw spectacular tropical birds and mango swamps. Steering problems and engine breakdowns continued, even after the overhaul.

Jak had reminisced about Parris Island, viewed from afar on their trip down, but on their return, mechanical difficulties forced them to dock there. A sergeant gave them a tour, and Jak enjoyed "old familiar sights." On April 21, at the landing from which they had begun their adventure, Betty met the scruffy boaters with the trailer. In two weeks they had cruised as far south as Daytona. They had experienced mechanical failures, drenching rains, heavy seas, gale-force winds, and human errors in judgment. Still they made it back safely. With many tales to tell, Joe headed for his typewriter to begin his story for the newspaper.

During their courtship, Jak and Betty continued dating others. Betty later stated that Jak encouraged her to have other dates because he wanted each of them to be certain before they settled into an exclusive relationship. Jak also encouraged her toward a new job in 1957. Alvin Creed was looking for a secretary-bookkeeper for his construction company, and Jak suggested Betty apply. Sears was a good company, Betty said, but as her job was in the complaint department, she thought a change was welcome. She set up an interview and got the job because of Jak, she said, since "I was a lousy typist."

When Jak proposed later that year and Betty accepted, Oscar and Mae were quite pleased. Everyone saw how happy the couple was, and they felt that Betty fit right into the family, and her kin also liked the match. When the engagement was announced in the *State* on December 19, 1957, coworkers could not resist teasing him. Jak entered the office to find posted a large layout sheet parodying one of his cartoon birds with a similar image and a note to the effect that his bachelor goose was cooked.

The marriage license issued March 4, 1958, listed Jak's age as thirty-four years and nine months, and Betty's as twenty-five years and four months. Sorting through personal effects preparing to transition from bachelorhood, Jak found a photograph of the marine buddy who helped him ashore after his tooth-shattering accidental fall disembarking in San Diego. On the back was the name and address of B. O. Smith. Anxious to get his teeth fixed permanently before he wed, Jak wrote Smith, requesting him to send the Veterans Administration a description of Jak's accident and aftermath. Smith, who clearly recalled the incident, complied. The VA accepted his account as confirmation of Jak's long-standing appeal

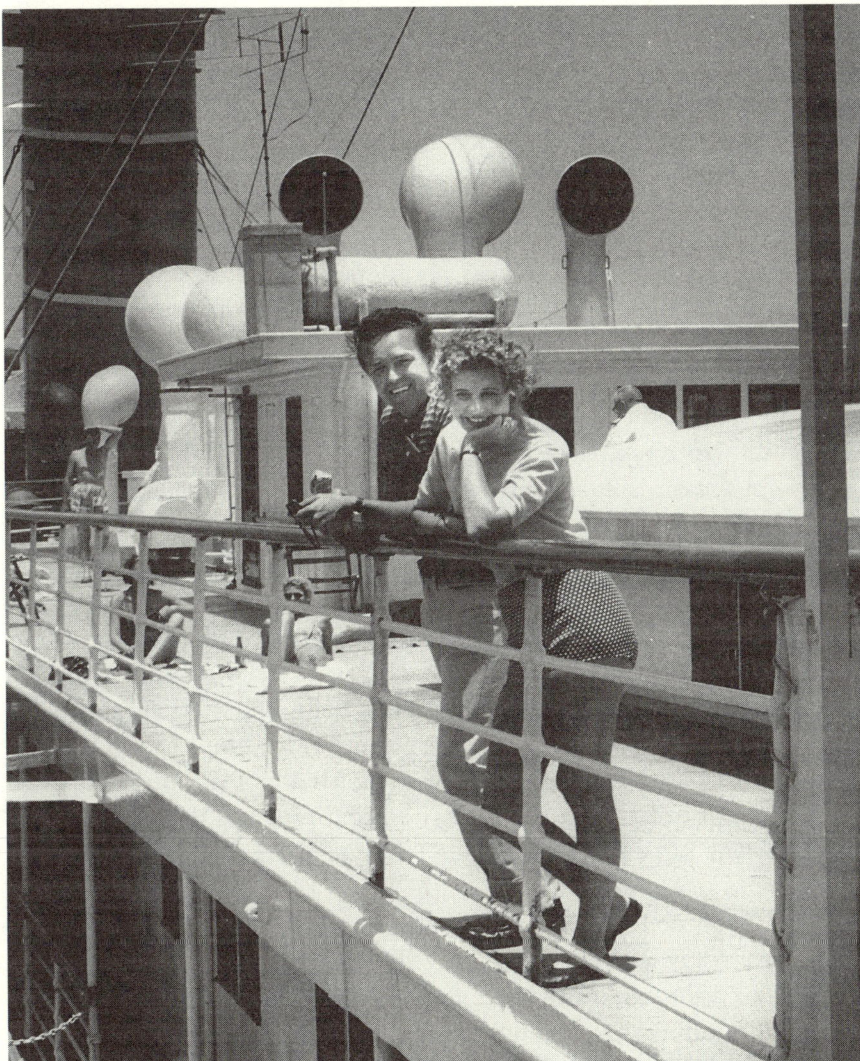

Jak and Betty aboard their honeymoon cruise ship in 1958. Courtesy of the family.

and authorized a Columbia dentist to "make and install a permanent bridge" in his upper jaw.

Flashing a new smile, Jak wed Betty on April 26 in Columbia's North Trenholm Baptist Church before family and friends of both bride and groom. After a cruise to the West Indies, Jak and Betty returned to make their home in the lakeside shack. Some improvements followed, although

Betty said they still showered outside rather than battle cranky plumbing inside. Betty was reasonably tolerant of Jak's friends, but both bride and groom became provoked when, in their absence, one of those friends without permission threw a party in their house and "honed in on hidden booze."

In 1958 Tom Nebbia left the *State* to work for *National Geographic* magazine. In a 2012 interview, he described how he got the position with the prestigious magazine. He was photographing South Carolina governor James F. Byrnes in his office when the governor mentioned knowing a *National Geographic* editor. Nebbia quickly asked for, and got, the governor's recommendation. The job followed. From assignments in far-flung locations around the world, he sent Jak frequent postcards. Vic Tutte on his travels wrote too, especially from annual trips to England. Jak and Betty kept the cards, looking forward someday to real-life distant travels themselves.

The "watering hole" that Jak and his newspaper colleagues were frequenting for postdeadline celebrations was the bar at American Legion Post 6 on Pickens Street. In a 2012 interview, writer Bill McDonald recounted an incident when spirits got out of hand. Jak was with coworkers when a managing editor with whom he had had some friction came in. In response to "some wise remark," Jak, atypically for him, threw his drink in the editor's face. He half expected to be fired, but nothing happened when he went in the next day. The late-night routines that Jak casually resumed may not have affected his job, but his marriage was another story.

Betty recounted that Jak was coming home long past the time she had his supper ready and expected him. She learned that wives of his colleagues faced the same situation. Betty thought it over. She did not ask Jak to stop joining his friends, but instead made a calm request—that he phone and let her know when he would be late, something considered polite as well as fair to her efforts to be ready for his arrival. Jak agreed to the mild request, and as he started calling home regularly, he began to think about negative effects of nocturnal habits on a happy marriage. He began arriving home on a timelier basis and gradually withdrew from frequent afterhours with coworkers. "Marriage takes working on," Betty said. "By two people."

Betty supported Jak's dream to rebuild at Holden Beach. She described visits when they slept overnight on the vacated beach lot. In the sand they drew house plans that he later sketched on paper. They secured a $5,000 loan "to construct a new cottage," receiving the proceeds on September 8, 1959. Jak had not engaged a builder and hesitated to impose again on his busy cousin Alvin, also Betty's boss. However, when Alvin heard Jak was ready to rebuild, he asked to see the plans, looked them over, and then announced, "I'll build this house if you'll rent it like you should and not give it away like you did with the other house I built for you." Alvin, like Betty, knew that Jak was "much too generous with some of his friends."

By summer 1960 the new house was completed. They named it the "Barnacle" in hopes that it would, like its namesake marine crustacean, hang on with determination to the place it was attached. On a map Jak drew for early renters, he described the cottage: "flat roof, multi-color asbestos shingles on sides, triangle window on back, random glass bricks inserted, porch with slanting supports on front . . . mid-century architectural style—on piers." Street numbers had yet to arrive on the island. It was a new and hopeful start, modern styled!

Jak continued supplementing wages with freelance work. In the late 1950s, officials with the Buck-a-Month Club, the forerunner of the University of South Carolina's Gamecock Club, approached him about improving the USC mascot. At the time, Jak said, the gamecock image resembled "some sort of prehistoric, wingless bird." The club wanted a more attractive logo to print on napkins for a big dinner. Researching the game bird and recalling what he had seen as a boy, Jak drew a gamecock in fighting stance with wings spread and spurs extended. Before long, his creation, for which he had been paid $10, was being reproduced on all types of USC paraphernalia—even being painted on the floor as the centerpiece of the basketball team's home court at the Field House on Sumter Street near the Horseshoe.

Jak was flattered that his design of the first "fighting gamecock" was so popular, but he saw a lot of other people making money from it without any recompense to him. Bob Gillespie in the August 26, 2007, *State,* described an educational moment. Jak asked a copyright lawyer, "What can I do, they are using my chicken?" The attorney told him, "You have to put your copyright mark on the very first one you sell or it's not copyrighted." Jak had not signed his logo. Its use was in the public domain. During Paul Dietzel's tenure as coach and athletic director, a Gamecock design in fighting stance was modified by an artist he hired and was copyrighted by the university. The new logo brightened the court floor of the new Carolina Coliseum in 1968 after the Field House burned. Seeing the proliferation of the new logo, Jak observed that if only he had signed

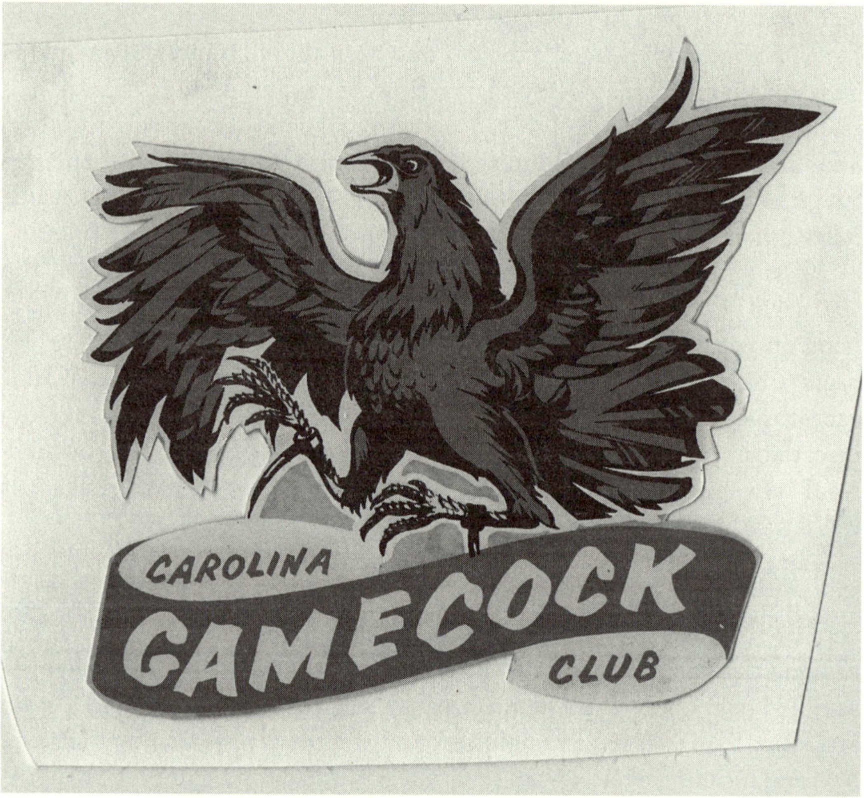

Carolina Gamecock Club decal featuring Jak's design of the "Fighting Gamecock." Courtesy of the University of South Carolina.

his name to the earlier one, his $10 chicken would have been worth a fortune.

By the 1960s Jak's statewide following knew to expect innovative designs and ideas from him. For example, to illustrate a September 3, 1961, feature in the *State* on the Darlington Southern 500, Jack positioned his art like a race track running around the edges of the page of text. Certain familiars came to life in his cartoons and illustrations. Actions of dogs and creatures of nature paralleled human experience. Jak's public asked about the "broke-tail dog" if one had not appeared for a time, and sometimes he offered a variation with other "tied-together" objects. Perky birds in funny hats became recognized as kindred spirits watching human action. Jak continued illustrating Carolinians in their common celebrations—sports, festivals, holidays, music—and in the natural and everyday world of which they were a part. His camera always with him, he kept his eye out for scenic views and human-interest shots, many of which he marketed to the Associated Press for widespread distribution via wire service.

Being established in his career, in the way that many do in maturity, Jak began to examine where he was in life and where he wished to be. It was a bit of surprise to Betty and him that their happy marriage had not quickly expanded into a household with a baby. Both had expected that as natural and had looked forward to welcoming an infant to a loving family such as each had known and continued to experience. Well, they had heard, sometimes these things take a while and a delay provides time to prepare for a big change when it happens. For now they would continue to hope.

Having gained recognition beyond state borders, Jak considered other options and job offers, for one traveling to Miami to interview for a more lucrative and prestigious position at the *Miami Herald.* He had always been drawn to Florida, to its warm weather and the closeness of the ocean surrounding its peninsular borders. He hesitated, however. In an undated letter about December 1961, Jak wrote Dan Wall, "Been back to Miami again also have job offer coming up in Orlando. If I take it, it's going to be rough being away from the beach house." A larger publication in a bigger market had an appeal, but Jak had weighed plusses and minuses before. The advantages of remaining in Columbia, with family near and his own place accessible at the beach, once again tipped the scales and kept him home. That decision made, Jak and Betty made another. They moved from the rustic cabin at Arcadia Lakes into a more modern bungalow on Satchel Ford Road. It was "a much more refined house, a sort of salmon brick," recalled Richard Creed. With casement windows mounted high and numerous shelves, the house was nicer and more modern.

Jak did not change jobs but instead focused on improving their home in Columbia and expanding dreams for the future. Between 1962 and 1969 Jak and Betty made contracts and began payments on seven beach lots at Holden Beach. One adjoined the Barnacle on the east, and two were second-row lots across Ocean Boulevard. Others lay to the east near the island's chapel. Betty agreed with Jak that investments made while the beach was rebuilding should prove valuable in the future. Besides, Betty shared Jak's belief that they were worthwhile "just for the beauty of the land." Nearly a decade would pass before they bought additional property as both worked hard to pay off their purchases.

Hopes of adding to the family with a child of their own would continue to elude them through the years, with doctors they consulted surmising Jak's age with lowered fertility counts the likely factor. Hearing this he painfully offered a divorce to Betty if she, nearly ten years younger, wanted to remarry for another chance to have a child. She replied with assurance that she loved Jak too much to imagine life without him. Devotedly they resolved to fill their hearts with one another, extended family, friends, and the pleasures of enjoying together whatever they would meet ahead.

From the late 1950s Oscar and Mae had been progressing toward the long-planned goal of building a pond for family use near the old Smyrl home place. On the acreage bought from the McDowells while Jak was in China, they selected a site across from the Flint Hill church. Damming a stream nestled between two hills created a fine little pond for fishing. To one hilltop Oscar moved a unique purchase, a nineteenth-century railroad dining car that had been converted to a diner near Fort Jackson. He and Jak were confident it would make a rustic getaway. Meanwhile Alfred, divorced, had been traveling the East Coast as an accountant with McKesson and Robbins. He wed Bonnie Ruth Litchfield, and while they were living in Miami Lakes, Florida, a son, Willie Alfred Smyrl, Jr., was born in 1964. Good reasons to visit Florida, as well as a pond retreat to anticipate at home, were added to Jak's interests in the 1960s.

A change at work also altered his responsibilities and staff relationships. In March 1962 the separate tabloid publication of the *State Magazine* ceased. Local Sunday features were blended into regular newspaper pages, and a slick nationally syndicated tabloid, *Parade,* was inserted. Jak's work, with reduced layout responsibilities, was more freely spread through *State* and *Record* sections.

Political issues and social changes of the 1960s defied complacency. Jak was not among the policy makers navigating editorial positions of the *State* in those turbulent times, although he was periodically asked to provide editorial cartoons on assigned current topics. He was not told what to draw, he said, or what position to take. Jak undertook such assignments with intent to illustrate a complex situation in an enlightening or thought-provoking way, he said, not to ridicule or demean a particular point of view. Instead of editorial cartoons, he preferred cartooning assignments that allowed him to express his opinions on topics of human nature in general and to deal with subjects of timeless concern.

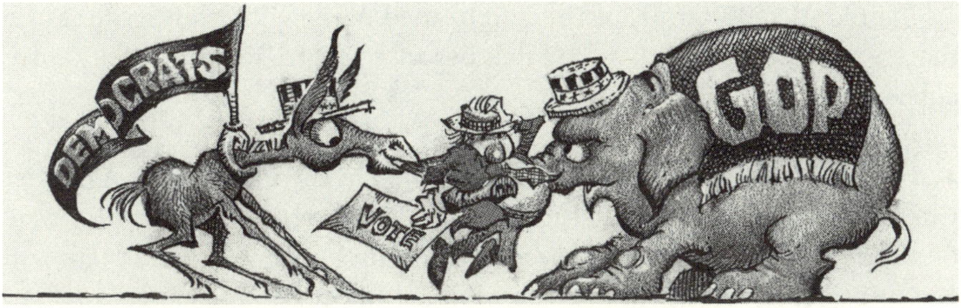

The voter's role in the contest of political parties, by Jak (*Random Rimes*).

Continuing to freelance also, in 1962 Jak illustrated with realism Zan Heyward's outdoor book for children *Swampy and Babs in Okefenokee.* Jak enjoyed the work, fascinated with the natural scenic area of the Okefenokee Swamp on the border of Georgia and Florida. When Heyward in 1965 wanted him to illustrate another book, *The Serpent Was a Salesman,* Jak was so busy he enlisted sister Lucy to help with illustrations. Named with him as co-artist, Lucy Brown assisted him on several other projects as well.

Freelancing for the South Carolina Auto Dealers Association yielded Jak perks for special events. In 1964 he and Betty were invited to travel with SCADA on a convention cruise. Lining up with other passengers to board the ship, Jak's hometown friend South Carolina senator John Carl West and his wife, Lois, greeted them. Presuming the Wests were simply on vacation, Betty remarked that she and Jak were traveling with a convention but "just for fun" and not for "any of those boring speeches." West replied with a grin, "Thanks, Betty. I'm the keynote speaker." Betty, embarrassed, felt "like jumping overboard," but the senator laughed with amusement. A few years later when he was elected South Carolina governor and making many public speeches, she humorously recalled her gaff.

On May 8, 1965, Jak and Betty set out on another type of trip, traveling from Columbia with Rhonda and Lucy towing their nineteen-foot Glastron powerboat. Destination was the Dry Tortugas, islands eighty miles out of Key West, Florida, in the Gulf of Mexico. Jak as usual kept a log. After a night in Orlando, the couples visited Alfred's family in Miami Lakes before departing for Key West, their launch point. They reached the East Key of the Tortugas on May 12 and continued onward. Three men living at historic Fort Jefferson gave them a tour of the fortified anchorage. The group hunted bottles on Loggerhead Key and climbed the 203 steps of the lighthouse to get "an eagles eye view." They returned to Key West on May

19, visited Alfred's family again, and headed home with photographs and more excursion plans. At home Jak began a feature on the Tortugas for subsequent publication.

That spring too Jak's niece Joan graduated from Winthrop College and began teaching at Camden High. In 1966 in the Camden First Baptist Church, she married USC student Glen Inabinet of Orangeburg. Mae blissfully sewed the wedding dress for her first grandchild, and Jak and Rhonda shared responsibilities as wedding photographers. They had encouraged Glen in his growing interest in photography, often describing experiences that they, sometimes with Alfred, had enjoyed with Gene Sloan as he worked on his recently published *Scenic South Carolina*. Sloan acknowledged contributions of Jak and Rhonda for photographs, thanked Betty and Lucy, and dedicated the book to his wife, Kitty, and, daughters Mary and Laura, who likewise shared its adventures. *Scenic South Carolina,* with 333 photographs of noted and remote locations, pictured the state from mountains to seacoast and added rich details in text, thus remaining a valuable resource.

Jak and Betty in early 1966 moved to another home, settling with satisfaction into a roomy two-story, older brick home they purchased at 1623 Heyward Street in Columbia. There was ample room for a studio. The home was convenient to Jak's work, close to the downtown city, and only a few blocks from Gene Sloan's family at 215 South Harden Street. Richard Creed remembered feeling that Jak and Betty had moved "into civilization, or big time" with the refined spaciousness, fireplaces, and better-cultivated yard of the traditional home. In a 2013 letter Mary Sloan Roby recalled, "At first Jak had his studio in one of the smaller bedrooms, but later took down the wall between the two rooms and had an expanded all-in-one studio, music room, and guest room." She remembered it "packed to the gills . . . with art projects in progress," citing, for example, "blocks of wood for carving . . . wrapped in cloth with exotic stamps from all over the world—sent to him by friends traveling overseas." She also remembered "*Playboy* magazines (racy!), trumpets, and harmonicas." Overall Mary observed that Jak "was very organized for an artist. His boxes and supplies were meticulously labeled."

Jak reveled in space to take on larger, more energetic projects such as wood carving. Besides working on his own carvings, he began giving his father lessons. Jak would help select two-inch-thick, fine-grained wood pieces, preferably cypress, and then draw a design for Oscar to work on. Knowing his father's interests, Jak thought wood carving would be a good

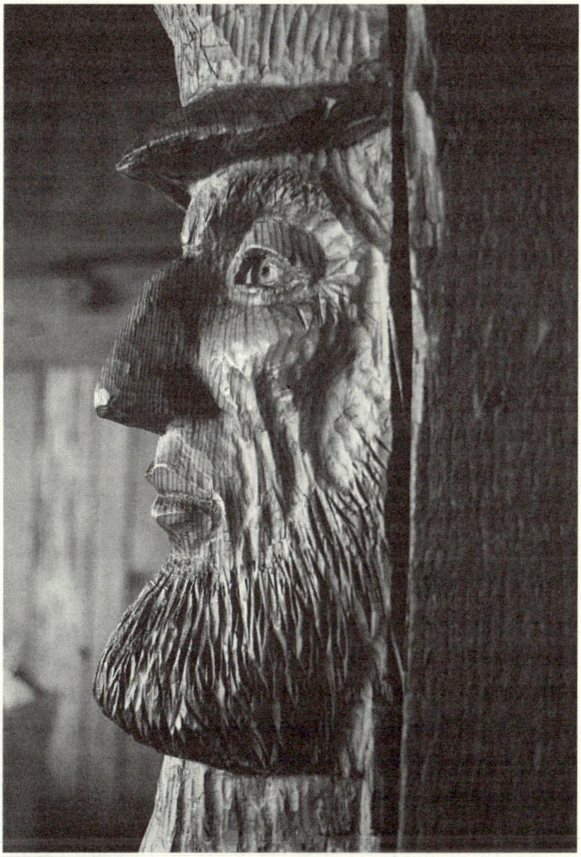

Jak's carving, the near-life-sized head of a sea captain carved in an exposed upright support beam at the center of his Holden Beach house. Photograph by Glen Inabinet.

hobby for his increased time. He had retired on January 1, 1965, ending nearly fifteen years managing the Midland Production Credit Association. Oscar and Mae continued their pleasures in extensive gardening as they landscaped grounds of their home and kept up large food and flower gardens.

In December 1966 the Smyrls' traditional holiday cheer was enhanced by the birth of Alfred and Bonnie's daughter Louise two days before Christmas. Joy turned to sorrow less than a month later when their toddler son, Willie, accidently drowned in the canal behind their home in Florida. A somber crowd gathered at Oscar and Mae's home to comfort the bereaved who had been so recently the blessed. In a cruel twist of fate, one of the youngest Smyrls was the first to be interred in a Quaker Cemetery plot intended for elders.

Always with his family in such times of personal sorrow, Jak returned to the work of this period that absorbed him with most intense concentration. By the late 1960s a number of Jak's illustrations for the *State* as well as for freelance projects included either representative or caricature portraits of local, state, or national personalities. Jak always maintained that drawing either type required close study of features, but the caricatures demanded the most. He aimed for them to be revealing, not insulting. Paying attention to individualized details of faces paralleled the increasing degree of detail that Jak added to other types of work as well. With excellent cartographic skill, Jak had always enjoyed drawing maps and adding illustrations to them for enhancement. He began filling every available space with details of factual and humorous interest.

Broadening the niche market of South Carolina interest that the *State Magazine, South Carolina Wildlife,* and *Scenic South Carolina* had tapped, in January 1968 the first issue of *Sandlapper* appeared. The slick and ambitious regional monthly magazine was established for subscription and rack sales by Lexington lawyer Robert P. Wilkins Sr. and wife, Rose, desiring to promote positive information about the state. Jak was delighted with the quality and look of the publication. Its first issue featured an article on his former professor influential artist Edmund Yaghjian, still at work in Columbia. Another feature described advantages of living in Camden. A third article, written by Kathleen L. Sloan, focused on historic architect Robert Mills, illustrated with photographs by Gene. The *Sandlapper* book section advertised *Scenic South Carolina* for sale and reviewed a new book, Eddie Finlay's *Down the Creek,* illustrated with "cartoons by Jack Smyrl." Finlay's lapse in using Jak's original name spelling may have been an accidental nod to the days they first collaborated at the *Columbia Record.* Jak just chuckled.

The third issue of *Sandlapper,* March 1968, featured Jak's map he was selling of Berkeley County's Hellhole Swamp, illuminated with native critters, comic moonshiners, careless hunters, and hapless travelers. He had illustrated an article in the *State* pointing out home places of several politicians born in that colorful corner of Carolina: Governor Robert McNair, Senator Rembert Dennis, Congressman Mendel L. Rivers, and Columbia's Mayor Lester Bates. So much interest had arisen in the map that Jak printed and sold copies for framing. It was the first but not the last caricature map he would privately publish and popularly sell. Beside the printed copyright at the bottom he urged viewers, "Order copies from Jak Smyrl, Columbia, S.C."

The levity that can make tension more endurable was certainly needed in the state and nation as social, racial, and political discord intensified in America and as war escalated in Southeast Asia. In 1968 the Smyrl family was apprehensive as another generation entered the military. Lottie and Lewis's son Robbie left for the army in June and their son-in-law Glen in September. The circumstances and mood of the country vastly differed from the times when previous family members had left for service. Mae, aged sixty-nine, kept a diary throughout 1968. It was an unusual action, as there is no evidence that she similarly recorded daily activities in previous years or after that year. Perhaps she recorded those particular events because her intuition suggested that it was a pivotal year in history. Perhaps she sensed her mind growing forgetful and sought to bolster memory. Whatever her motive Mae's entries provide an intimate view of family activities and document Jak's personal interactions with his parents.

In many ways Mae's diary reflects that life proceeded in a familiar pattern, with visits back and forth among family members, to North Carolina kin, and to Holden Beach. Oscar and Mae gardened and enjoyed their Colonial Lake home. They fished in their own little pond as well as in their front yard. They had salvaged two nearby sawmill buildings and moved them to the lakeside by their home, one to use as a "picnic house" for fish fries and another as a small guesthouse. While Jak worked with his father on wood-carving projects, Mae sewed, still an excellent seamstress.

As their parents developed signs of declining health and contemporary stresses, Jak and his siblings were attentive. In early 1968 Jak encouraged a change of scenery. On February 16 he, Betty, Oscar, and Mae took the train to Miami. They visited Alfred's family before departing on a four-day cruise aboard the *Jamaica Queen*. Mae recorded in her diary seeing communist Cuba "at the distance." Returning to Miami they visited three days with Alfred. For all it was an enjoyable break in winter doldrums.

Mae's March 10 diary entry reflected the interplay of family intimacy with health and cultural conditions: "It is raining today & cold. Did not go to church but listened to several good church programs. Cooked our dinner yesterday, so made this a quiet & restful day which I feel we all need in this restless age. Jack & Betty came to see us. We all went to Lotties a little while." Mae, often tired, had a medical checkup with X-rays in April. Oscar was hospitalized seven days in May for hernia surgery. Rounds of family visits attended his convalescence, including Alfred and family from Macon, Georgia, where they had moved. Mae reported the visits "grand" and Oscar doing well. On June 8, while the irises they had planted were in full bloom by the lake, family members gathered in the picnic house, bringing favorite dishes for a family meal. This time it was a supper for grandson Robbie, leaving for basic training in the army.

Keeping busy and involved with family helped Oscar and Mae cope with worry. In the summer Lucy's family stayed at Wateree Lake, and visits ensued back and forth. In July Mae wrote, "Jack & Betty came over for the 4th we had a grand dinner of Barbecued chicken, fresh veg. & peach ice cream." On September 5 Mae was bothered by current events: "Looked at T.V. tonight. 'Will it never end?'" She wrote of a family gathering at their home on September 11, "We had a supper for Glen. He is leaving for service in the army. Sure hated to see him go." A week later Oscar and Mae, with Alfred's family and Jak and Betty, left for several days at Holden Beach. On October 11 Oscar and Mae traveled to Durham, North Carolina, for Oscar's World War I reunion, came home to trade suitcases, and drove to a cabin in the mountains, where Alfred and Jack were already waiting for them.

On Thanksgiving Oscar and Mae "ate turkey dinner with Lottie & her family," and on Oscar's birthday, November 19, "Lucy's folks, Lotties folks Jack & Betty all came & had supper with us. We had a regular X'mas feed. Robbie was still here also. We had such a good time." Home on leave, Robbie was bound for Korea, so a Christmas menu now seemed just right for someone who would be away then. On November 24 Mae reported that Glen, who had not had Thanksgiving leave, would be home for Christmas. There was another big meal at her home on December 24, the holiday flurry giving anyone cause to be tired, but, as family hoped, also cheered. In one other notable event that month, Jak was in Camden on December 17 to serve as a pallbearer at the funeral of Newell Wimberly, his high school band director who had been so influential in his life. Jak remained loyal in keeping up with friends and in paying respects.

Although the late 1960s were tumultuous, Jak lightened public moods with caricature art that was revealing and entertaining. He illustrated an August 4, 1968, *State* article about South Carolina's importance in the upcoming GOP National Convention with caricatures of the three front-runners—Nixon, Reagan, and Rockefeller. His September 16, 1968, illustrations for a feature on Shakespeare's heroines depicted Romeo and Juliet and Cleopatra in an eye-catching style, lighthearted but not comical. In the following year, by December 1969, when Jak did several full-page spreads for Christmas, he had developed a comic strip character intended to be lovable and fun, Tee Bone, a chubby and cheerful dog with tied-

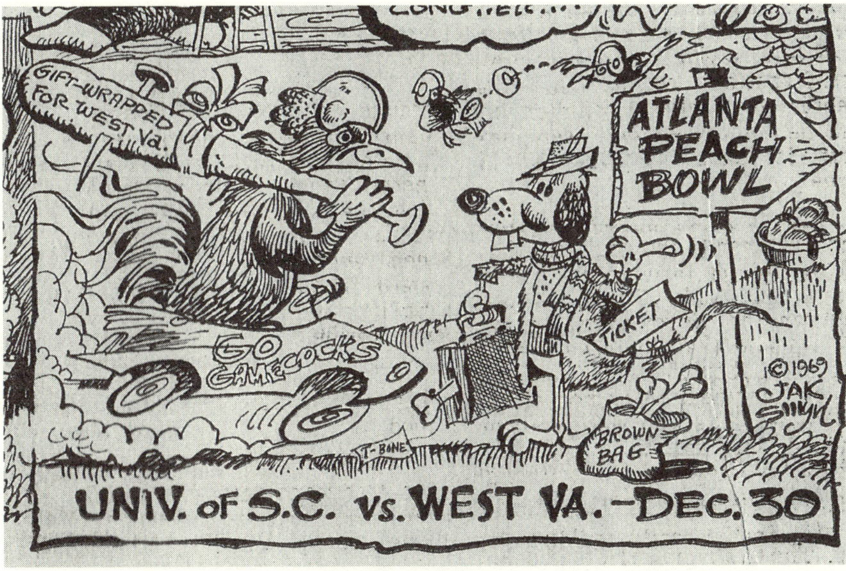

A detailed corner panel of Jak's December 1969 "Carotoons" in the *State:* Tee Bone and the helmeted University of South Carolina Gamecock head to the Peach Bowl, and helmeted birds toss a football overhead.

together tail. A cartoon titled "Carotoons—the Christmas Season Descends on Carolina" depicted Santa quizzically studying a South Carolina roadmap, his sleigh pulled by eight comic reindeer led by "Tee Bone (the Red-Nose Strange Deer)." Below, Tee Bone appeared in four scenes of holiday events. The same month "Carotoons—Christmas Comes but Once a Year" portrayed Tee Bone in various roles in fourteen of fifteen panels. Current sports and news were part of comic scenes—Fidel Castro popping out of Santa's bag to hijack his sleigh, demanding "Head for Havana"; Tee Bone in a conical Vietnamese hat delivering a Christmas card in a rice paddy to a grinning GI in camouflaged helmet; Tee Bone bearing a "Merry Christmas" sign beside a bearded, sandaled man with a sign reading "Hippie New Year."

In 1969 Jak witnessed a change he had long anticipated. Holden Beach incorporated. From the east end at Lockwood Inlet to the west end, Holden Beach encompassed Robinson Beach and Colonial Beach in one uninterrupted stretch. Having for twenty years been a landowner renting out his beach house each summer, Jak had watched area real estate increase, including the now-valuable lengthy section that in his penniless

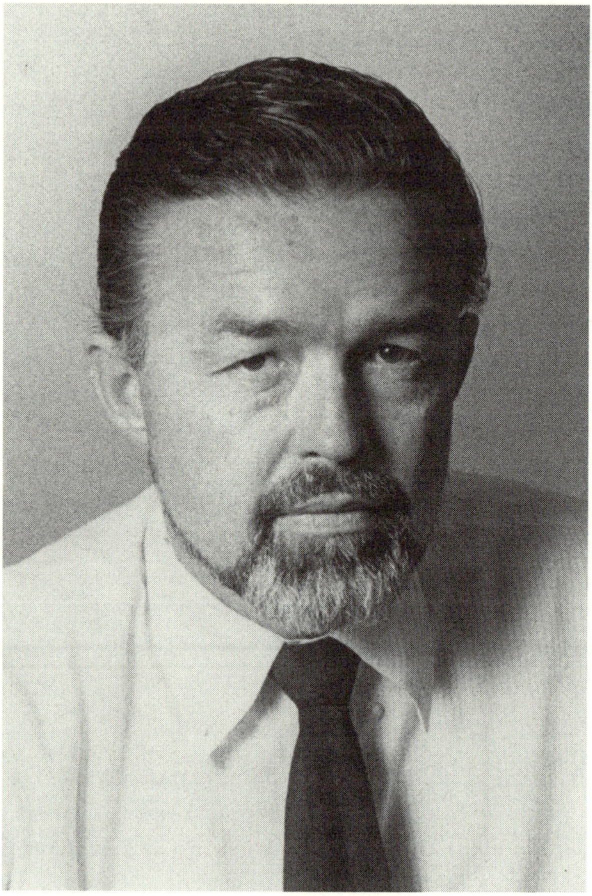

Jak at midcareer. Courtesy of the University of South Carolina.

days he had unsuccessfully longed to buy. Realizing that increased property values would follow incorporation, he urged friends and family to invest in beach real estate. “They are not making any more of this stuff! Once it’s gone, it’s gone,” Jak told them.

Many of the freelance jobs that helped fund Jak’s investments also appealed to his special interests, especially those related to the music he loved. He illustrated record album covers and advertisements for groups such as Larry Conger’s Two Rivers Jazz Band, and he drew brochure covers and announcements for the Carolina Summer Jazz Festival, which he regularly attended with enthusiasm. Researching his subjects by going to practice sessions and joining in for fun with his own horn was entertaining as well as effective in collecting material. He and Betty also enjoyed a number of social events as guests of music associates. With their busy life seeming to be going well, tragedy struck.

On April 6, 1969, Jak lost a best friend and kindred spirit. Gene Sloan, returning from an Easter morning walk on the beach, suffered a fatal heart attack at Hunting Island State Park. Gene had taken Kitty and their daughters with him on a working weekend to take photographs for another book. His camera was in his hand when he was stricken. Jak grieved. He and Gene had bonded closely through work and adventure. A memorable experience Jak described in his memoir notes recalled the time he, Alfred, and Rhonda had gone with Gene to find and photograph long-obscured Ellicott's Rock for a photograph in *Scenic South Carolina*. On a remote rocky granite crag in the early 1800s, U.S. surveyor Andrew Ellicott had inscribed the point where North Carolina, South Carolina, and Georgia meet. Gene had read of the marking in Ellicott's description, but the site was otherwise unknown except as an abstract compass point. Just as the four men were abandoning a long search, Jak's foot slipped, dislodging moss that obscured the inscription. Gene spotted the marking beneath Jak's shoe. It was a moment of excited disbelief.

Jak, in notes he made to deliver a memorial tribute, commented that with the passing of Gene Sloan, South Carolina had lost one of its best friends, a "visionary . . . teacher, philosopher, writer, photographer, historian." He emphasized that his forty-seven-year-old friend had "died as he lived—in pursuit of beauty."

Chapter 21

Place to Place

"A nut who just likes to draw"

In the year Jak lost his comrade Gene Sloan, he completed one of his most iconic works. Sized 19 × 24 inches, *A Caricature Map of South Carolina* was his private publishing venture. Appearing an attractive vintage map, it is revealed on close scrutiny to be what Jak called a "hysterical map." Printed in full color, designed for framing and close-up appreciation, it was packed with humorous and informative images representing the state's history, scenery, and culture. As he worked Jak thought often of how Gene would have appreciated the map. Recalling their times together at many of the places on the map no doubt salved grief.

Jak completed much of the work on weekends and holidays spent in seclusion at Oscar and Mae's private pond the family called Lake Luesta, named for "Uncle Lou" and "Aunt Esta," respected black storytellers who had lived on the property long ago. The railroad dining car had gradually been transformed into a quirky getaway in a Spartan setting. Jak and Betty brought in potable drinking water and swam in lieu of bathing. There was no phone to interrupt his flow of ideas. To minimize distractions they seldom informed others of their whereabouts. The only modern convenience was electricity in the train house, which gave Jak light to work into wee hours, as was his custom. Stars, winking fireflies, and hooting owls filled the nights outside. There was little use of an electric fan, which would disturb his materials. After the map was printed, Jak enlisted Oscar and Mae to help with sales. Trips to tourist shops and gift stores offered pleasurable outings.

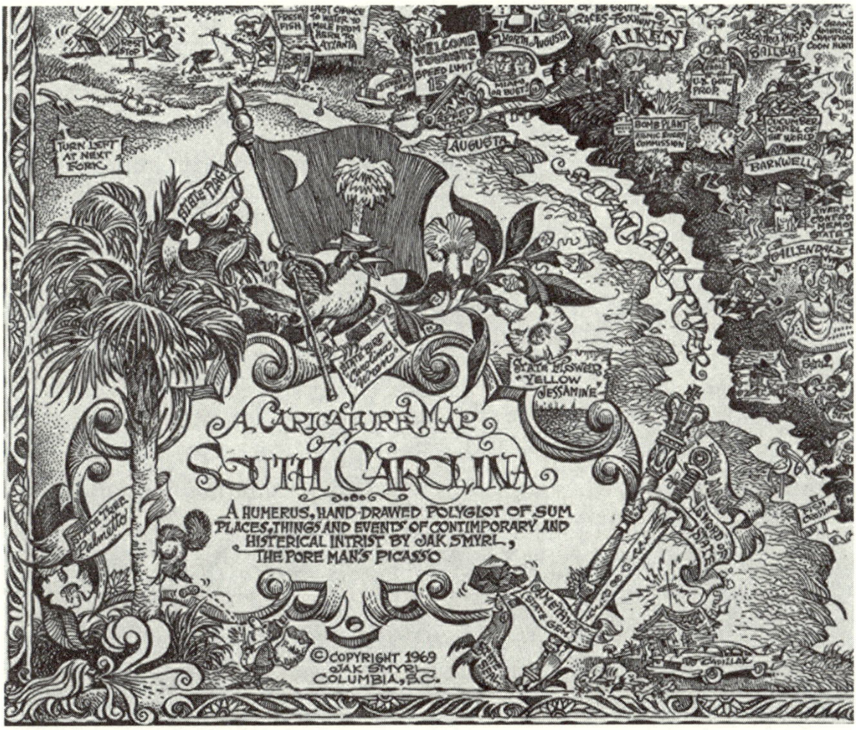

Title corner of Jak's 1969 *A Caricature Map of South Carolina,* including state symbols with playful touches such as the palmetto tree housing a squirrel and a state "seal" performing a circus trick. Courtesy of the University of South Carolina.

During the week Jak reported daily for work at the newspaper, no longer punching a time clock. A night owl, he usually got to the office around midmorning. His preferred assignments were features with some lead time. He was allowed to work at the office or in his studio at home as long as his assignments got turned in on time. The days when Jak had been given last-minute assignments and worked in a noisy environment amid a crowd of people gave way to more peaceful surroundings and more control of working hours. A freelance project in this period resulted in a series of graceful illustrations of musicians and instruments collected in a brochure for the Columbia Music Festival Association, *Musical Arts Drive, 1969–1970.* Jak's pen-and-ink sketches exemplified the association's various programs.

In September 1969, during Glen's service in Vietnam, Joan began a teaching assistantship and graduate study at the University of South

Carolina, while also doing freelance writing. She took Jak's advice to rent a room in Kitty Sloan's home until Glen's return in spring 1970. Living near the Sloans and Jak was another friend, scrimshaw artist Norwood Marlowe, Jak's former postman whose artistry and historical interest he encouraged. Joan wrote and photographed an article on Marlowe published in *Sandlapper.* Jak had a way of connecting people's interests by getting them involved in related projects.

Perhaps it was natural for Jak to plan something celebratory following the completion of his South Carolina map. Perhaps he recognized that his aging parents would eventually require more time and commitment. Unquestionably Gene Sloan's sudden and untimely death shocked him into a contemplation of his own mortality. Betty recalled their conversation driving to the beach one weekend in late 1969. While they were still able, Jack suggested, why not take leaves of absence from their jobs and travel around the world? Betty was taken by surprise but intrigued. Jak especially wanted to return to the Pacific islands and show Betty "the beautiful blue water."

They devised a strategy: they would sell one of their Holden Beach lots to finance the trip. Jak would write about, photograph, and illustrate their travels so that expenses would afterward produce compensating income and tax deductions. He had always had an ambition to write a book—what a perfect topic the world would be!

They began to make contacts and plan their itinerary. They advertised one of their beachfront lots. The purchaser was a chicken farmer who flew his private plane into a small airport near Shallotte, bringing to the closing the $10,000 purchase price in cash. He also brought them a live chicken. When they got back to the Barnacle, Betty said Jak wrung the chicken's neck, and they cooked and ate it. It was a fine celebration. With funds secured, they were ready for adventure.

With the immediate and specific time frame they presented their startled travel agent, there was no option to make all the arrangements in advance. "Don't worry," said Jak. "Just get us underway, point us in the directions, and we'll figure it out as we go." According to their travel records, Jack and Betty departed Los Angeles at 11:59 P.M. on December 31, 1969, arriving in Tahiti early on New Year's morning 1970.

The blue water of the Pacific was as breathtaking as Jak had described it, Betty said. Enjoying by motorbike the spectacular scenery of their next stop, Bora Bora, she took "a spill on the coral road." At a local infirmary, a nurse and her assistant stitched Betty's lacerated elbow but had no pain-killing drugs. Another tourist offered her codeine from a medical kit. The next day Betty rested while Jak and a newfound friend snorkeled in the lagoons. After returning to Tahiti Jak and Betty departed for Samoa with its "fales," wall-less huts where occupants ate and slept on the floor, cooled by the trade winds.

The traveling pair crossed the international date line, gaining a day, and landed in Nadi in the Fiji Islands. To explore the area, they took a sixty-four-foot vessel commanded by a "salty Aussie captain," assisted by two "native men in wrap-around skirts." To their surprise aboard ship Jak and Betty met a former Columbia, South Carolina, resident whose mother still lived there. In Suva an English doctor inspected Betty's healing injuries from Bora Bora and cleared her to swim. Their last evening in Nadi they spent sipping local coffee-like "kava" with newfound friends.

Arriving in Auckland, New Zealand, Jak and Betty settled into a modest boardinghouse hotel. From across the street, they watched police wearing "old keystone-cop hats" control a crowd of anti–Vietnam War demonstrators outside a luxury hotel expecting the arrival of U.S. vice president Spiro Agnew. They also met an American from Florida and Holden Beach. On their next stop, Australia, they spent a few nights in King's Row, Sidney's "Greenwich Village," then moved to a modest $6-per-night hotel on Bondi Beach, where they marveled at scantily clad sunbathers and surfers. Friend Tom Nebbia, on a *National Geographic* assignment in Melbourne, sent an invitation to join him. Almost 550 miles away, Jak and Betty regretfully declined. They viewed the remote outback from the plane's window departing for the Philippines.

Awed by the view, Jak requested and was granted permission for a panoramic view from the cockpit. He and the Filipino pilot, who turned out to be a portrait painter, developed an immediate connection. Leaving the copilot in charge, the pilot set Jak in his seat and went to the passenger section to meet Betty, where he "casually knocked out a sketch" of her and presented it as a gift. After coffee and conversation, the pilot invited Jak and Betty to be his guests at his home in Manila, where he invited friends and family to entertain them. The pilot and his wife toured the travelers about the area. Among the speeding automobiles, motorbikes, and buffalo carts, they spotted American Jeeps from World War II converted to brightly decorated minibuses. As they departed Jak and Betty took with them uncommon experiences and left behind more new friends.

Landing at the Tokyo airport wearing tropical clothing, Jak and Betty shivered in the thirty-degree chill of an early Japanese morning. Cab after cab ignored them until a street sweeper stopped one to take them to the monorail. When Jak accidentally left his wallet on the train, an unidentified passenger kindly gave it to the conductor, who chased them down and returned it intact. Their first nights in Tokyo they spent at a "ryokan," an authentic inn where the rarely seen manager spoke only a few English phrases. They bridged the language gap with sketches, hand gestures, and the few Japanese phrases Jak recalled from his Marine Corps days. In addition to museums, they toured "the beautiful poetic back country that has inspired the artists of Japan for centuries." They had a "splendid view of Fuji" on an unusually clear day. After bathing in hot sulfur springs, they took the bullet train back to a Western-style hotel in Tokyo's fashionable Ginza section.

Jak and Betty individually had different feelings about their next destination—Okinawa, where he had spent unforgettable months in 1945. The city of Naha, destroyed in the campaign in which he had been a part, had been rebuilt to the extent that Jak said he "never knew for a moment where I was." Dirt roads were now paved. Only the beach where he first landed and the mountains looked familiar as an English-speaking driver conducted their hired car over the island. Betty felt very uneasy as Jak recounted experiences there. Although this had been a part of his life before they met, Betty had experienced Jak's abruptly waking from its nightmares. She would never see Okinawa as he did.

The couple eagerly anticipated Hong Kong, but as interesting as this international trade center was, Jak could not look at the mountains of now-inaccessible "Red China" without wondering what had become of the people he had known in Tientsin. He and Betty visited Victoria Peak, Repulse Bay, and the floating village of Aberdeen. In the shopping district they gazed at price haggling and exotic food displays along the streets and alleys. In the harbor they took an excursion on a junk and dined in the floating Sea Palace.

On the flight to Thailand, Betty said she experienced anxiety when the pilot announced that they were flying over South Vietnam. They thought of Americans in combat below as they peered from the window. Glen was serving with an army artillery unit in the Mekong delta. They later learned that he, aware of their traveling, looked wistfully at commercial planes high above the rice paddies of the Mekong delta, wondering if they might be aboard. They thought too of Robbie, who had left Korea and they expected was in Vietnam by now too.

A landscape of rice fields, crisscrossed with canals and rivers, greeted the approach to Bangkok. Jak and Betty visited temples, browsed through the floating market, and observed silk makers. They read travel guide warnings to barter a fare with the driver before entering a taxi but missed warnings about touts on the streets. Betty recounted an experience that Jak did not write about. Conversing with several well-dressed, articulate men who asserted they had been educated in the United States, Jak and Betty were invited to accompany them on their way "to worship the Buddha."

Anticipating another unique experience, Jak and Betty followed them to a waiting taxi. A long, narrow powerboat sped them across the wide river to the temple, busy with worshippers burning incense before a big gold Buddha. Jak and Betty grew wary noticing their hosts stood at a distance, not participating in worship. Jak adamantly insisted they must return now. At midpoint in the river, the boat suddenly stopped. One of the hosts pointed at the boatman and said, "He wants your money." Knowing it safer to comply, Jak handed over his wallet, which contained about $60. The men returned his wallet and one dollar, asking for his watch, which he handed over. Betty said Jak sternly countered: "You have our money. Now take us back. If we do not return soon, our friends will be looking for us!" The boatman resumed to the other side, where the same taxi and driver were waiting. The men told Jak and Betty to give the driver the dollar and he would take them back to their hotel.

Once safely in their room, Jak and Betty comprehended that the taxi driver, boatman, and the other men were collaborators. Had these men searched and discovered that Jak was wearing a money belt containing $2,000, the two of them might have ended up at the bottom of the river. Shaken, they engaged the first flight out the next day, determined to be more guarded henceforth, but not to spoil their whole trip with one misadventure.

Sari-clad hostesses welcomed Jak and Betty aboard India Airlines. They flew over Burma, made a brief stop in East Pakistan, and touched down in New Delhi. They visited architectural sites, mosques, tombs, and "Thieves Market," and they witnessed the legendary poverty in Old Delhi. On a two-day trip to Agra, they found the Taj Mahal "indescribable," especially memorable under a full moon. From New Delhi they flew over the Indian Ocean to the "Dark Continent."

Landing in Nairobi, Kenya, Jak and Betty headed for Manyara National Park in Tanzania, camped on the crest of the rim of the Ngorongoro

Crater, and descended into the valley below, which teemed with wildlife and vegetation. After returning to Nairobi they embarked on a four-day photo safari a hundred miles through Maasai country to the Amboseli Game Preserve, where Jak photographed stunning landscapes and exotic animals. From their camp they gazed across the plains at snowcapped Mount Kilimanjaro. "Exhilarated" by the closeness to nature, Jak and Betty would recall the Kenyan experiences among the most outstanding of their world trip.

From Nairobi their flight the next day to Egypt paralleled half of the four-thousand-mile Nile River before they touched down in Cairo. Jak and Betty would later say they should have avoided the destination, however, because of flaring conflict between Egypt and Israel. They attempted to keep a low profile while seeing the sights: seven thousand years of Egypt's history in the Cairo Museum, the remains of the ancient capital of Memphis, underground tombs, the Sphinx, and the burial chamber of Cheops. They walked "into the edge of the Sahara just for the record." Along the road they passed machine gun emplacements. They were told "what to and what not to photograph." Their hotel manager "held our passports for a day for police checkups," nearly preventing them from leaving the Cairo airport. They were sent through a maze of "lines leading nowhere" and missed their flight to Nicosia. A sympathetic uniformed man attempted to help. Detained another hour they finally boarded "a rickety old prop plane" with razor-thin tires on which they embarked for Greece. Betty recalled relief of escape from such tense conditions.

Their Athens hotel overlooked the ruins of the Temple of Zeus, and Jak and Betty also visited the even larger ruins of the Acropolis. Views of ancient Greek statues must have reminded Jak of schoolbook illustrations and his early attempts to make art copies. He and Betty left Athens for Rome and more scenes of the classical world. They visited the Forum, tossed coins in Trevi Fountain, and descended into the catacombs where early Christians hid from persecution. They visited the world's oldest amphitheater and ruins of the Roman Coliseum, studied the architecture of the Basilica of St. Paul, and marveled at creations of Leonardo da Vinci and Raphael. In the Vatican City museum they viewed the Gutenberg Bible and Galileo's letter explaining the universe. Jak was awed by Michelangelo's achievement in the Sistine Chapel.

Taking a flight of unparalleled views over the French Alps, Jak and Betty landed in Paris, eager to enjoy more art, food, and scenery in the romantic city. There could never be enough time to spend in the Louvre, nor sufficient time or money to sample all the food, they would say. A highlight was sipping hot coffee in the Eiffel Tower at sunset as snow swirled around them. Crossing the English Channel, they settled into London for the last phase of their journey. They welcomed friendly taxis and the absence of a language barrier as they viewed Westminster Abbey, Soho, Buckingham Palace with its changing of the guard, Carnaby Street, Windsor Castle, Trafalgar Square, Piccadilly, and Big Ben. There were so many more attractions close at hand—museums and the English countryside, not to mention other parts of the United Kingdom—but time and money were short by now. They had visited twenty countries in eighty days.

Their Pan Am 747, the recently introduced "Jumbo Jet," made an uneventful hop across the Atlantic to New York City, where weather was cold but people "warm and friendly." They intended to go by Pittsburgh to visit Betty's brother Earl in the air force but learned that he had flown to Vietnam. They traveled south through Washington, D.C., to visit her brother Loyd and stop at Mount Vernon. A day later their two-story brick home on Heyward Street in Columbia was certainly a welcome sight. It was no match for the splendor of the Taj Mahal, its ceiling paled in comparison to the Sistine Chapel's, and it lacked rustic charms of Samoa, but its cozy familiarity was very agreeable. Kicking back and getting comfortable, they reminisced their adventures and began thinking where they might go next. For now it felt very good to be home.

Jak and Betty began quickly catching up on work. Immediately after his trip the *State* editors were eager to run his illustrated articles as a travel series, so Jak deferred intentions to seek a book publisher until after first appearance in the newspaper. Printing his film and piling together his notes and memorabilia, he tackled writing and illustrating his recent experiences. Some other projects Jak had in mind had awaited his return. Encouraged by the success of his Hellhole Swamp map, he also completed a map of Pawley's Island that year and had it printed for sale, encouraged to do so by local friends Reese and Sis Hart. In addition Jak took a step toward a change at Holden Beach. In late March 1970 he began to negotiate a trade of land near the chapel for another oceanfront lot near the Barnacle. The plan, set in motion, would take nearly eight years to be realized.

While Jak had much to share with his siblings about his world trip, they also began working together on a celebration of Oscar and Mae's fiftieth wedding anniversary. Lottie, Jak, Lucy, and Alfred recalled happy memories and shared concerns for their parents' health. Reserving for

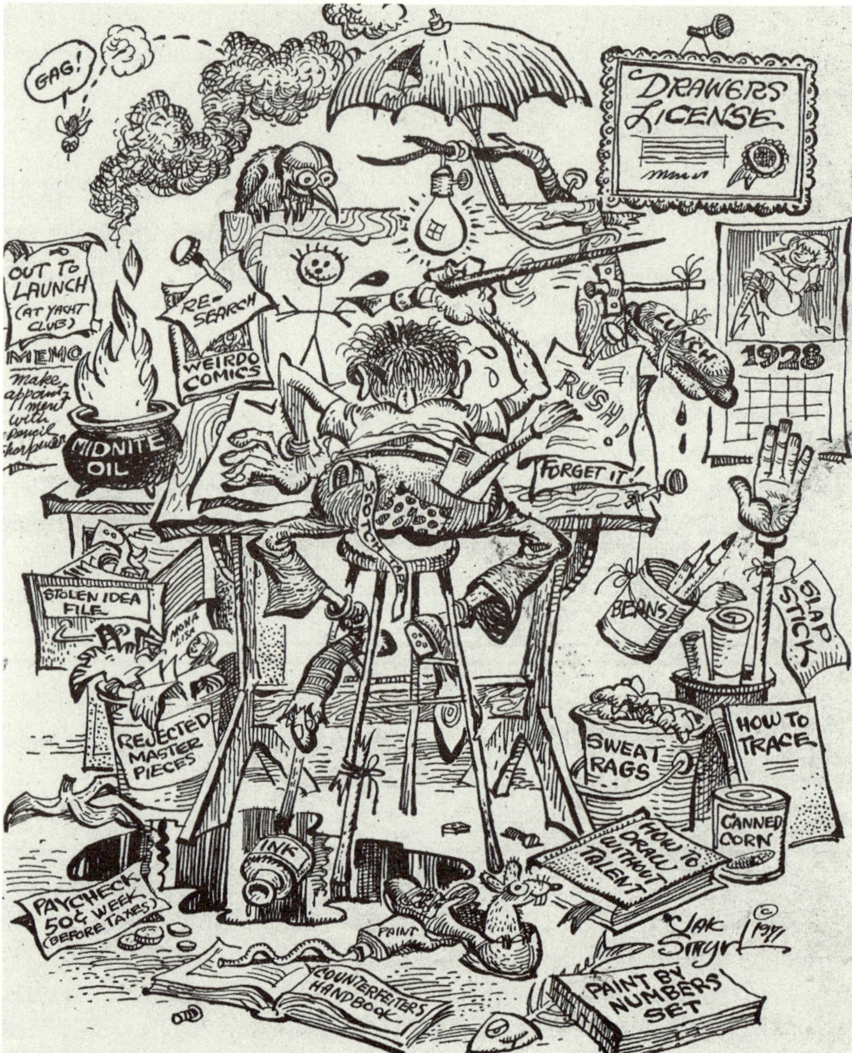

Self-caricature of Jak burning the midnight oil ©1971. Courtesy of the family.

May 30 the King Haiglar Room at Elizabeth Thomas Restaurant, where the community enjoyed many pleasant social functions, they planned a traditional theme: gold punch, white napkins with gold lettering, a white-iced tiered cake topped with a gold "50th" emblem, and Oscar's yellow-and-white Japanese irises. Mae, donning a mauve formal lace dress that she had made for Joan's wedding, remarked how pleased she was to wear it again to "such a lovely event." She and Oscar thoroughly enjoyed one of their lifelong pleasures—conversing with family and friends.

The *State* on October 11, 1970, began running a series of fifteen lengthy articles that Jak submitted of his and Betty's world trip, headed "Around the World with Smyrl." Each was illustrated with a mix of artistically composed photographs worthy of a travel brochure, realistic sketches, and signature satire. Jak's maps of foreign lands and exotic islands both amused and educated the reader, while realistic illustrations of people and places intermingled with comic ones. His text alternated between serious and humorous narrative, intended to entertain as well as provoke further study. Heavy on alliteration and comic word choice, "Trekking on Down to Tahiti," states, for example, "While changing our capitalistic decadent American dollars for quaint little French francs at the customs gate . . . we snorted up great snootfuls of the balmy breeze." Another article, "Foolin' Around in Faraway Fiji," includes a more evocative description: "Parts of the route led through mountain country that paradoxically looked like kissin kin to the Blue Ridge section of the Carolinas, complete with verdant valleys and grazing cattle."

The series of illustrated travel articles ran through spring 1971. From his processed and mounted slides, Jak arranged a chronological travelogue, an entertaining format to share experiences with family and friends. From his published articles he scaled illustrations and text to fit future book size and photocopied a mockup into a notebook. "Hmm," he mused, "it lacks the Americas . . . ," and he laid the project aside for now.

A variety of other assignments and projects had continued. For example Jak's color illustration for a feature on genealogy in the *State* on June 21, 1970, posed two monkeys in the top of a family tree, one of them reading Charles Darwin's book. Also pictured was a voluptuous, short-skirted female pulling a baby carriage and being led by a "bloodline" bloodhound. For a November 29 article titled "1900," Jak sketched a couple in contemporary dress, a barbershop quartet, a female talking on a wall-mounted telephone, and the interior of a store with a pot-bellied stove and men playing checkers atop a wooden barrel. Sports writers continued expectations of entertaining images to draw attention to highlights of their pages. No other artist, they said, could find as interestingly different ways to depict mascot or team action as Jak.

On his own Jak immersed himself in drawing a caricature map of Holden Beach. Of course it was imperative that they go there as frequently as possible to research facts and natural features that enriched the comic

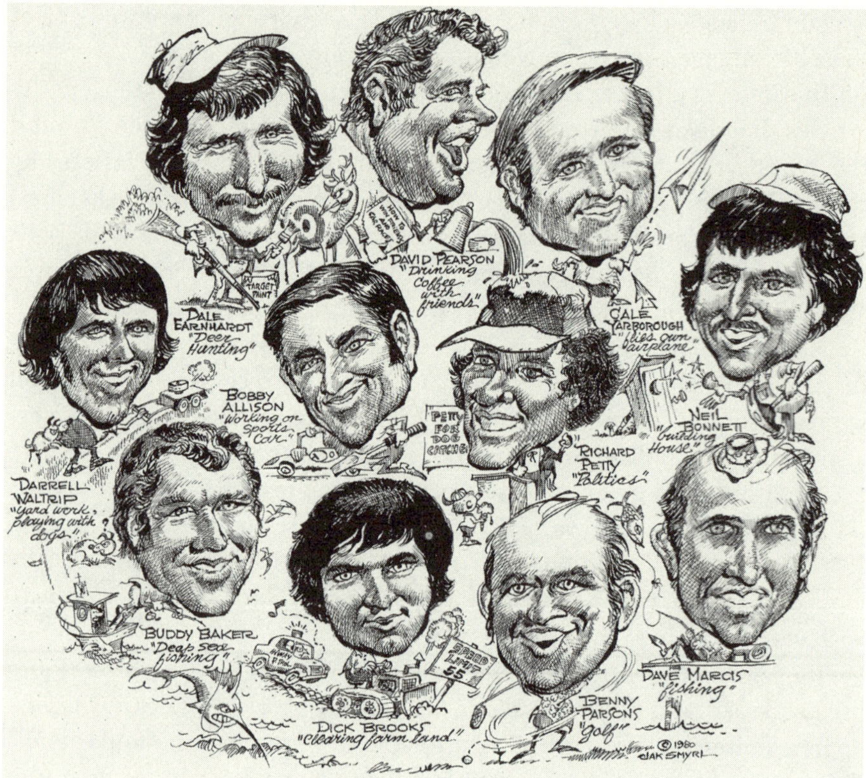

A sample of Jak's detailed caricatures of personalities, a collage of NASCAR drivers in 1980. Courtesy of the family.

scenes. He introduced a black-and-white map for sale in 1971, and Oscar and Mae helped wholesale it at the beach, suggesting it could be a coloring project for children or adults. For newspaper sports pages in September of that year, Jak used familiar style in delighting stock car fans with a minutely detailed rendering of the Southern 500 race at Darlington and completed it with caricatures of NASCAR's leading drivers. Coastal vacations and sports such as auto racing remained perennially popular.

Having indulged his and Betty's world travel desires, Jak was anxious in 1971 to share the thrill of new places with Oscar and Mae. Camping at state parks in his youth, the family had talked of traveling someday to national parks. He began planning a cross-country driving trip to show them America's natural treasures. Perhaps he could work them into his travel book?

As usual Jak kept a log. Oscar and Mae spent the night with them on May 1, and the carload of four headed out from Columbia early the next morning, eating lunch in Macon, Georgia, with Alfred, Louise, and Bonnie, who was expecting again. They visited Auburn University, with Jak delighting to drive them around his once-familiar haunts, and spent the night in Montgomery. Jak's log summarized: "Breakfast in S.C., Dinner in Georgia, Supper in Alabama." They spent the next night in Vicksburg after visiting the Civil War battlefield.

Over the next twenty days they traveled some seven thousand miles through twenty-two states and Mexico. They stopped at Weatherford, Texas, to visit relatives, the R. L. Smyrl family. They went down into Carlsbad Caverns, after which they drove to Juarez, Mexico, watching glassmakers at work. They visited Apache National Park, ate Mexican food that Jak noted was a first for his parents, and visited the Petrified Forest and the Painted Desert. They "saw ancient Indian pictures on rocks then drove to the Meteor Crater."

Along the way to the Hopi Indian reservation, the Smyrls met a gas station operator from Sumter, South Carolina, and Jak sold him a subscription to the *State*. They drove through a snowfall to Grand Canyon National Park, with a breathtaking view of the canyon from their motel. The next day they drove 312 miles to Las Vegas by way of Hoover Dam. They drove 380 miles through the Mojave Desert, making their way through a hailstorm into the Sequoia National Park to see the world's largest redwoods. Through the Big Sur region they followed the scenic route along the Pacific coast to San Francisco. While a service station changed the car's oil, the travelers took a popular Gray Line tour: Fisherman's Wharf, Inspiration Point, the Golden Gate and Bay Bridges, Alcatraz, the cable car, and Sausalito. Wood-carvers at the latter site were of special interest to Jak and Oscar.

The family left for Reno, Nevada, afterward driving along the Humboldt River and across the Great Salt Lake Desert on a "long, long, straight, fast road," reaching Graniteville 510 miles later. The next day they drove through northwestern Utah, stopping in Salt Lake City to visit the Mormon Tabernacle and to taste the water from the lake. On the way through western Wyoming to Jackson Hole, they saw a copper mine, went through the Snake River valley, and viewed lava formations. Heading north they passed through Grand Teton National Park on the way to Yellowstone National Park, where they saw Old Faithful erupt. A moose grazed next to their motel, adjacent to the wilderness. Passing oil wells and coal mines, they crossed through Shoshone National Forest and Bighorn National Forest. Jak commented, "Scenery of Wyoming—without parallel."

Entering South Dakota they traveled through Black Hills National Forest, finally pulling into Custer for the night. Seeing Mount Rushmore and the Crazy Horse carving in progress, the travelers drove through Badlands National Park and crossed South Dakota to South Sioux City, Nebraska. Jak stopped recording in his log with a partial entry on May 19: "Drove from South Sioux City to ———." At this point the Smyrls had traveled through parts of fourteen different states, completely traversing most of them. Recognizing that they had expended most of their time, Jak realized they needed to hasten home. He asked Mae to keep a log from that point so he could concentrate on driving and make better time. On May 21, 1971, they arrived home.

Back at home both Smyrl couples expressed an enhanced appreciation of the expanse and grandeur of their country. His mother had eagerly taken photos with the new Instamatic camera she loved. Jak selected an especially good shot Mae made of the Grand Canyon, enlarged and mounted it with currently popular decoupage. He carved the edges and burned them in the fashionable rustic touch and hung the colorful image above his parents' fireplace. He wanted his mother always to remember her trip and be proud of her photographic work recording it.

It was not until sometime after the trip was over that Jak read the notes Mae had taken for him driving back. She had always been very efficient and precise with such record keeping. With surprise he quickly realized that she had mixed up some dates as well as some words and was disappointed that her selection of details was not what he would have expected. Some entries were rambling, irrelevant, and at times incoherent. They were not useful for his writing, so to recall that portion of the trip, he would have to rely on brochures, his photography, and his memory, although he did not now have time to write about the trip anyway.

Return from vacation meant a hectic work schedule. Some examples of Jak's art in 1972 proved among his most popular works. For the twenty-first annual Sun Fun Festival, the Tempo section of the *State* on June 4 ran in color Jak's large caricature map *The Grand Strand of South Carolina,* which he privately printed for sale with his other maps. The *State* on September 24 accompanied an article titled "Apple Pickin' Time in S.C." with Jak's intricate collage of state festivals and scenes related to apples. Betty recalled that work as one Jak had especially enjoyed. Every fall she and

Jak went to the mountains with Oscar and Mae for at least a weekend, timing trips to bring home a variety of fresh apples and handmade cider.

Their thirst for distant travel not yet satiated, Jak and Betty had already planned their next trip. With winter and cold weather approaching, they were enticed to South America, where seasons are reversed. They departed Miami, arriving on November 25, 1972, in Bogota, Colombia. Their next stop was Quito, Ecuador, sitting squarely on the equator at an altitude of nine thousand feet. From Peru's capital of Lima, Jak and Betty left their plush hotel for a trek to Cuzco, the Western Hemisphere's oldest inhabited city, nestled in the Andes at 11,444 feet above sea level. They visited the Incan fortress ruins of Sacsahuaman, made of granite blocks weighing 250 to 500 tons that were moved from miles away and "fitted so finely a knife blade cannot slip between them."

For the three-hour trip of seventy miles to Machu Picchu, the Inca ruins discovered in 1911, Jak and Betty boarded a narrow-gauge train at Cuzco. The tracks ended at the base of Machu Picchu. A twenty-minute minibus ride took them the rest of the way. They marveled at the architectural genius of ancient builders. Still extant were the stone canals that provided water for the terrace gardens that provided subsistence. They saw the alpacas kept there to graze the terraces, thus subduing the vegetation that had obscured the village for so long.

The flight from Lima landed at La Paz, then the world's highest airport at 11,398 feet. Once their lungs adjusted to lowered oxygen levels, Jak and Betty were able to move about. The city was completely covered with tin roofs, Bolivia being home to the world's largest tin mines. Learning of the suggested link between indigenous Bolivians and ancient Egyptians, the couple were awed observing "Egyptian-style stone carvings of men with beards" and reed boats built by dwellers near Lake Titicaca identical to those pictured in Egyptian tombs, some of which the travelers themselves had observed there. Jak and Betty took a jarring bus ride to Titicaca, the world's highest navigable lake, then a hydrofoil to the Island of the Moon, where they drank water from an Inca spring at the ruins of a temple.

Departing Bolivia for Santiago, Chile, Jak and Betty were jarred back to modern times when they were X-rayed for weapons at the airport for clearance to fly to Buenos Aires, the "Paris of South America." A population of seven million made Argentina's capital the biggest city in the Southern Hemisphere, and its Ninth of July Boulevard the world's widest thoroughfare. Although their hotel was "considered the finest on the continent," Jak said he and Betty "slummed it up . . . in bowery style eateries," saving money for sightseeing.

Their next stop was Uruguay, South America's smallest and most democratic nation. In its capital, Montevideo, the world's least expensive city, "$200 per month means good living." Jak and Betty's convivial host in Uruguay owned a winery and a vineyard. After a flea market visit and a carnival with "horseback lancing and traditional gaucho dances," they were entertained at an evening "paradillada," or barbeque, complemented by the host's finest wines.

The travelers departed South America's smallest country for its largest, Brazil, the only one where Spanish was not the main language. Jak marveled at Copacabana Beach, 3½ miles long with scantily clad beauties. He identified their worst experience as paying "$19 (each) airport tax" to leave there December 16, 1972. As Jak had done following their global journey, he composed and illustrated articles on the South American trip in his inimitable style, a seven-part series in the *State* running March through April 1973. Again he interspersed personal experiences with geographical, historical, political, and cultural facts and illustrated each article with photographs, representative sketches, maps, and cartoons. He added photocopied pages of the articles, scaled to size, to the notebook version of his world book project, followed by a scaled article on the earlier boat trip to the Dry Tortugas off Florida. When he had time, he could add their trip across America.

In November 1973 Jak was honored by inclusion in an exhibition of editorial cartoons at the Gertrude Herbert Institute of Art in Augusta, Georgia. Since 1937 the institute had been a distinctive visual arts school and a distinguished contemporary art gallery housed in a historic mansion. Publicity for the exhibit stated that it was noteworthy that art galleries and institutes were beginning to recognize the importance of cartoon art. Five years later in the August 1978 *Sandlapper,* Ron Wenzell quoted Jak: "Generally speaking, cartooning is much better today than it was thirty years ago. It is becoming accepted as its own art form. And more and more, people are coming to realize the power of the cartoon to influence public opinion."

Wenzell reported that of modern political cartoonists Jak said his favorites were Patrick Oliphant and Jeff MacNelly, both of them Pulitzer Prize winners. Oliphant's trademark was a small penguin named "Punk" who added a comment on the subject of the cartoon. MacNelly the previous year had taken his political cartooning to a different level by beginning

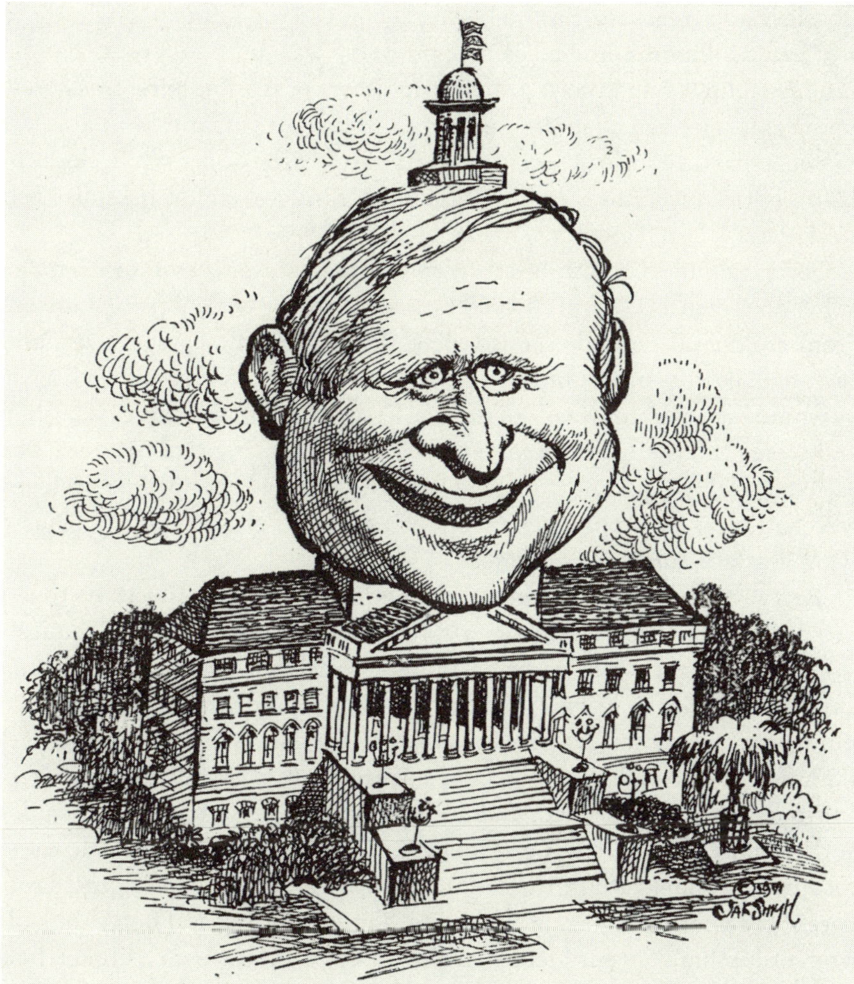

Political cartoon by Jak on election of John Carl West as South Carolina governor in 1970. Courtesy of the University of South Carolina.

the syndicated comic strip *Shoe,* about a cynical and rambunctious newspaper staff, all of them birds. Oliphant and MacNelly, respectively born in 1935 and 1947, were a younger generation of cartoonists dedicated to a specific type of cartooning, unlike Jak, a pioneer hired for general illustration as the newspaper's sole "staff artist" for most of his career.

In March 1974 Alfred retired and moved his family from Macon, Georgia, back to Camden. While he trained to assume a new position July 1 as city clerk and treasurer, he and his family moved for a time to Highway 97 into his childhood home place. The property was quite different than he and his siblings had known growing up. Rows of planted pine trees grew where chickens had been penned, produce had grown, and farm animals had been pastured. However, Alfred was happy to be home again, closer to his parents and siblings, and was anxious for his two children, Louise and John Patrick "Pat," to connect with their relatives.

Having enjoyed extensive air travel, perhaps it was inevitable that Jak in his do-it-yourself nature would take up learning to fly a plane himself. From childhood he had enjoyed views from different perspectives, and such had also been part of his training as an artist. With a pilot's license he would have greater freedom than as a passenger to fly where he wished and to see the earth from the perspective of a soaring bird. In the 1970s Jak began taking lessons from Don Watkins, a fellow newspaper employee who had recently earned his own pilot's license. Jak's memoir notes cite "Don Watkins (me, his 1st student)."

Betty recalled that Watkins, a stranger identifying connections to kin of Jak's, had knocked on the Smyrls' front door in the late 1960s, requesting that Jak teach him to use a camera. Watkins was charismatic and quick and eager to learn. They developed a friendship and Jak helped him get a job at the *State*. In 2012 interviews James Holton and Robert Kaminer both recalled graphic artist Watkins as very talented but free-spirited rather than settled, and undeterred by risk. Before long the pilot and his pupil began planning a trip to New Orleans, a flight that Jak would recount and illustrate in the *State* on April 14. In a single-engine, four-passenger plane, Watkins and his wife, Tanya, and Jak and Betty took off from Columbia's Owens Field. A shaky takeoff running over a broken bottle was followed by a rough landing on a flat tire in Vidalia, Georgia. There Betty's brother Earl aided them while the tire was fixed. A quick stop in Troy, Alabama, was followed by what Betty later recalled as a "harrowing experience circling round and round over Lake Pontchartrain" until air traffic controllers at the busy airport gave clearance to land. After sights, sounds, and tastes of Bourbon Street, and with a cold front moving east, they departed the next morning. After brief stops for weather checks, the group landed in Montgomery, Alabama, for supper and an overnight stay with Betty's other brother Loyd. The next day they rode the winds back to Columbia, just ahead of the front.

Instead of discouraging Jak, the flight to New Orleans induced him to continue his quest to become a licensed pilot. He completed training under Bob Tolhurst and on August 8, 1974, received his Solo Certificate flying a Cessna 150 from Owens Field. In his memoir notes, he recalled seeing a "man on bike on runway during 1st solo landing." Jak's flying experiences were often recalled with mention of the time he was flying back to Columbia and could not locate Owens Field. He frantically radioed its control tower with his predicament and was told, "Look under your left wing." He was directly over the airport but did not recognize it. Places he had no difficulty recognizing when he flew over northern Kershaw County, even taking aerial photographs of them, were the sites of the Lake Luesta train house, where he worked on his state map, and the Flint Hill church and the old Smyrl home nearby.

Oscar's sister Mamie had continued to live alone in the old Smyrl home place and to preserve it mostly unchanged, with neatly collected letters, memorabilia, and carefully folded clothing tucked in old trunks in the attic. Electricity had been welcomed, and the house was painted outside around midcentury, although other conveniences were resisted. Mamie continued to draw water with the bucket and windlass from the old open well. She did not think pumped water tasted as sweet and healthy. Visitors to the home agreed. On Oscar's insistence she agreed to accept installation of a telephone so relatives could keep in touch. In 1975 several years of events began when Mamie was hospitalized in Camden after a fall, and afterward she went to stay at the home of sister Nettie, leaving the old home just the same. When Mamie died on September 27, 1980, Jak was one of the pallbearers, all of them nephews.

While Mamie was living with Nettie, well-organized thieves broke into the unoccupied old Smyrl home, stole many items, and damaged or scattered others in making a hasty getaway during a rainy evening. When the break-in was discovered, family members helped salvage effects. Lottie, a librarian and family historian, paid special attention to collecting the strewn papers and documents that thieves had discarded from chests and trampled, including Civil War letters from Oscar's uncle Jim Smyrl. In the state's capital in the 1980s, the old Columbia Mill was being converted to house the newly established South Carolina State Museum. The Smyrl family donated to the institution many of the remaining antique tools and furnishings from the old family home. When the museum opened in October 1988, they proudly viewed those items in the displays.

When Jak and Betty visited the museum, she was also fascinated by the transformation of the old mill itself. While working as office manager for Creed Construction, she had begun expanding a lifelong interest in interior design. Her work with architects and blueprints had prompted her to take a class in interior design at the University of South Carolina. When she finished the class, she began a home-study course from the International School of Interior Design in Pittsburgh. Jak was quite supportive as he recalled the correspondence courses that had impacted his youthful learning. Betty and Jak talked it over, and after eighteen years with Creed Construction, she gave her notice and began to plan a new career at the end of her studies.

One of Creed's Columbia subcontractors, Bonitz Contract Design, learned Betty was not working and offered her a secretarial position. When they discovered her level of experience and the training she was undergoing, they offered her instead a job in design. When she talked the offer over with Jak, he adamantly opposed her taking it. Through the lens of his own experience, he believed that taking a job would mean she would not finish her education. Betty at first declined the job, but Bonitz made a compromise offer: work half a day and study half a day. Armed with that argument, Betty approached Jak using a tactic that reminded him of himself long ago: "So you see, Jak, I can take this job. No, it will not keep me from studying. In fact, the job will give me practical experience that will help me in the course, and the coursework will help me do the job better." Jak had to concur: "*That* Betty!"

Betty had worked for nearly two decades in the male-dominated construction industry. She had never lacked ambition or confidence, but now she could assert her worth as a professional. At first the CEO of Bonitz would introduce her as "Betty Smyrl, the wife of Jak Smyrl." Once she "felt more comfortable in her job," Betty told him, although "I was very happy and honored to be married to Jak Smyrl, to please let me establish my own identity as Betty Smyrl, Interior Decorator."

Like Betty's youthful interest in design, Jak's interest in music had never waned. In the mid-1970s, it tugged at him again. In a 2012 interview, Bill McDonald described the formation of a band of *State-Record* employees, consisting of Bob Pierce on saxophone, Sam McCuen on drums, and Bill and Jak on trumpet. They dubbed their group after a blues tune named for the old Winnsboro Cotton Mill in Bill's hometown. Bob, who at a different time had played in the same USC dance band as Jak, got the Winnsboro Cotton Mill Band "a booking at a little juke joint called Jeebo's on Assembly Street near the fairgrounds." The group enjoyed practicing together at Bob's house, "but Jeebo's closed" and they never performed there or anywhere else.

In spring 1975 Jak and Betty set out to explore a North Carolina coastal island accessible only by water. From May 5 to May 7, Jak and Betty accompanied Rhonda and Lucy on an excursion to Portsmouth Island, a mid-1700s fishing and lightering port abandoned in 1971. In earlier days cargos were unloaded there from transoceanic ships to shallow-draft vessels that could navigate the sounds accessing mainland ports. Jak's log shows the four travelers left Holden Beach in the Browns' Travelall, a two-ton behemoth with four-wheel drive. At Atlantic Landing they caught a two-vehicle ferry for the forty-minute ride to Portsmouth. After "difficulty unloading Travelall from ferry on makeshift ramp," they drove seven miles north of the landing where strong northeast winds created difficulties setting up their tent. The isolated location, dog flies, and swarms of mosquitoes challenged them along the eighteen-mile trail to a deserted village, where the visitors investigated and photographed old houses and other sites. They "played a hymn on the old foot-operated organ" in the church and climbed to a widow's walk atop one of the houses. Returning to the mainland by ferry, their vehicle was loaded with shells, driftwood, sketches, and photographs.

Following such interests Jak would soon become involved in various historic and natural preservation projects. Locally and across America, plans were materializing for a celebration of the national bicentennial, with the *State* giving wide coverage to celebrations and related historical topics. Joan and Glen headed a project from 1975 compiling local history in *Kershaw County Legacy*, published in 1976. In one article Oscar related Smyrl family experiences during Civil War times, when Sherman's troops ransacked the home place at Flint Hill. Jak illustrated this article with two realistic drawings, a scene of invaders at Grandpa Robert's house, and a postwar scene of two men pulling a plow themselves while a neighbor plowed with a milk cow. Many details lay in Jak's memories, his having heard his grandfather tell of those times he lived through.

Throughout the 1970s Mae's condition had deteriorated through different stages of what was coming to public attention as Alzheimer's disease. It was a painful time for all the family to watch her once-active mind slip away. Oscar, with help of his children and hired assistants, took care of her at home as long as possible. After a fall Mae was hospitalized in Lexington until 1978, when a bed became available in the new Karesh Long Term Care wing of the Kershaw County Memorial Hospital in Camden. Oscar spent a major part of each day by her side, and family visited often. With their mother's physical needs being met, Smyrl siblings gave extra attention to their father to conserve his strength and bolster his spirits.

In June 1978 Jak was saddened by news that old high school friend Bill Burns had died, not quite fifty-two years of age. Reflecting on experiences the two had shared over nearly four decades, Jak lamented conditions that had kept his friend from achieving longed-for dreams. When he recalled a youthful Bill playing his clarinet in the glow of a bonfire on the beach, Jak could not help but think, "Those were good times."

Jak kept in contact with a large number of friends. One was Paul Miller, his Marine buddy in China. Once on a visit to Jak and Betty, Paul and his wife, Jane, had gone with them to see the home place at Flint Hill and to drink from the well. In 1979 Jak wrote to the Millers, lamenting that the old house had been "ransacked by vandals." He told Paul about a visit from "another old Marine Corps buddy of mine from China, Cooper [Willie] Gore." Jak reported as well that Bill Robinson, "from Parris Island days who used to visit my home in Camden on liberty week-ends," had moved to Myrtle Beach, and they had enjoyed a recent reunion in Columbia.

Ron Wenzell interviewed Jak for the August 1978 *Sandlapper*, concluding: "At age 54, [Jak's] future is full to overflowing. In his second-floor studio in his ivy-covered house on Heyward Street, the chairs and tables are piled high with work in progress. The projects include a book of his cartoons, a book of his photographs, an illustrated history of the South Carolina Sea Islands and an illustrated book of his poetry." In the article Jak mused, "I could keep a staff of artists busy right here. I have so many different interests and get involved in so many things at once that I don't know quite where to begin. It's a weakness of mine, but isn't it exciting?" One of those interests that had not subsided was flying. In December 1978 he was taken on an aerobatic stunt flight by Roland Weeks and learned to do a loop.

At work a revival of a familiar feature of Jak's past appeared in September 1979 when the newspaper spiced up its Sunday editions by reintroducing the *State Magazine* as a weekly tabloid. By midsummer 1981 it sported a new design with contemporary graphics and once more featured freelance writers as variety. For the rest of his newspaper career Jak would continue in familiar swing, again illustrating for the magazine as well as for other sections.

In 1981 Jak marketed on his own a newly published "hysterical map" of Holden Beach, one larger, different, and more informative than his sold-out map of ten years earlier. It too was black and white like the older one, but

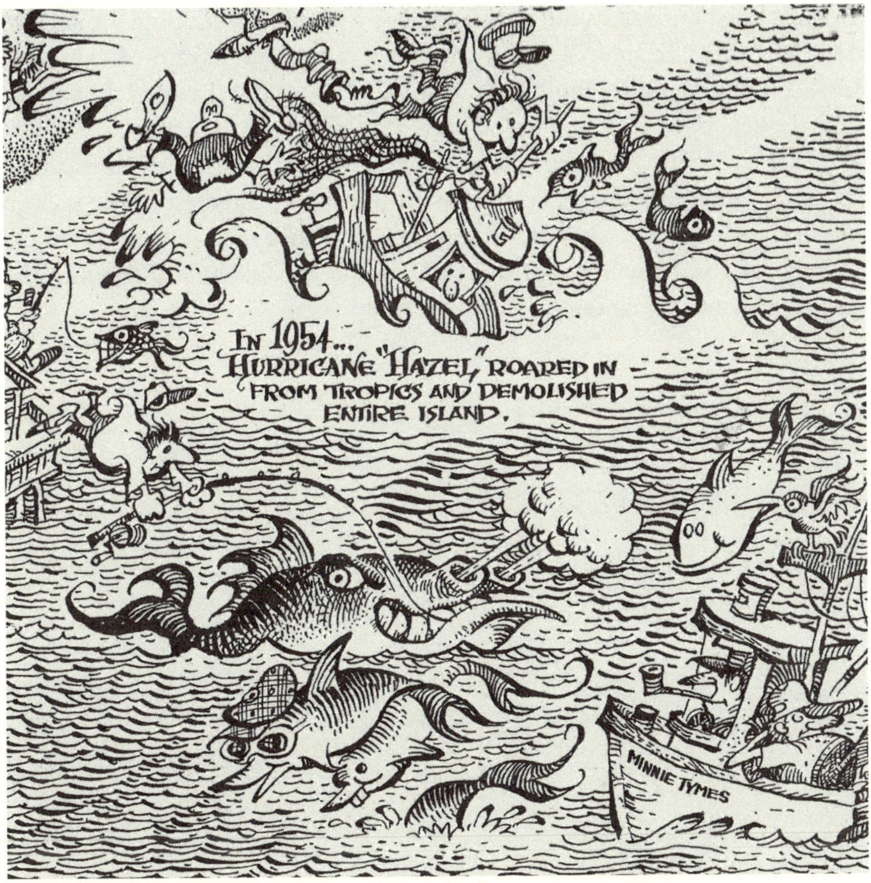

Portion of Holden Beach map ©1981 with historical fact of disastrous Hurricane Hazel in 1954 being interpreted with Jak's classic humor. Courtesy of the family.

he privately planned to do a color version, later when he had time. Computers were rapidly changing printing processes these days. The June 11 *Brunswick Beacon* of Shallotte, North Carolina, pictured Jak, stylish in a Panama hat, displaying the new map on which he had worked for five years. He told interviewer Demont Roseman that most of the map's facts came from his personal memory or hearsay from early families such as the Holdens. "Some things I imagined for fun," said Jak, whose map "mixed up the serious and the not-serious" with "some obvious jokes." He concluded, "My maps are just for fun. . . . They're a helluva lot of work and I don't make much profit, but I enjoy doing them."

Jak called himself "a nut who just likes to draw." Describing his style of detailed work, he said: "I'm like an ant bringing up a grain of sand at a time. Finally, there's a mountain of sand." His mountain was "thousands and thousands" of every form of art. "I'm the best collector of my own art," Jak said. "It's not especially great art, but it deals with things that have happened in South Carolina for 30 years. It's a record of the past in pictures." The article quoted Jak in predicting that the South Caroliniana Library of the University of South Carolina "probably will become the owner of Smyrl's collection."

Chapter 22

Full Circle

"It dawned on me I was already here"

For the fortieth reunion of his Camden High class (1941), Jak volunteered his help to produce a commemorative booklet. Inside his humorously illustrated cover, contents included members' vitae with their senior yearbook photos. Jak's own caption stated that he had been employed at the *State* thirty-three years and that his wife, Betty, was an "interior designer for Bonitz Co, doing commercial interiors of banks in S.C. and Georgia." Reminiscing on younger years with old friends prompted Jak privately to ponder dreams yet unfulfilled. He had most recently learned to fly and had seen the world from above. Now he turned his interest to another perspective. He had been scuba diving and wanted to explore deeper beneath the ocean surface, to view the world from the bottom up.

For diving instruction, Jak went to cousin Larry Ogburn, owner and operator of Wateree Outdoor Diving School in Columbia. Larry was leading a dive November 21–28, 1981, on beautiful and unspoiled San Salvador Island in the Bahamas. Jak and Betty signed up eagerly. On one dive during the trip, while Jak was happily photographing about fifty feet down, a large fish swam directly at him, knocking off his mask. Fortunately Larry was close and reattached his air supply. The incident inspired Jak's humorous color cover of the *State Magazine* on July 11, 1982. His travel article inside, "Move Over Cousteau," depicts in art, photography, and narrative the "undersea sortie to a history-hallowed island," where

Columbus first landed in the New World. Jak also sketched from life a portrait of one of the divers, actor Cliff Robertson, and described him as "a lovable, humble, kind man, untouched by fame." Jak continued about Robertson, "He told me that he was working on the movie, *Brainstorm,* with Natalie Wood. The news of her drowning, which occurred that week, was unknown to us. There is no newspaper on San Sal, and only one or two TV sets." The experience led to another *State Magazine* cover on January 30, 1983. Jak illustrated Ron Wenzell's feature "Modern-Day Adventurer" on Larry Ogburn, subtitled "Camden Man Deep Sea Dives, Parachutes, Catches Snakes."

Both Jak's and Betty's talents were on display in 1982. The *State* on October 7 featured a photograph of Betty's work as part of a Designers Showcase at Columbia's historic Boyleston House, part of the Governor's Mansion complex. Her profile in the American Society of Interior Designers brochure pointed out that she had been in the construction business eighteen years, the last ten as a designer. A number of articles and interviews were generated on Jak by a major exhibition of his work, *30 Years' Cartooning for Columbia Newspapers,* mounted at the Columbia Museum of Art and Science beginning on April 20. Established in 1950, after Jak had begun his career in a community lacking such facilities, the Columbia Museum had grown over the years into a significant influence for artists and the arts in midlands South Carolina. Jak was delighted to be recognized with his own show there. Many friends and colleagues reconnected as a result, and Jak's work likewise found new admirers.

Interviews in 1982 gave Jak opportunities for reflection on his life and career. He told Nancy Higgins in the *Chronicle-Independent* on January 19, "It seems like all my life, starting from childhood, I've been blessed with phenomenally good luck in the area of happiness." She recounted an important decision: "He knew artists who went to the big time, to New York City. That, of course is where the big money is made. However, they were saving that money to get back to the South. 'It dawned on me I was already here.'" The *State Magazine* on May 9 featured Jak's self-portrait on its cover, a prize honor. In that issue Bill McDonald quoted Jak's explanation for his myriad of interests and activities: "An artist's greatest fear is boredom, the fear you're going to get somewhere and be bored. It's just the nature of creative people. They're adventuresome. And what they experience other people can enjoy vicariously. I'm not a big deal at any of those things. But the more things you've got going for you, the richer your life is."

Of Jak's work as a cartoonist, McDonald stated: "Smyrl uses a musical analogy to describe the cartoonist's greatest challenge. He says the cartoonist is like a jazz musician, improvising from a single bar of melody, taking a note and transforming it into a symphony." McDonald offered his own description of Jak: "If you hopped into Smyrl's head, if you performed a frontal lobotomy, you'd find a madcap court jester wowing the king with his drawings of fat women in high-heeled humility, hungry vultures perched atop signposts and pencil-thin hound dogs sniffing the air." Jak had given himself labels before, such as "pore man's Picasso," and called himself for his style a "jazz artist." McDonald had offered a third colorful descriptor: "madcap jester." Fans agreed with the sentiment of Robert A. (Bob) Pierce's April 28 article summarized in its headline: "It'd Be a Shame If Jak Smyrl Grew Up."

Jak's illustrations continued to depict in changing variety the recurring rituals and celebrations of South Carolina. One of them, the State Fair, took place within sight of the newspaper building. A regular attender, Jak enjoyed the exhibits, animals, and food, especially the soft ice cream, but did not patronize the rides. Mostly, as elsewhere, he enjoyed studying the people. Betty was a member of the professional group Women in Construction, which yearly had a booth at the fair to raise scholarship funds. Once when Betty was publicity chair, she invited celebrated clarinetist Pete Fountain and band, performing there, to dine at the WIC booth. They accepted, and Betty called Jak to get some publicity in the newspaper. A fan of Fountain's music, Jak came there personally to meet him and, in usual style, struck up conversation. Fountain and his band accepted Jak and Betty's spur-of-the-moment invitation to be entertained at their home following his performance. Impulsive hospitality was typical of them.

With their Holden Beach house at a distance and often rented, Jak yearned to own a closer spot on the water for both work projects and relaxation. Eventually he traded a Holden Beach lot for a small place at Lake Wateree, where he had spent many happy days in his youth. In February 1983 Jak and Betty became owners of a rustic cottage on a beautiful, shaded lot with a panoramic view of the main water, broken only by two small islands near their shoreline, a natural home for numerous birds. The screened porch and front room provided workspace where Jak could create at his drawing board, distracted or inspired by glances at the lake scenes. There was no telephone, but for contacts Lucy and Rhonda now lived in a permanent home built on their lake property, only a mile distant by water.

In Jak's later years at the *State* numerous changes were underway in technology and in staff. A young artist who was hired, Robert Ariail, especially impressed Jak with his caricature skills and editorial perceptions, and Jak enjoyed getting to know him. Other young men were bringing word of computer programs that eliminated the need for white-out, tissue paper repairs, and tedious recopying that were part of everyday commercial art work he had done for years. Furthermore new computers and presses were ending the need for color separations, the time-consuming processes used for years. However, the strain of thirty-five years of deadlines, combined with Jak's desire to complete projects he had conceived but which lay unfinished or even unstarted, caused him to contemplate retirement. Besides he understood the toll Oscar's daily visits with Mae were making on his father's health. He desired to spend more time with them in their remaining years.

During these considerations the Kershaw County Fine Arts Center in Camden, only a decade old, requested to mount an exhibit of Jak's art in its new Bassett Gallery. Jak consented, glad to be a part of his hometown's evolving art interests and programming for artists. Advertisements for the event, commencing September 9, 1984, prompted Lottie's Winthrop roommate Dot Hendrix to write Oscar. She reminisced about "so many happy memories visiting in your home" and stated that she and husband G.T. regularly "search the State paper to see if [Jak] has some of his work in it." She recalled the role young Jak had played in her meeting her husband: "The first time I came home with Lottie, G.T. came up to your house to meet me. (This was a blind date to accommodate Lewis.) Lottie and I had gone somewhere when he came and Jak entertained G.T. with his drawings while he waited. . . . Jak made a drawing of me for him to see just what he was in for. Jak's drawing was so glamorous (of which I am so grateful) that G.T. waited around for us to return." A review of the reception the night before the exhibit opened reported "hundreds" in attendance, and hometown storytelling included many merry tales.

Jak had been visiting his mother often at the Karesh care facility. He would bundle her in her wheelchair, and with Oscar beside him, push her outside on the sidewalks or patio areas. At times he would put her in his car and take her for a drive, frequently to visit family. For a number of years Mae had lost the ability to communicate, but Jak deemed it important to treat her as if only her body, and not her mind, were impaired. On some visits he would bring art supplies and place a pencil or colored marker in her hand and guide it to create something. If visitors or staff

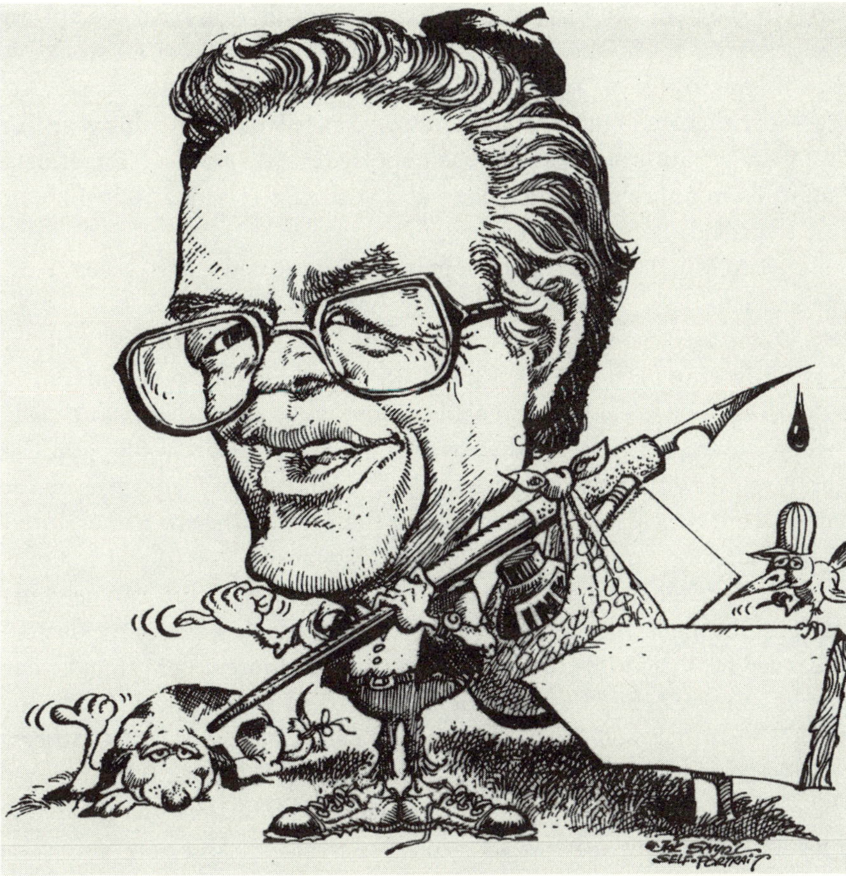

Retirement self-portrait of Jak, complete with dog and bird trademarks, with blank signboard he filled in for individual engagements. Courtesy of the family.

talked about Mae as if she were not present, he would remind them that she was "an intelligent lady" deserving of respect. At the suggestion, "But she doesn't know who you are," the response of Mae's children was always, "But *we* know who *she* is." In December 1984, just before Christmas, Jak and Betty invited the Smyrl clan to their Wateree Lake house and made his mother guest of honor.

There was a major change at the newspaper in early 1985. On February 12 company president Ben R. Morris sent employees a letter informing them of new company benefits, especially the Employee Stock Ownership Plan to "offer you stock ownership in your company. . . . When you are vested in the plan and leave the company, you will then have the option of taking your profit sharing in all cash, stock and cash, or all stock." A letter to employees on September 30 validated Jak's decision to participate. Morris wrote, "Our companies showed excellent profits this year. . . . [The] value of our holdings increased approximately 43%. . . . The efforts of all of us in improving efficiency, sales and waste elimination will continue to provide benefits for everyone."

Between Morris's two letters of good economic news, Jak received unexpected bad news. He and his siblings had lost their father. On July 6, 1985, Oscar was visiting Mae as usual when he had one of his spells of heart fibrillation in the hallway. The doctor checking on Oscar told him to lie down on a hospital bed and said he simply "went to sleep." Lucy was present, having come to see their mother, and Lottie was walking in the door. It was a swift and painless passing. The family was deeply grieved for their loss but considered it a blessing for their father that he had endured neither suffering nor long-term disability. Oscar was laid to rest in Camden's Quaker Cemetery near the grave of Alfred's son Willie. Jak used his artistic skill to design a tombstone for his parents, his distinctive lettering carved into the Winnsboro blue granite he admired. Less than a year later, in June 1986, Betty's father Odell Spires died and was buried in Nashville, Georgia. Jak and Betty each felt deeply the losses of two fathers.

Jak's career came full circle his last two years at the *State*. Bob Kaminer recalled in a 2012 interview that, anticipating Jak's retirement, the newspaper "started hiring other artists to replace him . . . and they were putting them all in a little office." With "three people in it, Jak couldn't work in that kind of condition . . . elbow to elbow . . . and he came to me." Kaminer had a big office space, and Jak asked if there was enough room for him to put in a desk. "So I said absolutely. I even got panels and everything and I put them up. He was facing the stadium, and he loved it in there." In a twist of fate, just as Jak had shared space in Bob's office at the beginning of his newspaper career, he ended it in like fashion.

In the 1980s there had been numerous changes in employee duties and equipment upgrades at Columbia Newspapers, Inc., as the State-Record Company had been renamed early in the past decade. Increased computerization significantly influenced job demands and was a bit intimidating to older employees. By middecade plans were underway for a new building, double the size of the existing plant, to be constructed around the corner on Shop Road. Jak had experienced the move from Main Street and did not relish another. He had been considering retirement for several years and decided it was the right time. He served notice that he would retire effective July 30, 1986, after thirty-seven and one-half years. Jak was leaning toward cashing in his stock but at the last moment decided to leave it in. Before long he would learn the effect of that somewhat casual decision.

Oscar had willed Jak his house and property on Colonial Lake. All his other children already had homes in Camden, and he thought Jak and Betty might want to live there in retirement. After renovations the Colonial Lake home was where they were living in September 1987 when they sent their friends a Jak-designed notice of their new address, complete with a sketched map and broke-tail-dog artwork. Betty, not yet retired, commuted to and from her job in Columbia, and Jak set about converting two rustic lakeside buildings into studio space where he would sort the collected works of his lifetime and devote himself to his projects.

Jak found it pleasant to have time to work on his accumulated projects and easy to adapt to life without daily press deadlines. Sometimes he reflected how different his job would have been had he remained at the newspaper given sweeping changes that soon occurred. Less than three months after his departure, his former coworkers were caught off guard by the announcement that Miami-based newspaper giant Knight-Ridder had purchased the company. Publisher Ben Morris summoned department heads to a meeting the afternoon of October 27, 1986. Robert Pierce was present and described in *Palmettos and Oaks* the manner in which Morris addressed the gathering with a statement about the longtime owners that was often quoted by those present: "The descendants of the Gonzales family are scattered and they have many interests." He then introduced seven new executives, strangers to most of the crowd. The newspaper's family ties to its founder ended, and so did local ownership.

As the buyout progressed through its phases in the following weeks, stock value more than tripled. Jak wrote in his memoir notes, pleased by his unexpected gain, that he had "left 20 shares in State Co. upon retirement. Few days later they sold Co. to Knight-Ridder. Made just under $40,000 in one day. (Knight-Ridder bought out shares at 3 times value.)" Another change that would have affected Jak had he still been at the newspaper was the announcement in January 1988 that publication of the *Columbia Record* would end with its April 1 issue. Previous owners had recurrently considered closing it, and Knight-Ridder had discarded unprofitable operations in other buyouts. The ups and downs of the corporate world he could now view at a distance.

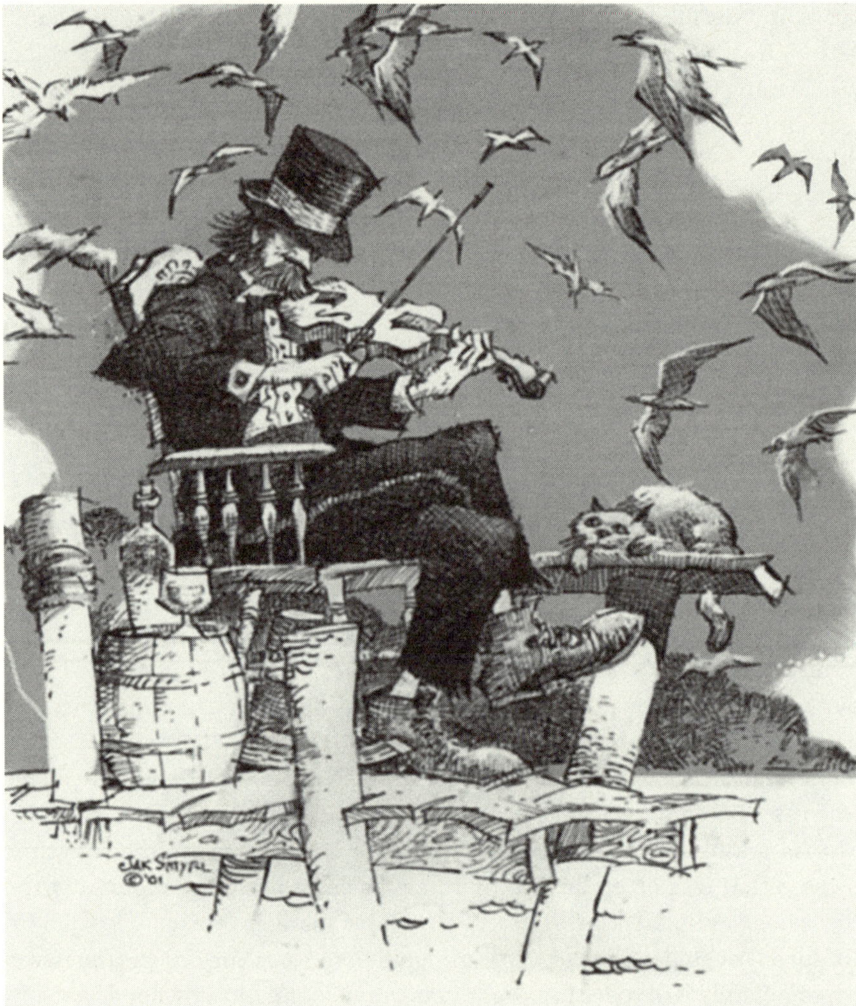

Jak's illustration of his poem "The Hermit." The subject is absorbed in nature, music, and contemplation, reflective of Jak's own interests (*Random Rimes*).

Retired, Jak had more time for all interests besides the freelance work he did from time to time. Stray and rescue dogs and cats found their way into his life, and special ones remained. He planted tomatoes and cultivated grapes. He experimented with wine and cider making. He collected wood for carving and rocks for landscaping projects. He cleaned out the swimming area at his lakefront. He and Betty moved their memberships to the First Baptist Church, where Jak had belonged as a boy. Every day was filled with activity, planning, and action. Jak began making longer lists. He wanted to write an autobiography and kept thinking of what to include. He was also compiling a book of his poems, working on illustrating them, and even composing music to accompany them. There was also business to take care of.

In 1986 at Holden Beach, a modern, high-curving bridge provided unobstructed access to the island. Beach erosion was the current concern of owners, especially those of older structures built close to the water. The Barnacle, as one of the oldest beachfront cottages, was the closest to the water of any nearby structures. With diminishing dunes extreme tides caused by full moons or storms would splash beneath the structure. Jak began gathering paperwork to aid in dealing with the issue. By 1988 he was looking at insurance allowances for moving back erosion-threatened buildings. A note in Jak's hand stated the erosion rate on Holden Beach was two feet per year.

Coastal property owners lived with the realization that a major hurricane could wipe away investments. Jak had experienced such losses before. A decade after losing his first cottage, "a waterspout danced in from the ocean in full view of everyone on the beach," he said in memoir notes. "It came inland and took the roof off just one house, mine." In mid-September 1989, when weather reports began tracking a massive storm, Jak began to steel himself. After wreaking havoc on Puerto Rico and the Virgin Islands, a category 5 hurricane named Hugo was downgraded to a category 2. Jak breathed a little bit easier but could not totally relax. The National Weather Service was unable to predict with certainty if or where it might come ashore. Hurricanes had a mind of their own, and a direct hit by a category 2 storm might still mean the end of the Barnacle.

By September 21, 1989, Hugo had intensified. Near midnight the storm had been reclassified category 4 when it made landfall slightly north of Charleston, South Carolina. Contrary to usual patterns, Hugo continued inland, devastating a swath through South Carolina and going on through Charlotte, North Carolina, and into Virginia. The eye passed through Camden, toppling trees and utility poles, and damaging or destroying houses. Power would not be restored for most residents for a week or longer. Several huge pine trees that lay across Jak and Betty's driveway had to be cut and removed before they could leave their yard.

Though Jak's beach home had been spared a direct hit, exceptionally high tides had ravaged North Carolina's south-facing beaches. The Barnacle remained on its pilings but had not escaped unscathed. No dunes remained to offer protection. Early in 1990 Jak mailed renters a comic letter saying that "wicked waves sent by Hurricane Hugo" did not destroy but managed to "sweep away the sun deck, back porch, all steps and everything under the house." The letter continued, "Strange as it may seem, the house itself remained untouched. Out on a flat, duneless beach it bravely stood daring the tide to come one step closer. Hurricanes come and hurricanes go but the Barnacle is here to stay." The house had been repaired although "for the moment no one on Holden is allowed to build sun decks until the new, man-made dunes stabilize." The first change one familiar with the cottage would notice was that a new pitched roof had been placed over the old flat roof and indoor renovations included paddle fans in all rooms. The storm damage had been a nuisance, not a tragedy.

Among friends who continued to rent or visit with Jak and Betty at the Barnacle were members of Gene Sloan's family. When Mary became engaged to Clint Roby in 1990, Jak walked her down the aisle in Summerville and played his trumpet at the reception. Her matron of honor was sister Laura, married to Birdie Crosby, and an artist crediting Jak for inspiration. Another artist who remained a longtime renter was Mary Winstead. Her own cottage at Holden Beach had been lost years before to Hurricane Hazel. She began annual rentals at the Barnacle in the 1970s, enjoying its natural, vintage atmosphere. Jak liked to reminisce with Mary about the days when she flew and landed her own airplane on the beach, pulling the craft up into the sand dunes in front of her cottage until her return flight. Before leaving for the beach from her Roxboro, North Carolina, home, Mary would telephone for tide reports in order to arrive when the beach was wide enough for a landing.

Jak developed a friendship with a Holden Beach developer who arranged a swap. The developer would build the Smyrls another house, and furnish it, on their lot next to the Barnacle in exchange for the deed to an undeveloped lot. The specifications were dated February 22, 1991, and construction shortly began on the "Spindrift." On April 19, two months before Jak's new beach house was completed, Mae passed away in her room at the Karesh care facility, where she had been a patient for thirteen years. She was interred in Quaker Cemetery beside Oscar. In 1989 Betty's mother, Lorena "Rena" Spires, had moved from Georgia to Camden, where on September 17 Betty found a house for her in the subdivision of Edgewood, about two miles from Colonial Lake. At the same time Betty's brother

Loyd Spires and his wife, Mary, also moved to Camden. Betty and Jak had more members to include in family gatherings.

In the settlement of properties with the passing of their parents, Jak and siblings made decisions regarding the Highway 97 farm tract where they had lived in their youth. A Dutch investor who was developing Pacoma Farms, a horse-training facility on adjoining property, wanted to purchase a part of the Smyrl tract. Alfred decided to keep his share, but the others in 1991 sold the developer what he needed. The remaining area was eventually divided, and four of Oscar and Mae's grandchildren built homes there.

Chapter 23

Standing Firm

"Blessed with the chance"

Sobering reflections filled their lives. By early 1992 both Jak and Betty were diagnosed with cancer and sought treatment. On June 21, 1992, Jak wrote Laura Sloan Crosby, "Betty and I have been blessed with the chance to conquer our cancer threats by having them discovered early on and thank the Lord we live in a country where medical help is available. I have completed 35 radiation treatments and Betty, who is undergoing chemotherapy, is soon seeing the light at the end of the tunnel. She has 3 more treatments and then some radiation."

Determined not to let the cancer and its treatments control his life, Jak resumed work on his projects and became involved in his hometown in a number of ways. For a time he played his trumpet in the Camden Community Band and made new friends. In a later interview, Mitch Santiago, who joined the band about 1994, recalled Jak's sitting down next to him and introducing himself. Santiago knew him by reputation. After they conversed a bit, Jak said that, although he had played the trumpet for some fifty-five years, he had never learned to read music. He asked if Santiago, a retired band director, would teach him. He went to Jak's studio at Colonial Lake a few times, noting that while he made some progress with notes, "he was more interested just spending time playing with another human being." Trumpeter Mike Clyburn, son of Jak's old friends Bill and Peggy, also inspired, taught, and played with Jak, who also took up beginning piano lessons. It was a surprised group of primary school youngsters whose recital included among their performances one of a smiling, white-haired senior citizen.

From his Colonial Lake home, Jak was able to spend more time at his Lake Wateree cottage. He kept projects underway there as well as in his home studio. He and Betty had joined the Wateree Home Owners Association soon after they purchased the lake property. In 1995 he was asked to be area representative on the association board. He typed a letter of introduction to other property owners, encouraging them to join the environmentally minded organization. He wrote, "My family's association with Wateree goes back four generations to the pre–Civil War days when it was still a river only." He outlined some of the things WHOA was doing on behalf of its members regarding "the quality of life on Lake Wateree." His illustration on the top of the page was a cartoon of a fisherman in a boat waving, "Howdy Naybor!"

Unfortunately Jak's radiation three years earlier had not ended his battle with cancer, which reappeared in 1995. In his memoir notes Jak referred to "much time (about 2 years) used up recovering from cancer surgery." On January 27, 1996, while still recovering, he wrote niece Linda Brown thanking her for her "wonderful letter [which] lifted my jaded spirits." It was typical of Jak to make such a response to a kindness paid him by another. Printed in brown ink on lined paper, it was both a sincere gesture of appreciation to her and a comment on human beings coping with unfortunate circumstances in their lives. The letter was meticulously embellished with humorous cartoon characters in color: a bluebird in a hat perching on the greeting; a broke-tail dog putting his paws in his ears to mute the sounds of a bugler; an arm with a long finger pointing at a billiard ball "2" on the second page, at the bottom of which was a smiling snake; a comic character with outstretched twisted arm on which was perched a red bird; and, to denote the third page, a kite with a "3," the top of which was in the grasp of another crow-like bird. Holding on to the kite string was a lad who was airborne and losing his shoes, socks, and pants. Even at a time when Jak was facing a crisis in his own life, he used his creative talent to bring smiles to others.

Jak used his talent in civic efforts as well. The Laurens Street building in which Jak had attended high school had been demolished, and the property was to be dedicated as a park honoring teachers and staffs of the schools that had been located there. Asked to assist with the project, Jak designed the memorial stone, which included a sketch of the building. Jak stated, "I am pleased to help honor such outstanding teachers as Miss Etta Zemp and Mr. C. T. Baldwin. I remember these two in particular as encouraging me to become an artist." The dedication took place on March 20, 1996. Several days earlier the *Chronicle-Independent* published Jak's "Night before the Cup," a parody for the Carolina Cup of the classic "Night before Christmas," accompanied by Jak's humorous illustrations.

Late in 1995, continuing estate settlements, the Smyrl heirs sold Lake Luesta, including the train house. In spring 1996, while Jak was still recovering from his cancer surgery, Lottie was diagnosed with pancreatic cancer. With surgery impossible she took radiation and chemotherapy to no avail. Lottie died on September 7 in the home she and Lewis had shared for fifty years and was buried in Quaker Cemetery.

One of Jak's old friends who sometimes vacationed at the Barnacle was artist Tom Jung, acclaimed in Hollywood especially for movie posters, such as those for the reissued *Gone with the Wind* as well as *Star Wars* and *The Empire Strikes Back*. In an undated letter to the Jungs, Jak thanked Tom for sending a "package of drawings, sketches and fabulous illustrations." Jak mentioned his new beach house and two major storms that damaged the Barnacle and dunes. Needing to move it "back from the encroaching ocean," he revealed that he was selling the Barnacle to the builder of the Spindrift. Jak lamented the shortness of time "to maintain social contacts that give life its joys and sweet memories" but admitted, "This scarcity of time is 90% my own fault for being too interested in doing too many things. I'm addicted to variety and involved in a bunch of junk." He did not need to explain that his art also helped him cope with daily difficulties.

The Barnacle was sold in May 1995. Jak, unwell from the recurrence of cancer and surgery, continued to worry about the old beach house. When the buyer indicated intent to sell instead of keep and repair, Betty suggested they repurchase the house and see to moving it back from the ocean. In June 1997 their offer was accepted to swap a second-row beach lot for the equity in the Barnacle. In spite of the work ahead, Jak was elated to own his beloved beach house once again. Working to preserve it cheered his spirits. Jak's memoir notes state that they had the Barnacle moved back fifty feet. Movers said it was unnecessary to remove anything from the house, and Betty was amazed they were so skilled that not a single dish or glass was broken in the move.

In 2000, after twenty-five years as an interior designer with Bonitz Contract Design, Betty retired to have more time with her mother and

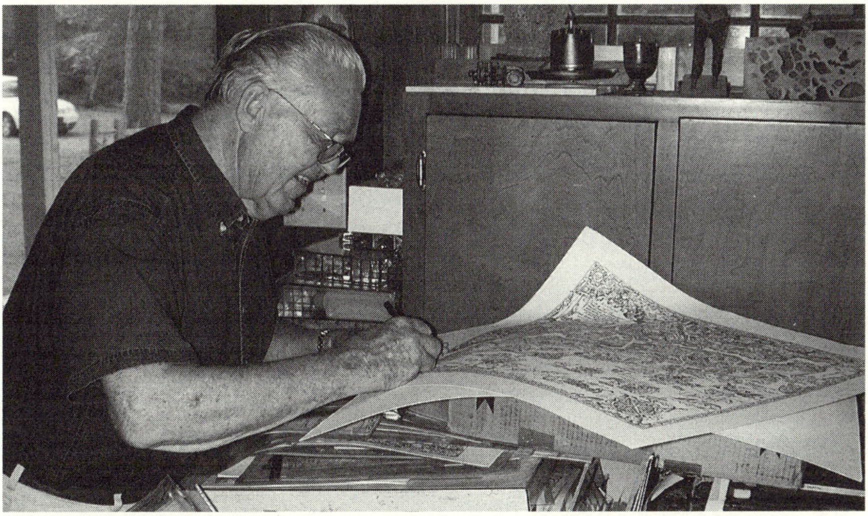

Jak in his Colonial Lake home studio during a 2003 family reunion, signing one of his colorfully detailed South Carolina maps. Photograph by Julie Inabinet Putnam.

Jak. She set up a home office and continued to do contract work for about five years. With his health declining, Jak conceded that maintenance of two beach houses was a bit daunting. He and Betty decided to keep the Barnacle but put the Spindrift on the market. With some sadness they sold it in 2002.

Jak cultivated family rapport with another generation, always especially promoting interests in art and music. For example he encouraged photography and musical interests of great-niece Julie Inabinet. He invited her, nephew Pat Smyrl, and their high school band friends to come to his studio and "jam" with him. When Bill Inabinet was working on a wood-carving project for Boy Scouts, Jak helped him carve a sailboat, and when Greg Inabinet played trumpet in the high school band, Jak gave him one of his horns and took him to hear Doc Severson perform. On December 3, 1998, Greg wrote to thank him, adding a postscript that he had gotten first chair with "Thanks for your encouragement." Encouragement was something Jak gave many.

Arrival of a new millennium did not bring the major numerical disasters that were predicted, but it did bring considerable sorrow to the Smyrl family in a series of deaths in only a few years: Bonnie Smyrl, 2001; Robbie Anderson, 2003; Lucy Brown, 2004; Lewis Anderson, 2006; Rhonda Brown,

2007. Oscar had often remarked that in childhood he had been told by an elderly man, "One of these days, you'll look around and realize that you are the oldest person you know." At age eighty-four, having watched so many loved ones slip away, perhaps Jak understood his father's sentiment reflecting on the statement. Growing stronger in the spiritual faith he had followed since childhood, Jak held to belief that his greatest adventure would follow the close of his life. Meanwhile he would appreciate each day as much as he could.

Jak had always enjoyed extended family reunions, which the Smyrl family had held at various intervals and locations over the years, and he hosted some of them himself. When younger members of the family expressed a desire for a reunion in 2003, Jak and Betty offered the use of their Colonial Lake property. Invited were all the family lines Jak had known as a boy—Smyrls, Campbells, Creeds, Ogburns, Shaws, Clyburns, Kellys, and related folks. September 27 was a gorgeous fall day. Some seventy attendees served themselves from the buffet of picnic foods laid out in Jak's studio and enjoyed the fellowship outside on the grounds. Children looked for minnows along the lake's edge. Older folks reminisced about similar gatherings from the past. Many of them remembered when Oscar and Mae hosted similar events there. Jak reveled in being the emcee. Not unexpectedly he produced his trumpet and played a bit of jazz.

Recognition continued for Jak even in retirement. Sheila Riddick McKinney characterized him as a "Renaissance man" in a full-page feature in the *Chronicle-Independent,* on May 26, 2003. After visiting his art-filled studio at his home, McKinney stated that although Jak was "best known for his cartoons and caricatures, he also does illustrations, wood carvings, art photography, writes ballads and plays the trumpet." Ongoing projects were in evidence throughout his studio, as well as collected works from his past years. From September 26 to November 20, 2003, Jak's work was included in an exhibit hung in the Bassett Gallery at the Fine Arts Center of Kershaw County. *Roots on the Wateree* also included other local artists Lisa Boykin Adams, Robert Ariail, Patty Blackwell, Claude Buckley, Chet Goff, Mariah Kirby-Smith, and Maci Scheuer.

Much of Jak's career as an artist of outdoor life was reviewed and a number of his illustrations reprinted by former colleague Pat Robertson in the November–December 2006 issue of *South Carolina Wildlife.* "Pore Man's Picasso" emphasized its key point: "Pioneering staff artist at *The State* newspaper and frequent contributor to *South Carolina Wildlife* magazine in its early years, Jak Smyrl created hundreds of cartoons that brought

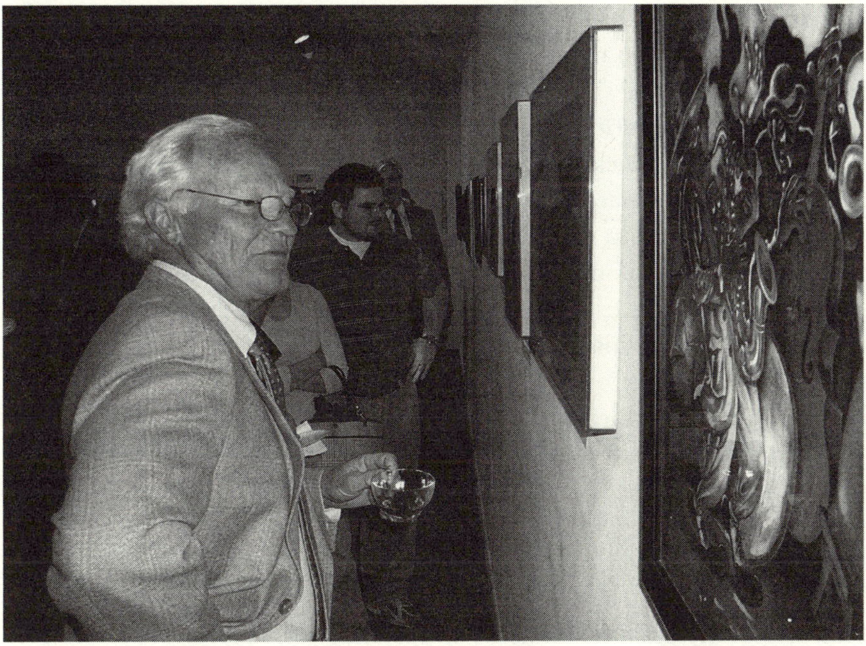

Bill Denton reacting to Jak's colorful painting *Jazz Combo* exhibited in Camden's Bassett Gallery. Photograph by Glen Inabinet.

writers' ideas to life." Robertson commented that "although Smyrl never went hunting or fishing with [*Wildlife* editor Eddie] Finlay he had an ingenious knack for finding the particular element in Finlay's columns that he could satirize in a cartoon panel." Robertson himself once wrote an article reminiscing about his grandfather and "the wonderful days I'd spent as a boy fishing with him." The writer asked Jak to provide an illustration and was astonished when he saw the results. Although Robertson had provided no description, Jak's drawing "could have passed for a portrait of my Grandfather, who always wore long-sleeved khaki shirts with bib overalls and a snap-brim fedora," just as Jak portrayed the old man "sitting under a tree and fishing with a cane pole."

Jak's last few years were a blur—hospital stays punctuated with cards, flowers, and visits from family and friends, treatments that offered glimmers of hope that too quickly faded. He would sit outside at their Colonial Lake home, sometimes with a blanket to ward off chills, and would look appreciatively at the flowering shrubs, bulbs, and trees Oscar and Mae had planted and painstakingly cultivated many years earlier. Occasional honking of geese would direct his attention to the waterfront. One day Joan and Glen found him seated outside with Betty, watching in amazement as a king snake slowly swallowed another snake. He was always fascinated by such experiences with nature.

Jak now tired quickly and expended what energy he had on revising and reshaping the materials for an illustrated book of his poetry that he desperately wanted to see in print. In more energetic days, he had loved reading the poems aloud to visitors and even made double-track tapes of the poems with music he performed to accompany them. Betty drove Jak to Holden Beach to his beloved Barnacle, but the joy of being there was tempered by exhaustion from the long ride and, once there, by the difficulty of getting up the steep stairs.

With determination Jak summoned his strength to enjoy a highlight of his life on June 6, 2007, when he proudly stood in the State House to be recognized before legislators and senators by a concurrent resolution "To Recognize and Honor Jak Smyrl." There would be one final family gathering. On July 4 Alfred and his family, Lucy's children, Lottie's children and grandchildren, and a few cousins and friends gathered in the evening at Jak and Betty's Wateree River lake house to watch the annual Independence Day fireworks stream from the sky, casting colorfully distorted reflections over the shimmering water. Jak's mind was alert, but he was tired, and his voice was weak.

Perhaps the fireworks reminded him of older family members shooting skyrockets down DeKalb Street when he was a boy living in town. Maybe the colors and the booms brought back memories of Okinawa. Perhaps he was reminded of other family gatherings to watch the annual fireworks at the lake, sometimes from Lucy and Rhonda's place, later from his and Betty's. Perhaps he thought of old days with his family relaxing on an island in the lake. Whatever his thoughts were, he kept them to himself, content to be surrounded by those he loved and who loved him. Perhaps, sitting there listening to familiar voices droning about him, he felt as he had another time long ago, when he returned from the Pacific, riding home with Oscar and Mae, too ill and exhausted to carry on conversation, but peaceful with familiar voices in his ears and the assurance that he was in the care of those who loved him.

Chapter 24

Legacy

"Life, Softly Satirized"

"Renowned artist, writer, and raconteur, Oscar Jackson Smyrl died Tuesday, August 7, 2007. He was 84." Thus began the announcement on the front page of the August 8 *Chronicle-Independent*. Associate editor Jim Tatum interviewed several friends and colleagues for comments. Camden physician Mac McCorkle described his old friend as "quite a character." High school pals who played together in a jazz band in the 1940s, Jak and Mac had corresponded while in military service. Mac said, "He was sort of a non-conformist type; a great guy with a great sense of humor," adding that he was also "a great punster." Friend and retired editor of the *State* Tom McLean thought Jak marched to the beat of a different drummer when he first met him but stated, "The longer I knew him, the more I understood Jak *was* the drummer—a drummer whose keen sense of self enabled him to lay down a smooth cadence on every march he made in life. I envied him. All of his friends envied him."

Another friend, Claudia Smith Brinson, a former editor of the *State Magazine,* began her reflection in the *State* on August 8, "On a Jak Smyrl map the scale was aimed at happiness: One inch equaled one smile." She described his signature characters: "buzzards flying overhead, big-hipped women in stilettos and an ever-present dog with a broken tail, the wag tied back on with string." She quoted editorial cartoonist Robert Ariail's saying of Jak, "He commented on the human condition, always in the Smyrl style; it was unique." Former columnist Bill McDonald said of his friend, "He left a giant footprint in the '50s, '60s, '70s and '80s. He loved every day, he really did. Jak told me one time one of the greatest moments in his life was discovering he could make a living with a blank sheet of paper and a No. 2 pencil."

One week after Brinson's article, Jim Tatum entitled a *Chronicle-Independent* column "Jak Smyrl One of Truly Unforgettable Ones." Tatum, who had known Jak only recently, paid tribute to a man who left lasting impressions. The most memorable interaction with Jak had occurred less than three weeks before his death. Tatum spent "a magical three hours with Jak and his lovely wife, Betty, listening to him tell hilarious stories, showing me his workshop and various projects and just having a grand time." When Tatum made the appointment, he had no idea "just how sick he was, which was exactly how he liked it. He wanted to entertain. He loved being around people and people loved being around him." And as most visitors to their home, Tatum did not leave empty-handed: "I finally left with a bag of tomatoes and probably the last two signed Jak Smyrl prints in this world." Tatum observed that of the multitudes of people one encounters in life, "most slide into obscurity. . . . We remember every detail about [the jerks] . . . who always seem to stay around forever. But the truly unforgettable ones, the ones who touch our lives in such a positive, profound way, are the ones who will live forever. They are few and far between, and any time spent with them is never nearly enough. . . . Jak Smyrl was one of those people. Simply unforgettable."

Bob Gillespie, another friend and colleague at the *State,* reviewed Jak's influence on sports in his column on August 26, 2007, titled "Drawn to Sports." Gillespie began, "Who knows what might have happened if Jak Smyrl had been really good at sports?" Instead he kept up at "his true calling" and never lost his love for sports. He and Betty often went to USC games, especially enjoying the old Big Thursday games when Carolina played host to Clemson during the week of the State Fair. Jak caricatured Carolina and Clemson coaches and mascots without iniquity. Although he had attended USC, his illustrations never showed bias. He parodied both schools with equal humor. Gillespie quoted Betty, "We'd go to games, but he didn't keep up with scoring. He loved the hustle and bustle of the games."

Tatum wrote another article on December 12, 2007, about Jak's final project, *Random Rimes,* a whimsical, illustrated book of his poetry released after his death. Tatum interviewed Jak's niece Mary Ann Blaskowitz about her decade of working with her uncle in his efforts to prepare the book for publication. She said that Jak "didn't do computers," and would bring her "a batch of hand-written poems" to type. He would then "go over them again and make changes." As a result "he probably re-did most of those poems 10 to 15 times." Other family members, including Betty, Alfred, and Joan, helped with the process, as did Julie Putnam, who scanned all of Jak's artwork into digital forms. Betty told Tatum that Jak's "one wish was to live long enough to see this project in print. Happily, he was able to do so." Mary Ann described how special it was to put a printed proof copy in Jak's hands and turn the pages so he could see what the published book would look like. While *Random Rimes* was being printed, Jak's cancer was also in its final stages.

In the year following his death, the Kershaw County Fine Arts Center mounted a retrospective exhibition, *A Tribute to Jak Smyrl,* in the Bassett Gallery from October 28 to November 14, 2008. In the October 24 *Chronicle-Independent,* FAC director Kristin Cobb stated, "Jak was truly a gifted artist full of enthusiasm for how the arts touch our lives daily." The exhibit's publicity drew a number of its biographical comments from the wording of the House and Senate's concurrent resolution on June 6, 2007, which concluded in appreciation to Jak "for lightening the hearts of uncounted South Carolinians."

A preview opening of the exhibit complemented a program titled "The Life and Art of Jak Smyrl," presented by the Kershaw County Historical Society at the Fine Arts Center on October 26. An appropriately chosen speaker for the occasion was Robert Ariail, Jak's colleague. Ariail's own pen had earlier already spoken more eloquently of feelings for Jak. On the editorial page of the *State* on August 8, 2007, Ariail's cartoon had evoked a ritual tribute to a fallen soldier. A stilled artist's pen, topped with a beret, was stuck upright beside an inkwell on a stack of drawings. Mourning beside it was a Jak-styled and tagged "broke tail dawg," a tear streaming from his eye. In time Betty would also choose a dog image to etch into the back of blue granite stone over Jak's resting place beside his parents. It was his own wistfully smiling dog, tail tied hopefully and held upward.

Two years after Jak's death, McKissick Museum, University of South Carolina, opened a major exhibition. *Southern Satire: The Illustrated World of Jak Smyrl* ran from August 8, 2009, to January 23, 2010. Jason E. Shaiman, chief curator of exhibitions, commented, "Throughout all of his work there was a common thread, he had a light-hearted manner. He was never malicious." Among persons viewing Jak's work opening night and in the six months afterward were many persons familiar with it and many too who were viewing it for the first time. Shaiman remarked at the

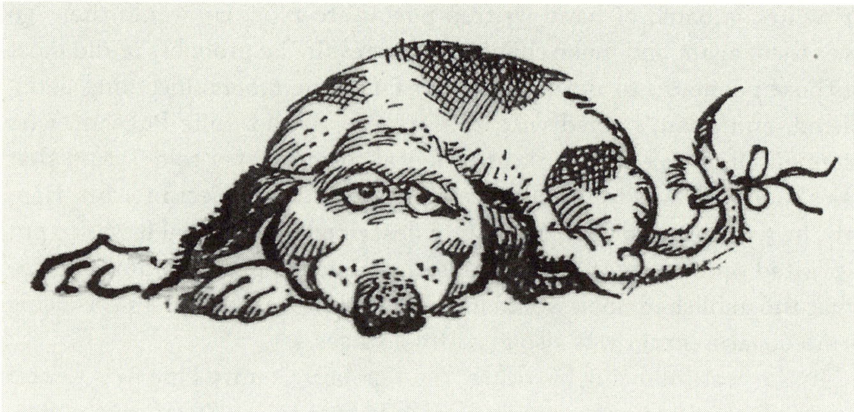

Jak's broke-tail dog, a different dog in each appearance, in the artist's latter years appearing comfortably fed and still reflecting cheerful hopefulness (*Random Rimes*).

exhibition's end that despite the age of Jak's work, children and adults of all ages had responded to its "timeless" and "universal" appeals. Shaiman had suggested, for fun, searches for tied-together tails and hatted birds, and even children had understood the implied messages.

In his life and his art, Jak was interested in the reaction to an action. At a football game, he enjoyed the drama of the spectators as well as the players on the field. At a parade the varied humanity lining the street was as interesting as the clowns and floats passing by. Doug Fisher, USC journalism instructor, employed that technique of observing reaction when he attended the McKissick exhibit. His observations, titled "What Jak Smyrl Can Teach Us," appeared in his January 2010 column in *Common Sense Journalism:* "I spent a pleasant evening recently watching dozens of people thoroughly engrossed in the newspaper. One after another, young and old, they went from page to page. They pointed out things on the pages. They discussed them with one another. They smiled. They frowned. Sometimes they were just transfixed by the information they were absorbing. It was a publisher's and editor's dream. The pages, unfortunately, were on the wall of a museum."

Fisher pointed out that Jak's collective work covering the walls of McKissick Museum were "typical of what you could find among the papers of the era, not just words but illustrations and photo pages that engaged and engrossed readers and extended their involvement with the journalism. Far from being frivolous, such illustrations were a journalism of their own, sometimes poking fun at pomposity, sometimes putting complex matters in a way readers could chew on bit by bit, sometimes bringing just a knowing chuckle." He lamented that in recent newspaper layoffs "some of the first to go were the illustrators and the editorial cartoonists." Fisher considered such a trend "a bad move for 'serious' journalism when our audiences are becoming more visually literate and sophisticated." He advocated that "these folks are journalists, just as much as any 'word' person, who can explain complicated things in ways that engage audiences."

Mary Bentz Gilkerson, a first-place winner for critical writing for the 2008 South Carolina Press Association, commented on the McKissick display and Jak's legacy as a southern satirist. In "Smyrl: Southern Life, Softly Satirized" in the September 23, 2009, *Free Times,* she stated that "he never lost his connection to the rural small town perspective even though his own grew much larger." Whereas many other satirists used stinging barbs, "Many of his pieces gently poke at puffed-up pretensions, mainly by reminding us of our common humanity with a total lack of irony." Gilkerson illustrated Jak's technique of caricaturing "politicians and other public figures" by "taking them gently down a notch," by citing an example. She observed that Jak's illustration "commemorating the election of John West as governor shows West's grinning head wedged between the main structure of the State House with the dome sitting on top like a hat. It celebrates West's election, but at the same time jokes about the inflated egos of all politicians." She wrote that "Smyrl literally drew the landscape of South Carolina both geographically and culturally, creating fabulously detailed maps that captured the essence of broad cultural topics." In summary Gilkerson stated, "Smyrl passed away in 2007, and with his generation passes the era of the staff cartoonist. Exactly what role the cartoonist will play and where that will be remains to be seen."

The role that Jak, among others, played in newspaper history was recognized on August 1, 2013, when the State-Record Hall of Fame was established at the State office building, Shop Road, under its owners since 2006, the McClatchy Company. Inaugural inductees included Jak along with three other employees in the *State-Record*'s 120-year history—founder N. G. Gonzales, Marilyn W. Thompson, and Lee Bandy. A committee of former employees made the final selections of the four charter members, who were recognized in a ceremony attended by executives, employees, and family of persons honored. Clearly the influence of a genial artist must have been considered very significant for him to have been selected from among so many employees over more than a century.

Betty, Alfred, and other family, as well as former colleagues, knew that Jak would have felt surprised, humble, and very honored.

In interviews from 2011 to 2013, a number of colleagues and other acquaintances shared recollections of the character and traits of Jak, the man behind the images that he created. Bill McDonald at his Winnsboro home stated that "Jak's heart was in South Carolina. Had he been born in New York City, no telling what he could have done with all the available art schools. He could have gone wherever he wanted with his talent." He observed that Jak became a citizen of the world but still chose to live in the region he loved best among the people he loved most. In reference also to Jak's choice, Tom Nebbia, who traveled the world as a renowned photographer for *National Geographic,* made the observation at his North Carolina home that "I was successful but not very happy. Jak was happy all the time."

Bob Kaminer in an interview at his Columbia home remarked that "Jak could see something good in anything, and it didn't matter what it was. It could be ugly to me, but he could see something that was good in it. It could be a puddle of water with a shadow in it. I didn't even see anything." McDonald recalled Jak's "artistic temperament" and a "compulsion to create." To illustrate effects of Jak's attraction to beauty, McDonald told of the time that he, model Millie Lewis, and Jak were judges for a college beauty contest. When the tabulator came to collect the scorecards, Jak's were blank. He had been gawking at the girls but not marking his cards. They had to march the contestants back out, delaying the contest thirty minutes. The audience grew impatient and began clapping, stomping, and jeering at the judges.

Interviewed at a USC exhibit, Tom Priddy recollected Jak's work habits: "I was his boss for a while, but being boss for Jak was kind of like Obama trying to control Congress. You know, you're sorta in charge of a little bit of the program but not really everything." Priddy explained that "Jak would always do his own thing. We'd talk about issues and ideas, and I'd have an idea of what he was going to do, and he'd always do something just miraculous. It was a lot of fun to think about, to dream up those things with Jak and then watch him go off." About Jak's process of working, Priddy stated, "He never liked anyone to watch him work. When he was working on a final piece, you never saw him. He always did that privately. He'd come back, and it'd be completed. It was like drawing back the curtain and just seeing the final production. It was quite a trip, a treat to be able to work with Jak."

It was in the last years of Jak's career that Priddy came to the *State*, in the process of upgrading technology. While the rest of the art department transformed to a computer graphics department, Priddy said, "We knew Jak was Jak, and there was never a thought to make him digitize. You don't want to mess with something like that." Priddy commented on advantages of digitization while adding, "but Jak was always Jak. He was a genius with the knife, the pen, the ink, the scratching, and the white-out, a lot of white-out, lots of white-out all over the place."

Tom McLean, on a visit to the late artist's Camden home, referred to Jak's studio and workshop, which were still housing his years of collected art, as a "veritable museum of Jak's life." Those items were also pertinent to the history of his profession and much more. Historian Harvey S. Teal, who viewed the collected materials after Jak's death, recognized their value for use of general, cultural, and political historians as a "capsule of the times" and a "mirror of South Carolina." Teal was also interested in the fact that a number of Jak's works were in themselves well-researched representations of historical topics. Correspondence and photography added further depth of interest.

A special gathering at the University of South Carolina on July 13, 2013, celebrated the acquisition of the Oscar Jackson "Jak" Smyrl, Jr., Papers by the South Caroliniana Society. The event in the Hollings Room at Thomas Cooper Library was not the beginning of the process, for the transfer of papers and the work of curating the collection had begun some two years earlier. Nor was it the end, for work to publish an art book and a biography were also underway. Before a crowd of Jak's colleagues, friends, family, and university associates, and other interested persons, Betty stood at the podium.

Speaking briefly of her late husband, Betty said, "He loved people of all walks of life and never met a stranger. . . . He was a 'Gentle Man.'" She referred to "Jak's love of his native State of South Carolina and the University of South Carolina." She recognized a list of Jak's former coworkers present, thanked the Caroliniana Society and a list of persons for helping preserve the collection, and stated, "This will ensure his legacy will live on."

The Oscar Jackson "Jak" Smyrl, Jr., Papers were described by its curator, archivist Edward Blessing, as "the majority of Jak's oeuvre, bringing together a vast array of materials that provide a unique insight into the life of this prolific artist." The collection he described includes thousands of "papers, drawings, notes, sketches and doodles," as well as "homemade

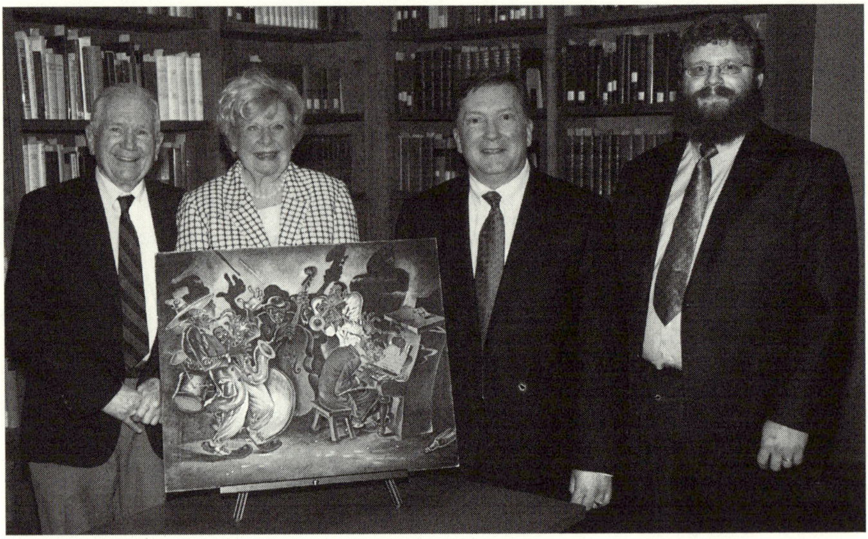

At the celebration of the acquisition of Jak Smyrl's papers by the South Caroliniana Library, Bill McDonald, Betty Smyrl, Caroliniana director Henry Fulmer, and archivist Edward Blessing with Jak's 1948 painting *Jazz Combo*. Photograph by Jason Ayers.

audio recordings, photographs, freelance artwork, World War II and postwar correspondence, personal diaries, childhood sketches, and hundreds of drawings and doodles." After remarks by Blessing, along with Caroliniana director Henry Fulmer, director of USC Libraries Thomas McNally, and guest speaker Bill McDonald, the guests viewed samples from the collection and listened to music performed by Jak's friend Dick Goodwin and his band. "Jak would have expressed his enthusiasm by 'sitting in' with the band," remarked Betty.

That the Smyrl collection will continue to be studied and will continue to reveal more is clear. Artist Laura Crosby from personal knowledge referred to Jak as "a connoisseur of people." Remarking that "he was a person who had all the time in the world to sit down and talk to you," she said that "during those conversations, you had his undivided attention." Tom McLean also observed, "When Jak met people, he focused on their interests." Laura Crosby added, "In retrospect, there are thousands of questions I wish I had asked him. The answers, though, are in his works. The works of artists have always been their lens to the world. To the viewer, his paintings and cartoons say, 'Within this work are the things we could have talked and laughed about. Talking to you would have been my pleasure.'"

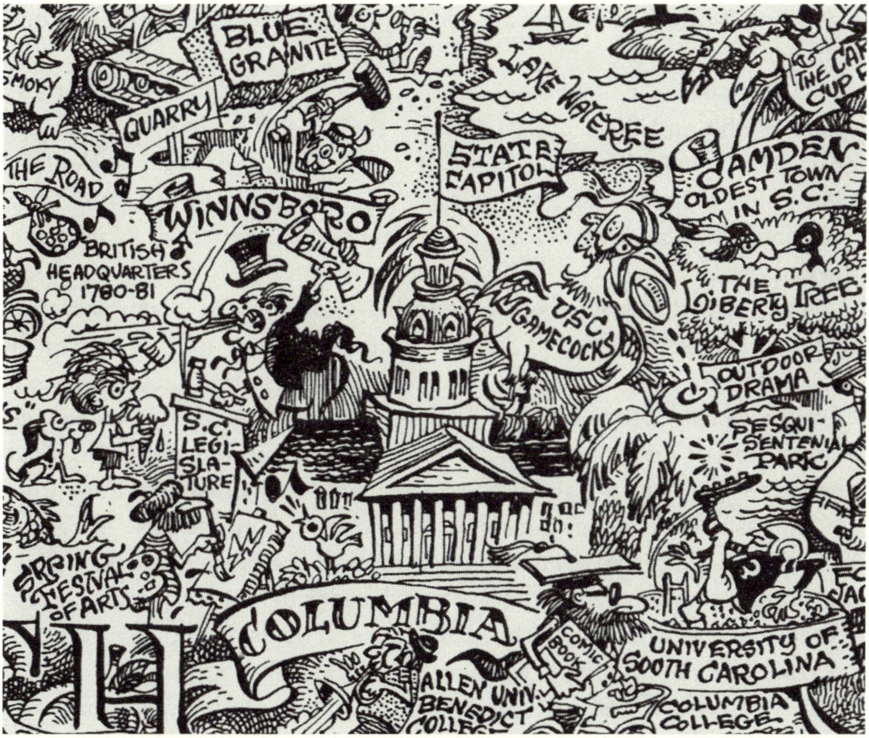

A midsection of Jak's *A Caricature Map of South Carolina* ©1969 weaves together many scenes familiar in his life—State House politics, Gamecock football, area universities, local arts, Fort Jackson, blue granite, Lake Wateree, Camden. Courtesy of the University of South Carolina.

A real-life conversation with Jak was filmed in 1988 when Lise Swensson, curator of Art at the South Carolina State Museum, interviewed him in his home studio in Camden at the time of the museum's exhibition of what they titled his "festoons"—his cartoon maps of South Carolina's numerous festivals. Swensson questioned Jak about the broad body of his work and his collection in his studio. After Jak's passing the edited short feature film was posted online by a friend and continues to be widely viewed.

Though brief the film survives as a fitting epilogue of Jak's long and productive life. Swensson's voice begins: "It was 1949. Harry Truman was president, Strom Thurmond was governor of South Carolina, and the windows of the State Newspaper Company overlooked Main Street. That was when World War II veteran Jak Smyrl began drawing South Carolina history."

As Jak speaks to Swensson nearly four decades later, his southern syllables ebb and flow, punctuated by chuckles and his half-apologetic grin. He tells her with amusement that he thought he would work at the *State* only "a short time, and then Walt Disney would call, and I'd be in Hollywood—making millions." He laughs. She reports, "Disney never did call."

While showing scenes of Jak and his varied works, Swensson comments, "He has poked fun at South Carolina and its people, . . . and at the same time his more than two thousand cartoons are a record of South Carolina's past." Sitting at his drawing table, Jak gives her an earnest explanation of his humor: "You want to make it fun but not harm, hurt, anybody—but have a way for them to laugh—at themselves, hopefully."

Swensson, in closing, muses of Jak, "I don't think he has thought of himself as a historian, but when you look at the body of work, he is—pictorially." The interview, almost two decades before his passing, anticipated many of the values that colleagues, friends, and other admirers posthumously accorded his work.

Through the words and works of artist Jak Smyrl, the wacky and wonderful world he lived in, loved, and shared—even in dark times—will continue to influence minds and lighten hearts.

Selected Bibliography

Manuscript Collections

Inabinet, Joan A., and L. Glen Inabinet. Smyrl and related family papers and images. Community research collection. Interviews and correspondence.

South Caroliniana Library. Oscar Jackson "Jak" Smyrl, Jr., Papers.

Books

Edmund Yaghjian: A Retrospective. Columbia: South Carolina State Museum, 2007.

Fisher, Jacquelyn Felix, and E. W. Goodman. *The Art Institute of Pittsburgh.* Charleston, S.C.: Arcadia, 2009.

Holden, John F. *Holden Beach History.* Wilmington, N.C.: New Hanover, 1988.

Inabinet, L. Glen, and Joan A. Inabinet, eds. *Kershaw County Legacy: A Commemorative History.* Camden, S.C.: Kershaw County Historical Society, 1976.

———. *Legacy II: Kershaw County History and Heritage.* Camden, S.C.: Kershaw County Historical Society, 1983.

Inabinet, Joan A., ed. *A History of Camden High School (Incorporating Jackson High School).* Camden, S.C.: Midlands, 1991.

Inabinet, Joan A., and L. Glen Inabinet. *A History of Kershaw County, South Carolina.* Columbia: University of South Carolina Press, 2011.

Johnson, Bill, comp. *Gridiron Legends: The Camden Bulldogs.* Edited by Joan A. Inabinet. Camden, S.C.: Pine Tree, 1991.

Latimer, S. L., Jr. *Almost Four Score: The Story of* The State, *1891–1969, and the Gonzales Brothers.* Columbia, S.C.: State Printing, 1970.

McGuirt, Charles W. *Alice the Elephant and Other Stories of Growing Up in Rural South Carolina.* Camden, S.C.: Midlands, 2004.

Moore, John Hammond. *Columbia and Richland County: A South Carolina Community, 1740–1990.* Columbia: University of South Carolina Press, 1993.

Pedlow, Franda Dobson. *Sand and Sea Fever: An Early History of Holden Beach.* Wilmington, N.C.: New Hanover, 1994.

Pierce, Robert A. *Between the Sheets: The Journalist and His Lore,* privately published by Dianne Chinnes, no date.

———. *Palmettos and Oaks: A Centennial History of* The State, *1891–1991.* Columbia, S.C.: State-Record, 1991.

Shaw, Henry I., Jr. *The United States Marines in North China: 1945–1949*. Washington, D.C.: Marine Corps Historical Reference pamphlet, 1968.
Sloan, Eugene B. *Scenic South Carolina*. Columbia, S.C.: State Company, 1966.
Smyrl, Jak. *Random Rimes*. Camden, S.C.: Lulu, 2007.
United States Army, Center of Military History. *United States Army in World War II: The War in the Pacific. Okinawa: The Last Battle* by Roy E. Appleman, James M. Burns, Russell A. Gugeler, and John Stevens. Washington, D.C.: Government Printing Office, 1948.

Newspapers and Periodicals

Camden Chronicle. Camden, S.C.
Carolina Review. Columbia: University of South Carolina, 1946–48, 1951.
Chronicle-Independent. Camden, S.C.
Columbia Record. Columbia, S.C.
Gamecock. Columbia: University of South Carolina, 1946–48.
State. Columbia, S.C.
State Magazine. Columbia, S.C.

Articles

Blessing, Edward. "South Carolina's Everyman Artist: The Oscar Jackson "Jak" Smyrl, Jr., Papers." *Caroliniana Columns*, Faculty and Staff Publications, University Libraries (33), 15–26.
Brinson, Claudia Smith. "Ex-Artist at *The State* Dies." *State*, August 8, 2007, B1, B7.
Dunlap, Dick. "Cartoonist Jak Smyrl Made Plant Contributions." *May Times*, October 1984.
Fisher, Doug. "What Jak Smyrl Can Teach Us." *Common Sense Journalism*, January 2010. http://www.jour.sc.edu/news/csj/CSJJan10.html.
Gilkerson, Mary Bentz. "Smyrl: Southern Life, Softly Satirized." *Free Times*, September 23, 2009.
Gillespie, Bob. "Drawn to Sports." *State*, August 26, 2007, 10C.
Higgins, Nancy. "An Illustrious Career." *Chronicle-Independent*, January 19, 1982, 1–10.
McDonald, Bill. "Jak Smyrl." *State Magazine*, May 9, 1982, 8–10.
McKinney, Sheila Riddick. "From the Tip of His Pen." *Chronicle-Independent*, May 26, 2003, 6A.
"Remembering Jak Smyrl—and His Brilliance!" *BLine* (Bonitz), July–August 2007, 16–17.
Robertson, Pat. "Pore Man's Picasso." *South Carolina Wildlife Magazine*, November–December 2006, 12–17.

Roseman, Demont. "Smyrl Puts Holden 'On the Map' Again." *Brunswick Beacon,* June 11, 1981, 1, 5.

Tatum, Jim. "A Few Moments with Jak Smyrl." *Chronicle-Independent,* July 23, 2007, 1, 4A.

———. "Jak Smyrl One of Truly Unforgettable Ones." *Chronicle-Independent,* August 15, 2007, 3A.

———. "Random Rimes." *Chronicle-Independent,* December 12, 2007, 1, 5A.

———. "We Enjoyed Him While We Had Him." *Chronicle-Independent,* August 8, 2007, 1, 4A.

Wenzell, Ron. "Jak Smyrl: Artist." *Sandlapper Magazine,* August 1978, 38–39.

Index